Story

In jeder *Unit* gibt es zwei längere englische Originaltexte mit vielfältigen Aufgaben. An **Story 1** knüpft die **Skills**-Seite und die **Unit task** an. **Story 2** ist ein optionales Angebot.

Skills und Unit task

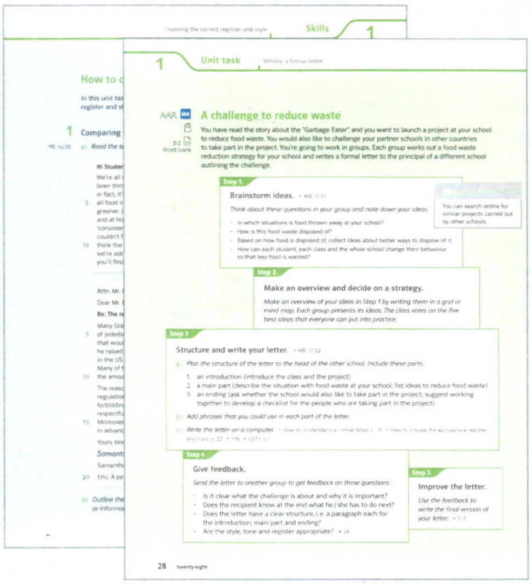

Auf den **Skills**-Seiten werden spezielle Fertigkeiten eingeführt, die für die Unit task wichtig sind. Die **Unit task**-Seiten beinhalten kreative, kollaborative Aufgaben, die neu erlernte Fertigkeiten zusammenführen und festigen.

Check-out

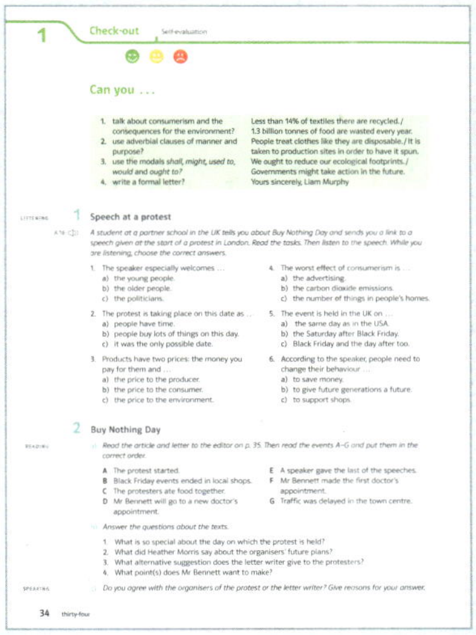

Auf den **Check-out**-Seiten kannst du deine Lernfortschritte überprüfen. Die Lösungen findest du im Anhang. Manche Aufgaben machen dich mit dem Format der ZP10 vertraut.

Der Anhang

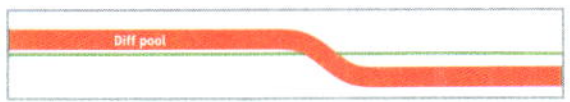

Der **Diff pool** enthält neben einer zur *Unit* passenden Aufgabe, an der du im Laufe der *Unit* immer wieder arbeiten kannst, weitere Übungen mit Angaben, wann du diese am besten erledigst. Die Lösungen dazu findest du im Anhang.

Auf den **Grammar**-Seiten findest du nicht nur Regeln, Beispiele, Tipps und Übungen zum grammatischen Lernstoff aus den **Stations**, sondern auch viele Übersichten und Übungen zum Wiederholen. Die Lösungen findest du im Anhang.

Der **Skills**-Anhang enthält alle wichtigen Methoden und Lerntechniken übersichtlich zusammengefasst. Tipps zum Umgang mit Medien erkennst du am MK -Symbol.

Im **Vocabulary** steht der Lernwortschatz des jeweiligen Moduls in chronologischer Reihenfolge. Jedes Modul ist auf der Grundlage des Vokabelstands von Green Line 5 G9 angelegt.

Symbole

- Partnerarbeit
- Gruppenarbeit
- Produkt für dein Portfolio
- <> fakultative/s Übung / Kapitel
- MK Aufgaben und Tipps zur Entwicklung und Stärkung der Medienkompetenz
- 1 Aufgabe zur Vorbereitung auf die ZP10
- ○ Hilfestellung / zusätzliche Aufgabe
- ● anspruchsvollere Aufgabe
- WB Übung im Workbook
- G Grammatikanhang
- S Skillsanhang
- A1 Audio: Gespräch, Interview etc.
- V1 Video: Filmsequenz
- D1 Dokument: Template, Word bank, Script etc.
- I1 interaktiv: Diagramm, Zeitstrahl

Den Zugang zu den Audios und Dokumenten findest du in deinem **Workbook**, Green Line-**eBook** oder in den **Medien zum Schulbuch**.

Green Line 6 G9 für Klasse 10 an Gymnasien

ISBN 978-3-12-835060-8 (fester Einband)
1. Auflage 1 5 4 3 2 1 | 2027 26 25 24 23

ISBN 978-3-12-835061-5 (flexibler Einband)
1. Auflage 1 5 4 3 2 1 | 2027 26 25 24 23

Alle Drucke dieser Auflage sind unverändert und können im Unterricht nebeneinander verwendet werden.
Die letzte Zahl bezeichnet das Jahr des Druckes.

Herausgeber: Prof. Harald Sonntag-Weisshaar, Bisingen
Autorinnen und Autoren: Jennifer Baer-Engel, Göppingen; Carolyn Jones M.A., Beckenham; Jon Marks, Ventnor; Alison Wooder, Ventnor sowie Louise Carleton-Gertsch, München; Geraldine Greenhalgh, Morrinsville; Cornelia Kaminski, Fulda; Karoline Wellner, Dachau
Beratung: Nilgül Karabulut-Klöppelt, Aachen; Silke Krieger, Castrop-Rauxel; Michael Rogge, Mülheim an der Ruhr

Entstanden in Zusammenarbeit mit dem Projektteam des Verlages.

Externe Redaktion: Joanne Popp, editing etc., Korntal-Münchingen *(Vokabular)*
Layout: Petra Michel, Essen
Umschlaggestaltung: Koma Amok, Stuttgart
Titelbild: U1.1. Unsplash, Montréal, QC (Daniel Novykov); **U1.2** plainpicture GmbH & Co. KG RF, Hamburg (DEEPOL)
Satz: Miriam Brusniak | Preiselbeerdesign, Berlin
Reproduktion: Schwaben-Repro, Stuttgart
Druck: Mohn Media Mohndruck GmbH, Gütersloh

Printed in Germany

Green Line

6 G9

von
Jennifer Baer-Engel
Carolyn Jones
Jon Marks
Alison Wooder
Louise Carleton-Gertsch
Geraldine Greenhalgh
Cornelia Kaminski
Karoline Wellner

herausgegeben von
Harald Sonntag-Weisshaar

Ernst Klett Verlag
Stuttgart · Leipzig

Dieses Lernmittel ist Eigentum der Stadt Gelsenkirchen
Es wird leihweise zur Verfügung gestellt. Das Lernmittel ist pfleglich zu behandeln. Der Benutzer hat darauf zu achten, daß das Lernmittel auch den nachfolgenden Schülern in ordnungsgemäßem Zustand übergeben werden kann.

Datum der Ausgabe	Datum der Rückgabe	Name des Schülers	Klasse

Contents

Module 2

Across cultures 2 Exploring culture in new dimensions

Page		Learning objectives	Linguistic competence
46		You learn about ways of accessing culture from home and their pros and cons.	VOCABULARY/PHRASES Words and phrases to talk about AR and VR **46**

Unit 2 The digital age

Page		Learning objectives	Linguistic competence
50 52 55 59 60 63 64 65 68	Check-in Station 1 Station 2 Action! Story 1 Skills Unit task ‹Story 2› Check-out	You learn about the digital age and its impact on us. You learn about aspects such as the future of education, social media and gaming.	VOCABULARY/PHRASES Words and phrases to talk about education and technology **53** | Words and phrases to talk about the future of school **53** | Definitions **56/62** | Words and phrases to discuss game developers' responsibilities **62** | ‹Story 2: Descriptive language› **67** GRAMMAR the will-future progressive and the will-future perfect **52–53** | relative clauses with *which* to comment on the main clause **55–56** | relative clauses with *when* and *where* **55/57** ‹Revision: tenses referring to the future› **G6** | ‹Revision: relative clauses› **G9**

Text and media smart 2 Dealing with factual texts

Page		Learning objectives	Linguistic competence
72 73 78 81	Check-in Station 1 Station 2 Options	You learn how to sum up and analyse factual texts as well as how to write an argumentative text.	VOCABULARY/PHRASES Words and phrases for writing a summary **75** | Words and phrases to argue for or against a point **79** | Words and phrases for presenting arguments **79** GRAMMAR ‹Revision: tenses referring to the present› **G12**

Module 3

Across cultures 3 Canada

Unit 3 Discover Canada!

Text and media smart 3 Dealing with plays

Die in diesem Band aufbereiteten Inhalte stellen ein Angebot dar, sie sind nicht obligatorisch durchzunehmen. Maßgeblich für die Auswahl der Texte und Übungen ist der Lehrplan Ihres Bundeslandes bzw. Ihr schulinternes Curriculum.

Der Verlag orientiert sich bei der Bezeichnung von marginalisierten Gruppen an Begrifflichkeiten, die sich zum Zeitpunkt des Erscheinens als Selbstbezeichnungen mit breiter Akzeptanz durchgesetzt haben. Dabei respektieren wir ausdrücklich die Belange der Betroffenen und die Vielfalt der Positionen in der Diskussion um korrekte bzw. präferierte Bezeichnungen. Wo diese Bezeichnungen umstritten oder historisch nicht mehr akzeptiert sind, werden sie in einfache Anführungszeichen gesetzt, um dieser Tatsache Rechnung zu tragen. An manchen Stellen ist die Verwendung von nicht eigens ausgezeichneten (Fremd)bezeichnungen unvermeidlich, weil sie z. B. in Originaltexten vorkommen oder in einer bestimmten Community, die in dem Material zu Wort kommt, gängig ist.

Making your voice heard

Having a voice and making it heard are key aspects of democracy and participation in society. There are many ways that people can make their voices heard at a local, national and international level and you're going to look at some of them on these pages.

READING

1 A personality quiz

WB 2/1

*Do the personality quiz. Choose **one** sentence that best describes your attitude for each point. Note down how many of each colour you chose.*

How far would YOU go to have your voice heard? Do the quiz and find out!

1
- **a)** If I were on a student council, I'd want to lead it and make change happen.
- **b)** I'd like to be on a student council, but I wouldn't want to lead it.
- **c)** It's important to have a good student council, but I don't need to be on it.
- **d)** Who needs a student council? What a waste of time! How boring!

2
- **a)** Why vote in elections? How can my vote make any difference?
- **b)** I can't believe that some people never vote in elections. What losers!
- **c)** People have fought for our right to vote. It's disrespectful not to vote if you have the opportunity.
- **d)** If you don't understand the issues, it's best to leave it to others to vote in elections.

3
- **a)** I admire political activists who do dangerous stunts, like climbing skyscrapers to put up protest banners.
- **b)** In my opinion it's crazy when activists do crazy stunts.
- **c)** It doesn't change anything and it's illegal too. Protest is OK, but why do dramatic stunts? There are other ways to make your point.
- **d)** I can imagine doing a dangerous stunt to get people's attention and make them think about an issue I really believe in.

4
- **a)** I would sign somebody else's petition, but would I start one myself? No thanks.
- **b)** Yes, I would be happy to collect signatures on the street for a petition.
- **c)** I can imagine starting my own petition about something I feel strongly about.
- **d)** I would never waste my time on petitions. I'm not interested in stuff like that.

5
- **a)** I respect people who take part in protest movements. Perhaps I should do more myself.
- **b)** Lots of my classmates take part in protests, so I don't need to go.
- **c)** If people think I'm wasting my time when I go to protests, then that's their problem not mine.
- **d)** I'm always so busy. I don't have time to go to protests every week.

6
- **a)** When we buy clothes, we can make a statement about child labour and animal protection.
- **b)** I love it when protesters throw paint at people in fur coats. They deserve it. How can people be so cruel to animals?
- **c)** Clothes are just clothes. They have nothing to do with politics so why waste a thought on them?
- **d)** I wouldn't wear fur myself – but if others do, that's fine. Having a voice doesn't mean you can tell others how to live their lives.

SPEAKING

2 Discuss your results

WB 2/2

Now see what your results in ex. 1 mean below. Say if you agree with your result or not, and why.

Mostly red: You think it is important to make your voice heard. You express your opinion and like to persuade others to join you. You would go far – too far perhaps – to stand up for your beliefs.

Mostly yellow: You see how important it is to get involved. It's just that you prefer other people to take the lead. Maybe you haven't yet found an issue you feel really strongly about?

Mostly green: You're happy to sit back and let other people do the work. Maybe you don't believe you could make a difference, but don't forget that being involved can be worthwhile.

Mostly blue: You live in a world of your own and you really aren't interested in politics or in any wider issues. But your voice and your actions are valuable. Don't just run and hide!

VIEWING

3 Having a voice at local level

V1

a) *Watch the film until 03:38. Sum up what the Student Council at Thomas Tallis School does and who is involved in it.*

Useful phrases

discussion | to discuss | to feel strongly about sth | to nominate sb | participation | to participate | representative | to represent

b) *Watch this part of the film about the Student Council and the Student Voice at Thomas Tallis School again and take notes on the details that you think are the most interesting. Explain why.*

c) *Watch the rest of the film. Sum up why the members are in the Student Voice and how they are making a difference.*

d) *Compare the Student Council to the Student Voice. Use your notes from a) and c).*

A

B

4 Your turn: Having a voice at your school → S19

SPEAKING

a) *Does your school have a student council? If so, what things can this group do or have they done to change things at your school? Interview your representative for the school council to find out. Take notes.*

WRITING

b) *Use your notes to write an email to Laura in the film in English and explain how student representation works at your school. Use the phrases in the Useful phrases box for ideas.*

Useful phrases

to represent students | to organise projects | to point out issues such as … | to mediate when … | to give advice | …

5 Having a voice at a national level: Votes for teens → S1

READING

a) *You are in Debate Club at school and the next question you are going to debate is "Should 16- and 17-year-olds be allowed to vote in German national elections?" You look online for information and find this text. Take notes on the voting ages in other European countries and the reasons for and against lowering the voting age.*

Votes for teens: Is 16 the new 18?

For some time now, people have been saying "50 is the new 40", and even "60 is the new 40" … Around the world retirement ages are rising. In the UK people often live ten years longer than they did in 1980. What has this got to do with lowering voting ages? It shows that what it means to be a particular age is changing.

In almost all countries of the world, the voting age is 18, and has been for a long time. In the UK the voting age was lowered from 21 to 18 in 1969. Back then 18-year-olds usually had little experience of the world outside the area where they lived. Getting the latest news was difficult and they were mostly influenced by their parents' political views. Since then the quality of education has improved dramatically, and teenagers are very likely to have a much wider understanding of the world. Anyone with a smartphone can get news around the clock, and many teenagers are well-informed about politics. Research shows that parents' political views now have far less influence on teenagers than their friends' views.

The main argument against lowering the voting age is that people who are younger than 18 cannot make good political decisions. However, in Austria and some states of Germany, where the voting age has been lowered to 16, there is no evidence that the quality of voting choices among the under 18-year-olds is any worse than that of older voters. The number of people who make poor voting choices, such as voting or not voting for a party because of the leader's appearance, seems to be similar across all age groups.

In a recent survey in the UK, 53% of the young people polled said that the voting age should be lowered to 16. In Scotland 16- and 17-year-olds have been allowed to vote in Scottish elections since 2013. Maybe the rest of the UK will follow Scotland's lead soon so that, politically at least, "16 is the new 18".

SPEAKING

b) *Compare your notes. Then read the Across cultures box and think of more reasons for and against lowering the voting age.*

Across cultures

In the UK people who want the voting age to be lowered to 16 often argue that 11-year-olds can open a bank account with their parents' permission, 13-year-olds can have a part-time job, and 10-year-olds in England and Wales can be arrested for a crime. How appropriate do you think these three minimum ages are?

c) *Agree on a voting age that your group thinks appropriate. Explain your reasons in class.*

READING

6 Who does what in the UK?

I1 Diagram

Find out about the UK's political system. Outline the role of the monarchy as well as the roles of the government and parliament. Who has the power in the UK? Why do you think so? Give reasons for your answer.

7 A visit to the capital → S29

SPEAKING WB 3/3

a) *Look at the photo on the right. What's the name of the building? Where is it? What job does the person have who lives there?*

LISTENING A1

b) *Copy the diagram into your exercise book. A family from England is on holiday in Washington D.C. Listen to the conversation and complete the diagram with these words:*

make can suggest law check

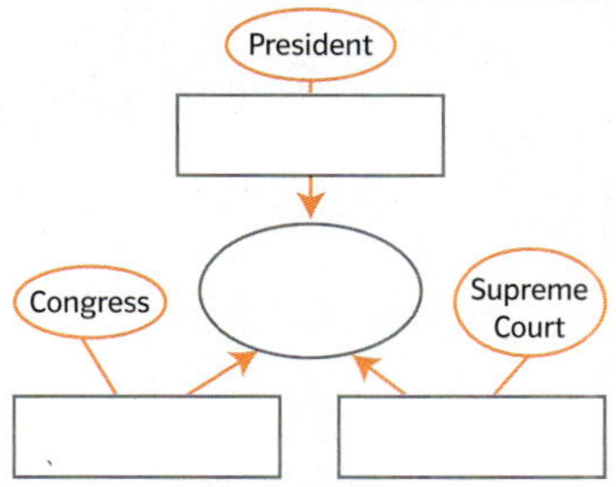

c) *Listen again and answer the questions:*

1. What does the US president do?
2. How long may someone be president?
3. Who decides who will become president?

8 What about the German political system? → S19, S34

MEDIATION MK V9

a) *A student at your partner school in the UK is doing a project on democracy in Europe and has asked you about the German political system. Find out about the roles of the German president, the* Bundeskanzler/-in, *parliament and the* Bundesrat.

b) *Write an email in English to the student at the partner school with the information you have found.*

Tip

What is the *Bundeskanzler/-in* called in English? How can you explain the *Bundesrat*?

9 Talking about Sustainable Development Goals

SPEAKING WB 3/4

a) *Look at the Sustainable Development Goals (SDGs) which were adopted by the UN in 2015. What can an individual, a student council and a government body do to achieve these goals?*

b) *Choose* ***one*** *of the goals. Discuss ideas how everyone at your school can work towards it.*

Unit 1

Never enough?

A

B

C

D

SPEAKING

1 Our lifestyle → More practice ● 140/1 → S11

a) *Look at the photos on this page and describe the situation in each one. Then explain in 2–3 sentences how the photos are related to the title of this unit and also to our lifestyles.*

b) *Look at the photos on p. 15 too. Outline the link between photos A and 1, B and 3, C and 2, D and 4. Write your ideas in a grid with these headings: action, impact.*

Word bank

to consume | choice | waste | disposable | to exceed | product | packaging | to persuade | to take away | to expect | shopping

MK

c) *Your turn: Find a photo of something you can't get enough of. Show the photo to your partner and think about the impact this might have.*

VOCABULARY

2 Working with word families → S37

Find verbs, nouns or adjectives for each of the words in the Word bank in ex. 1 and write them down. Use a monolingual dictionary for help. Sometimes there is more than one word for each part of speech.

Example: to consume → consumption, consumer

In Unit 1 you learn

… about consumerism and consumer protection.
You learn:

- how to talk about consumerism and the consequences for the environment.
- how to use adverbial clauses of manner and purpose.
- how to use the modals shall, might, used to, would and ought to.
- how to write a formal letter.

1

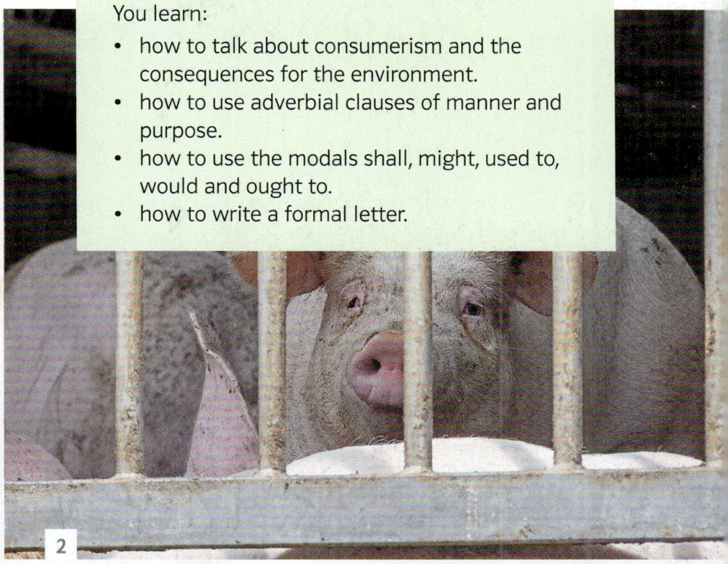
2

3

4

3 Young people and activism

→ More practice ○ 140/2 → More practice ● 140/3 → S29

LISTENING A2 WB 4/1

a) *Listen to a talk show with three activists. Note down what the speakers say about the following points: their cause, the origin of the movement, means of protest and their achievements.*

b) *Listen again. Add more information to your notes. Then present each movement.*

SPEAKING

c) *Your turn: Your school will let students off homework once a week in the summer term if they show social commitment. Read the Across cultures box. Which of the causes in the box or in a)/b) can you identify with the most, and why? How could you get involved? Would you collect signatures for petitions, hand out flyers, boycott something or raise money?*

Across cultures

If you're too young to vote or join a political party, there are other **ways of making your voice heard**. In Britain sisters Amy and Ella Meek, who were 10 and 12 at the time, started a project in 2016 to try to stop plastic waste. "Kids against Plastic" has since become a charity. In 2016 Muzoon Almellehan, who now lives in Newcastle, fled from Syria. She has spoken up about the right of every child to an education since she lived in a refugee camp in Jordan. Which activists in Germany do you know? Which causes do they fight for? How do they protest and what have they achieved?

A3

The life cycle of a T-shirt

SPEAKING

1 Before you read

→ More help 141/4 → S28

D1 Survey

Use an online survey tool to prepare a survey on these questions: Where do you get your clothes? How do you decide what you need? On average, how long do you keep your clothes? How do you dispose of clothes you don't wear any longer? Decide which options you want to give to answer each question. Also decide who will put the questions into the tool and who will organise and present the results. Give the survey to the class to do and present the results in class. Which ones are surprising?

The environmental impact of a T-shirt

Environmentalists are worried about the textile industry's carbon dioxide emissions and the fact that it causes 5%–10% of global pollution every year. A study of the ecological footprint of textiles looks at the five phases of the life cycle of a cotton T-shirt: raw materials, production, shipping, use and disposal. The last two phases have often been ignored as though they have little effect on a T-shirt's ecological footprint. However, this is not the case.

The main raw materials needed for a T-shirt are water and cotton. To produce one T-shirt, more than 2,000 litres of water are used. Globally, almost 25 million metric tonnes of cotton are produced every year, but less than 1% of this is organic. Instead, a lot of farmers use pesticides in order to make their fields more profitable. These pesticides can be harmful to the health of field workers.

After the raw cotton has been picked, it is taken to production sites in order to have it spun and made into fabric. From the US, for example, the cotton could travel more than 12,000 miles to textile factories in Bangladesh by plane or ship. Before the cotton can be turned into clothing, a lot of energy and water are used so the fabric can be bleached and dyed. If the water used in production is not treated, the chemicals in it can contaminate the groundwater. The textile workers who make the clothes later come into close contact with the harmful chemicals just as the field workers who produce the cotton do.

After this the finished T-shirts are transported thousands of miles to stores in order to sell them.

The next phase is use. The amount of money spent on clothes by an average family in California in a year is about 2.5 times higher than what one of the four million textile workers in Bangladesh earns. It is important to point out the environmental impact of this phase in case people forget that their T-shirts will of course be washed a lot. In the US one load of washing uses about 100 litres of water and the average American family does 400 loads per year so that we can say that every T-shirt has a large ecological footprint.

The T-shirt's life cycle isn't over quite yet, but unfortunately, its use is often much too short. Many people treat clothes like they are disposable. Globally, about 92 million tonnes of textiles are thrown away every year. In the US for example, each person throws away about 37 kg of clothes in the same period. Less than 14% of textiles there are recycled and the rest end up in landfill or are burnt. Having been treated with chemicals, the clothes release harmful emissions in the process. According to some sources, it looks as if at least one-fifth of clothing in the US is never actually worn.

2 Understanding the article → S1, S26

READING

a) *Read the article on p. 16 and sum it up in 2–3 sentences.*

WB 5/2

b) *Are these statements true or false? Give evidence from the text by quoting short passages from the text.*

1. The last two phases in the life of a T-shirt have a much smaller effect on its ecological footprint than the first three phases.
2. A lot of water is needed to produce cotton T-shirts.
3. Every year about 25,000 metric tonnes of organic cotton are produced worldwide.
4. Transporting T-shirts to stores is the only time in their life cycle that they travel long distances.
5. Each T-shirt is washed 400 times a year.
6. 14% of the textiles that are thrown away are burnt.

WRITING WB 5/3

c) *Create an infographic which shows the different phases in the life cycle of a T-shirt.*

SPEAKING

d) *Your turn: Compare what the article on p. 16 says about consumer behaviour with the results of your survey in ex. 1. How are they similar? How are they different?*

Media skills

To make an **infographic** you should:

1. Choose the points you want to include and write a short text about each one.
2. Find pictures to go with each text. Also use statistics and visuals if possible.
3. Put the information into a logical order.
4. Think of a catchy title or caption for each element and also for the infographic itself.

VOCABULARY

3 Finding synonyms

Find synonyms in the article on p. 16 for these words and phrases: environmental

transport | throwing sth away | not thought about | produced without harmful chemicals

made white | coloured | effect | site where waste is disposed of

GRAMMAR

4 Find the rule: Adverbial clauses of purpose and manner → <G1>, G2

WB 6/4

a) *Look at the adverbial clauses from the article on p. 16. Which adverbial clause describes* **why** *something is happening in the main clause (***purpose***)? Which adverbial clause describes* **how** *something is happening in the main clause (***manner***)?*

1. The last two phases have often been ignored **as though they have little effect on a T-shirt's ecological footprint.** (ll. 9–12)
2. Instead, a lot of farmers use pesticides **in order to make their fields more profitable.** (ll. 18–20)

b) *Find more examples of adverbial clauses of purpose and manner in the article on p. 16 and write them down in a grid in your exercise book.*

Tip

Adverbial clauses of purpose can use the linking words *so, so that, in order to* and *in case*. Adverbial clauses of manner can use the linking words *like, as though/as if* and *(just) as*.

GRAMMAR

5 What we could do better → G2

WB 6/5
WB 7/6

a) *A group of activists is trying to think of ways in which everyone can reduce the ecological footprint of clothing. Use the* ***linking words*** *to join the adverbial clauses of purpose and manner with the main clauses. Sometimes there is more than one correct answer.*

(just) like | as though | as if | as | so that | in order to | in case

Joe: People could buy fewer clothes and wear them for longer **1** they can reduce their ecological footprint. What do you think, Meg?
Meg: Consumers need to realise that they can't treat clothes **2** they were disposable.
Cal: And people also often wash clothes at a high temperature **3** they don't get clean at a lower temperature, but that isn't true.
Pat: No, it isn't. We also need to inform consumers about the poor working conditions in textile factories **4** they might not realise how 'fast fashion' is produced.
Kate: That's right. We've found that consumers who are aware of working conditions in textile factories are more careful when they buy new clothes, **5** you would expect.
Cara: Well, we could boycott certain fashion labels **6** stop companies using child labour.
Dan: That's a good idea. We want each person to feel **7** they can make a difference if they change the way that they shop. Anyone can boycott a fashion label.

b) *Each of you thinks of more ways to reduce the ecological footprint of clothing and writes sentences with the linking words in a). Then read out your sentences to your partner but leave out the linking words. Your partner should guess the correct linking words.*

WRITING

6 Alternatives to landfill → G2 → More help ○ 141/5

WB 7/7

a) *Look at these ways of treating clothes and other products in a sustainable way. Note down any advantages and disadvantages you think of.*

to repair torn clothes / broken machines | to share items with neighbours / friends | to buy second-hand | to sell things online | to regift items | to upcycle clothes | to sell items at a flea market

b) *Use your notes to write a post for your blog #sustainableliving, in which you give tips on how to give clothes a longer and more useful life cycle. Include adverbial clauses of purpose and manner.*

SPEAKING MK

7 Your turn: Sustainability projects → S30

WB 8/8

a) *Divide the class into six groups. Each group finds out about* ***one*** *of these sustainability projects. There might be one in your town or area. Take notes on the project and how it works.*

a repair café | a clothing swap | a flea market | sharing or swapping things using apps | a second-hand shop | selling second-hand items online

b) *Present the project in class in a two-minute talk. Describe the project and say why you think it is worthwhile. Suggest ways that people can participate in it.*

WRITING

8 Consumer trapped ir shopping trolley → S11

VIP File
Banksy is a street artist who is we l known for making critical comments on social issues. Their real identity is unknown. "Consumer trapped in shopping trolley" was created for the Cans Festival, London in 2008

a) *Describe the painting in the photo on the right.*

b) *Analyse it… message. What do you think the artist is trying … t consumerism? Give reasons for your answer.*

1 so that
2 as if / as though
3 " "
4 in case
5 as (just) like
6 in order to
7 like / as if / as though
p18 (5)

…es

… | The black and white graffiti shows … | upside down | bars | figure of … | …lp | to remind sb of sb / sth | cage | factory farm

VOCAB…

…rstand a formal letter → More help ○ 141/6 → S34, S37

…r and find out the meaning of the abbreviations using a dictionary. …em with the numbers 1–6.

pp. | Ref. | Enc. / Encl. | c/o

… | Unit 17 | Brennan Road Industrial Estate | Dublin 11 | Ireland

Rheinische Str. 209
44147 Dortmund
Germany

12 October 20..

1 Head Buyer, 2 Mr Elias Schröder, Assistant Buyer

3 Your recent order, 4 4892G

Dear Mr Schröder,
As of January next year, all our T-shirts will be produced with 50% recycled cotton. These products will have the comfortable feel customers expect; however, the environmental impact will be reduced. While it is better for the planet, recycled cotton comes at a slightly higher cost to us. For this reason, our T-shirt prices will increase by 12.5%. If you wish to cancel your recent order, we will refund your prepayment. Of course, we hope that you will not wish to do this and will share our goal of a more sustainable clothing industry.

Yours sincerely,
Liam Murphy

5 **Niamh O'Callaghan, Managing Director**
6 New eco-cotton products brochure, revised price list for all products.

MEDIATION V9 ▷ b) *Your boss asks you to sum up the letter in a short email. You should mention the increase in the price of the products and the reasons for this. Write the email in German.*

A 4

What shall I cook for dinner?

How can we all reduce our ecological footprint?

Overshoot Day draws attention to food consumption worldwide

"Shall we have meat or fish tonight?" asks a parent. "Can we have something vegetarian?" asks the teenager. In the past families used to have conversations like this about personal preferences, but now more people are becoming aware of the ecological impact of what's on their plate.

Overshoot Day is the day in the year when consumption of resources exceeds what our planet can regenerate in that year. In 2021 Earth's Overshoot Day was July 29. We all know we ought to reduce our ecological footprints in order to help push Overshoot Day back. It's easy to say, 'The government ought to do more about this'. While governments might take action in the future, we shall all need to play our parts in the years ahead. One of the easiest ways to do that is through our food choices.

The best tip is to eat less or no meat. The CO_2 emissions of a food aren't the only factor in calculating its environmental impact, but they can be a good guide. As shown in the chart below, 1 kg of lamb generates nearly 40 kg of CO_2. Just imagine a small bedroom filled with CO_2 gas. That is how much CO_2 is released when a family shares a kilo of lamb for dinner. Reducing global meat consumption by 50% would push Overshoot Day back by 17 days.

The best choice from the planet's point of view is a vegan diet. Second best is a vegetarian diet, preferably reducing the consumption of dairy products. If you can't say goodbye to meat, take an example from the past when people used to eat less meat than they do now. Many of our ancestors ate meat only as a rare treat.

A shocking 1.3 billion tonnes of food are wasted every year. This is about one-third of the total amount of food produced. Reducing food waste by half would bring Overshoot Day back by 13 days. Plan your meals, and only buy what you need. Also, go food shopping more often, buy less each time and only the things on your shopping list. That way you won't find things at the back of the fridge that have gone past their 'use-by' date. If you do find that you've bought too much food, give it to your local food bank.

People didn't use to eat apples in June or tomatoes in January or other food that wasn't 'in season', because it wasn't available. So, what did they use to eat? They used to enjoy fresh, locally produced food at the time it was ready to eat. Fruit and vegetables that you eat outside of their season have either been transported from far away or they have been grown in heated greenhouses with lots of chemical fertilisers. People often aren't aware of the natural seasons for fruit and vegetables in their region. Take the time to find out. Sometimes food websites give you ideas for seasonal recipes too.

A diet that is healthier for the planet is healthier for us too, and it might also be cheaper. Do your planet, body and purse a favour – think green every time you choose what to eat.

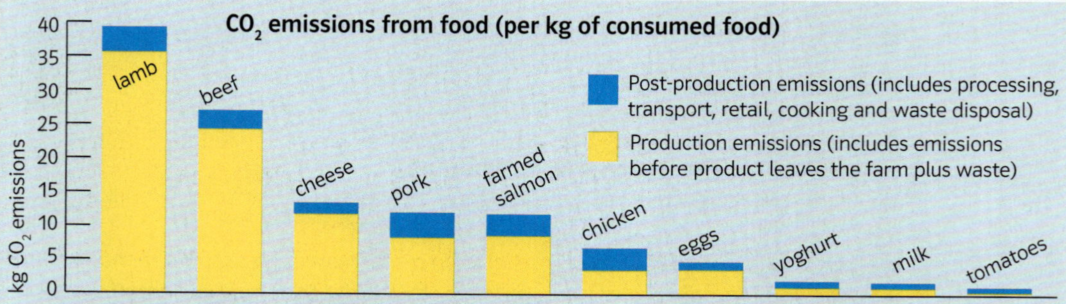

Source: Environmental Working Group (2011)

READING

1 Understanding the article → More help ○ 141/7 → S1

WB 9/9

a) *Read the article on p. 20 and write a list of tips to reduce a person's ecological footprint.*

b) *Explain what these figures in the article refer to:*

29 | 40 | 50 | 17 | 1,300,000,000 | $^1/_3$

VOCABULARY

2 Talking about environmental issues → More help ○ 142/8 → S2

Read the definitions and match them with words in the article on p. 20.

1. an amount which is used
2. make something grow again
3. finding out a figure
4. produces or causes production of
5. what is usually eaten
6. making something less
7. buildings for growing plants
8. substances that help plants to grow

GRAMMAR

3 Find the rule: The modals *shall, might, ought to, would* → <G3>, G4

WB 9/10

a) *Look at the sentences from the article on p. 20 and translate them into German.*

1. **Shall** we have meat or fish tonight? (l. 3)
2. The government **ought to** do more about this. (ll. 16–17)
3. While governments **might** take action in the future, we shall all need to play our parts in the years ahead. (ll. 17–19)
4. Reducing food waste by half **would** bring Overshoot Day back by 13 days. (ll. 42–44)

Tip

Which sentences can you translate with forms of *sollen, können / könnten* or *würden*?

b) *Complete the conversation with the modal auxiliaries from a). Use each one once.*

Alice: I think the school cafeteria **1** have vegan options as well as vegetarian ones.
Nathan: I agree. It **2** probably make the menu better for everyone, not just for vegans.
Alice: **3** we write a letter to the head teacher?
Nathan: One letter **4** not make much difference. Let's start a petition.

WRITING

4 What's for lunch? → More practice ○ 142/9 → More practice ● 142/10

WB 10/11

Look at the menu from your partner school in the UK. Make suggestions on how to improve the choice of food so that it is healthier and has a smaller ecological footprint. Write down your ideas. Try to use the modals ***shall, might, ought to*** *and* ***would*** *in your answer.*

Menu from November 11–15

MONDAY	TUESDAY	WEDNESDAY	THURSDAY	FRIDAY
► Lasagne and chips ► Apple crumble	► Beef burger and chips ► Banana yoghurt	► Chicken wings, green beans and a baked potato ► Strawberry trifle	► Hot dog in a bun ► Chocolate ice cream	► Chili con carne and rice ► Cherry cake

GRAMMAR

5 Find the rule: used to do sth → G4

WB 10/12

a) *Read the sentences with **used to + infinitive** from the text on p. 20. What information do we get about the action in the sentence?*

1. Take an example from the past when people **used to eat** less meat than they do now. (ll. 36–38)
2. People **didn't use to eat** apples in June… (l. 52)
3. So, what **did they use to eat**? (ll. 54–55)

b) *Translate the sentences in a) into German. What do you notice?*

c) *Find other examples with **used to + infinitive** in the article on p. 20 and translate them into German.*

GRAMMAR

6 Time to change → G4

a) *At the end of last year, Joe, Nadiya and Alfie were so worried about global warming that they decided to change some things in their lives. Compare the things that they **used to do** or **didn't use to do** a year ago with what they do / don't do now. Use the words and phrases.*

disposable cup | to waste electricity | short distance | travel mug | to turn off | public transport | devices | to drive on one's own / with a colleague | to prefer to take … | to have sth on all of the time

A year ago

Joe

Nadiya

Alfie

↓ ↓ ↓

Now

b) *Your turn: Think about yourself five years ago. Talk about things you used to do or used to like, but don't do or like any more. Also say what you do or like to do now instead.*

Example: I used to love meeting my friends in a skatepark, but now I prefer to play basketball with my club.

Beware of 'greenwashing'

VOCABULARY MK **1**

Warm-up: Vocabulary → S37

WB 11/13

a) *Write down definitions for these key words and phrases, which you will also hear in the video. You can use a dictionary for help.*

eco-conscious shopping | not legally defined | biodegradable | sustainable products | to mislead | green claim | the fine print | certification

b) *Exchange your definitions in a) with a partner and improve them. Then present your results in class.*

VIEWING **2**

Talking about greenwashing → S15

V2 WB 11/14

a) *Watch the documentary. Sum up the message of the film in 2–3 sentences.*

b) *Watch the documentary again. Take notes on the term 'greenwashing'. Explain how it works and outline the consequences for consumers.*

SPEAKING MK **3**

Examining green claims → More practice ○ 142/11 More practice ● 143/12 → S30

WB 11/15

a) *Choose **one** product which is described by its producer as eco-friendly. Examine the product and its packaging and try to answer the questions to find out if it is as green as it claims to be.*

- What green claims are written on the product / its packaging? How does the producer support these claims?
- What symbols of certification are printed on the packaging to suggest that it is environmentally friendly? Does the product carry any certification by a third party or an independent body? What does the certification mean?
- Where was the product produced? What does its production site tell us about the product's claim to be green?
- Is the product biodegradable? Is the packaging biodegradable or recyclable?

Tip

Check online what the symbols of certification on the product mean. What information does the company's website give about the product's ecological footprint?

b) *Present your findings in a three-minute talk.*

SPEAKING MK **4**

< Using apps to check products >

a) *Find apps which tell you about the ethical and ecological footprint of products. Then choose **one** app and try to answer these questions:*

- How does the app work?
- What information does it give about products, e.g. about sustainability, origin, biodegradability?
- How well does the app work when you actually use it in a shop?

b) *Compare your experiences in class. Would you recommend the app that you looked at? Is it helpful or not? How many stars out of five would you give the app?*

A 5–9

The Garbage Eater

SPEAKING

1 Before you read

What happens to the food that hasn't been eaten in your school cafeteria?
What could be done with that food instead?

James Hoff is a 17-year-old high school student who keeps a diary about his life and activities. He is involved in a campaign to save wetlands[1] near his town and has collected signatures for a petition. His ex-girlfriend, Sadie, is also involved in the campaign.

A **THE NEW GUY**

So I'm sitting in the lounge with Jessica and some other people, and Rich Herrington comes over and starts talking about this new guy and something he did in the cafeteria. I don't know what he's talking about, but he's very excited. So is everyone else. They've all heard about this new guy. Other people join in the conversation. Did you hear what he did? *Did you hear what he said? What's his name, anyway? Where's he from?* I've never seen people at my high school get like this.

People in my high school usually don't care about anything.

As it turns out, what this new guy does – drumroll[2], please – is stand by the garbage cans in the cafeteria and take food people are going to throw away. He takes it off their trays, apples, rolls, whatever they don't want, whatever's edible. He's very polite about it, but people still freak out. The first time he did it, one of the cafeteria ladies with the plastic bags on her head came out and yelled at him. Then a real teacher tried to make him stop and there was a big argument. He got sent to the principal's office. But then he did it again, in direct defiance[3] of the principal.

Which is kind of impressive, I have to admit.

B People are calling him the Garbage Eater. His real name is Jedediah Strock. "Jedediah" strikes me as a pretentious name. Especially if you're not calling yourself Jed but going for the long version, which sounds like you're a pioneer homesteader[4] or some dude out of the Bible. The garbage gathering is apparently a political statement. He's against waste. Big deal. Who isn't? Also, he has this straggly[5] beard and long straggly hair that he pulls back with one of those girl scrunchy things. People say how intense he is. People talk about his piercing blue eyes. I'm not buying it. He sounds too obvious. Anybody can stand there eating garbage in front of the whole school.

What's your point?

I see Sadie after school, and since we're petition partners and saving the wetlands together, she comes right over and asks me if I've heard about Jedediah. I say I have. She wants to know if I've actually seen him collecting the stuff off people's trays. I haven't. "That's pretty daring, don't you think?" she asks. She's all flushed[6] and excited about this guy. I don't answer. I ask her how the petitions went, out at the airport. She says good, they got a lot of signatures. She says she heard I did well, too, that I got sixty-five signatures. She says she couldn't believe I got so many. I say, "I'm actually quite charming when I want to be."

She says, "Yeah, when you *want* to be."

C Where the hell did this Jedediah guy come from? During fourth period he sits in the

1 **wetlands** ['wetləndz] wet area that is the home to certain plants and birds | 2 **drumroll** *(ironic)* ['drʌmrəʊl] a number of fast beats on a drum | 3 **in direct defiance of sb** [ɪn də'rekt dɪ'faɪəns əf] clearly not doing what sb tells you to do | 4 **homesteader** *(AE, historic)* ['həʊmstedə] one of the first people to have a farm in the West | 5 **straggly** ['strægli] hanging in an unattractive way | 6 **flushed** [flʌʃt] having a red face

middle of the main lawn, playing his guitar and *singing*. And doing Buddhist chants. What is up with that? He wears trashed Converse low-tops that are held together with duct tape[7], his T-shirts are so old you can see through them. He doesn't have enough facial hair to have a beard, but he has one anyway. The mystical hippie dude thing: Don't you have to be outta[8] high school to pull that off? I heard some jocks are planning to beat him up. I feel jealous.

The jocks[9] used to beat *me* up.

I see Sadie talking to Jedediah. God, I hate that guy. Supposedly his parents are missionaries and he lived in India for five years. Go back to frickin'[10] India, bro. Sadie is so kissing his ass. Asking him questions. Maybe they can go into the helping people business together. He can sing songs of love and understanding, and she can get a new bike path approved.

I hate bike paths.

D I finally see him doing it. He's been forbidden to do it by every authority known to man, but there he is, during Wednesday lunch, collecting the garbage off people's trays.

> **Stop and think:**
> What do you think happens next? How do the students react?

He does it for like thirty seconds and then Mr. Greco, the gym teacher, swoops down[11] on him. Mr. Greco grabs Jedediah's very skinny arm and yanks him away from the garbage cans. All the apples and unopened milk cartons and stuff go spilling across the floor. Mr. Greco is an ex-Marine[12]. He grabs the Garbage Eater by the back of his shirt and marches him toward the principal's office. But here's the killer. As he's being led away, people begin to clap. Everyone in the cafeteria starts clapping and standing up. Soon the whole cafeteria is on their feet giving him a standing ovation, as Mr. Greco practically rips his shirt off. I have to stand up or look like a total jerk.

I don't clap, though.

In the meantime, while the Garbage Eater is getting all the attention at school, I'm stuck downtown trying to get crazy people to sign my stupid petition. That's my own demented[13] sense of honor. I said I'd do the petitions, so I do them. One good thing, I finally meet Alice Weitzman. She's the head of Save the Wetlands. But a lot of good that does me. I'm still standing in the street getting signatures, while Sadie is somewhere else, getting all sparkle-eyed[14] over Jedediah. Everyone thinks he's so rad. They love that he keeps doing the garbage thing no matter how many times they bust him. Of course his parents have been called. That's the latest news everyone is buzzing about.

What will the missionary parents do?

I don't think Sadie is really in love with Jedediah. But who knows? He keeps getting in trouble and now his parents are involved. Apparently, his mother screamed at Mr. Brown about how racist our school is. Sadie is all worked up about it. People are saying Jedediah has a First Amendment[15] right to express himself. Collecting garbage is freedom of speech. Other people (me) think he's a show-off. Someone interviewed him for the school paper and it turned out he has been thrown out of a couple different schools for similar escapades. The teachers all know he isn't hurting anything, but at the same time they can't let him do stuff he's been told not to do.

I can just imagine Mr. Brown sitting in his office rolling his eyes.

E I see the Garbage Eater and Sadie sitting out on the main lawn during lunch. His guitar is lying gently on the grass, he's sitting cross-legged, his ancient[16] Converse duct-taped to his feet. Sadie's doing her "attentive" pose, her "help me be a better person" posture.

7 **duct tape** ['dʌkt teɪp] long piece of fabric used to stick things together | 8 **outta** *(AE, infml)* ['aʊtə] out of | 9 **jock** *(AE)* [dʒɒk] sb who plays a lot of sport | 10 **frickin'** *(AE, slang)* ['frɪkɪŋ] a rude word | 11 **to swoop down on sb** ['swu:p ˌdaʊn ɒn] to move fast towards sb | 12 **Marine** *(AE)* [mə'ri:n] soldier in a special unit | 13 **demented** [dɪ'mentɪd] crazy | 14 **to get all sparkle-eyed** [get 'ɔ:l ˌspɑ:kl‿'aɪd] to look excited | 15 **First Amendment** *(AE)* [ˌfɜ:st ə'mendmənt] right to freedom of speech | 16 **ancient** ['eɪnʃənt] very old

So I decide to go see for myself. Maybe I've been too harsh on this guy. We are on the same side, after all. Probably Sadie will tell him about our petition. I'm the guy who got sixty-five signatures on my first day. So I walk over and say hi and sit down, and Jedediah pretends I'm not there. He's busy going on and on about India, the conditions there, the poor, the way his parents taught him to never give in to structure or authority or meaningless directives[17]. He is a very earnest dude. I try to roll with it. I nod and agree that starvation is bad. But he barely acknowledges me. He is totally focused on Sadie. They are bonding[18] in a deep do-gooder trance of self-righteousness and high self-esteem energies. The bell's about to ring and I have to go so I say good-bye and stand up. They barely notice. Sadie could have helped. She could have said, "Jedediah, this is James. He's helping me save the wetlands." But she doesn't.

Sixty-five signatures in one day. Keep that in mind, Mr. Strock.

From: Blake Nelson, *Destroy all cars*, 2009 (abridged)

READING

2 Understanding the story → More practice ○ 143/13 → More practice ● 143/14

a) *Describe James' reaction to Jedediah. Compare his reaction to the reactions of the other students and the staff at the school.*

b) *Write a characterisation of James and Jedediah, in which you compare their behaviour, and their ways of dealing with each another and with other characters.*

c) *Explain what James means when he says, "We are on the same side, after all" (ll. 146–147). Use quotations from the text to support your answer.*

VOCABULARY

3 Looking at language → S1

Find the informal phrases in the story which have the same meaning as these phrases:

are upset and angry | What is the reason for …? | broken | man | trying hard to make sb like you | this is the exciting thing | a stupid person | great | stop sb committing a crime | to accept a difficult situation

READING

4 Analysis: Narrative perspective and language → S6

a) *Analyse the narrative perspective in the extract and the effect it has on the reader.*

b) *Comment on the language in the extract by referring to examples of humour, exaggeration and rhetorical questions. What does the language tell the reader about the character of James?*

WRITING

5 Options → More help ○ 143/15 → S8, S17

WB 12–15/16–19

*Choose **one** of the options:*

A Read the story again up to l. 121 and write a blog entry from Jedediah's point of view. How does he feel about what happened in the cafeteria with Mr Greco? What does he think will happen when his parents visit Mr Brown?

B Write an article for the high school yearbook, in which you present Jedediah and what he did. Is the tone serious / funny / shocked? Think of a good title for the article.

17 **directive** [də'rektɪv] instruction | 18 **to bond** ['bɒnd] to make one's relationship stronger

How to choose the appropriate register and style

In this unit task you are going to write a formal letter. This page will help you to choose the correct register and style for the letter.

1 Comparing language and style → More help ○ 143/16 → S8

WB 16/20 **a)** *Read the texts and explain both situations. Who is communicating with whom, and why?*

A

Hi Student Council! Please check and correct this draft and send the letter to Mr. Brown.

We're all really angry that our new friend Jedediah Strock (aka 'the Garbage Eater') has been thrown out of school. What he did in the cafeteria did no harm to anybody and in fact, it's made a lot of us think about this problem. Did you know that about 40% of all food in the US is thrown away? Wasting less of it would make the whole country greener. Jedediah has inspired lots of us to reduce how much food we waste at school and at home. Anyway, Jedediah was expelled because, according to the teachers, he 'consistently disobeyed school regulations'. We've checked all the school rules and we couldn't find anything about collecting food that's been thrown away at school!!! We think the teachers ought to show us the regulations they're talking about. On top of that, we're asking the principal to let Jedediah come back to school right now. In this envelope you'll find a petition with 90 signatures from Grade 10 students. Thanks, Sadie

B

Attn. Mr. Brown, School Principal

Dear Mr. Brown,

Re: The recent expulsion of Jedediah Strock

Many Grade 10 students have asked us to express their disappointment at the expulsion of Jedediah Strock from our school. The actions he took to find a use for unwanted food that would otherwise have been thrown away were completely harmless. Furthermore, he raised awareness of a serious issue. They would like to point out that 40% of all food in the US is wasted. Reducing that waste would reduce this country's ecological footprint. Many of the students have found his actions inspiring and have started trying to reduce the amount of food wasted at school and at home.

The reason given for expelling Mr. Strock was that he had 'consistently disobeyed school regulations'. Having examined the school rules, the students can find no regulation forbidding a student from saving food that has been thrown away at school. They respectfully ask the school authorities to produce evidence of any such regulation. Moreover, they request Mr. Strock's reinstatement as a student at this school. Thank you in advance for your consideration of this matter.

Yours sincerely,

Samantha Torres

Samantha Torres, President of the Student Council

Enc: A petition with 90 signatures calling for Jedediah Strock's reinstatement

b) *Outline the differences in structure and style between the two texts. Refer to examples of formal or informal phrases, grammar, politeness and linking words.*

MK D2 Word bank

A challenge to reduce waste

You have read the story about the "Garbage Eater", and you want to launch a project at your school to reduce food waste. You would also like to challenge your partner schools in other countries to take part in the project. You're going to work in groups. Each group works out a food waste reduction strategy for your school and writes a formal letter to the principal of a different school outlining the challenge.

Step 1

Brainstorm ideas. → WB 17/21

Think about these questions in your group and note down your ideas:

- In which situations is food thrown away at your school?
- How is this food waste disposed of?
- Based on how food is disposed of, collect ideas about better ways to dispose of it.
- How can each student, each class and the whole school change their behaviour so that less food is wasted?

Tip

You can search online for similar projects carried out by other schools.

Step 2

Make an overview and decide on a strategy.

Make an overview of your ideas in Step 1 by writing them in a grid or mind map. Each group presents its ideas. The class votes on the five best ideas that everyone can put into practice.

Step 3

Structure and write your letter. → WB 17/22

a) *Plan the structure of the letter to the head of the other school. Include these parts:*

1. an introduction (introduce the class and the project)
2. a main part (describe the situation with food waste at your school; list ideas to reduce food waste)
3. an ending (ask whether the school would also like to take part in the project; suggest working together to develop a checklist for the people who are taking part in the project)

b) *Add phrases that you could use in each part of the letter.*

c) *Write the letter on a computer.* → How to: Understand a formal letter, p. 19 → How to choose the appropriate register and style, p. 27 → S18 → <G1>, G2

Step 4

Give feedback.

Send the letter to another group to get feedback on these questions:

- Is it clear what the challenge is about and why it is important?
- Does the recipient know at the end what he / she has to do next?
- Does the letter have a clear structure, i.e. a paragraph each for the introduction, main part and ending?
- Are the style, tone and register appropriate? → S8

Step 5

Improve the letter.

Use the feedback to write the final version of your letter. → S17

A 10–15

The Carbon Diaries

SPEAKING

1 Before you read

Have you ever experienced a power cut that went on for a number of hours? What did you do? What things couldn't you do? How did you feel?

The Carbon Diaries 2015 *was published in 2008. The science-fiction novel is set in London and is written in the form of diary entries by 16-year-old Laura. Climate change is causing natural disasters like blizzards, droughts and wildfires, and politicians in the UK have decided to introduce carbon rationing[1] in order to reduce the use of fossil fuels[2]. In 2015 Britain was still a member of the EU.*

A

We're going in, boys!

8/01/15

UK to commence 60 % Carbon Rations

Government sets date

In a historic parliamentary speech, the Prime Minister today announced the date of full UK entry into a nationwide carbon rationing system. As of[3] January 8th 2015, the UK will be the first nation state within the EU to implement the system. It's an emotive date, exactly 63 years to the day the nation last endured[4] food and petrol rationing in WW2[5].

Fri, Jan 2nd

I wanted to watch the news and check out the countdown to rationing, so I switched on Channel 4 News. They've got this big countdown clock in the studio with massive Day-Glo carbon symbols instead of numbers on its face. It was kind of like kid's TV cept it's so real. Messed up. Anyway, today's symbol was about food miles. The presenter stood in front of a split video screen and waved his arm towards the left-side screen, where there was a South African farmer holding out a juicy mango. On the other side there was a farmer in Kent holding a wrinkled apple. Basically a 12,000-air-mile mango versus a 40-minutes-in-the-back-of-a-dirty-old-truck apple. The carbon maths[6] is a no-brainer, but life is definitely going to be a lot less glamorous.

This 60 % reduction is way over the top. We were supposed to get there by 2030, but after the Great Storm everything changed and it all became more hectic. Even so, why is the UK going first? I know we were hit the hardest in the storm – that was one messed-up time; houses literally ripped out of the ground, thousands of people homeless over the whole winter, no petrol for a month. I guess something really happened to people then. It was like everyone went *That's enough. Stop now.* Europe's going to follow – I mean, they've got to in the end – but right now it's like they're happy for someone else to do it first. So looks like we're the stupid guinea-pig freaks[7], giving up everything while the rest sit back and watch.

1 **carbon rationing** ['kɑ:bn 'ræʃnɪŋ] system where people are only allowed to produce a certain amount of carbon | 2 **fossil fuel** ['fɒsl ˌfju:l] material, e.g. oil, gas, which is used to produce energy | 3 **as of** ['æz‿əv] starting on a certain date | 4 **to endure sth** [ɪn'djuə] to deal with a difficult situation | 5 **WW2** [ˌwɜ:ld wɔ: 'tu:] World War Two | 6 **carbon maths** ['kɑ:bn mæθs] the amount of carbon produced by sth | 7 **guinea-pig freak** ['gɪni: ˌpɪg 'fri:k] sb who takes part in an experiment

B

Sat, Jan 3rd

Dad sat us all down again tonight and took us thru a disgusting government online form to work out what our family CO allowance actually is. It's heavy. Basically we've got a carbon allowance of 200 Carbon Points per month to spend on travel, heat and food. All other stuff like clothes and technology and books have already got the Carbon Points built into the price, so say you wanna buy a PC but it's been shipped over from China and built using dirty fossil fuel then you're gonna pay a lot more for it in Euros – cos you're paying for all the energy that's gone into making it.

At first they set up a free trading system so that if you were rich you could just buy up carbon in cash and live how you wanted – but after the riots last September the Gov backed down and changed the rules so that no one's allowed to buy more than 50 extra points a month.

And the worst thing is, on top of all this, me and Kim have to give up loads of our points for the family energy allowance, which leaves us some pathetic amount for travel, college, going out. ... Using the car's gonna be cut way back, all of us get access[8] to the PC, TV, HD, stereo for only 2 hours a day, heating is down to 16°C in the living room and 1 hour a day for the rest of the house, showers max 5 minutes, baths only at weekend. We've got to choose – hairdryer, toaster, microwave, smartphone, de-ioniser (Mum), kettle, lights, PDA, e-pod, fridge or freezer and on and on. Flights are a real no-no and shopping, travelling and going out not much better. It's all kind of a *choice*.

C

Mon, Jan 5th

Carbon cards came today ...

They've got these little blocks down one side going from green to red and as you use up your year's ration they fade away[9] one by one till you're down to the last red and then you're all alone, crying in the dark. Kim won't unwrap her card, she says if she touches it then that's all her youth gone. I felt pretty shaky[10] unwrapping mine, not that I really have a youth in my family. My sister's got it.

Thurs, Jan 8th

Rationing.

Back to college, and I got in late cos I had to take Mum to her bus stop. Her eyes filled up with tears as we walked past the Saab. She whispered, "It's not for ever," and stroked the bonnet. I pretended not to see – it's better than her being positive.

We missed the first bus cos her high heels were rubbing, so we had to wait 15 minutes in the drizzle till the next one. When it finally came I leapt on, swiped my card and was hurrying upstairs, only to see Mum behind me going thru her purse, bag and pockets, throwing fluff and Conran receipts everywhere. She looked up at me.

"Laura, darling, I can't find my card. Can you lend me some ..."

The driver shook his head. "No carbon card, no ride, love."

"But, please ..."

A woman out in the rain shouted: "Get off, yer stoopid cow! You're holding us up."

And then Mum started to cry. I went back down and walked her off the bus. "We'll have to go home and get your card, Mum."

"Found it! In the lining! Bastards!" Mum shook the green plastic at the bus, now rumbling off into the traffic.

8 access ['ækses] being able or having the right to use sth | **9 to fade away** [ˌfeɪd‿ə'weɪ] to disappear slowly | **10 shaky** ['ʃeɪki] weak because one is upset

D **Weds, Jan 14th**
I woke up this morning and it was freezing, freezing cold. I'm only allowed heat on in my room between 7 and 8. I went and looked at the Smart Meter in the hall. It's this thing that tells you everything that's going on with energy in the house. Even for our one hour of heat Dad's locked the bedroom temp at 15°C. What a joke – it's not even enough to melt the frost on the windows.

Thurs, Jan 15th
There's heavy snowstorms all over Southern Europe.

Mon, Jan 19th
The blizzards in Europe are getting worse – and spreading north. Italy has just lost all its electricity. The news showed this footage of the Vatican going black, window after window. Later they started up emergency generators so they could power up the Pope saying something into a microphone in Latin to a couple of cardinals. Whatever.

E **Tues, Jan 20th**
We had a power cut in the night. The house is so cold now, it feels like 200 years of evil chill creeping into my bones. Reminds me of the Great Storm. Cuts are scary – you know when you go to switch the light on and it's dead? It was so freezing I went shopping with Mum and Dad just to keep my blood moving. Super-strange experience.

Stop and think:
What do you think Laura's shopping experience was like? How was it different to the time before carbon rationing?

It was all dark inside the shop cos they'd switched off loads of lights and the aircon and those fans that spread baking-bread smells around. It was just like a big warehouse[11]. It was pretty funny, all the nice middle-class people pretending they weren't panic buying and that it was completely normal for them to be pushing six trolleys around, totally bulging[12] with stuff. The staff kept making people put things back at the checkout cos they'd gone over their CO points.

My mother nearly had a fight with this other woman over a multi-pack of garlic and basil passata.

They both put their hands on the box at the same time and gave a little jerky tug[13] and then went "Excuse me," followed by another tug and an *Aha, ha, ha*, knuckles starting to whiten around the edges of the packet. Then my mother really went for it.

"I wouldn't insist normally but this is one of the few foods my daughter" (stroking my hair) "can eat – she has an acid deficiency. Her skin comes out in boils if she gets low."

The other woman backed off like a defeated animal in a nature programme.

11 **warehouse** ['weəhaʊs] big building in which thousands of products are kept | 12 **to bulge** [bʌldʒ] to be completely full | 13 **jerky tug** [ˌdʒɜ:ki 'tʌg] pulling hard on sth

F **Thurs, Jan 22nd**

Italy has only just got its power back. They've found out the cause of the blackout – a tree fell on a live cable on the Swiss border. A bloody *plant* wiped out a whole country for 60 hours. Loads of old people have died. So strange. I never knew that cold could kill people like that. France is under deep snow now, and it's coming our way.

We had a Sunday roast, the first one ever. Mum is so desperate[14] for everything to be normal, and even Dad joined in. He came into the kitchen rubbing his hands going, "Mmm, that smells good," like he was a dad in a happy-family sitcom.

Kim refused to come out of her room and eat with us, even though my father begged her. This is unusual cos normally she softens up for him, if a crocodile *can* soften. Finally Mum lost it[15]. She shouted from the kitchen:

"I've spent the whole afternoon cooking this dinner for you, so you can at least have the manners to come and eat it."

Kim's door opened for a second. "Don't pretend you did it for me. You did it for you. You make me sick!" Slam!

The really annoying thing about Kim is although she's a total bitch, she is also the most honest person I've ever met. She's raised her game[16] to a whole new level right now, though – basically used the cancellation of her gap year to New York to start a war against my parents. They're doomed[17].

As a special Sunday treat we watched separate movies in separate rooms. That was *so* the best thing about unrestricted[18] carbon. The freedom.

I don't know if our family can survive being *together*.

From: Saci Lloyd, *The Carbon Diaries*, 2015 (abridged)

SPEAKING

2 Your reaction

Outline your reaction to the extract from the science-fiction novel. What do you think of the situation that Laura finds herself in? Is the family's reaction to carbon rationing understandable / exaggerated / unrealistic? Give reasons for your answer.

READING

3 Understanding the text → S1

a) *Sum up what happens in the extract in 4–5 sentences.*

b) *The main theme of this extract (and of the book) is presented on three levels:*
1. *a global level,*
2. *a national level,*
3. *an individual level.*

Name the parties involved at each level and describe the conflicts between them. Give examples from the text.

Word bank

to pretend | to cry | to try to stay in control | to feel scared | to rebel against sb / sth | to react emotionally | to be annoyed with / by | to get angry with sb | to seem tough | to express his / her / … anger

c) *The parents and the children in the family react differently to carbon rationing. Describe each character's reaction and say who you identify with the most, and why.*

d) *In the extract Laura writes about two concepts: 'choice' (l. 80) and 'freedom' (l. 214). Explain how she defines these terms. Why are they important for the plot?*

14 **to be desperate** ['desprət] *here:* to really want sth to happen although it probably will not | 15 **to lose it** *(infml)* ['lu:z‿ɪt] to lose control of one's emotions | 16 **to raise one's game** ['reɪz wʌnz geɪm] to do more to achieve one's goals | 17 **to be doomed** [bɪ 'du:md] to be certain to have a very bad experience | 18 **unrestricted** [ˌʌnrɪ'strɪktɪd] without a limit

VOCABULARY

4 The consequences of carbon rationing → S2

Collect words and phrases in the extract relating to the consequences of carbon rationing. You can write them in a grid with the following headings: at home / lifestyle / transport / shopping.

READING

5 Literary genre: Diary → S4

a) *Read the skills box and find examples in the extract of the features you would expect in a novel written in the form of diary entries. Give line numbers.*

b) *Analyse the effect that these features have on you, the reader.*

Reading skills

A novel that is written in the form of **diary entries** usually has the following features:

- Readers are given information about the protagonist's thoughts and feelings.
- Events are in a chronological order.
- The setting is limited to places that the protagonist knows.
- The register and language are informal.

SPEAKING

6 Stylistic devices: Imagery → S9

a) *How does the narrator describe the people in her family? Find examples of any imagery that she uses.*

b) *What impression do you get of the characters? What does the imagery tell the reader about the narrator's relationship with each person?*

SPEAKING

7 Language: Tone → S8

a) *The text has a serious topic, but it isn't written completely in a serious tone. Find examples of the types of tone used in the diary entries.*

b) *What effect do the types of tone have on the reader? How would the effect be different if the writer had only used a serious tone?*

c) *Compare the tone used in Story 1 and Story 2. How are they similar? How are they different?*

Writing skills

The following elements create a specific **tone**:

- very short or one-word sentences,
- very informal register, as if speaking rather than writing,
- language written as if it is spoken informally instead of with the usual spelling.

8 Options

*Choose **one** of the options:*

WRITING

A Imagine you are living in the same town in Britain as Laura during carbon rationing. Write a diary entry in which you outline the problems it creates and describe your feelings.

SPEAKING

B Read the diary entry for 3rd January when Laura's family have a conference. Take notes on any questions each character could ask or points they might make. How could each character react? Use your notes to make prompt cards. Prepare and act out a role play in class.

Start: Dad: We've got a carbon allowance of 200 Carbon Points per month to spend on travel, heat and food. Unfortunately, girls, you must also give some of your points to …

Can you ...

1. talk about consumerism and the consequences for the environment?	Less than 14% of textiles there are recycled. / 1.3 billion tonnes of food are wasted every year.
2. use adverbial clauses of manner and purpose?	People treat clothes like they are disposable. / It is taken to production sites in order to have it spun.
3. use the modals *shall, might, used to, would* and *ought to?*	We ought to reduce our ecological footprints. / Governments might take action in the future.
4. write a formal letter?	Yours sincerely, Liam Murphy

LISTENING

1 Speech at a protest

A 16

A student at a partner school in the UK tells you about Buy Nothing Day and sends you a link to a speech given at the start of a protest in London. Read the tasks. Then listen to the speech. While you are listening, choose the correct answers.

1. The speaker especially welcomes ...
   a) the young people.
   b) the older people.
   c) the politicians.
2. The protest is taking place on this date as ...
   a) people have time.
   b) people buy lots of things on this day.
   c) it was the only possible date.
3. Products have two prices: the money you pay for them and ...
   a) the price to the producer.
   b) the price to the consumer.
   c) the price to the environment.
4. The worst effect of consumerism is ...
   a) the advertising.
   b) the carbon dioxide emissions.
   c) the number of things in people's homes.
5. The event is held in the UK on ...
   a) the same day as in the USA.
   b) the Saturday after Black Friday.
   c) Black Friday and the day after too.
6. According to the speaker, people need to change their behaviour ...
   a) to save money.
   b) to give future generations a future.
   c) to support shops.

2 Buy Nothing Day

READING

a) *Read the article and letter to the editor on p. 35. Then read the events A–G and put them in the correct order.*

A The protest started.
B Black Friday events ended in local shops.
C The protesters ate food together.
D Mr Bennett will go to a new doctor's appointment.
E A speaker gave the last of the speeches.
F Mr Bennett made the first doctor's appointment.
G Traffic was delayed in the town centre.

b) *Answer the questions about the texts.*

1. What is so special about the day on which the protest is held?
2. What did Heather Morris say about the organisers' future plans?
3. What alternative suggestion does the letter writer give to the protesters?
4. What point(s) does Mr Bennett want to make?

SPEAKING

c) *Do you agree with the organisers of the protest or the letter writer? Give reasons for your answer.*

→ Solutions p. 276

Town centre Buy Nothing Day protest

Protest during Black Friday events

Hundreds of protesters gathered in the town centre in order to protest against consumerism and the damage it causes to the environment. The Buy Nothing Day protest was planned for the same day as Black Friday events in stores and online. The organisers claimed that more than 1,000 people attended. The local police put the figure at around 900. The protest began at 11 a.m. with speeches in George Square. The protesters then walked along Castle Road, South Street and Park Avenue before arriving at around 12:30 p.m. in Victoria Park for more speeches and a 'picnic against climate change'.

One of the organisers of the event Heather Morris told the *County News*, "We organised this event to make the people of this town remember that our consumerism cannot just go on as if we had decades to solve the climate emergency and our other environmental problems. Almost everybody now knows that people in rich countries ought to consume less, but real change still isn't happening. This is not just about one protest today. We shall continue to raise awareness of this issue as much as we can. Shop less, live more. System change, not climate change."

The protest ended peacefully, and nobody was arrested. Meanwhile, Black Friday events continued as planned in local stores, with many price reductions and some stores reporting their busiest day of the year so far.

Dear Editor,

I am writing because I would like to comment on your article "Town centre Buy Nothing Day protest" published on 30th November. The article did not report the impact of the protest on local residents such as myself. At the time of the protest, I was driving to a doctor's appointment[1] for which I had waited several days. As a result of the traffic delays[2] caused by the protest, I missed my appointment. This wasted my time and, far more importantly, it wasted the doctor's time. Moreover, it was not possible to book another appointment until early December, causing a further delay to my treatment[3].

I do not disagree with the protesters' message. However, I do disagree with the protesters' way of spreading the message. Stopping town centre traffic so that they can make a political point which most people are already aware of and generally agree with is unacceptable. I believe they would get better results by trying to persuade politicians and business leaders to act directly. Causing problems for people like me achieves nothing. What is worse, it might make people associate environmental activism with problems for themselves.

Edward Bennett

photo: **greed** [griːd] wanting power and money | 1 **appointment** [ə'pɔɪntmənt] date and time you agree to meet sb | 2 **traffic delay** ['træfɪk dɪ'leɪ] when cars must go more slowly | 3 **treatment** ['triːtmənt] *here:* medical help when sb is ill

WRITING

3 What do you think?

*Choose **one** of the options:*

A Based on the article, "Town centre Buy Nothing Day protest" on p. 35, write a letter to the editor with your opinion of Buy Nothing Day.

B Write a letter to the editor in which you give your reaction to Edward Bennett's letter on p. 35.

VOCABULARY

4 Water: A key resource

Choose the correct words to complete the text.

A raw 1 that is used in production and is often ignored is water. The problem is that our 2 has a big 3 on limited fresh water supplies such as rivers and lakes. In dry areas factories and farms may rely on 4, a resource which will take centuries to 5. There are further problems when the time comes to 6 things we don't want any more. Harmful 7 from items that have been 8 can escape from 9 and 10 water supplies. An 'organic' label on some products may in fact be an example of 11. No 12 were used, but how much water was needed? The 13 industry is a very big consumer of water. Buying an organic 14 T-shirt is better than buying a non-organic one, but wearing the T-shirts you already have is better still.

1. a) substance b) material c) stuff
2. a) consumerism b) consumer c) consuming
3. a) damage b) influence c) impact
4. a) groundwater b) rain c) rivers
5. a) generate b) regenerate c) produce
6. a) transport b) store c) dispose of
7. a) clothes b) materials c) chemicals
8. a) thrown b) thrown away c) disposed
9. a) landfills b) homes c) schools
10. a) clean b) contaminate c) reduce
11. a) advertising b) certification c) greenwashing
12. a) fertilisers b) pesticides c) colours
13. a) clothes b) textile c) dress
14. a) summer b) plastic c) cotton

MEDIATION

5 Apps and food waste

You often visit an online forum which shares ideas about reducing our ecological footprint. Most of the forum members are in the UK and they have asked you about apps in Germany which help people to reduce food waste. You have found this article online. Write a comment in English for the forum in which you explain how each of the apps works.

Apps gegen Lebensmittelverschwendung

In Deutschland landen jedes Jahr mehr als elf Millionen Tonnen Lebensmittel im Müll. Neben Händlern und Restaurantbesitzern werfen auch Verbraucherinnen und Verbraucher übriggebliebenes Essen weg, etwa weil das Mindesthaltbarkeitsdatum abgelaufen ist. Mit den Apps „Beste Reste" und „Too Good To Go" können Verbraucherinnen und Verbraucher jetzt schon etwas gegen Lebensmittelverschwendung unternehmen. Die App „Beste Reste", die Teil der Kampagne „Zu gut für die Tonne!" ist, bietet mehr als 700 Kochrezepte, die mit Lebensmittelresten gekocht werden können. Auf der Suchseite der App lassen sich bis zu drei Zutaten miteinander kombinieren. Die App schränkt die Auswahl automatisch auf mögliche Kombinationen ein und wirft passende Kochrezepte aus. Die App „Too Good To Go" vernetzt Restaurants, Bäckereien und Supermärkte mit Verbrauchern, die übriggebliebene Lebensmittel vor der Mülltonne retten wollen. Die Gerichte oder Produkte werden zu einem wesentlich geringeren Preis verkauft. Auf diese Weise bekommen App-Nutzerinnen und -Nutzer leckeres Essen und gleichzeitig leisten sie einen Beitrag gegen Verschwendung.

Quelle: Die Bundesregierung, 5. August 2019.

→ Solutions p. 276

GRAMMAR

6 Your ideas ...

Complete the sentences with your ideas based on the theme of this unit.

1. We ought to reduce waste so that ...
2. ... as though our planet has unlimited resources.
3. ... in order to protect the environment for future generations.
4. ... like never before in human history.
5. ... as people did when consumer technology was more expensive.
6. .... in case it can be repaired.
7. It sometimes seems as if ...

GRAMMAR

7 A family conversation

a) *Rewrite the conversation with* ***shall, might, ought to*** *and* ***used to****.*

1 b material
2 a consumerism
3 c impact
4 a groundwater
5 b regenerate
6 c dispose of
7 c chemicals
8 b thrown away
9 a landfills
10 b contaminate
11 c greenwashing
12 b pesticides
13 b textile
14 c cotton

Imogen: Do you think we should try
ecoming vegetarians?
aybe. I was a vegetarian when
was younger.
know, but Mum may not be very
appy about it.
/hen we were at university, we
ften cooked vegetarian food.
o you agree it's a good idea to ask
Mum what she thinks?

e next part of the conversation with a form of ***used to*** *where possible.*

How often did you cook together in those days?
Quite often. We lived in the same student house, so we shared a kitchen.
That's how we got to know each other.
Back then, did you go to protests together too?
No, at that time we had very different interests. She certainly didn't like my protests
and I didn't do much else!

SPEAKING

8 You, the consumer

a) *In small groups discuss these strategies for reducing waste. How much do you think they can help the environment? Would you think about doing them? Explain why or why not.*

1. Buy only three new items of clothing per year.
2. Buy second-hand alternatives to new things whenever possible.
3. Always try to repair things instead of throwing them away.
4. Try to have a most zero food waste.
5. If you're not already, become a vegetarian.
6. If you're not already, become a vegan.

b) *Read the quotation and then comment on it. Do you agree with it or not? Think of arguments for and against it.*

"As consumers we have so much power to change the world by just being careful in what we buy."
Emma Watson

Check-in

Text and media smart 1

Dealing with advertising

You're going to learn about different types of advertising and their features.
At the end of Text and media smart 1, you're going to create a print ad or commercial.

1 Warm-up: What type of customer are you? → More practice ○ 144/1 → More practice ● 144/2 → S12

VOCABULARY WB 18/1

a) *Make notes about ideas that come to mind when you hear the word 'advertisement'. Make a mind map with your ideas. Then compare your ideas with another pair and add more ideas to your mind map.*

READING

b) *What do you think? Are you an advertiser's dream customer or are you sceptical of advertising? Follow the arrows in the flow chart to the statements that are true for you. Only choose one per row. Then read about the type of customer you are.*

On your favourite social media platform they mention a big sale at a clothing store in the shopping mall. They're offering two T-shirts for the price of one. And it's your favourite brand!

You go to the shopping mall right away to look for the T-shirts in the ad.	You're going to the shopping mall anyway so you'll have a look while you're there.	You don't pay attention to ads on the internet or social media or anywhere.
At the mall they don't have any T-shirts in your favourite colour. But you love a bargain, so you decide to buy two anyway.	You don't like the T-shirts in the sale. But you see another T-shirt that looks great. Maybe you'll buy it.	You don't need one new T-shirt, so why would you need two just because there is a sale? Forget it!
You see people giving away samples of a new chocolate bar. You take one. Mmm, good! Then you decide to buy one.	You see people giving away samples of a new chocolate bar. You take one, but you probably won't buy one later.	You see people giving away samples of a new chocolate bar. You know they just want you to buy one. You aren't stupid!
You see your favourite film star on a shampoo ad. He / she has perfect hair so the product must be good. You decide to try it so you buy a bottle.	You see your favourite film star on a shampoo ad. You aren't happy with the product you're using now. Maybe you'll try this one; maybe not.	You see your favourite film star on a shampoo ad. You never buy products that are advertised by celebrities. They probably don't even use them.
You seem to be an advertiser's dream customer! You're open to ads and interested in buying new products.	You're interested in new things, but you don't react right away to every new offer that advertisers try to sell you.	You seem to be sceptical of advertising and you don't often buy new things. Ad people won't have an easy time with you!

SPEAKING

c) *Does the description match what you said about yourself in b)? Explain why / why not.*

Did you see that new ad?

1 The features of print ads → S14

READING WB 18/2

a) *How would you advertise fair trade coffee? Which aspects would you include in an ad?*

b) *Describe how the product is presented in the advertisement. What claim do the advertisers make about it?*

c) *Read the skills box and match the four parts of the AIDA formula to different parts of the ad. Then explain how the ad works. What makes this product different to other brands?*

Reading skills

The **AIDA** [eiːdə] formula is often used in marketing. It describes how to sell products or services:

- Catch the target group's **attention** with an eye-catching slogan, visual etc.
- Hold their **interest** (e.g. with attractive ad copy, someone using the product).
- Create **desire** for the product (e.g. show its unique features).
- Get the target group to take **action** (e.g. to buy the product).

d) *Find examples of (strong) adjectives and adverbs, double meanings and persuasive language in the ad copy (also see below). Then say what effect this language has on the target group.*

FAIR TRADE COFFEE
Buying fair trade coffee helps the thousands of families in Africa and Latin America to live with dignity out of their work. This way, they can improve the lives of their families and their community.

Useful phrases

The visual / slogan / ad copy catches the reader's attention by … | It explains / shows / presents … | The ad copy tries to persuade (target group) to buy / to think about / to find out more about … | The ad aims to … | In my opinion, the ad is entertaining / memorable / funny / surprising / …

SPEAKING

e) *Your turn: Find an ad that you think is interesting and use the AIDA formula to analyse it. Take notes and prepare a three-minute presentation with your ideas. Present the ad in class.*

VOCABULARY

2 Buy it now! → More help ○ 144/3

WB 19/3

a) *Look at the photos. Find suitable adjectives for each of the products.*

A a power bank

B a muesli bar

C an electric toothbrush

b) *Match the slogans with the photos. (There are more slogans than you need.) You can also suggest better slogans if you want.*

1. The power to help your business to succeed
2. Great taste, small price
3. Find out what clean really feels like!
4. Power for an active life
5. Fight that Monday morning feeling
6. The taste of outdoors in every single delicious bite

c) *Complete the ad copies for the products in a) with suitable words. You can use a dictionary for help.*

A You're watching a **1** on the bus, looking through social media with your mid-morning latte, chatting to friends – suddenly your **2** goes dead, and it's FOMO time! But you don't have to have that awful feeling ever again. Give your digital life some extra **3** anytime anywhere with a VoltPak from Durabatz.

B Whether you are hiking in the hills or working hard in the office, an Uncle Gordon's Oatastix **4** will give you the energy you need to reach your next goal. Always all-natural **5**, and now the great taste you love comes with 20% less **6**.

C Normal **7** can miss those hard-to-reach places. The new Rototronic AquaVibes **8** with Enamel Protection Pulse Technology will make your **9** feel fresher than fresh every time you use it. What a fresh way to start – and end – the day!

d) *Define the target group for each product in a).*

WRITING

MK 3 Slogans and ad copy → S14 → ⟨G5⟩

WB 19/4

Choose ***one*** *product that you know well. Write an eye-catching slogan and some ad copy with reasons to buy the product. Refer to the AIDA formula on p. 39 and take notes on which parts of your ad will catch attention, create interest and desire, and lead to action. Where possible, try to use (strong) adjectives, a double meaning and persuasive language. Here are some ideas to help you:*

product	**reasons to buy it**
fair trade T-shirts	cool / comfortable / the people who grew the cotton and made the T-shirt were paid fairly
solar-powered watch	attractive and modern design / never needs a new battery
natural energy drink	gives you energy / tastes good / only natural ingredients / doesn't contain any chemicals

VIEWING MK **4** **Understanding and analysing a commercial** → More practice ● 144/4 → S14, S15

V3 ▷ **a)** *Watch the commercial for "Meat free Monday". Take notes and do these tasks:*

1. Sum up the storyline in 1–2 sentences.
2. Describe the setting and the characters that you see in the commercial.

b) *Watch the commercial again. Explain how it catches the viewer's attention. Think about the dialogue and the music as well as your results from a). What kind of atmosphere is created?*

c) *The advertisers work with humour. Make a note of examples of this stylistic device in the commercial. Explain the effect this device probably has on the viewer.*

Word bank

setting:	is filmed in … | shows people's halls, living rooms …
characters:	mainly children / adults | between … and … years of age
dialogue:	very little | natural | typical of …
music:	lively | playful | light | uses instruments such as …
effect:	to make sb think about sth | to create interest in … | to entertain sb | to give the impression that … | to impress sb | to persuade sb

d) *One of the children sums up the message in a slogan at the end of the commercial. What is the slogan? What message do the advertisers want to convey with this slogan? What action do they want viewers to take? Explain your ideas.*

e) *Choose camera shots and camera movements in the commercial which you think are effective. Make a grid like the one below in your exercise book and take notes.*

time slot	camera shot	camera movement	point in storyline	setting	characters
Example: 00:04	medium shot	tracking shot	a little girl has come home from the shops; she is having fun with a pumpkin	a hall in a house	a little girl, her mother

f) *Read the skills box. Then explain the effects of these camera shots and movements on the viewer.*

Film skills

By using different **camera shots**, the advertisers try to catch and hold the viewers' attention. In commercials, which are normally short, the type of shot used often changes quickly. Sometimes special effects are added in post-production; for example, a scene or part of a scene is shown in fast or slow motion. The function of each type of shot varies, e.g. a close-up brings the viewer into the story, and a long shot creates a distance to events and provides an overview of a situation. Different **camera movements** also make a scene more interesting. For example, the camera operator can zoom in on characters or objects to emphasise them while the movement created by a handheld camera can make the viewer feel that they are a part of the scene.

g) *Match parts of the commercial to each element in the AIDA formula on p. 39.*

Example: The activity in the first scenes and tracking shots of the children catch the viewers' attention. Then …

How advertising works

VOCABULARY

1 What does it really mean? → More help ○ 145/5 → S37

a) *Complete the claims from food packaging. You can use a dictionary for help.*

added | artificial | balanced | energy | fat | goodness | ingredients | iron | preservatives | nutritious diet | vitamins | whole grains

Made with **1** | No **2** sugar | low **3** | Forms part of a **4** diet | Part of a **5** | Bursting with natural **6** | All natural **7** | Contains six **8** | High in **9** | Free from **10** colours, flavours and **11** | Gives you the **12** you need to start your day

b) *Each claim could be misleading about how healthy that food really is. Explain why.*

VIEWING

2 Food advertising to kids → More practice ○ 145/6 → More practice ● 145/7

a) *Brainstorm ideas about the tricks which companies use to sell food products to customers.*

V4 WB 20/5

b) *Read the information below from the first part of the film and watch this part. Think of questions with question words which have these answers. Then ask / answer your questions.*

A. What is advertising? (00:18–02:31)
1. to get people to buy a product or service 2. $4.6 billion 3. to buy specific snack foods and visit certain fast food restaurants 4. between 12 and 21 ads 5. unhealthy fast food

c) *Watch parts B, C and D of the film and make notes about at least five pieces of information. Then think of questions to go with this information and ask your partner.*

B. How does food advertising contribute to childhood obesity? (02:32–04:23)	**C.** What are some techniques advertisers use? (04:24–07:09)	**D.** What other food advertising techniques should kids be aware of? (07:10–11:56)

WRITING

3 Your turn: Banning marketing tricks

WB 20/6

Do you think any of the marketing tricks described in the film should be banned? Which ones? Write a short comment for the website of an advertising watchdog in which you express your opinion.

SPEAKING MK **4** **Before you read**

What products are often advertised by influencers? Have you ever bought a product which was advertised by an influencer?

A 17

Trust me, I'm an influencer

How honest are influencers really?

A The earliest known printed advertisement comes from China around 1,000 years ago. It says, "We buy high-quality steel and make high-quality needles." This sounds surprisingly modern, and the ad also features a picture of a rabbit holding a needle and a logo for the brand. The first TV ad was broadcast in the US in 1941. Traditional forms of advertising have developed over decades or centuries, and over that time regulations have been made which aim to make sure that advertising is (reasonably) honest. But what about the promotion of products by internet influencers? This form of marketing is still very new and it exists in a grey area between advertising and entertainment. Unfortunately, advertising watchdogs don't always keep up with the latest developments.

B You are watching the online video channel of a popular influencer. She holds a bottle of shampoo up to the camera and says, "This is my favourite shampoo. I use it every day." Which of the following do you think? a) It is her favourite shampoo and she just wants to tell everyone about it; b) it is her favourite shampoo and the company that makes it has paid her to say this; c) it is not really her favourite shampoo, but the company has paid her to say that it is. Answers a) and b) are possible, of course, but c) is the most likely.

C There is no legal problem when influencers are paid to advertise a product if the influencer acknowledges that it is a paid advert. In the UK this rule applies to any online activity, from a busy video channel to a three-word social media post. However, in 2021 the UK's advertising watchdog, the Advertising Standards Authority (ASA), examined influencers' social media posts. They found that nearly 25% of the posts that they checked were ads, but only 35% of them were identified as ads. The influencers and the companies whose products they were promoting were not named in public by the ASA, but they were warned to follow the rules in future.

D Children influencers (or 'kidfluencers') are some of the biggest stars on the internet, whether they are enjoying the latest toys, playing a new video game or just looking cute while their parents promote products. In countries where child labour is illegal (which is most countries), the adults who are producing the material may be breaking the law. The parents may argue that the children are just having fun, and it is the adults who do all the work. However, another way of looking at it is that it's not play if they're making money. There are increasing calls for child labour laws to be updated to protect children from this type of exploitation.

E It is easy to introduce regulations that make advertising more honest and stop the exploitation of children. Harder to police are influencers who associate themselves with socially progressive views, but still promote products which don't match those values. For example, an influencer may promote environmental awareness and responsibility while also advertising products that are actually damaging the environment. Are that influencer's well-known 'green values' giving the misleading impression that the products they advertise are also 'green' in some way? If an influencer who often makes anti-racist comments is hired to promote products by a company that has a poor record as an equal opportunities employer, is that company misleading us? Is the influencer misleading us?

F Advertisers and influencers who are paid to promote their products put a lot of care and attention into their promotional activities. We – the targets of this marketing – must be equally aware of the ways that we react to their advertising.

READING

5 Understanding the text → More help ○ 145/8

WB 21/7

a) *Read the article on p. 43. Match the photos with the paragraphs that describe each type of influencer.*

1

2

3

b) *Match the headings below with paragraphs A–F. There is* **one** *heading you don't need.*

1. How influencers advertise
2. Misleading advertising
3. Policing the internet
4. Work or play?
5. A short history of advertising
6. Knowing your reaction to advertising
7. Laws on influencer advertising

c) *Sum up the three problems that the article identifies.*

VOCABULARY

6 Understanding new words

Explain the meanings of these words and phrases from the context in the article. Then write definitions for them.

reasonably (l. 13) | advertising watchdogs (l. 18) | acknowledges (l. 34) | breaking the law (ll. 54–55) | to police (l. 64) | socially progressive views (l. 66) | equal opportunities employer (l. 78)

SPEAKING

MK 7 Your turn: More online advertising issues

a) *Read the article about online advertising. Then say how much of the information you already knew. What information was new to you?*

Ads on websites
If you don't use an ad blocker with your browser, visiting a website can mean also seeing large amounts of advertising. When you visit a website, cookies will probably track your activity. Companies use this to build up a profile of your digital footprint. They will then use this information about you to show you targeted ads, and they may also sell it to other companies. Websites must ask you to accept cookies if they are used, and may offer you options about how your visit is tracked. However, disabling cookies may not protect you from clickbait. These are links that seem attractive but actually lead to poor quality web pages full of advertising.

b) *Read the situations below. Have you had similar experiences? Describe what happened.*

1. You are doing online research for a school project on the history of Greece. Then you notice that websites are showing you ads for holidays in Greece.
2. You start using an ad blocker and now some websites won't let you view them.
3. On the side of a web page, you see a link to an article which looks very interesting and you click on the link. However, the article is short, uninteresting and badly written.

MK **1**

Writing options

a) *You are doing work experience at an advertising agency. You are helping some colleagues with a project: A chain of ice cream parlours wants to persuade people to visit its ice cream parlours on Ice Cream for Breakfast Day. Divide into groups and choose **one** of the options in c) below.*

> **Across cultures**
>
> Ice Cream for Breakfast Day is celebrated on the first Saturday in February. The idea was started by a woman in Rochester, New York, because her children were complaining about the cold. She suggested that they have ice cream for breakfast and the tradition was born.

b) *Decide who your target group is. Think about:*

- What kind of people will be most interested in Ice Cream for Breakfast Day?
- Why should they come to your ice cream parlours rather than eating ice cream at home?

c) *Do the tasks for your group: A or B. You can refer to the AIDA formula on p. 39.*

Group A: Print ad → S14

1. *Discuss the pros and cons of the photos. Choose the **one** you think is the most suitable.*

2. *Write the ad copy to go with the photo you chose or a similar Creative Commons licence photo. Refer to your ideas in b). Use strong adjectives / adverbs and the correct register.*
3. *Choose a font size and colour for the ad copy that is easy to read. Where should you put the ad copy / the photo / the slogan in your advert?*

Group B: Commercial → S16

1. *Decide on a storyline. What setting/characters do you want to use?*
2. *Plan the scene(s) and write the dialogue. You can draw the storyboard by hand or use an online storyboard tool.*
3. *Organise props and rehearse the scene(s). Then film your commercial.*
4. *Edit the commercial. Add sound effects and music from Creative Commons licence sources.*

d) *Present your ad or commercial in class. Say how useful the AIDA formula is when creating print ads or commercials.*

Exploring culture in new dimensions

SPEAKING

1 Another reality

a) *Look at the photos. What are the people doing?*

Word bank

to hold a tablet / smartphone / controller | to wear a VR headset / AR goggles | to use an application | to scan sth | to appear (on a device) | to do a virtual tour | to see sth in 3D | to use a game console | to immerse oneself in sth | to interact with sb/sth

Media skills

Augmented reality (AR) is a digital technology that **enhances** the real-life environment by adding computer-generated images on a screen. For example, point your phone's camera at a historical monument and see a live view plus written information.

Virtual reality (VR) is a digital technology that **replaces** the real-life environment with computer-generated images and sounds that the user can interact with. The experience seems almost real. For example, put on a VR headset and walk with dinosaurs or stand in a city square thousands of miles away.

b) *Read the skills box. Match the photos in a) to the correct category: AR or VR.*

c) *Your turn: If you have tried AR or VR before, what did you use it for? Share your experiences. If you haven't, would you like to? Give reasons.*

d) *Compare the situations in the photos with the 'real world'. What's the same? What's different?*

A 18 LISTENING WB 25/1

2 Welcome to the metaverse

a) *Listen to the podcast about the future of AR and VR. Take notes on the pros and cons of the technologies and the opinions of the podcaster (Gabby) and her guest (Theo). Then sum up your findings in your own words.*

b) *Listen again. Explain why these words and numbers in the podcast are important:*

metaverse | 2019 | 10,000 | 70% | 'vomity reality' | 'phygital'

VOCABULARY

c) *Choose **one** of the words and explain it to your partner. Take turns.*

three-dimensional (3D) | immersive | sceptical | unwieldy

SPEAKING

d) *Your turn: What is your prediction for the future of AR and VR?*

SPEAKING

3 What does 'culture' mean?

D3 Placemat

In groups of four, use a placemat to note down what 'culture' means to you. Then discuss your ideas and write the ones you agree on in the middle of the placemat. In class, present and compare your results.

READING MK

4 Go see the world – from home

WB 25/2

a) *Marissa is a travel blogger. Read her latest post about virtual tours. What does she aim to do in her post? How does she present the virtual tours? What advantages does she mention?*

Some of the world's best virtual tours

Natural History Museum, London

The Natural History Museum's huge collection of objects from the natural world has long been popular with locals and tourists. Can't visit in person? Our interactive online guide is the next best thing: It will bring you up close and personal with dinosaurs, whales, birds, tigers and so much more. Didn't have time to see everything on your visit? No problem – come back in virtual form as often as you like. Click here to visit.

Sydney, Australia

Start with an amazing 360° view of Sydney harbour, then take a tour in any place you like in Australia's largest and most exciting city – including a boat trip to admire the city's waterfront sights. You'll also be invited to join guides (every one is a 'Sydneysider', as the locals there are known) and learn about some of Sydney's best-kept secrets. Ideal for planning a real-life visit, or just as a way to get to know Oz's top tourist destination. Click here to visit.

Yosemite National Park, California, USA

As a change from hectic Sydney, how about a virtual visit to one of America's most popular national parks? Hike up trails, cycle down valleys, cross lakes and even take a peek inside a hotel – all from the comfort of your home. Make sure your audio is turned on. The sounds of the wind, water and wildlife are an essential part of the immersive experience. After your visit, you can head (virtually) towards the coast and San Francisco! Click here to visit.

Now it's your turn! Try the tours and tell me what you think about them in the comment section below.

Advertising disclosure: This post may contain affiliate links for your convenience. View my full advertising disclosure here.

SPEAKING

b) *Would you like to do a virtual field trip to one of these places? Explain why or why not.*

WRITING

c) *Go on a virtual visit to* ***one*** *of these places (you don't need any VR devices for them). Then write a comment on your experience on Marissa's blog. What did/didn't you like about your visit? What did you learn? Did it make you want to visit the place in person? Explain why or why not.*

Media skills

All advertising is usually regulated by law. In some countries social media posts and blogs which promote a product or service must include a disclaimer. Why do you think disclaimers like this are required? Find out what the regulations are in Germany.

5 The pros and cons of virtual concerts

SPEAKING

a) *Have you ever been to a concert? If so, who was the artist, what type of music did they play, what was your experience with regard to the atmosphere, audience and how you felt? If you have never been to a concert, whom would you like to see and what do you think might the concert be like?*

READING

b) *Read the post and comments about a hybrid rock concert. Make a list of the pros and cons.*

The1999

34,739 likes

Big thanx to all our fans who attended our concert in New York last night, and we mean all – 9,000 in the stadium, and more than 100,000 who were with us virtually! A first for us, and we wanna know what you guys think. Virtual gigs – hot or not?

layla_rocks 2h ago Loved the online gig. Who wants to be in row Z99 when you can be right at the front – and without some tall guy with a big head in front of you! Plus – and I know this isn't very rock 'n' roll – but it's awesome to control the volume. No ringing in your ears afterwards! Oh, and no $100+ ticket price, either! What's not to like?

michael13 1h ago Mixed feelings. No way was I gonna get there from New Zealand, but it kinda made me feel sad I wasn't there in person. Also, my internet connection isn't fantastic. Just getting to a big chorus and… oh no, frozen again! And, of course, when I say 'big chorus' there's a limit to how big anything's gonna sound on a laptop …

WRITING

c) *Think of more pros and cons and add them to your list. Then add a comment to the post in b).*

MEDIATION

6 Virtual reality and student exchanges

A19 V9

a) *You want to present the idea of a virtual student exchange to your class and class teacher. Listen to the advertisement you have found and take notes: What does the programme offer? What are the advantages of a virtual exchange?*

b) *Use your notes to prepare and give a two-minute talk in German for your class and teacher. Present the programme and say why it is better than a traditional one.*

7 Virtual and augmented reality: Are they all good news?

READING

a) *Malik is a blogger who interviews people about the latest technology trends and the impact on their lives. Read his blog post and make a list of the pros and cons of virtual interaction.*

More and more people around the world are interacting with other people and places in virtual ways, whether via virtual reality (VR), augmented reality (AR) or basic online communication platforms. This increased dramatically during the COVID-19 pandemic and continues to grow.

Virtual technologies have much to offer in educational contexts, and in particular can create great opportunities for cultural exchange activities with other students from almost anywhere in the world. But is this entirely good news? Carlos from Argentina is not so sure, "It's great that I can join in so easily and cheaply, but, of course, it's not as immersive as experiencing a new place in person. For one thing, it's only for a short amount of time each week. I've got to know a few people, but I'm not sure I really know them that well. I certainly don't feel like I understand much about where they live. How could I if I can't experience it myself? My older sister went on a traditional exchange visit to Australia a few years ago, and she's still talking about it. I don't think my virtual exchange programme is going to make that much of an impression."

The possibilities for immersive language learning are huge though. Hitomi from Japan shares her experiences, "For me, it's really good that I can practise English virtually. I feel much more relaxed than when I speak English in real life. On the other hand, I'm not really meeting people. I'm just sitting alone in my apartment."

A good virtual tour can also be an enjoyable alternative to visiting a place in person. Akeyo, a young digital imaging technician in Kenya, helped with creating a virtual safari. "We hope that our virtual tour will encourage people to come and see the real thing," she says. "What we don't want is people saying, 'Now I've seen those animals in the wild, I don't need to go there'. We really need those tourism jobs."

VR technologies have been enthusiastically adopted by the gaming world, and the latest technical advances in VR often appear in gaming first. However, the effects of excessive VR gaming are not known. There are few controls, and some gaming can be violent. Fighting and killing enemies on a flat screen is one thing; doing it in what feels almost like real life may be another, with different psychological effects.

Finally, there is also a danger of a two-tier virtual world: full immersion for those who can afford expensive VR equipment, and a very much second-best experience for those using a flat screen. The future may be virtual, but we must also try to make it fair.

WRITING

b) *Write an online comment on this post in which you give your personal opinion on virtual interaction.*

SPEAKING

MK 8 Your turn: Create a virtual tour

a) *In groups of five, plan and create a virtual tour or field trip:*

1. Choose an interesting place or places in your area.
2. Use a 360-degree camera or an app on your phone / tablet to take 360-degree photos of the place you chose. You could also use Creative Commons 360-degree photos.
3. Find and use an app to upload your photos and add informative texts (written or spoken) that tourists might find interesting. Your tour should make people feel like they have been to the place.

Tip

You can also find the place you chose in an online map, enable street view and do a screen recording while moving around. Upload the video in an app to add text.

b) *Share your tour in class. Give each other feedback.*

Unit 2

The digital age

A

SPEAKING

1 Photos and quotations → More practice ● 146/1 → S11

a) *On your own, look at the photos and decide which one represents the digital age best. Then describe it and explain your choice to a partner.*

b) *Read the quotations and match them to the photos on pp. 50–51.*

"To understand their world we must be willing to immerse ourselves in that world. We must embrace the new digital reality. If we can't relate, if we don't get it, we won't be able to make schools relevant to the current and future needs of the digital generation."
Ian Jukes (speaker, author)

"Social media is changing the way we communicate and the way we are perceived, both positively and negatively. Every time you post a photo, or update your status, you are contributing to your own digital footprint and personal brand."
Amy Jo Martin (author, speaker, entrepreneur)

"Video games foster the mindset that allows creativity to grow."
Nolan Bushnell (engineer, businessman)

c) *Your turn: Choose the quotation that speaks to you most. In small groups, explain what this quotation means to you. Then discuss the message of each of the quotations.*

In Unit 2 you learn
… about the digital age and its effect on us.
You learn:
- how to talk about the digital age,
- how to use the will-future progressive and will-future perfect,
- how to use *which* to comment on a main clause,
- how to use relative clauses with *when* and *which*,
- how to create a talk show.

B

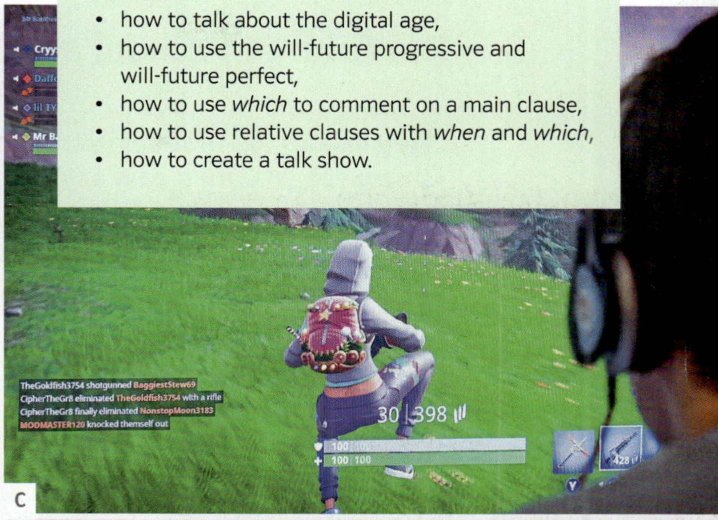
C

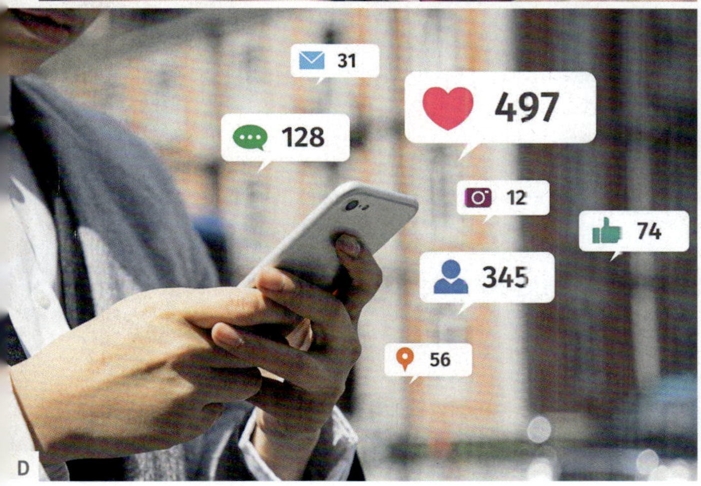

D

E

MK 2 Look on up → More help ○ 146/2 → S10

LISTENING A 20 WB 26/1

a) *Listen to the song "Look on up" by Relient K and sum up what it is about.*

b) *Listen again and describe the music. Think about the genre it belongs to, the instruments you can hear, the rhythm and how it changes, and the effect it has on the listener.*

READING

c) *Read part of the lyrics on the right. Sum up the message of that part in one sentence.*

WRITING

d) *Comment on the last two lines. "It's time I put down my devices and I start to live my life."*

I'm fighting the temptation not to look
But I'm still leafing through the pages like the world's my open book
Why don't I got something else to do?
Feeling trapped behind the viewfinder to share it all with you
And that's not what it's about
I'm so tired of missing out
I look on up to the sky
I wonder why I put a filter between beauty and my eyes
I look on up into your eyes
It's time I put down my devices and I start to live my life

Words: Relient K

A 21

The future of school and learning

Welcome to the first newsletter of NewSchoolUS, a new school with a new approach to learning.

For most students in the US today, education is based on a model that has changed little since the 19th century. Every student in a class should learn the same thing at the same time. Every 60 minutes students change to a different subject and follow another lesson which is probably based on the next few pages of a textbook.

By the time students have completed their education, their teachers will have presented tens of thousands of facts to them, but how much will students really have understood? Will they have learned the things they really need to be successful in their adult lives? At NewSchoolUS, we do not believe that they will have developed the skills they need for the future that lies ahead. A few years from now, most of them won't be doing jobs that are related to a typical school curriculum. It is far more likely that they will be working in roles where the emphasis is on having the ability to develop new skills quickly, collaborate in digital environments, adapt to fast-changing situations and most importantly to do what they personally are best at doing.

When we launch our first school this September, we will be offering a more personalised approach to education that meets the needs of life in the 21st century. We believe that motivation is the key to success in both education and work. Using our innovative digital learning platform, students will have more control over what they learn and how, when and how fast they learn it. At certain times in the school day, students in the same space will be working on completely different things. They will be free to follow their interests with help from their teachers. We believe that this is much more motivating than the mass-production model of traditional education.

Gaming technologies will have an important role in our classrooms. 'Gamification' in education can be highly motivating and provides really good opportunities for trial-and-error learning strategies. We have developed innovative ways to use virtual reality and augmented reality for creative, immersive personalised learning experiences. Over the coming months, we will be developing an exciting VR-based collaborative learning program with partner schools around the world.

We will open fully next year. By then, the trial program to test our approach will have finished. We believe that all students in the trial program will have performed significantly better than average in all standard tests and exams. On completing a NewSchoolUS education, students will have benefitted from a personalised education that meets their needs, and will also have prepared for higher education. We believe that when they leave us, they will be starting their adult lives from the best possible position.

Enrollment into this exciting new educational opportunity is now open.
For more information click here.

MK 1 Understanding the newsletter → S1

READING

a) *Read the newsletter. Who is it from? Who is it aimed at? What is the main point it is making?*

b) *Make a list of the innovations that are described. Add notes about how they are connected with the school, technology and education.*

SPEAKING

c) *Your turn: Compare NewSchoolUS with your own school. Would you like to go there? Explain why or why not.*

VOCABULARY

2 Working with words: Talking about technology

Make lists of words and short phrases from the text that relate to a) education and b) technology. Some words / phrases can go in both lists.

GRAMMAR

3 Find the rule: Will-future progressive / perfect → More help ○ 146/3 → <G6>, G7, G8

WB 27/2

a) *Match the uses of the* ***will-future progressive*** *and the* ***will-future perfect*** *A–D to the sentences 1–4 from the text. Which uses belong to which tense?*

A to express that an action or event will have been completed at a certain point in the future
B to describe an action that will be in progress at a certain time in the future
C to describe an action that will be in progress when another action or event happens
D to describe an action that will be in progress for a certain period of time in the future

1. A few years from now, most of them **won't be doing** jobs that are related to a typical school curriculum.
2. Over the coming months, we **will be developing** an exciting VR-based collaborative learning program with partner schools around the world.
3. We believe that when they leave us, they **will be starting** their adult lives from the best possible position.
4. We will open fully next year. By then, the trial program to test our approach **will have finished**.

b) *Find more examples for each of the two future forms in the text on p. 52. Note down any signal words that are used with these future forms. For each example, say why this future form was used.*

GRAMMAR

4 More from the school website → G7, G8

WB 27/3

Complete some more sentences from the NewSchoolUS website with the ***will-future progressive*** *or the* ***will-future perfect****. Then match the sentences with the uses A–D in ex. 3a).*

1. At the end of each school year, our students ___ (to complete) everything on the state curriculum, but in their own way and at their own pace.
2. When we welcome our first students, all our technology ___ (to work) and ready to use.
3. The teachers ___ (to review and to check) students' progress regularly during the first year.
4. We believe that 20 years from now our approach ___ (to become) the standard model for education.
5. We hope that by 2035 we ___ (to open) more schools, and thousands of students ___ (to learn) with our innovative approach.

SPEAKING

MK 5 Your turn: A look into the future → More practice ○ 147/4 → More practice ● 147/5 → G7, G8

a) *Work together in groups of four. Imagine your school ten years from now. In what ways* ***will*** *it* ***have changed****? What* ***will*** *students and teachers* ***be doing*** *in class? Brainstorm ideas using a placemat.*

b) *Discuss your results and write the ten best ideas in the middle of your placemat. Present your vision in class.*

a decade from now | by the time | classroom activities | timetable | subjects | exams | more / less emphasis on | to become normal / unusual

MEDIATION MK **6** **The future of education** → S34

V9

Your American pen pal Sanjay is in Debate Club at school and has to give a speech about how schools should prepare students better for the future. You came across the following website in German and want to support him. Send him a voicemail in which you sum up the important information from the website, focusing on the things that students should learn in school in addition to the traditional subjects.

Prinzipien für die Bildungswelt von morgen

Kompetenzen für das 21. Jahrhundert

In Zukunft kommt es auf ein Set von analogen und digitalen Kompetenzen an, die junge Menschen erwerben sollten. Neben den bekannten Grundkompetenzen Sprachen, Rechnen, Lesen und Schreiben, Geschichte, Naturwissenschaften, Wirtschaft und Politik werden in Zukunft vier analoge Kompetenzen wichtig: Kommunikation, Kreativität, kritisches Denken und Kollaboration. Kreativität ist die Kunst, Probleme zu lösen und steht für die Fähigkeit, auch unkonventionell zu denken. Kreative Schülerinnen und Schüler sind in der Lage, aus gewohnten Denkmustern und Normen auszubrechen und auf neue Ideen zu kommen. Kritisches Denken ist die Fähigkeit, eigenständig und vernetzt zu denken und ein Bewusstsein für globale Trends und Zusammenhänge zu entwickeln. Dazu gehört auch der Umgang mit falschen Informationen (Fake News) und sozialen Medien. Kollaboratives Lernen und Arbeiten in Teams ist zentral für das soziale Miteinander und das Erarbeiten von Wissen und Kompetenzen. Der Alltagsbezug und die Frage nach dem „Warum" und „Wofür" werden dabei wichtiger.

Der Europäische Referenzrahmen DigComp zählt zu den Kompetenzen, die in Schulen erworben werden sollten, außerdem die Auswahl von digitalen Tools, die Erstellung digitaler Inhalte und Datensicherheit. Immer wichtiger wird die aktive Nutzung digitaler Lernplattformen und Tools, etwa für die Kommunikation oder die Aufbereitung von Daten und Informationen. Da die neuen Freiheiten und Möglichkeiten, die mit der Digitalisierung einhergehen, oft auch mehr Stress bedeuten, wird die Fähigkeit zur Selbstdisziplin und -organisierung immer wichtiger.

Resilienz und Selbstwirksamkeit

Den gemeinsamen Nenner der analogen und digitalen Kompetenzen bildet ein selbstbewusster Umgang mit Unsicherheit und Komplexität. Resilienz ist die Fähigkeit, Krisen zu bewältigen. Entscheidend ist dabei nicht nur eine Kultur der Beweglichkeit und Offenheit mit Spielräumen, in denen Kreativität, Experimentierfreude und Innovation gedeihen können: Ebenso wichtig ist die Gewährleistung von Stabilität und Sicherheit. Zur Resilienz gehört auch das Prinzip der Selbstwirksamkeit: die Fähigkeit, mit Veränderungen umzugehen und dabei das eigene Gleichgewicht zu bewahren. Die eigene Zukunft wird von Umbrüchen geprägt sein, die Arbeits- und private Welt ändern sich regelmäßig. Zur Selbstwirksamkeit gehören Selbstvertrauen, Selbstreflexion und Selbstdisziplin.

Agilität

Wenn Schulen in einer sich ändernden Gesellschaft noch relevant bleiben wollen, müssen sie sich ebenfalls ändern. Agilität ist die Fähigkeit, eine flexible und aktive Kultur der ständigen Verbesserung und der Innovationsbereitschaft zu entwickeln. Gemeint ist Mut zu „kreativem Scheitern". Agilität setzt nicht auf endgültige Lösungen, die es aufgrund der digitalen Veränderungsgeschwindigkeit nicht mehr gibt, sondern auf haltbare Zwischenlösungen.

Dr. Daniel Dettling, *Schulen der Zukunft* website, 2020

A 22

Creating your own reality

SPEAKING MK **1**

Before you read

Have you ever used apps to modify your photos for social media? Explain why or why not.

Teenagers show the scary effects of editing apps

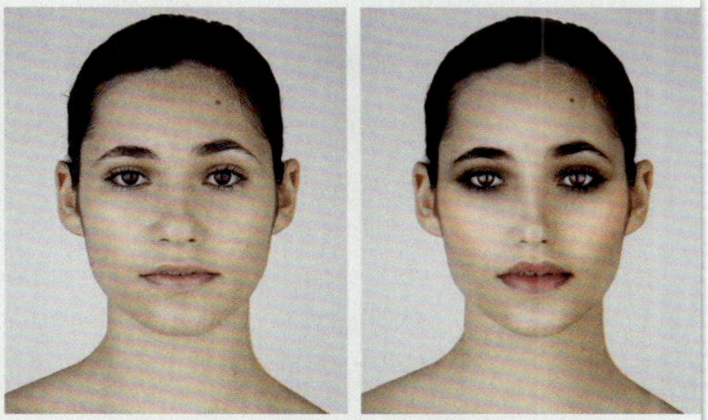

Photo editing has become an open secret in the land of social media, where image is everything. Apps have made it so easy for us to change the way we look – through filters, retouching or a combination of both – that it's becoming harder to determine what's real and what's not. We'd also argue that these apps are enabling us to perpetuate a homogenized expression of beauty, as opposed to celebrating true individuality.

British photographer Rankin (born John Rankin Waddell) explored these apps and their potentially harmful effects in a recent photo series, which is titled 'Selfie Harm.' For the project, Rankin photographed a group of teenagers and then asked them to edit their own portrait until it was "social media ready".

The before and after images offered a striking look at what can happen on occasions when people use simple apps to alter photos of themselves.

Rankin had noticed social media sites where people often retouched their own photos. He came up with the idea of using photography to show the ways individuals, particularly young people, use digital tools to alter their appearances.

"What I was particularly scared by was how much like a game it is to do it," he said. "You take a picture of yourself and, as you're changing it, you can look at a before and after very easily. It also makes you feel very inadequate about what you look like in this game-y way." Photo editing apps, Rankin noted, are increasingly easy to use. "Anybody can do it," he said. "That's where the project came along."

The photographer, whose photography subjects have included David Bowie and Queen Elizabeth II, took portraits of 15 individuals wearing minimal make-up. Some of the teenagers were models and others were invited from a local school, which meant they covered a good variety of face types. The only precondition was that they didn't use retouching apps regularly.

"I didn't want it to be about what people do personally but how you can use the app to change yourself even if you don't know much about it," Rankin said.

As he witnessed the girls and boys edit their photos, he realized that they all seemed to do the same things, e.g. enlarge their eyes and plump their lips, which was a reflection on how people see beauty at the moment. Interestingly, he said, the individuals didn't really like the altered versions of themselves, but they did feel like the edited images would get more likes on social media.

Rankin's goal for the project wasn't to blame apps or the people who created them. Instead, he wanted to raise awareness that these apps exist and people are using them to alter their faces to fit an ideal that has become extremely homogenous.

Rankin's opinion is that being the better version of yourself is about looking like yourself, not someone else, which is hard to disagree with.

Julia Brucculieri, *Huffington Post*, 2019

READING

2 Understanding the article → More practice ● 147/6 → S1

a) *Read the article on p. 55. Then briefly describe Rankin's project, its goal, the results and his evaluation.*

b) *Sum up what the teenagers who participated in the project think about their own modified selfies.*

VOCABULARY

3 Working with words

WB 28/4

Find the verb forms below in the article on p. 55 and match them with the correct meanings.

retouching | to determine | to perpetuate | homogenised | celebrating | to alter | witnessed | to enlarge | to plump

1. to make sth fatter
2. saw an event (often used for crimes)
3. focusing on the positive aspects of sth
4. changed so that everything is the same
5. to make sth bigger
6. to change
7. to work out or find out
8. to make sth continue
9. making small changes to the appearance of sth, especially a painting or photo

GRAMMAR

4 Find the rule: Non-defining relative clauses with *which* → <G9>, G10

WB 28/5

a) *Compare the sentences with* ***non-defining relative clauses****. In which one does the relative clause refer to the* ***entire main clause*** *and in which one to a* ***single word or group of words****? How would you translate* which *into German in each sentence?*

1. British photographer Rankin (born John Rankin Waddell) explored these apps and their potentially harmful effects in a recent photo series, **which is titled 'Selfie Harm.'**
2. Some of the teenagers were models and others were invited from a local school, **which meant they covered a good variety of face types.**

b) *In the article on p. 55, find other relative clauses that start with* ***which*** *and that refer to the main clause in the sentence. How would you translate the relative clause into German?*

GRAMMAR

5 Posting photos → G10

WB 29/6

Ayla is an influencer. Read what she says about posting photos on social media. Combine the sentences with ***which*** *so the second sentence becomes a clause that comments on the first sentence. Don't forget the comma before* ***which****!*

1. I retouched a photo of myself so I looked completely different. It was a fun thing to do.
2. Some people post unflattering photos of me. That can really hurt.
3. That photo I posted got lots of negative comments. That was unfair.
4. I took some photos with a proper camera instead of my phone. It's something I hadn't done before.

GRAMMAR

6 Find the rule: Relative clauses with *where* and *when* → G11

Find a variation of the following sentences in the article on p. 55. How can the ***preposition + which*** *be replaced?*

1. Photo editing has become an open secret in the land of social media **in which** image is everything.
2. The before and after images offered a striking look at what can happen on occasions **at which** people use simple apps to alter photos of themselves.
3. Rankin had noticed social media sites **on which** people often retouched their own photos.

GRAMMAR

7 Should I post it? → More help ○ 147/7 → G11

WB 29/7

Ryan and Ellie are talking about their last holiday. Combine the sentences 1–7 with the relative adverb ***where*** *or* ***when****. You will need to decide whether the relative clause is defining or non-defining and needs a comma.*

Ryan: **1** That was the beach next to our hotel. You took a really nice photo of me there.
Ellie: Oh, I remember. **2** The day was very cloudy. I took this photo then.
Ryan: Do you think I should post it? **3** I don't usually put photos of myself on social media. There's always a risk of getting negative comments there.
Ellie: That's true. **4** I'd really like to live in a perfect world. Everybody is really polite on social media there.
Ryan: **5** Do you remember this time last year? You first started posting content then.
Ellie: I do. Fortunately, I haven't had any negative experiences so far. **6** But at my school, they've decided to ban mobile phones. Cyberbullying has become very common there.
Ryan: That's so sad. I don't know. Maybe I shouldn't post it.
Ellie: It's your choice. **7** Sometimes I wish I hadn't started using social media last year. I didn't care that much about my online image then.

SPEAKING MK

8 Having a discussion → S32

Have a discussion in small groups. Choose ***one*** *of the options:*

A There are several counter-movements against the use of filters on social media, for example #nofilter and #bodypositivity. What do you think about such movements? How helpful are they when it comes to fighting unrealistic body images?

B Influencers in Norway must label retouched photos on social media with a particular sticker. This rule applies when changes are made to the influencer's body shape, height or skin. The law is supposed to fight unrealistic beauty standards. Do you think this law would be a good idea in Germany too?

MEDIATION MK

9 Media use during lockdown[1] → More help ○ 148/8 → S12, S34

V9

Your exchange partner in the UK has to give a talk about media use by students in different countries during the lockdowns of 2020–2021 and asks you for help. You find these statistics. Write an email in English. Sum up the changes in social media use and gaming from September 2019 to May 2021.

Nutzungszeiten sozialer Medien und Gaming über vier Messzeitpunkte

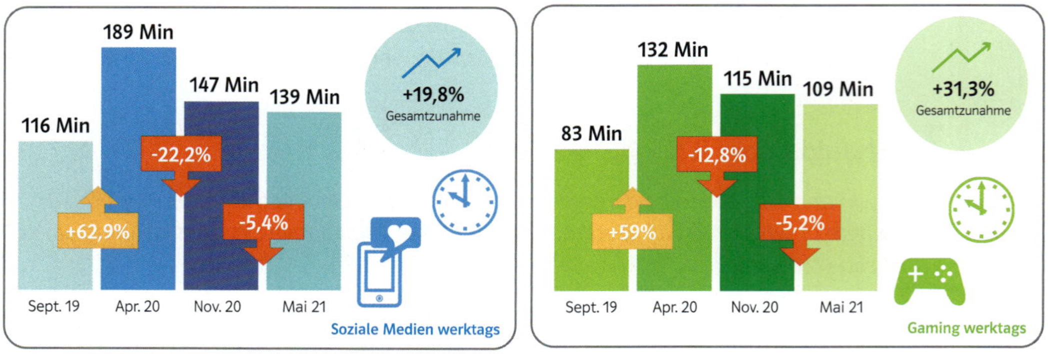

Messzeitpunkte: Sept. 2019: Vorkrisenniveau; **Apr. 2020:** 4 Wochen nach Beginn des 1. Lockdowns; **Nov.–Dez. 2020:** Nach vorübergehenden Öffnungen erneute Schließung von Geschäften und Freizeitstätten; **Mai–Juni 2021:** zunehmende Lockerungen der Einschränkungen

Source: DAK-Gesundheit

LISTENING

10 How to: Understand a talk show → S29

A 23 WB 30/8

a) *Listen to part of a talk show about gaming and esports. Take notes about the guests. Who are they? What do they do? Why have they been invited?*

b) *Listen again. Sum up who makes which point about:*

internet gaming disorder (IGD)

esports as a college subject | time limits in games | the process of developing new games

Listening skills

Talk shows often have a main topic, and each guest has a different perspective on that topic. Knowing each guest's background can help you to identify their perspective and follow the conversation. Listen carefully when the host introduces each guest.

WRITING MK

11 Cartoons → S11, S13

WB 31/9

a) *Describe the cartoons. Which aspects of gaming do they deal with?*

b) *Analyse the cartoons.*

"These online fantasy worlds are great fun. I can be 'Dave the Accountant' from Birmingham."

1 Due to the COVID-19 pandemic in 2020–2021, social interaction in Germany was restricted by a number of lockdowns and students were homeschooled for longer periods.

Gone too far

SPEAKING **1** **Warm-up: What is cyberbullying?**

What is cyberbullying? How is it different from physical bullying? How is it the same? Discuss in small groups and write a definition. Include adjectives to describe the feelings of a victim and a cyberbully.

VIEWING **2** **A film about cyberbullying** → S15

V5 WB 31/10

a) *Watch the film. What's your first reaction? How did the film make you feel?*

b) *Watch it again. Sum up the situation that Jason finds himself in. Describe Ben's and Jenna's reactions to Jason's situation.*

c) *Describe how Jason and Charlie feel in the course of the film.*

d) *Sum up the message of the film.*

VIEWING **3** **Film analysis** → S15

V7 WB 31/11

Analyse how the film conveys Jason's and Charlie's feelings. Choose ***one*** *scene for each character. Think about their body language, facial expressions, tone and choice of words. How do music, camera shots, camera movements and lighting help to show their feelings?*

MK **4** **Getting help** → More help 148/9

SPEAKING

a) *Brainstorm ideas about ways of dealing with cyberbullying: How can you protect yourself? How can you help victims? Where can you get help? Who can you talk to? Take notes.*

WRITING

b) *The producers of the film want to include one or two informative slides at the end of the film to help victims and those who want to support them. Use your notes in a) to create your slide(s).*

SPEAKING **5** **Role play** → S15

a) *Choose* ***one*** *of the film stills. Describe the situation and how it relates to the plot of the film.*

b) *How could people in the scene have reacted differently? Rewrite the scene so that the characters actually say how they feel, discuss ways to stop the bullying and find help. Use your ideas in ex. 4. Then act out your role play in class. You can also film it.*

A 24–27

Video game murder

SPEAKING

1 Before you read

Do you play video games? Explain why or why not.

Kiera Johnson is a seventeen-year-old teenager and one of the few Black students at her school. She is also the game developer of the secret online VR game, SLAY – a video game which is meant to be a safe space[1] for the Black community worldwide. She is in the school cafeteria following the news on one of the TVs there when she gets to know about the murder of a SLAYer.

A The banner now reads something new that strikes me.

Boy shot in his sleep over video game.

My chest tightens at the reminder of how cruel people can be. As a game developer, I'm not just an artist. I'm not just a coder. I feel a certain responsibility for the people who play my game. Their characters are an extension[2] of them, after all. There are real people behind those characters, and I suddenly feel sorry for whoever developed the game behind this murder. I watch and wait to see which game it is, although I suspect it's *Legacy of Planets*, that MMORPG[3] Wyatt always plays. That game has millions of players, some of whom have died of pulmonary embolisms[4] from blood clots[5] that can develop after sitting still and doing nothing but playing for days in a row. With how serious people take *Legacy*, I wouldn't be surprised to hear of someone being killed in real life over it.

As I'm staring up at the TV, the closed-captioning appears below a boy who looks a few years younger than me, tears streaming down his face.

It was over a damn game, man. It was a game! That's my brother in there.

And what game is that? asks the reporter.

S'called SLAY. *Homeboy[6], Jamal, and I been playing every night for forever.*

B The words freeze me where I sit, and I read them again to make sure I'm not imagining it. *SLAY.* My mind can't process the words. It takes me a moment to realize and I suddenly feel like throwing up.

We ran a hustle together. We spent hours SLAY*ing, dueling, stacking coins. We put all our coins in Jamal's account so he could buy stuff for us. He tried to hold 'em for ransom[7] for real dollars, and ... this dude we never shoulda been playing with, he's bad news, man. Came and shot Jamal. He shot Jamal in his sleep for hijacking[8] damn game coins, man! That was my brother!*

It all washes over me so fast. I navigate through the swarms of students and disappear down the hallway to the bathroom, where I shut myself inside and try my best to breathe.

1 **safe space** ['seɪf speɪs] a place or situation in which (a group of) people are protected from emotional / physical damage | 2 **extension** [ɪk'stenʃn] *here:* another part of sb's personality | 3 **MMORPG** massively multiplayer online role-playing game | 4 **pulmonary embolism** ['pʌlmənəri 'embəlɪzəm] when the blood is stopped from flowing into the lungs | 5 **clot** [klɒt] sth that blocks the blood flowing | 6 **homeboy** ['həʊm bɔɪ] *(AE, infml)* close friend; member of your gang | 7 **to hold sth for ransom** ['həʊld fə 'rænsəm] to make sb pay in order to get sth back | 8 **to hijack sth** ['haɪdʒæk] *here:* to take control of or use sth that is not yours

C *Kiera decides to skip class for the rest of the day and go home to log into* SLAY.

Does this make me a murderer? Did I kill Jamal?

I've been staring at my VR screen so long my eyes are dry. My back and feet hurt from standing for too long. My hands are sweaty inside my gloves.

Anubis is standing in front of me. I found him in the Desert, exactly where his human – Jamal – left him. He's moving slightly, swaying slowly from side to side as if he's real.

Have I killed him? Was it me? It feels so painfully real now to remember there are actual people behind the characters I see in my headset. This Egyptian god of a character that stands before me, who's an epic warrior here in the SLAY universe, is just a kid in the real world – around my age. Was a kid. I can't stop shaking. This is my fault. I should've been more careful. I should've included in the list of game rules that you can't trade real money for SLAY coins. Not like it would've done anything. People do what people do. But ... I can't shake this feeling that I could've done something.

D I think back to that day I came home from Harper's house three years ago, when we both played *Legacy of Planets* – it was the very first time I was called the n-word. After I had finally customized my character who had to be a dwarf if I wanted to make her skin as dark as mine is in real life, I went to the first character I saw on the map – I don't even remember his username – and he took one look at my character and whipped out that word. I never told Harper or Wyatt because I didn't want to ruin the game for them. In fact, I kept playing. I wanted so badly to love *Legacy of*

Planets, because who doesn't love the idea of having a virtual miniature them who can go on campaigns and fight dragons with no risks except for virtual character damage and loss of coins? Who doesn't want to have a world at their fingertips – where you can do whatever you want within the limits of the game, where your actions have no consequences, and where you can hide behind a keyboard without being held responsible for what you say or do? Everyone wants that freedom. And whenever I played *Legacy*, I'd hear all the things people wish they could say to people in real life.

I remember creating Emerald, making her skin my shade, just a few shades shy of passing the paper bag test[9], wondering how I could share her with everyone I knew who needed a world like this. I never thought the game would get this big, this time-consuming, or this dangerous. I never thought a boy would lose his life because of me. I stare at Anubis, still swaying slightly, looking silently at me. I hold out my hands and look down at them, at Emerald's hands. Would I still have created her if I had known?

From: Brittney Morris, *SLAY*, 2019 (adapted)

SPEAKING

2 Your reaction → S1, S2

a) *Describe your first reaction to the novel extract.*

b) *Would you like to read the rest of the novel? Explain why or why not.*

9 the paper bag test *(AE)* refers to a test within African-American communities which compared sb's skin colour to a brown paper bag. If their skin colour was darker, they sometimes didn't get certain privileges, e.g. going to social events. This test dates back to the time of slavery where darker-skinned slaves had to work outside while the lighter-skinned often worked inside the slave master's home.

READING

3 Understanding the story → More help ○ 149/10 → S1

a) *Briefly describe each of these people or things in the extract on pp. 60–61. Who or what are they?*

Legacy of Planets | Wyatt and Harper | Jamal | Anubis | Emerald

b) *Sum up what happens to Kiera, the protagonist of the story.*

c) *Find information in the extract about the effect of video games on developers and on users. Take notes in a grid like the one below. Give line numbers.*

	advantages and possibilities	downsides and real-life consequences
developers	– video games can be a form of art / creative expression (ll. 5–6)	– they are responsible for the negative effect of games on users (ll. 6–8) – …
users	…	…

VOCABULARY

4 Looking at language

Find these words in the extract on pp. 60–61 and write down definitions for them.

closed-captioning | to run a hustle | to customize | dwarf | shade | to sway

READING

5 Analysis: Narrative perspective and character → S6, S7

a) *Analyse the narrative perspective and explain its effect on the reader.*

b) *Explain why Kiera's attitude towards the murder changes during the extract.*

c) *Write a characterisation for Kiera by focusing on her motivation to create video games and her feelings of responsibility for the boy's death.*

SPEAKING MK

6 Game developers' responsibilities → S32

Read Kiera's statement. Then discuss whether you think game developers are responsible for the users' actions or not.

"As a game developer, I'm not just an artist. I'm not just a coder. I feel a certain responsibility for the people who play my game." (ll. 5–8)

Word bank

(un)intended consequence | (un)fortunate result | (un)avoidable outcome | negative effect | to predict how players will … | to try to ensure that … | to do one's best to … | to wish for / that | to keep / to lose a sense of perspective | to be / to get sth out of proportion | excessive | to get sth wrong

WRITING

WB 32–35/12–14

7 Options → S17, S22

*Choose **one** of the options:*

A Write a chat between Kiera and her best friend in which she tells them about what happened.

B Write a news report (for a popular or quality newspaper) about what happened. Include comments from the gaming community.

How to work in a team

In the unit task you're going to create a talk show in a team. This page will give you some useful tips on how to work successfully with other people.

1 Collaborating successfully

WB 36/15

a) *Read the advice about collaborating from a website below. Which advice is the most helpful in your opinion? Can you add any further tips based on your own experiences?*

Improve your collaboration skills

Step 1: Plan how you are going to work
Are you going to work on different aspects individually / in pairs and share your ideas with the group? Or are you going to work together from the start?

Step 2: Assign roles
If the project involves different roles / tasks, agree who will do what. Take responsibility for completing your tasks well and in the time available.

Step 3: Make a schedule
Check how much time you have for your project. Agree on the result you want to have by the end of the available time. Then divide your work into small goals and set milestones.

Step 4: Work on your tasks
Depending on your choice in Step 1, work together or individually on your tasks. Try to stick to your schedule. If you have trouble finishing in time, communicate your delay as soon as possible and ask for help if necessary.

Step 5: Check your progress
Check the group's progress regularly, e.g. when you have reached a milestone. Assess the work you have done carefully and honestly. If the work isn't going well, change what you are doing and / or how you are doing it. Remember that sometimes the best solution is to start again!
During your project work, give feedback respectfully. Listen carefully to other perspectives and inputs. Accept constructive feedback on your work and be willing to change it. Remember that nobody is right all the time! If necessary, one person must mediate in order to reach a group decision. Accept the majority decision even if you disagree with it.

b) *For each of the steps 1–5 think of phrases that could be helpful when working together.*

2 Using digital tools for collaboration → S36

WB 36/16

a) *Have you ever used any of the apps or tools in the skills box? If so, make a grid with four columns: What was the* ***name*** *of the app or tool? What did you* ***use*** *it for? Why was it* ***easy*** *or* ***difficult*** *to use?*

b) *Go online and find free apps and tools for the other categories in the skills box or alternatives to the ones you found difficult to use in a). Add them to your grid.*

Media skills

Suggestions for collaborative tools
- Use a planner app to arrange meetings etc.
- Use a project management tool to plan and visualise your milestones.
- Use a conference app for meetings outside the classroom.
- Use an online mind-mapping tool to brainstorm ideas.
- Use a presentation app to present your ideas or the results of your research to the group.

MK

A collaborative project: Creating a talk show

D4 Word bank

In this unit task you're going to organise and record a short talk show (10–15 minutes) about game developers' and the gaming community's responsibilities.

Step 1

Plan how you are going to work. → WB 37/17

Get together in groups of six or seven. Then read Steps 2–6 and decide whether you will work on them together or separately.

→ How to work in a team p. 63 → S36

Step 2

Assign roles.

Organise the roles and tasks in your team.

1. Who are your guests?
2. Who is going to prepare which guest role?
3. Who is going to be the host?

Step 3

Make a schedule.

How much time do you have to prepare the talk show? What are the milestones of your project? Set dates / times for each milestone.

Step 4

Work on your tasks. → WB 37/18

Guests:

1. Why have you been invited to the show? What experience do you have, e.g. are you a gamer, developer, parent, expert? Do some research if necessary.
2. Write a short profile for your role, which the host can use to prepare.
3. Decide on at least four arguments. Prepare reasons and examples to go with your ideas.
4. Compare your arguments with those of the other guests to make sure that you don't use the same ones.
5. Write key words on prompt cards to use in the talk show.

Host:

1. Think of introductions for the show and the guests.
2. Think of questions that you can ask your guests. Write notes on prompt cards.
3. Think of ways to react: What will you say if your guests stop talking, interrupt each other or nobody has any questions?
4. Think of ways to end: Sum up or give the most convincing argument for one side of the debate.

→ S35, S37

Step 5

Check your progress.

For each milestone, have a meeting with your team. Check your progress, exchange results and give each other feedback. Also check your schedule and practise the talk show.

→ How to: Understand a talk show p. 58 → S32

Step 6

Act out the show and give feedback.

Act out your talk show in class or record it. Give each other feedback on how it went.

Step 7

Reflect on your collaboration in your group.

How well did you collaborate? When should you have communicated more / better? How could the next collaboration be more successful? Which tools or apps have been helpful, which haven't?

A 28–30

The Disconnect

SPEAKING MK **1**

Before you read

Imagine one day without your phone. How would you feel? Why?

Esther, a 16-year-old girl, goes to school in Britain and lives with her mum and her stepfather Avi. Her dad lives in the United States with his new wife, Esther's older sister Rosa and Rosa's baby boy, Zack. Esther uses her phone to stay in touch with her family. She'd like to go and see them, but unfortunately her mother can't afford the journey.

A On Monday at school, I can feel my phone vibrating in my pocket. I'm going to have to find a way to sneak a look at it when I get out of assembly.

Ugh, what a rubbish weekend. When the girls actually saw what I looked like in that top, they sort of smirked. And a lot of pictures were taken. And now they're all over Insta, all over Snapchat. The comments will be coming in thick and fast, either fake nice or downright rude.

I should switch off my phone. That's what we're meant to do at school. But it could be something urgent. You never know. Dad likes to know he can contact me any time. And what if something happens to Rosa and Zack? I do worry about them, because they're thousands of miles away. And so is Dad, of course.

Maybe I can ease it out of my pocket ...

But we're in a special assembly and someone would see. And I really can't afford to have my phone taken away.

We aren't normally called into assembly in period two. I should be doing History. The whole of Year Eleven are here. The head teacher's talking about some special guest. Must be the woman sitting next to him.

She's very smart[1] and looks a bit scary. Her silver-blonde hair's all puffed up and she's wearing a tailored jacket and a white blouse with a floppy bow. Plus a chunky silver choker and earrings. She looks like she might be here to close the school down. But I don't think she is, because then Mr Lamarr wouldn't be smiling, and the school would probably send letters home to our parents rather than break the news in a Year Eleven assembly.

B "So, I'd like to welcome Dame Irene Irvine back to the school," Mr Lamarr says. "She was a pupil here back in the 1970s, and since then she's become one of our most successful former students."

Something stirs in my memory. Dame Irene Irvine. Mobile phones. Billionaire. Super impressive.

"She's got news of a very exciting new programme for you in Year Eleven," Mr Lamarr goes on, "which I hope you'll all get involved in. It's a fascinating social experiment, and I think you'll find it something that can help to improve both your exam results and your social skills ... It might even increase your happiness."

I don't know what he's going on about. It's a well-known fact that schools only care about exam results. But anyway, how can Dame Irene Irvine make us happier? Give us all free phones with unlimited data?

"Thank you, Mr Lamarr!" Dame Irene begins. "And it is so good to be back here again. I've just been treated to a tour of the grounds and I can tell you that a lot has changed since 1979! In my day, a lot of classes were taught in temporary classrooms with leaking roofs. There were no computer suites or dance studios. But there's still a lot that's familiar."

I'm not interested in a history lesson, especially when I've been pulled out of a History lesson, so my mind starts wandering a bit. I think about how Natalie has gone a bit crazy about boys lately. How she likes it when they message her or like her pictures. How she's always going on at me to friend different boys. And how I find the whole thing a bit annoying but could never say so.

1 **smart** *here:* elegant; chic

"So, mobile-phone technology has been my life," Dame Irene is saying. "And I am proud of what I've achieved. A few decades ago, no one could have predicted the sort of impact[2] technology would have on our lives today."

I can't imagine a life without phones. Mum talks about it sometimes, and it just feels so strange that someone I know lived like that. It's like knowing someone who remembers Henry VIII beheading his second wife. "Phones are a vital part of our everyday life," Dame Irene says. "We use them to communicate, to socialise[3], to share information and photographs, videos and links."

Typical older person with a really limited view of what phones are for. What about finding our way to places? How do you do that without GPS? How about googling stuff? And meeting people online?

"My challenge now is to look to the future," Dame Irene continues. "What role will phones play in the decades to come? What can we do better? How can technology grow to help us even more? And that's where you come in. Year Eleven, I want you to help me."

The room buzzes with excitement. For a minute we forget to be silent and we turn to each other, words spilling out of our mouths as we try to work out what Dame Irene means. Then Ms Mohammed (head of discipline and decorum) blows her whistle and we're silent again.

C "I'm creating a task force to tell me about mobile-phone culture," Dame Irene says. "And I thought there'd be no better way to recruit[4] people than by looking to your generation. You're digital natives. People who have grown up with this technology."

Dame Irene pauses, gazes intently at us with her piercing blue eyes, and adds, "You know more about mobile phones than I do. They've always been part of your life. You can tell me exactly what's good – and bad – about the way technology affects us. I'm sure each and every one of you could help me. But I need to find the best candidates. People who show discipline and determination[5]. So I have a challenge for you."

A ripple of anticipation[6] spreads across the room.

"My challenge is this," Dame Irene says. "You have to give up your mobile phone."

Every single one of us gasps in horror. Well, everyone I can see, anyway.

"The challenge will last for six weeks," Dame Irene continues, "until half term. Anyone who manages to go six weeks without their phone will win £1,000 and become a member of my task force. They'll be paid to attend meetings. Their ideas will help change the future. Those who want to take part will get simple phones, which you can use for calls and texts. You won't be out of touch in an emergency. I'll trust you not to cheat, and as the weaker participants drop out I'll announce ways of monitoring[7] you further. A letter has gone to your parents today, outlining the challenge, and I'll need their permission for you to take part. I know it won't be easy. But I think and hope that we will all learn a great deal from this challenge, which I've called The Disconnect."

My head splits into two, like it's a watermelon and Dame Irene has taken an axe to it. One half of my brain is all "My phone? My phone? She wants to take my phone away?"

But the other is "One thousand pounds! One thousand pounds! Wow! Yes, please!"

From: Keren David, *The Disconnect*, 2021 (abridged)

Across cultures

Every year the British monarch awards individuals with honours such as the **Order of the British Empire** (OBE). People who get this award can use the title 'Sir' (for men) or 'Dame' (for women) before their name. What honours are given in Germany? What have people done to be awarded?

2 **impact** [ˈɪmpækt] effect | 3 **to socialise** [ˈsəʊʃlaɪz] to make friends and spend time with them | 4 **to recruit sb** [rɪˈkruːt] *here:* to find sb to do a particular task | 5 **determination** [dɪˌtɜːmɪˈneɪʃn] quality that makes you continue doing sth although it is difficult | 6 **a ripple of anticipation** [ˈrɪpl əv ænˌtɪsɪˈpeɪʃn] a feeling that sth interesting is going to happen | 7 **to monitor sb** [ˈmɒnɪtə] to check what sb is doing

2 Understanding the novel extract → S1

READING

a) *Answer the questions about the extract:*

1. Why does Esther say "Ugh, what a rubbish weekend"? (l. 5)
2. How do Esther's feelings about the assembly change? Why?
3. Who is Dame Irene? What is her challenge about?
4. How does Esther respond to the challenge? Why?

b) *Find and list the arguments which Dame Irene uses to motivate the students to take part in the challenge.*

SPEAKING

c) *You want to persuade the students at your school to take part in the challenge. Write a speech or make a poster for the school noticeboard to invite them to join the experiment. Use the arguments you found in b) and think of additional convincing arguments.*

d) *Your turn: Would you take part in the challenge? Explain why or why not.*

VOCABULARY

3 Descriptive language → S37

The writer uses some words with very specific meanings to describe events and appearances. From the context, try to explain the difference between each pair of words or phrases. Then check your answers using a dictionary.

1. to sneak a look (l. 3) | to have a look
2. to smirk (l. 7) | to smile
3. puffed up (l. 29) | big
4. chunky (l. 31) | big
5. to be treated to sth (l. 61) | to be given sth
6. spilling out (l. 103) | coming out
7. to gaze (l. 114) | to look
8. to gasp (l. 128) | to breathe in

READING

4 Analysis: Characterisation and language → More help ○ 149/11 → S7, S8

a) *Based on the extract, write a characterisation of the narrator, Esther. Include quotations from the extract to support your findings. Give line numbers.*

b) *Analyse the narrator's language. Focus on the register and tone that she uses.*

c) *Analyse Dame Irene's register and tone and compare them with the narrator's. Use your findings from b).*

WRITING

5 Options → S4, S17

*Choose **one** of the following options:*

A Esther decides to take part in the challenge. Write her letter to her father in which she tells him about the challenge and describes how her life has changed since she gave up her phone.

B Esther takes part in the challenge. After one week, she realises that one of her friends is cheating and secretly using another friend's phone. What does Esther do? Write this part of the novel.

Can you …

1. talk about the digital age?	We must embrace the new digital reality.
2. use the will-future progressive and will-future perfect?	A few years from now, most of them won't be doing jobs that are related to a typical school curriculum.
3. use *which* to comment on a main clause?	Rankin's opinion is that being the better version of yourself is about looking like yourself, which is hard to disagree with.
4. use relative clauses with *when* and *where*?	Rankin had noticed social media sites where people often retouched their own photos.
5. create a talk show?	In a talk show, the host interviews their guests and gets them to discuss a controversial topic.

LISTENING

1 Edutainment

A 31

In this episode of the podcast 'Forward Thinking', the host interviews a professor about 'edutainment'. Read the tasks. Then listen and choose the correct answer or give short answers.

1. What does 'edutainment' mean?
2. Young people are … they were in the past.
   a) more patient than
   b) as patient as
   c) less patient than
3. What's the effect of edutainment on learning?
4. What has happened to the sales of game-based learning products?
5. Name two of the three possible disadvantages of edutainment that Professor White mentions.
6. Edutainment will … students when they start work.
   a) connect
   b) help
   c) distract

SPEAKING

2 Your experiences

a) *Describe the cartoon and analyse its message. Say whether you think it is realistic or not.*

b) *Discuss the following quotation:*

"Everyone is comparing lives on social media and wants the perfect body, perfect image, perfect outfit, perfect life – we're striving for this perfection, and it's so unhealthy because there's no such thing as perfection."
Emily Atack (actor)

"Wow! What graphics!"

→ Solutions p. 279

MEDIATION MK **3**

Online friendships

Your cousin thinks making new friends online isn't worthwhile. You disagree and you come across this article when you look for arguments online. Write an email to your cousin in German in which you sum up the arguments in the article which show that online friendships are worthwhile.

Online friendships – real or fake?

Online friends are often thought incorrectly to be nasty people or fakes. But with that mindset you miss out on the honest and open-minded people whom you could form a long-lasting friendship with.

But what exactly is friendship? Well, according to Aristotle, there are three types of friendships: friendships of utility[1], pleasure, and virtue[2]. Friendships of utility happen "by accident[3]" and are not permanent at all. Both people get some kind of benefit from the exchange, but there is no intimate connection. Then there are friendships based on pleasure, also known as a shared interest. They end once that interest changes. The most long-lasting, most intimate[4], and most "complete" form of friendship is the one that is based on the appreciation[5] of each other's virtues. These friendships take time to form, and you go through ups and downs together.

Sure, the internet did not exist 2,000 years ago, but I am sure that Aristotle would have come to the same conclusions about friendship if he had chatted to people online.

If the friendships we can make online and offline are the same and we assume that both are based on mutual goodwill[6] (something essential according to Aristotle), why do we still label online friendships as fake or something you can't trust?

Actually, online friendships are even better than offline friendships in some ways. I am Asian-American, queer, and socially awkward. Online no one knows who I am. That means that I face a lot less prejudices. People do not judge me for the way I look or for liking T-shirts with funny slogans.

When you belong to a minority group, you will not only find less prejudice, but (often) also much more understanding online. I have met one of my best friends online through a queer support group. Even though we live hundreds of kilometres away from one another, they are essential for my happiness and health because I can talk to them about what it means to be queer in a small town in the Midwest – something my nonqueer friends wouldn't understand. We have supported each other through some tough times and talk or video chat almost every day.

Also, it can be hard for me to start a conversation in real life because I feel awkward or judged. Starting a conversation online feels a lot safer. I can think about what I want to write, and I can leave a conversation whenever I want. Talking to strangers on the internet has also helped me improve my social skills. I now know how to get from a meaningless "hey what's up?" – "nothing much. u?" exchange of words to having an actual conversation.

Last but not least, I can find people with the same interests and hobbies online. People who agree Pokémon is cool and who share my love for Minecraft. Plus, meeting people with the same interests from around the world can add cultural perspectives and allow for deeper conversations.

All in all, I would say that the quality of an online friendship depends on yourself and what you want from it, your commitment and openness towards the other person. In conclusion, online friendships should not be quickly judged and labelled as fake or "not real" but need to be assessed individually.

Daya Davis, *Student Magazine*, 2022

1 **utility** [ju:ˈtɪləti] *here:* usefulness | 2 **virtue** [ˈvɜ:tʃu:] a good quality in a person | 3 **by accident** [ˌbaɪ ˈæksɪˈdnt] not planned | 4 **intimate** [ˈɪntɪmət] deep; close | 5 **appreciation** [əˌpri:ʃiˈeɪʃn] seeing the good features of others | 6 **mutual goodwill** [ˈmju:tʃuəl ɡʊdˈwɪl] friendly feelings towards one another

MK **4**

A fresh start

After losing her father and being bullied online, Anna and her mother move from Birmingham to the small Scottish village of St Monans to make a fresh start. Even though she has made some friends at her new school, Anna is worried that one day people will find out about her past.

Rounding a corner, I find my path blocked by a group of boys I don't know. But, as I try to walk past, one of them purposely steps in front of me, blocking my way. I move to walk round him and he sidesteps, trapping me between him and the lockers. "Hey, Anna," he sings in a teasing voice, "fancy[1] a threesome[2]?" Some of the others laugh rowdily[3]. I try to push past him, but he moves sideways again, backing me against a locker door. "C'mon," he croons[4], "don't be like that. I know you want it ... I've seen your Facebook page." He moves closer, his breath hot on my face. "Isn't this what you like, Anna Clark?" And then his voice drops to a whisper. "Or should I say Anna Reeves?" A shock runs through my body like electricity. I dive sideways and escape, running down the corridor. I hear laughter and shouts behind me. How does he know that name?

I stumble through the main door as the bell rings for the next period. I have to see it. I have to know. I stumble down a few streets, far enough away from school to avoid the risk of being spotted. I sink down against the trunk of a tree and pull out my phone. I google "Anna Reeves Facebook", and find what I'm looking for almost immediately. Someone has set up a new profile and it's not exactly easy to miss. I can't log in, but I don't need an account to view it – the profile is public. Of course it is. How did I ever think I could outrun[5] this?

The main profile picture is an old one of me, cropped from a photo on someone else's account. I'm at a party and the side of someone else's smiling face is still just visible next to mine. Under "work and education" it says: "Founder of Sluts[6] United". And then, underneath, there it is. The picture I've been running away from, the feeling I literally left the country to escape, the shame that's been trying to get back inside my mind ever since we got here. The photograph I've tried over and over to forget, the one I've deleted all copies and evidence of. And yet here it is again, turned against me like a weapon. I feel sick and close my eyes. My blood is rushing loud in my ears. Everything else is quiet.

Whoever created the profile must have searched for St Margaret's and it looks like they've added practically everyone in our year. Some are people I've slowly started making friends with; some I've barely[9] even met. Well, they all know me now.

Panicking, I tap hard at the picture, desperate[10] to delete it, to make it disappear. I create a new profile. As soon as I'm in, I return to the Anna Reeves page and click again on the photo, looking for the report button. I hesitate.

– It's a bad photo of me
– It's inappropriate
– It makes me sad
– It's embarrassing

Where's "All of the above" when you need it?

From: Laura Bates, *The Burning*, 2019 (adapted)

READING

a) *Sum up what happens to Anna in the novel extract.*

b) *Describe how Anna's feelings change in the course of the extract. Give line numbers.*

WRITING

c) *Write Anna's diary entry for that day, explaining what happened and how she felt.*

1 **to fancy** ['fænsi] to want (to do) sth | 2 **threesome** ['θri:səm] *here:* when three people have sex together | 3 **rowdily** ['raʊdəli] noisily | 4 **to croon** [kru:n] to speak quietly and in a friendly way | 5 **to outrun** [ˌaʊt'rʌn] to escape from sth | 6 **slut** [slʌt] offensive word for a woman who (supposedly) has many sexual partners

→ Solutions p. 279

VOCABULARY

5 VR in every home and school?

Choose the most suitable words to complete this information about VR.

Virtual reality offers amazing 1 (free-time / successful / personal) and educational activities. This 2 (important / immersive / independent) experience is much better than just using a standard 3 (game console / VR headset / browser) or other 4 (analog / personalised / screen-based) device. It 5 (demonstrates / enables / blames) us to immerse ourselves in virtual worlds and to experience video gaming, far-away places and new ways of learning like never before. By the 1990s VR had most of the features that are typical of it today. Then why isn't VR 6 (celebrated / allowed / enabled) more? Why don't millions of homes have a VR system? Why doesn't every school have a VR room when there is no doubt about the great 7 (disadvantages / benefits / consequences) of using VR to teach subjects? In addition, the latest VR system costs about the same as a good laptop. VR systems are also not difficult to 8 (fix / build / use). The reason that the 9 (danger / potential / possibility) of VR is not used widely yet may be that it does not so far have that 10 (all-important / great / large) 'killer app' – an app such as a browser, which is so useful that millions of people adopt a new technology in order to use it.

GRAMMAR

6 The future of digital media

Complete this extract from an article with a form of the ***will-future progressive*** *or* ***will-future perfect****.*

50 years from now, digital media 1 (to be) around for so long that people 2 (not to write) articles like this. It 3 (to become) such a basic part of life that we won't even think about it – like water from taps now, for example. Of course, some aspects of it 4 (to change) by then. I hope that people 5 (to learn) from the mistakes that we are making now, and when I'm 66 everybody 6 (to use) social media in a more sensitive way that they were when I was 16. I imagine that by then, people 7 (understand) that being mean online can have serious consequences. But perhaps I will be disappointed, and teenagers 8 (to cyberbully) each other the same as they are now!

GRAMMAR

7 Mixed bag

Correct the relative pronouns and/or the use of commas in the following relative clauses where necessary.

1. I never play video games which makes me unusual at my school.
2. That's the classroom which we're going to start a coding club.
3. Can you remember a time where you didn't use social media every day?
4. We found that AR software is really easy to use when we weren't expecting.
5. Major esports competitions where can win a lot of money attract thousands of spectators.
6. During people's teenage years, which cyberbullying can become a serious problem, it is especially important to be careful on social media.

Check-in

Text and media smart 2

Dealing with factual texts

On these Text and media smart pages, you're going to learn how to sum up and analyse factual texts as well as how to write an argumentative text to discuss a topic.

SPEAKING

1 Summing up information

a) *Summing up is helpful in a lot of everyday situations – when it's done right. Read the dialogue between Tom and Rachel.*

Tell me about that new series. What is it about?

Well, it's about this group of friends who solve crimes together. And you know what's funny? The series is based on a book that I loved to read as a kid. I don't usually watch movies or series that are based on books. They're just never as good as the original. They cut or extend the story in the weirdest places and that just makes me angry and disappointed, you know …

b) *Look at the photo which was taken while Tom was answering Rachel's question. What information did she probably expect to get? What did she probably* ***not*** *want to know?*

c) *Role play: Take turns asking the everyday questions below and giving answers. Try to decide what information is important and unimportant.*

How was your day? | How did you celebrate your last birthday? | How did you get to school today? | What are your plans for tonight? | What's your favourite book / film about?

SPEAKING

2 Analysing: the author's intention, tone and register → More practice ● 150/1

Compare the types of text on the right, considering the questions below:

1. What's the author's intention?
2. Does the author give their personal opinion?
3. Which tone and register does the author use?

film review | interview-based article with a sports star | news report on an earthquake

SPEAKING

3 Discussing the pros and cons

a) *In which of these types of texts does the author discuss an issue from different points of view?*

letter to the editor | book review | comment | speech | invitation | itinerary | news report | survey | yearbook article | blog entry

b) *Your turn: Which of these types of text have you already written at school or outside school? What was the reason for doing so?*

Summary and analysis

MK **1** "Honey, let's track the kids" → S1

SPEAKING

a) *Do you have any experience of using location-tracking apps on your phone? How would you feel if someone, e.g. a parent, used an app to track you?*

READING

b) *Read the article. Then compare your ideas in a) with the responses quoted in the article.*

A 32

Honey, let's track the kids: the rise of parental surveillance

Phone apps now allow parents to follow every move their children make. But does keeping them safe come at a price?

A recent survey of 4,000 parents and guardians in the UK found that 40% of them used real-time GPS location tracking on a daily basis for their children; 15% said that they checked their whereabouts "constantly".

At best, location-tracking apps can feel like an extension of helicopter parenting; at worst, they might feel like stalking. Consequently, location tracking has become a battleground in many families, bringing up issues of trust, privacy and personal growth. However, not all teenagers find location tracking an invasion of their privacy. "It makes me feel safe, because I know that Mum or Dad knows where I am," says Lola Pethybridge, a 17-year-old student from south London. "It's just that safety net where you can say, 'I need help.' Or, 'Can you come and get me?'"

The issue is more contentious with other families. Alicia Hardy, a solicitor from Hampshire, encouraged her two children, Ben and Louise, to use a location-tracking app. Ben, who was 17 at the time, lasted for about a month. "At that point in my life, I wasn't necessarily that happy about Mum knowing where I was all the time," says Ben, who is now 23.

Louise, meanwhile, was 14 and went along with her mother's request; six years later, they both still use the app. "I introduced it not because I wanted to catch my kids out doing stuff wrong, because frankly, I did stuff wrong, but for me it was more an anxious-mother thing," explains Alicia. Louise agrees that, at times, location-tracking apps have made her feel safer, but still has some conflict about them. "As a kid you're meant to do stuff that your parents don't know about," she says. "You're meant to make mistakes, you're meant to mess up. So them always having an eye on you takes away from childhood a little bit. But Mum is a worrier, so it's just a case of keeping her a bit sane."

The Hardy family are clearly very open with each other, and that's important according to Philippa Perry, a psychotherapist and the *Observer Magazine's* agony aunt. For Perry, location tracking, like most technology, is neither good nor evil: what matters is the boundaries you set and everyone being comfortable with the negotiation. She says, "If you want your children to be open with you and feel like they can tell you anything, don't react angrily or negatively or dismissively when they confide in you. If you have done this in the past and now you have a mute teenager, try to repair that rupture by telling them where you overreacted in the past without making excuses for yourself and say you'll do better next time. And do better next time."

Whether the use of these apps keeps children safer is disputed, but there is obviously the potential to affect relationships between parents and their offspring: certainly where trust has been damaged, location tracking is unlikely to repair it.

Tim Lewis, *The Guardian* website, 2022 (abridged and adapted)

READING

2 A model summary → S23 → <G12>

a) *Read the skills box. Then note down the main point(s) in each paragraph of the article "Honey, let's track the kids" that you would include in a summary.*

b) *Read a model summary of the article. Which of the key points you noted in a) are included?*

Writing skills

A **summary** briefly outlines the main ideas in a non-fictional text or retells a story. It leaves out details, personal opinions and interpretations. Its length depends on the original text. For shorter texts like articles, 30–40% of the original text is recommended. For longer texts, e.g. novels, one to three pages are enough.

In an article entitled "Honey, let's track the kids: the rise of parental surveillance" by Tim Lewis, published on The Guardian website in 2022, the writer reports on the use of smartphone location-tracking apps by parents to check their children's whereabouts.

The writer begins by referring to a survey which found that 40% of parents and guardians in the UK use these apps daily, and 15% use them constantly. The writer discusses the effects on families and illustrates these effects by quoting the reactions of both parents and children who have used these apps.

The writer goes on to quote Philippa Perry, a psychotherapist and agony aunt. According to her, the important thing is that everyone is comfortable with whatever has been negotiated around the use of location-tracking apps. She also advises parents not to overreact when teenagers tell them things. If parents do overreact and damage communication with teenagers, they should admit their mistake and try to do better in the future.

The author concludes the article by pointing out that it has not been proved whether these apps keep children safer and suggests that where trust has been damaged, location tracking is unlikely to repair it.

c) *Compare the model summary with the original article. Point out information which the summary writer didn't feel was relevant enough to include. Think of possible reasons.*

WRITING

3 A checklist for summary writing → More help ○ 150/2 → S23

D5 Checklist

a) *Compare this checklist for summary writing with the model summary in ex. 2. Correct the mistakes in the checklist and write the correct checklist in your exercise book.*

- *reduce the text to 30–40% of the original article / one to three pages for longer texts*
- *introduction: state title and main point (plus source and publication date if it's an article)*
- *main part: structured in paragraphs; not every new point needs a new paragraph*
- *conclusion: not needed*
- *order of points: either chronologically (combined in a new, logical way) or thematically (as in the original)*
- *include details, examples, quotations and your own opinion*
- *copy original lines word for word*
- *use an informal register*
- *use the past tense if you describe the actions of the author, e.g. "The author concludes ..."*

b) *Exchange checklists and peer-edit your results. Then add tips of your own to the corrected checklist. Maybe there's something you feel you need to pay special attention to.*

VOCABULARY

4 Useful phrases for writing a summary

a) *Find useful phrases in the summary in ex. 2 which describe how the writer, Tim Lewis, wrote the article on p. 73.*

Example: The writer reports on …

b) *Complete the useful phrases for writing a summary with words from a) and any other suitable words you already know. There may be more than one solution for each useful phrase.*

1. The writer ___ the issue / problem by / with …
2. The author ___ explain / describe / quote …
3. The writer ___ the issue of …
4. The author ___ an expert / a witness …
5. The writer ___ a survey / a report / statistics.
6. The writer ___ that …
7. The author ___ the article / report / review with / by …

READING

5 Differences in summary quality → S23

a) *Read this example of an **unsuccessful** summary of "Honey, let's track the kids". Note down what you think is wrong with this summary. Refer to your checklist in ex. 3.*

In the article, Tim Lewis (the writer) described how a recent survey found that lots of parents use tracking apps on their children's phones to track their whereabouts. I was really surprised that the number of parents who do this is so high.

Tim went on to talk about stuff like how the apps "can feel like an extension of helicopter parenting" or "might feel like stalking" (He's not wrong!) and quoted some people who've used them. One kid called Lola said she thinks using the app is OK because it makes her feel safe. But a guy called Ben stopped using it after a month because he wasn't necessarily that happy about Mum knowing where he was all the time. His sister, on the other hand, continued using it, partly to stop her mum worrying about her. However, "As a kid you're meant to do stuff that your parents don't know about," she says. "You're meant to make mistakes, you're meant to mess up. So them always having an eye on you takes away from childhood a little bit." I totally agree with that.

In the next part of the article, Tim quoted somebody called Philippa Perry. For Perry, location tracking, like most technology, is neither good nor evil: what matters is the boundaries you set and everyone being comfortable with the negotiation. Then there's some stuff about parents not overreacting and if they do, trying not to do it again.

At the end, Tim said nobody knows if these apps actually do any good or not, and that where trust has been damaged, location tracking is unlikely to repair it. I thought it was a well-written article about an interesting topic. I wouldn't want one of those apps on my phone though, that's for sure!

b) *Use your checklist in ex. 3 and your notes from a) to compare your findings and exchange your ideas about the quality of the summary.*

MK **6** ## Writing a summary → S17, S23

READING

a) *Read the article. Then tell your partner about its main message to make sure you understood the key information.*

A 33
WB 38/1

China limits young gamers to three hours a week

New rule means young gamers can play online for one hour per day on Fridays, weekends and holidays.

Aiming to control what the government has described as 'youth video game addiction', China has ordered online gaming companies to reduce even further the amount of time young gamers are allowed to spend playing online games. In 2019 a new government restriction limited playing time for users under the age of 18 to 1.5 hours on weekdays and three hours per day at weekends. That has now been reduced to just one hour in the evenings on Fridays, Saturdays, Sundays and holidays. Players cannot choose the time: This is fixed at 8 p.m. to 9 p.m. local time. There are also new regulations to make sure that young players cannot get around the restriction by using a borrowed adult ID and to limit how much money they can spend on in-game purchases.

The government has stated that the restrictions are necessary in order to protect the physical and mental health of young people from the effects of what they believe can be a damaging habit which can lead to addiction. However, many young gamers disagree, claiming that most gamers do not play excessively and noting that in China a 16-year-old can go to work in an adult job but cannot relax by gaming online in the evening. It has also been pointed out that online video games are not the only type of game available – games that work independently of an internet connection existed for decades before online gaming became widely available, and interest in standalone games for computers and game consoles is expected to increase again.

Another cause for concern among the Chinese gaming community is the effect on esports. This is increasingly being recognised as a proper sport. In 2021 the first 'Olympic Virtual Series' took place, with cycling, rowing, sailing, motorsport and baseball as esports events. So there is a real chance that esports will eventually become a proper Olympic sport. Competitive esports players tend to be young, and to have started developing their gaming skills as children. The new restriction could put China at a disadvantage in future international esports events.

Despite the anger expressed by many young gamers, many parents, teachers and child development experts have welcomed the new limits.

WRITING

b) *Sum up the information about the restrictions on young gamers given in the article. Each of you writes an introduction and a first paragraph for a summary. Then peer-edit each other's results: What works well? What can be improved, and how?*

c) *On your own, write the rest of the summary. Refer to your checklist in ex. 3 and the useful phrases in ex. 4.*

READING

7 Text analysis: Comparing two examples → More help ○ 150/3

a) *Two students have analysed the article on p. 76 based on how **well written**, how **convincing** and how **interesting** it is. Read their results below and compare them.*

A	B
This is an article about an amazing thing that's happened in China. The government there now won't allow people younger than 18 to do online gaming for more than three hours a week. I couldn't believe it! I thought the article was quite easy to read and it presented some interesting facts. The author's style is objective and right for a news story, but there's more information about young gamers' complaints (obviously, they're not pleased!) than there is about the government's reasons for doing this. I would have liked a bit more information about the problems online gaming has been causing. I would also have liked to see some quotations from people in China. (Maybe the writer didn't have time to get any good quotations.) In general, the writer did an OK job, but I thought it could have been a bit more balanced and needed more quotations.	The article aims to inform the reader about a new restriction in China that limits online gaming for players under 18 to three hours per week. The writer presents the facts clearly and raises some interesting points. The writer spends more time discussing the arguments against the restriction than for it. The article would be more balanced with more information about the negative effects of excessive online gaming in China. However, the writer deals with the topic objectively and leaves the reader to make up their own mind about the issue. The article has a clear and logical structure. It is written in a formal register and the writing style is appropriate for a serious news story. Overall, the writer presents information that is relevant to the story in a way which is clear, objective and easy to follow.

b) *Exchange ideas on which analysis is better. Use the skills box for help.*

Writing skills

For a **successful analysis**, consider these points:
- **Step 1:** Choose one or more **aspects** of the text that you want to **describe and explain in detail**, e.g. why an article was written ('author's intention'), how objective it is, how convincing the argument is, how a character's feelings change in the course of the story, what made a character do what they did. Make sure you understand the aspects of the text you are going to explain.
- **Step 2:** Write an **outline**. Your text should have an **introduction**, **main body** and **conclusion**. Introduce each new idea in a new paragraph.
- **Step 3:** Describe and explain the aspect(s) you chose in Step 1. You should give examples from the text to justify your ideas. Use a **formal register** (i.e. no short forms). Do not give your personal feelings about the text or the information in it.

WRITING

8 Analysing "Honey, let's track the kids" → S4, S17

D6 Peer-editing

WB 39/2–3

Analyse the article on p. 73. Choose the aspect(s) that you want to focus on. Refer to the skills box in ex. 7.

Argumentative texts

READING **MK** **1**

Reading: Unrealistic images → S1

a) *Think about the people you follow on social media. Discuss whether the photos they have posted give a realistic image of what they look like in real life.*

b) *In a post for his school's blog, Nick Shaw from Leeds discusses the issue of unrealistic body images in the media and how this affects people. Read his post and sum up his main points.*

A 34

The media are harming us with unrealistic images of people

All across the media – in adverts, on social media, on TV, in films and in video games – we are confronted with images of what we are expected to look like. This can cause real damage and should change, as the following arguments will show.

Firstly, I would like to discuss how the body types shown in the media can make us feel bad about ourselves. While it is true that we see more variety than in the past, including 'plus size' models and more people with physical disabilities, we are still presented with a huge number of images of people with an 'ideal' body type: tall, slim, athletic and usually with an 'ideal' face too, i.e. clear skin and perfect symmetry.

On the one hand, one could see this as the media giving us what we want: It seems we prefer to see especially good-looking people. On the other hand, it is irresponsible to present perfect images of people as if they were typical. The fact is that 'perfect'-looking people are the exception, not the rule. After seeing these images their whole lives, many of my friends feel unattractive, and this has affected their confidence. A friend of mine with a minor physical disability told me that he sometimes cries about how he looks before going to school.
It also puts pressure on us to waste our energy worrying about our appearance and to spend money we can't afford on clothes, make-up etc.

Even more worryingly, I have heard many stories of people our age risking their health with steroids, plastic surgery and extreme diets. I believe that all my friends and everyone else can be proud of their own unique look, and we should stop comparing ourselves with media images. It is also important to remember that these images often feature professional models working with professional make-up artists, and even then, the images are often edited using a filter or professional software.

Secondly, I would like to focus on the way that the huge number of media images of 'perfect' people encourages negative comments on social media when somebody's appearance does not match those ideals. Of course, it is well known that social media are full of cruel comments of all types, and it is our responsibility to stop making them – a small change in behaviour which would be a real improvement. Having said that, I believe there would be less temptation to post critical comments about people's appearances if the media focused less on people's looks.

In addition, perhaps social media influencers our age should spend less time making themselves look perfect before they turn on the camera, and show us instead what they really look like.

To sum up, the media still focus too much on unrealistic ideas of physical perfection, and it is damaging for us to compare ourselves and others with these images. My suggestion would be for the media to present realistic images of people as the rule rather than the exception.

Nick Shaw (staff writer, Year 11)

Leave your comments **here.**

2 Understanding the text → More practice ● 151/4 → S1

READING

a) *Nick presents three arguments for and three against the statement that the media are harming us with unrealistic images of people. Take notes on his arguments.*

SPEAKING

b) *Your turn: Discuss your attitude to the statement and to the arguments Nick presents.*

Word bank

I agree / disagree with Nick when he says that … | Nick is right / wrong when he says … | I partly agree / disagree with … | In my experience … | I have / haven't seen many examples of … | An important point Nick missed is … | Nick could have mentioned …

3 Argumentative texts → S25

READING V8

a) *Read the skills box about two types of argumentative texts on the right. What type of argumentative text is Nick's blog entry? Give reasons.*

Writing skills

Two types of argumentative texts:
- A **comment** presents one's **own opinion** clearly and supports one's own view with examples and reasons.
- An **essay** discusses a controversial topic, issue or statement, presenting it from **different points of view** in a clear and logical way. The writer gives arguments or reasons for and against, **discussing the pros and cons,** and then comes to a **well-founded conclusion**.

WRITING

b) *Read the skills box below about the elements of argumentative texts. Then show that you understand how the text on p. 78 works by writing an outline of it with a partner. It should name each section of the text and **briefly** sum up what each section is about.*

Example:
- The introduction is from lines … to … It presents … Some key words / ideas include …
- Paragraph … introduces a pro. The important facts are …

Writing skills

Elements of argumentative texts:

1. In the **introduction** briefly outline the issue, question or statement and take a stand.
2. Divide the **main body** into paragraphs in which you introduce and explain your arguments. State your argument in the first sentence of a paragraph, then support it with reasons and examples in the sentences that follow.

   In a **comment** explain your personal opinion. Give reasons and examples.
   Start with your weakest and end with your strongest argument.

   In an **essay** discuss the pros and cons of the issue. Choose **one** of these structures:

Paragraph 1: Pro 1 – Con 1	**or**	Paragraph 1: Pros 1–3
Paragraph 2: Pro 2 – Con 2		Paragraph 2: Cons 1–3
Paragraph 3: Pro 3 – Con 3		

3. In the **conclusion** state your own opinion again, taking into account the arguments that you gave in the main body.

VOCABULARY

c) *Go back to Nick's blog entry and find words and phrases that you can use to present arguments. Make a list of useful phrases.*

Example: Firstly, I would like to discuss …

WRITING MK **4**

Smartphones at school

→ More help ○ 151/5 → S17, S24

a) *As a member of the student council, Vanessa is part of a group that is examining the regulations on smartphone use at her school. Another student submits a petition to include the following change to the regulations:*

From Year 11 (age 15/16), all students should be allowed to use their smartphones as much as they like at school.

The head teacher asks Vanessa to discuss the change with the members of the student council and comment on the rule from their point of view. With a partner, brainstorm pros and cons. Then decide if you are for or against the new rule.

b) *Use three of the pros and cons that you found in a) to write Vanessa's comment. Use the example and information on p. 79, ex. 3 for help.*

c) *Compare your comment to a partner's (who has chosen another point of view). Which one would the head teacher find more convincing, and why?*

Tip

Start with an outline. Order your arguments from weakest to strongest.

WRITING MK **5**

Structuring and writing an essay

→ More help ○ 151/6 → S17, S25

WB 40/4

a) *Read the statement below which you are going to discuss in an essay. Make a list of all the ideas that come to mind when you think about the issue. Then organise your ideas into categories. Which ones go together?*

The minimum age in the US for social media accounts is 13. This should be raised to 16.

b) *Do research on the topic to find examples and facts that support both sides: for and against raising the minimum age.*

c) *Look at your results from a) and b) again. Decide whether raising the minimum age for social media accounts would be a good idea. Decide how you want to order your arguments and the supporting information.*

d) *Write an introduction. You can use your notes from a) for ideas on how to present the issue.*

e) *Write the main part in which you discuss the pros and cons, and a conclusion in which you state your own opinion.*

Tip

Remember that the arguments you give in the main part should support and lead to the conclusion that you make at the end.

WRITING

1 Summary and text analysis

a) *Read the article. Sum up the information about limiting young people's phone use.*

A 35

Tech bosses limit their kids' time on smartphones: why shouldn't we?

As children and young people spend an increasing amount of time with screens – more than six hours a day according to one US survey – parents have begun to wonder if spending this much time with screens is safe.

An increasing amount of research suggests it is not. Young people who use screens this much are 52% more likely to sleep less than seven hours a night – a significant amount of sleep deprivation with potential consequences for both physical and mental health. The more time young adults spend on social media, the more likely they are to be depressed or lonely.

Here's the twist: the people who designed these electronic devices and apps knew that over-using them wasn't safe, especially for children. When *New York Times* reporter Nick Bilton interviewed Apple co-founder and chief executive Steve Jobs in late 2010, he asked Jobs if his kids loved the iPad. "They haven't used it," Jobs said. "We limit how much technology our kids use at home."

Given the consequences of overuse, setting time limits is just as important as restricting access to content. For instance, parents could limit the amount of time certain apps are used, restrict hours of total phone use, or shut the phone down after bedtime.

Limiting teenagers' phone use might sound like the beginning of a huge parent-child fight. However, it might not be as bad as you think. When I interviewed young people for *iGen* [a book about the generation born after 1995], I was surprised how many were aware of the negative effects of spending so much time on a phone. Several complained, just as adults do, that they hated it when their friends or parents were looking at their phones when they were talking.

Since then, I've spoken to several teachers who asked teenagers to put their phones away for an hour or two for a project. All said that their reactions were much more characterised by relief than anger. Teenagers often feel constant pressure to respond instantly to texts and social media posts, and welcome a break.

Should we just take teenagers' phones away? The research suggests this is not a good idea. Young people who don't use smartphones or social media at all are less well-adjusted than teens who use them a little – perhaps because teen social life these days requires at least some digital media.

I expect that parents, policymakers and tech companies will be working over the next few years to come up with workable solutions. In the meantime, smartphone owners of all ages should be thinking about how to use their devices safely – meaning for a few hours a day, not for most of it. Let your phone be a tool you use – not a tool that uses you.

Jean M. Twenge, *The Guardian* website, 2018
(abridged and adapted)

b) *Analyse how Twenge presents her arguments to the reader.*

WRITING

2 Comment

D7 Peer-editing

a) *Comment on the statement on the right from your point of view. Give reasons and examples to support your arguments.*

b) *Exchange texts with a partner and peer-edit each other's work.*

Teachers should be allowed to track their students' smartphones on class trips for their safety.

Canada

READING

1 General information on Canada → S35

a) *What do you already know about Canada? Complete the sentences to find out.*

1 ... is the capital of Canada.
a) Toronto
b) Vancouver
c) Ottawa

2 Canada has a population of about ... people.
a) 36 million
b) 329.5 million
c) 144 million

3 It's the ... country in the world, but it only has 0.5% of the world's population.
a) second largest
b) third largest
c) fifth largest

4 Its currency is the ...
a) Canadian franc.
b) Canadian pound.
c) Canadian dollar.

5 Its national symbols are ...
a) the whale, the glacier and the lake.
b) the maple leaf, the beaver and the Canadian horse.
c) the maple leaf, the whale and the bear.

6 The country is a leader in ...
a) shipbuilding, mining and fishing.
b) the film industry, banking and tourism.
c) agricultural production, telecommunications and energy technologies.

7 The head of state is called ...
a) the governor-general.
b) the British monarch.
c) the prime minister.

8 Canada has ...
a) one official language, English.
b) two official languages, English and French.
c) no official language.

9 If you went from east to west in Canada, you would travel 4,700 miles (7,560 kilometres) and cross ...
a) six time zones.
b) seven time zones.
c) nine time zones.

10 The national sports are ...
a) swimming and skiing.
b) basketball and skating.
c) ice hockey and lacrosse.

11 The country is divided into 13 states: There are ...
a) three territories and ten provinces.
b) ten territories and three provinces.
c) eleven territories and two provinces.

MK

b) *Compare your answers. You can use the internet for help to check your answers.*

MK 2 A poem: Together we are Canada → S29, S9

LISTENING A36

a) *What do you think the poem "Together we are Canada" could be about?*

b) *Listen to the poem. While listening, find the provinces and territories that are mentioned on a map, e.g. an online map or the map at the back of your book.*

D8 Grid

c) *Make a grid with the names of Canada's provinces and territories. Then listen again and match these key words to the right places.*

West Coast | forestry and fishing | oil | French | open space | mountains | prairies | ice and cold | democracy | cows | wheat | potatoes | government | Atlantic Coast

READING

d) *Get together in small groups. There should be one group for each of the eight stanzas in the poem that mention provinces and territories. On the internet find more information that relates to the province / territory in your stanza and add it to your grid. Also find photos to go with it and explain why you chose them.*

VOCABULARY

e) *Your turn: If you had to write a poem like this about a country you feel you belong to, what places and things would you mention? Collect ideas. (If you want, you can write the poem.)*

MK 3 A short history of Canada → S34

MEDIATION
V9
I2 Time line
WB 46/1

While the US is often compared to a 'melting pot', Canada's culture is referred to as a 'mosaic'. You have to give a presentation in German in your history class about the historical events that created this mosaic. Read the time line and write down key words for events that created the mosaic. Then use the key words to prepare the slides for your presentation.

4 Indigenous peoples, an umbrella term

VOCABULARY

a) *Read the Across cultures box. Then explain the term 'Indigenous peoples' in German.*

Across cultures

Indigenous peoples is an umbrella term which, in Canada, is used to refer to First Nations peoples, Métis and Inuit. In the past Indigenous peoples were referred to as "Indians", a term which dates to colonial times and is offensive. **First Nations** peoples are the original inhabitants of the land that is now called Canada. They often live in territories south of the Arctic. According to the 2016 census by Statistics Canada, 977,230 people identified as being of First Nations heritage, making them the largest group of Indigenous people in Canada. There are 634 First Nations communities in Canada, speaking more than 50 different languages. **Métis** communities developed after European fur traders had married First Nations or Inuit women. Hence, Métis culture has European and Indigenous influences. Today the Métis are the second largest group of Indigenous people in Canada. They mostly live in Manitoba, Saskatchewan, Alberta and Ontario. The **Inuit** make up the smallest group of Indigenous people in Canada. Their homeland, known as Inuit Nunangat, is mainly located in the snow and ice of the Arctic.

SPEAKING D9 Statistics

b) *Look at the bar charts. How has the distribution of Indigenous people in Canada changed over the years? How does their distribution compare to that of non-Indigenous people?*

5 The impact of colonisation on Indigenous peoples → S1, S32

READING WB 46/2

a) *With the passing of the British North America Act in 1867, a federation called the Dominion of Canada was created and the Canadian parliament was given the power to make laws concerning all "Indians and lands reserved for the Indians." By passing the Indian Act in 1876, the government began an assimilation policy which aimed to integrate First Nations communities into a Europeanized Canadian society and to control many aspects of their lives. Until 1950 the government did not allow First Nations to organize themselves politically or perform cultural activities. Read the texts to find out how the Indian Act affected – and still affects – the First Nations communities.*

Governance

When the Indian Act became law in 1876, the Canadian government replaced the First Nations traditional governance systems with elected or appointed Band Councils, i.e. basic units of government consisting of a 'chief' and councillors that run the communities. Through the Band Councils the government had more control over local First Nations communities.

Reserves and the pass system

Settlers and Roman Catholic missionaries from France had established the first reserves in New France at the beginning of the 17th century in order to convert locals to Catholicism. The British, however, weren't interested in establishing reserves when they first arrived. But the Indian Act paved the way for the creation of reserves and the British crown reserved land only for the use of the First Nations peoples. If a First Nations people didn't sign a treaty, the Canadian government had them moved to a reserve without their consent. The Canadian government established over 80% of the reserves in remote and less fertile areas. This made farming difficult and denied the First Nations access to goods and services.

In 1885 the government introduced the pass system. Originally introduced to stop First Nations resistance to government policies, the pass system later prevented them from leaving their reserves. The system remained in place until 1951 to segregate First Nations peoples in the prairies from settlers and newly-arrived immigrants. The government didn't allow First Nations people to leave their reserves unless they had written permission to do so from an Indian Agent (today also referred to as a Government Agent), a Canadian government representative on the reserve. If a First Nations person was found outside their reserve without a pass or with a pass that had expired, the police could arrest them.

Residential schools

In 1879 residential schools became the official government policy for educating Indigenous children aged 7 to 16.

Until the mid-20th century, the government removed more than 150,000 Indigenous children from their families and communities to attend distant Christian schools. There, they were forced to speak English or French and to adopt European culture and religion. The last residential school didn't close until the mid 1990s. Before that the government removed another 20,000 Indigenous children from their homes and forced them to live with white middle-class families. These forced removals have caused great damage to the individual children as well as to the cultural identities of Indigenous peoples. It is estimated that between 3,200 and 30,000 children died in residential schools, and many were victims of physical and sexual abuse.

The fate of these children still concerns Canada and the Roman Catholic Church today. In 2008 Prime Minister Stephen Harper officially apologized to all the children that were put into residential schools and in 2017 the Canadian government promised to pay compensation to those affected. An apology was also made by Pope Francis on behalf of the Roman Catholic Church in 2022.

Culture and traditions

For the Indigenous peoples of the Pacific Northwest, totem poles have always been a way of telling their stories. However, at the end of the 19th century, Christian missionaries believed totem poles to be a form of 'idol worship'. Hence, they made Indigenous people stop creating them and they destroyed existing ones.

Between 1884 and 1951, the government also banned ceremonies such as the potlatch, ghost dance and sun dance. The police arrested anyone who performed them. Wearing traditional and ceremonial clothing was also illegal.

SPEAKING

b) *Do you know other Indigenous peoples who were oppressed and had their rights taken away in a similar way? Point out similarities.*

6 A diverse country → S29

LISTENING A37

a) *Make a grid like this in your exercise book. Then listen to a podcast with three Canadians who are talking about their towns and take notes on the topics in the grid.*

town	language(s)	population/sq. mi	climate	interesting fact
Iqaluit	*Inuktitut, ...*	...	...	...
Montreal	...	...	...	...
Vancouver	...	...	...	...

SPEAKING

b) *Your turn: Add a line to your grid in a) and fill in the information for your town. Then say in which ways your town is similar or different to the Canadian towns described.*

7 Travelling or moving abroad → S11, S13

VOCABULARY

a) *Your turn: Canada is a popular tourist destination. Collect ideas in a mind map on how you would prepare for a trip there.*

WRITING

b) *Describe and analyse the cartoon.*

SPEAKING

c) *Because of the job opportunities it offers, Canada has always been an attractive country for immigrants to live and work in. What could go wrong or be difficult when moving abroad? Discuss your ideas. Then think of how difficulties can be prevented or avoided.*

to speak the language | to have a job | to find a place to stay | to need savings | to know about the country, its culture and people | to adapt to a country | to fit into a society | ...

MK 8 What not to do in Canada → S35

READING

a) *If you are visiting Canada and don't want to annoy or upset people, you should try to* ***not*** *do the following six things. Can you think why? Use the internet for help.*

1. Don't comment on the relations between the English- and French-speaking communities.
2. Don't compare Québécois French to French from France.
3. Don't say that Canadians are like Americans.
4. Don't comment on the fact that the British monarch is on Canadian money.
5. Don't criticize Tim Hortons, a popular fast-food chain.
6. Don't get onto public transport until everyone has gotten out.

SPEAKING

b) *Present and compare your ideas in class.*

WRITING

c) *For people who want to visit Germany, write a list of six to eight tips similar in style to the ones in a). What should they do or not do to avoid annoying or upsetting people?*

Unit 3
Discover Canada!

Becoming a Canadian citizen

The term 'mosaic' is often used to describe Canada because in some ways it is many nations in one. Descendants of British and French immigrants make up about half the population. They are followed by other European, Asian and Black immigrants. Indigenous peoples make up about 5% of the population. Immigrants who want to become Canadian citizens have to take the 'Oath of Citizenship', according to which they swear to be faithful to the British king or queen, to observe the laws of Canada and its Constitution and to recognize the rights of Indigenous peoples.

The Inuit

The Inuit have lived in the Arctic region of Canada for more than 1,000 years; most of their members live in the Yukon and the Northwest Territories, but others have moved to cities across Canada. They traditionally live on fishing and hunting seals and caribou. The entirety of these animals is used, which includes making the skin into a coat. Animal rights activists criticize this use of animal skin, without considering the Inuits' traditional lifestyle.

1 First impressions → More practice ● 152/1, 2 → S11

SPEAKING

a) *Each partner describes two of the photos A–D to the other partner.*

b) *What impression do the photos give you of Canada? Give reasons for your answer.*

It looks like Canada is … | Canada seems to have … | Looking at photo …, you get the impression that …

Word bank

flag | ceremony room | waterproof / smart clothes | port | to dress smartly | snowmobile | to hunt | industrial park | sparsely / densely populated | suit | Indigenous peoples | Inuit | deposit of oil | citizenship certificate | open space

READING

c) *Read texts A–D. Say which of the details mentioned were new or surprising to you.*

2 Word families → S2

VOCABULARY

WB 47/1

Look at these words from the texts and find more words from the same word family for each one. Then use a dictionary to check your answers. Write down example sentences for the words you found too.

immigrant | officially | to declare | hunting | fishing | settler | explorer

In Unit 3 you learn:
... about Canada and its people.
You learn:
- about its history, landscapes and environmental issues,
- how to use the past perfect progressive,
- how to express probability,
- how to turn written text into an audio adaptation.

C View from Grouse Mountain in Vancouver

Canada's big cities like Montreal, Toronto and Vancouver are near the border with the US, but the rest of the country is quite rural. Its spectacular geography includes high mountain ranges, lots of rivers, about two million lakes and huge forest areas. There are also Arctic landscapes like the tundra which is covered in snow and ice in the winter and where species like the polar bear or the caribou live. The land and its wilderness has always appealed to settlers and explorers. And today it's popular with Canadians and tourists who like the outdoors.

D The oil sands of Alberta

Natural resources like coal, oil, gas, minerals and fish make Canada a rich country. Its oil reserves are the third largest in the world, after Venezuela and Saudi Arabia. Most of Canada's oil comes from the oil sands of Alberta. The huge oil reserves make Canada less dependent on other countries, but the extraction of oil is expensive and causes pollution. Canada also has huge forests, meaning it can export large amounts of paper and wood.

3 Maple syrup shortage → S29, S30

LISTENING A 38 WB 47/2

a) *Read the Across cultures box. Then listen to a podcast by Canadian sister and brother Shannon and Liam and answer the questions.*

1. Which part of Canada produces most of the world's maple syrup?
2. What breakfast foods are mentioned?
3. Why was there a shortage of maple syrup in Canada in 2021?
4. How is maple syrup produced?
5. What is the 'strategic reserve', and what is its purpose?

READING MK

b) *Your turn: Find typical Canadian recipes that use maple syrup. Then present them in a gallery walk. Which one would you like to try?*

Across cultures

Beavers have played an important role in North American history for a long time. Their fur was sold by Indigenous people to the Europeans during the 19th century. Also, the way beavers change their environment by building dams has shaped the Canadian landscape. So the beaver almost made it onto the Canadian flag. But in 1965 the Canadians decided on the **maple leaf** instead. Today Canada is the world's biggest producer of maple syrup. What are Germany's national symbols? What do you know about their history and the reasons they became symbols?

A 39

Adventures in Eastern Canada

Hi, it's Leon again! OK, everyone (classmates, teachers, friends and family 😀) – I've been living with my host family in Toronto for almost eight months (it's been amazing) and last week it was time for me to be the host when my parents came all the way from Dusseldorf for a visit! So, check out our adventures in Eastern Canada. We were really busy!

Days 1–2: Toronto **(✈ Dusseldorf – Toronto: 3824 miles/6154 km)**

My parents and I spent the first day sightseeing in Toronto. First, we visited the CN Tower, which was built in 1975 and is still one of the tallest of its kind at 553 m. The view from the observation deck is great, but going on the Edge Walk was even more exciting! My mom didn't want to come down again.
We'd been walking around Toronto since 10:00 a. m. on the second day when we discovered a police museum. Even though I've seen lots of Toronto already, I'd never heard about it. But I bet we didn't really find it by accident. My mom is a police officer and a good detective, like Sherlock Holmes! Did you know that Toronto was among the first cities to allow Sikh police officers to wear turbans? In the afternoon we boarded the ferry to Toronto Island Park on Lake Ontario to enjoy the view of the skyline and later we did some kayaking.

Day 3: Day trip to Niagara Falls **(🚌 Toronto – Niagara Falls: 80 miles/128 km)**

We'd been hoping to take the train to Niagara Falls, but we found out that it wasn't possible to do the trip in a day. We hadn't been planning on staying overnight so we took the bus instead – it was cheaper and faster, but it still took the bus almost two hours to go 128 km. We'd been talking about booking a package tour but realized it was cheaper to do it on our own. We saw the falls from three different perspectives: walking behind them, sitting in front of them on a boat, and looking down on them from Skylon Tower 233 m in the air! And then it was time to get on the bus again. We didn't have time to see the town (I think it's nothing special). Maybe next time! But we did learn something. The hydropower from the falls provides 25% of the power in Ontario and New York State. Wow!

Days 4–5: Montreal **(🚆 Toronto – Montreal: 335 miles / 540 km)**

Five hours on the train and talk about a culture shock! It's all French now. Merci to Mme. Steiner in Germany for all the valuable French lessons! Montreal has LOADS to offer but our highlights were the views of downtown from Mount Royal and eating poutine, the world-famous dish made with cheese curds, gravy and fries. Dad is totally into ice hockey and for months I'd been saving a big surprise for him – tickets to a Montréal Canadiens game! He loved it! 🙂 We could have spent more time here.

Days 6–7: Ottawa **(🚆 Montreal – Ottawa: 125 miles/200 km)**

The train ride here was only about two hours, so we had more time in Ottawa than in Montreal. Mom had been talking about Ottawa since the day they booked their flights. And Ottawa was even better than she had expected. We took a walking tour the first day and learned neat stuff about Indigenous women in the arts, culture and history of Ottawa. This morning we rented bikes 🚲. First, we cycled across town and stopped at some sights like the National Arts Centre and Bytown Museum. In the afternoon we took the Ottawa River Route. We cycled past the Rideau Canal and crossed the Champlain Bridge into Quebec. April weather is still too cold for the beaches along the river, but maybe I can come back in July!

1 Understanding Leon's blog → S1

READING WB 48/3

a) *Read the blog and name …*

1. the two towers they visited.
2. at least three forms of transport they used.
3. three bodies of water they visited.
4. at least five facts from the blog.

VOCABULARY

b) *Find synonyms in the blog for these travel words. Then use some of the words from the blog and below to write a short blog entry about a (day) trip you went on.*

went to | panorama | got on | excursion | trip | hired | path

SPEAKING

c) *Leon and his family visited four different cities in a week. Discuss whether it's a good idea 'to rush' through a country.*

GRAMMAR

2 < Find the rule: The past perfect progressive > → More help ○ 152/3 → <G13, G14>

a) *Look at these two sentences from the blog. Say how you form the* ***past perfect progressive****.*

1. For months I **had been saving** a big surprise for him.
2. Mom **had been talking** about Ottawa since the day they booked their flights.

b) *Find more examples of the* ***past perfect progressive*** *in Leon's blog.*

c) *Look at the tip box and the sentences from a) and b). Write down the rule of how the* ***past perfect progressive*** *is used. Compare it to the use of the* ***present perfect progressive****.*

Tip

The train arrived. NOW

They had been waiting for 20 minutes.

I arrived here in September. NOW

I have been living here for 8 months.

3 < Mom's birthday present: CN Tower Edge Walk > → <G13, G14>

GRAMMAR WB 48/4

a) *Last month it was Leon's mom's birthday. As a birthday present, Leon and his dad gave her a voucher for the CN Tower Edge Walk. Complete what Leon tells his host family about their experience. Use the* ***simple past*** *or* ***past perfect progressive****.*

"I was so glad we'd reserved our tickets. When we **1** (get) there, some people **2** (stand) in line for two hours. The Edge Walk was amazing! We **3** (look forward to) it for weeks, but it **4** (be) much better than you could ever imagine. You're taken to a glass platform at a height of 365 m and you walk around the edge with nothing to hold onto. But it's completely safe because you're tied to a rail over your head. I've never been so excited in my life! And my mom **5** (look) so happy because the moment she **6** (wait for) had finally arrived."

SPEAKING

b) *Your turn: Would you do an Edge Walk? Explain why or why not.*

GRAMMAR

4 < Working in the forestry industry > → More help ○ 153/4 → <G13, G14, G15>

WB 49/5

Complete what Leon says about his host dad. Use the verbs in the correct tense: ***simple past, present perfect simple, present perfect progressive*** *or* ***past perfect progressive****.*

"Since I **1** (to arrive) here, I **2** (to try) to learn all about unique jobs in Canada so that I can write about them in my blog. My host dad **3** (to work) as a field crew supervisor in the forest industry for more than 20 years. He **4** (to plan) to study Forestry at university but then his father **5** (to lose) his job and they **6** (not to have) enough money. He **7** (not to give up) though and eventually **8** (to find) a job that was suited to his interests. He **9** (to be) in charge of his crew for ten years. He's responsible for forest development and harvesting, wildfire protection and road system layouts. He **10** (also / to work) on developing a new GPS system for a few years now."

MEDIATION

5 A tour of the Bell Centre → S34

A 40
V 9

Leon's host dad has a brother in Montreal, so they decide to visit him for the weekend. This time there's time to do a tour of the ice hockey arena, the Bell Centre. The audio guided tour is in English. While listening, Leon takes notes so he can write an email in German to his grandad, who is a big fan of ice hockey. Listen and take notes on important moments in the Montréal Canadiens' history and a typical game day. Then use your notes to write Leon's email in German.

WRITING

6 Your turn: Applying for a school exchange → S17, S18, S20, S21

WB 49/6

You are at Leon's school in Germany and are following his blog. You have written him a message because you are interested in going on a school exchange. In his answer Leon sends you this advertisement and you decide to apply for the exchange programme. Write your application email and your CV to apply for a place on the programme.

Improve your English and have the experience of a lifetime by spending a year at a high school in Canada!

Exchange students will live with a Canadian host family and attend a public or private school. You can rank your destination preferences by province / territory and we will try to fulfil each wish.

Get ready to experience the diversity of Canada!

For further information, please contact: Ed Forster at e.forster@exchange.com.

SPEAKING

7 Your turn: The interview → More help ○ 153/5 → S33

WB 50/7

a) *After you have sent your application form, you are invited for an interview and want to prepare for it. Look at the topics the interviewer might ask about. Then brainstorm questions for each of them.*

your background | your characteristics | what you know about the programme | resilience and judgment | school life | host country

b) *Think about how you would answer the questions you came up with in a).*

c) *Take turns to role-play the interview.*

Tip

Use icebreakers to start the interview. Also use the correct register, try to have positive body language and be polite and honest.

VOCABULARY MK

8 Canadian English → S35, S37

Leon quickly noticed the similarities in spelling between Canadian, British and American English (p. 259). But he had problems understanding Canadian English words like ***chesterfield, loonie*** *and* ***toonie, parkade, runners, snowbird*** *and* ***washroom****. What German translation, if any, do translation tools provide for the words* ***above****? What other ways are there to get a translation of / an explanation for them?*

A 41–44

Western Canada and its environmental issues

Read these news reports extracts about environmental issues in Western Canada.

Experts say that ski resorts have a negative impact on the environment. Firstly, it's the transportation to the resorts – often by plane, usually by car and seldom by train. Next in line are wildlife disturbances and deforestation. Finally, the use of large amounts of water to make artificial snow and the massive use of fossil fuel energy. The resort town of Whistler is supposed to be environmentally friendly. So why is there no information about how the hotels and ski lift owners actually put this into practice?

A

You'd better hurry if you want to see Athabasca Glacier in Jasper National Park. In just one generation, 20 years from now, it is likely to have disappeared. The glacier has been retreating at an alarming rate for the last 125 years and has shrunk by almost 1.5 km, which means it has lost half its volume. However, because of its accessibility, it is one of the most visited glaciers in the world. Environmentalists hope that visitors learn important lessons about climate change and believe that through the experience people are certain to change their behaviour and lifestyles. But aren't tourists adding to the problem?

B

Stanley Park in Vancouver is said to be all about caring for natural spaces in urban places. Vancouver residents are encouraged to get involved by helping with wildlife surveys (counting birds), dealing with invasive species (digging out Himalayan blackberry plants) and restoring habitats (carrying boulders to streams). But there's much more to be done.

C

"Fracking has allowed us to extract natural gas that we couldn't get to before," explains Clara Hall, an expert on energy technology in Calgary. But not everybody supports fracking. It uses a mixture of chemicals, sand and water which is put into the ground under great pressure in order to break open rocks that hold gas. When the gas rises, it can be collected. The chemicals are said to endanger and pollute rivers. The areas where fracking is done also happen to have a higher risk of earthquakes.

D

1 Understanding the news reports → S1

READING WB 51/8

a) *Based on the news reports extracts on p. 91, make a list of the environmental problems that Canada faces.*

SPEAKING

b) *Your turn: Which of the problems can you also see in Germany and other countries?*

VOCABULARY

2 Working with words → S37

WB 52/9

a) *Make a grid with these words and complete it with synonyms from the news reports extracts on p. 91. Then add their antonyms. Use a dictionary to check your answers.*

rarely | fake | to take out | to move back | scary | to contribute | to look after | to get smaller

word	synonym from the text	antonym
rarely	…	…

b) *Collect environmental words from the news reports extracts on p. 91 in a mind map. Then add more environmental words that you know.*

GRAMMAR

3 < Find the rule: Expressing probability > → More help ○ 154/6 → <G16>

WB 52/10

a) *Look for these words in the news reports extracts on p. 91:* ***likely, supposed, happen, certain, said.*** *Write down the phrases they are used in.*

b) *Identify the parts of speech and verb forms that are used in the phrases.*

c) *All of the phrases express the probability of something happening. Rank the phrases on a scale like the one on the right. Then compare your ideas with those of your partner.*

low **probability** high →

GRAMMAR

4 < It's likely to happen! > → <G16>

WB 53/11

a) *Complete the news report extract with phrases from ex. 3.*

After a company has finished extracting oil or gas from a well, it **1** clean up after itself. However, in the province of Alberta this **2** (not) be the case for more than 73,000 inactive wells. Environmentalists in particular **3** be unhappy with the present clean-up rate of closed wells. New laws which were introduced in 2021 **4** make it clearer who is responsible for the clean-up – the oil and gas companies – but environmentalists think that companies **5** find ways around these laws, just like they did in the past.

b) *Complete the sentences with your predictions about the environment.*

1. Temperatures are likely to …
2. The amount of plastic we use is certain to …
3. Young people are said to …
4. In the future fossil fuels are supposed to …
5. Glaciers don't happen to …

LISTENING MK **5**

Conserving Canada: The Okanagan Desert → S29

A 45 WB 53/12

a) *The Okanagan Desert, which goes from British Columbia to Washington State in the US, contains unique wildlife. Find photos of the desert to get an impression of the landscape. Then use the Word bank to collect problems that can occur in the desert landscape. Also think about how these problems can be prevented or solved.*

Word bank

ecosystem | unique | endangered | vital | habitat | invasive species / plants | water shortage | non-native insects / plants | seed | root | food web | to protect | to conserve | to damage | to breed | to notice changes in the landscape | to destroy | to educate | to care about | to identify

b) *Listen to a podcast which is part of the series* Conserving Canada. *Take notes to answer these questions.*

1. How does a boardwalk through the desert contribute to conservation?
2. How are invasive plant species fought in the desert?
3. What challenges does the western rattlesnake face in the Okanagan Desert?
4. Explain the comparison of land to a mother in your own words.

c) *Is the creation of a national park a solution to the problem? Which arguments are given by the cattle ranchers and the Osoyoos Indian Band? Explain whose side you are on.*

WRITING MK **6**

A cartoon → More help ○ 154/7 → More practice ● 154/8 → S11, S13

WB 54/13

a) *Find out background information on Vancouver to help you to understand the cartoon.*

geographical location | places to see salmon

changes in temperature and precipitation

b) *Describe and analyse the cartoon.*

Backyard salmon farming becomes the newest hobby in Vancouver.

SPEAKING MK **7**

A presentation → S30

WB 54/14

a) *Think about criteria that make a good presentation. Agree on six to eight criteria and write a checklist that you can refer to when you prepare your presentation and that your classmates can use later.*

b) *Choose* **one** *of the problems or places mentioned in the news reports extracts on p. 91 and find out more about it. What caused the problem? How does it affect animals, plants and humans? What solutions have been found? Which groups or people don't see the issue as a problem?*

c) *Decide which materials you need to visualize your findings, e.g. as part of a slide show, multimedia presentation or handout. Find suitable photos, statistics, headings or extracts from news reports, audio and video clips.*

d) *Write prompt cards with your main points and practise giving your group presentation.*

e) *At the beginning of your presentation, present your checklist to your classmates. Ask them to take notes on the criteria you listed so they can give you feedback later. Then give your presentation.*

Ice fishing in the Yukon

SPEAKING MK **1**

Warm-up: The Yukon

Look at a map of Canada and find the Yukon. What do you expect it to be like? Think about the landscape, climate and population density. Share your ideas in class.

2

A documentary → S15

VIEWING V6

a) *Watch the documentary and take notes on these questions:*

1. What do you learn about the lifestyle of the community shown?
2. What do you learn about the landscape and climate conditions the people live in?
3. What skills are the children in the documentary taught?
4. What is the children's attitude towards nature?

SPEAKING

b) *Compare the children's skills with the ones you have learned from your community. Take notes. Then exchange your ideas and discuss which skills everybody should have.*

MEDIATION **3**

A role play → S34

V9

Your younger sister was watching the documentary with you, but she understood very little of it. She asks you: Wer sind die Personen im Film?, Wo in Kanada befinden sie sich?, Worüber unterhalten sie sich? *Use your notes in ex. 2. Partner A and B role-play the conversation in German. Partner C listens and gives feedback: Did the conversation flow properly? Was the information that was given correct?*

MK **4**

How to: Find out about culture portrayed in films → More practice ● 154/9 → S15

WRITING WB 54/15

a) *Read the skills box. Then choose the still below that you think shows the greatest contrast to your own cultural background. Describe the still and explain how it is different to your experience.*

Film skills

When watching a film, pay attention to details that indicate it is about a **culture** different than your own. Think about customs, skills, clothing, buildings, special items, how the landscape is portrayed, any special words they use and (background) music.

A

B

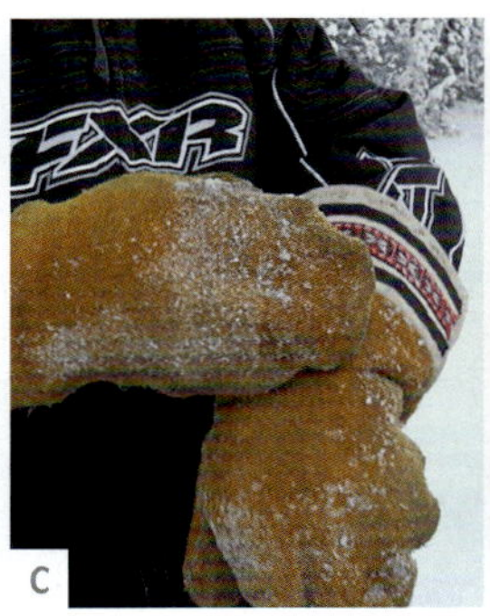
C

D

SPEAKING

b) *Watch the documentary again and choose another situation that is different or similar to your own cultural background. (You can stop the film, note down the time code and/or make a still.) Describe the situation and explain why you chose it.*

Migwite'tmeg: We remember it

MK 1 Before you read: Celebrating the 150th anniversary → S35

READING

a) *In 1867 the Province of Canada, Nova Scotia and New Brunswick united to form the Dominion of Canada. In 2017 the country of Canada celebrated the 150th anniversary of this event. Do some internet research and find out more about the Dominion of Canada and what the British North American Act meant for the people there. Present your findings in class.*

SPEAKING

b) *These 150 years in Canadian history are shown from the perspective of Indigenous peoples in the graphic novel anthology,* 150 years retold. *This anthology includes ten different stories told by Indigenous artists. Why do you think they felt it was necessary to publish their own book about the experiences of Indigenous peoples in Canada?*

2 Signing treaties

WRITING

a) *Write a definition of the word "treaty".*

SPEAKING

b) *Read the Across cultures box. Why did the British sign treaties with Indigenous peoples in Canada? Why did the Indigenous peoples sign them? What other reasons might both sides have had to sign treaties?*

c) *When Christopher Columbus travelled west to find a sea route to India, he ended up in the 'Americas'. It is believed that he named the people he met there 'Indians' because he thought he was in India. The term was also used in treaties because it was then used to refer to Indigenous peoples in North America in general. Discuss why this name has been used for more than 500 years and why it is offensive to Indigenous peoples.*

Across cultures

Especially in the 1700s, the French and the British competed for control of North America and what is now Canada. The third party involved were the Indigenous peoples, who fought battles and wars both on the side of the British and the French. Both sides signed **treaties** with the Indigenous peoples to secure them as allies. One important treaty was the *Peace and Friendship Treaty* (1752) between the British Crown and the leader of the Mi'gmaq (also often spelled Mi'kmaw), Jean Baptiste Cope. The treaty reads: "The said tribe of Indians shall not be hindered from, but have free liberty of hunting & fishing as usual … and shall have free liberty to bring for sale … skills, feathers, fowl, fish or any other thing."

MK 3 A graphic novel

SPEAKING

a) *Have you ever read a graphic novel? Did you enjoy reading it? Explain why or why not.*

WRITING

b) *Find information on the three people who were involved in creating the graphic novel* Migwite'tmeg: We remember it *(2019). Write a short profile of each of them:* ***Brandon Mitchell (author), Tara Audibert (illustrator), Donovan Yaciuk (colourist).***

Migwite'tmeg: We remember it → S2

HEY, EASY THERE, GWIS*. WHAT'S THE PROBLEM?
FROM MI'GMAQ: *SON.
THEY'RE BACK AGAIN?!
LET'S GO TELL YOUR FATHER.

QPP Quebec Provincial Police

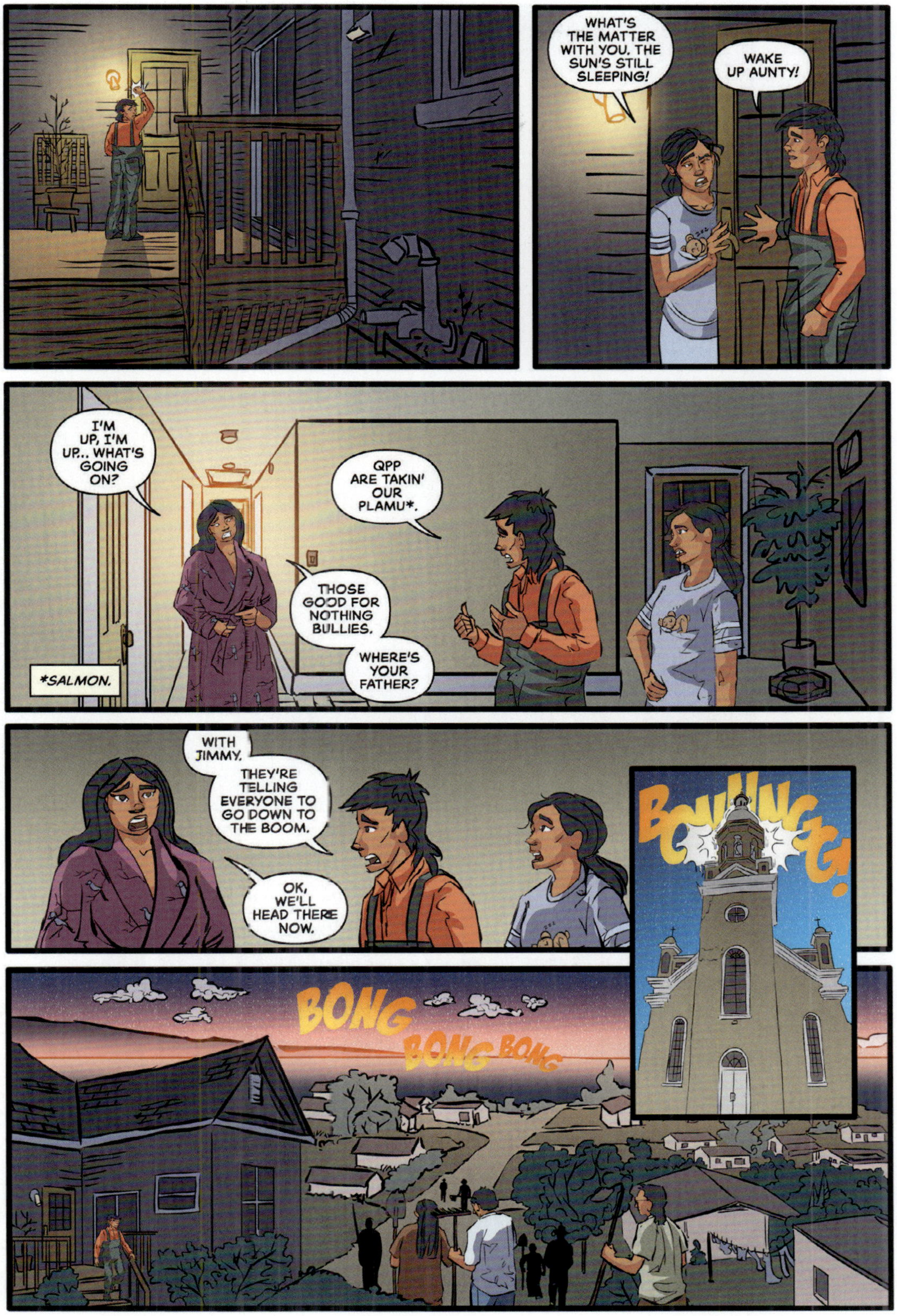

boom [bu:m] structure across a harbour to stop ships going in and out

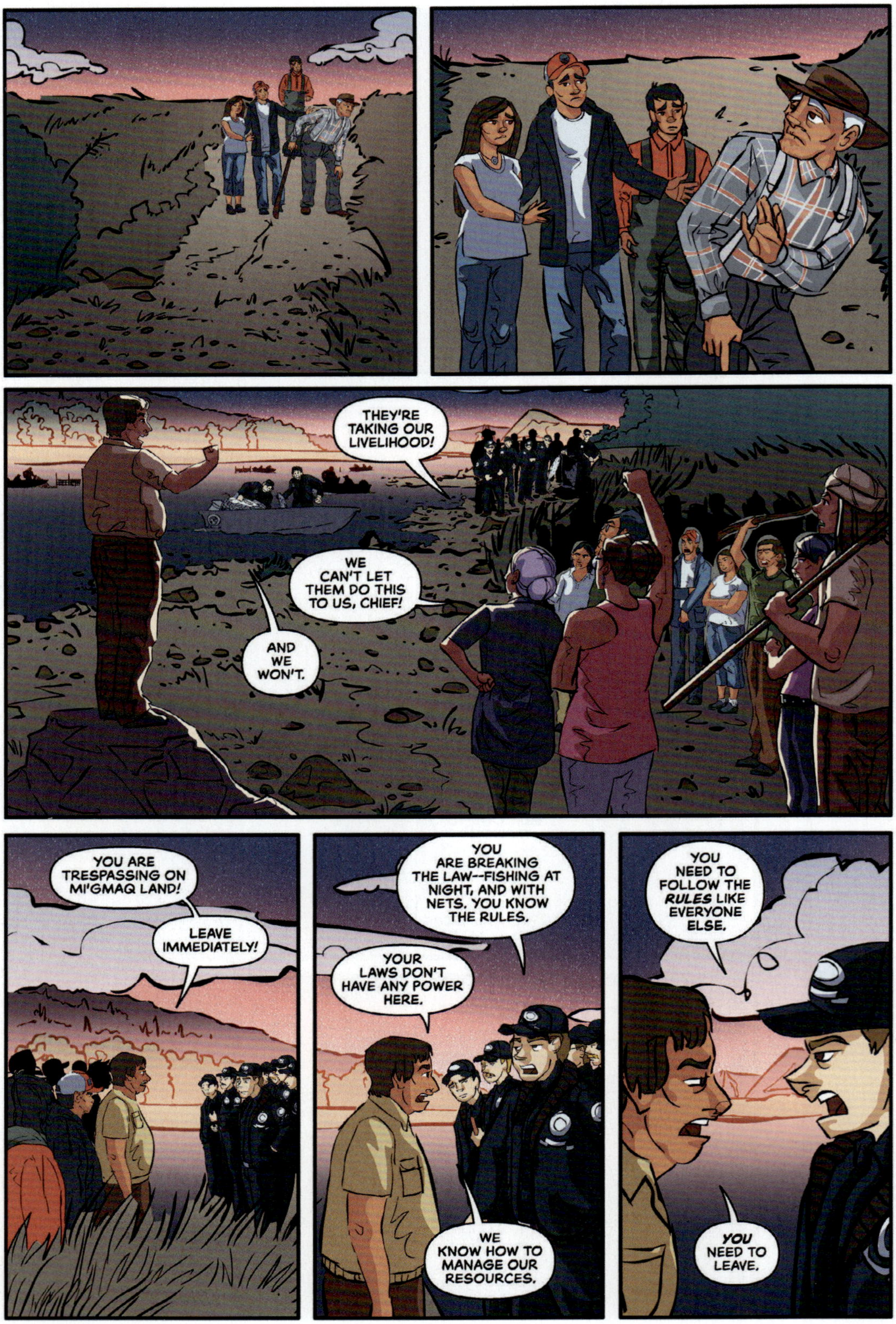
THEY'RE TAKING OUR LIVELIHOOD!
WE CAN'T LET THEM DO THIS TO US, CHIEF!
AND WE WON'T.
YOU ARE TRESPASSING ON MI'GMAQ LAND!
LEAVE IMMEDIATELY!
YOU ARE BREAKING THE LAW--FISHING AT NIGHT, AND WITH NETS. YOU KNOW THE RULES.
YOUR LAWS DON'T HAVE ANY POWER HERE.
WE KNOW HOW TO MANAGE OUR RESOURCES.
YOU NEED TO FOLLOW THE RULES LIKE EVERYONE ELSE.
YOU NEED TO LEAVE.

THIS IS WHERE YOUR LAWS STOP.
You are entering Restigouche MI'GMAQ TERRITORY Please Drive Safely
DON'T THINK THIS IS THE END OF THIS.
IT IS FOR NOW.
ULA ETA NA TMG. APAJA'TIGL...*
*THIS IS ONLY THE BEGINNING. THEY WILL COME BACK...

Minister of Recreation, Fish and Game [ˈmɪnɪstə əv ˌrekriˈeɪʃn, fɪʃ ənd ɡeɪm] government official responsible for the environment in the province of Quebec

(salmon) run [ˈsæmən ˌrʌn] time in a salmon's life when it swims upriver to where it was born

to gut [gʌt] to remove the organs from inside a fish | **sack** [sæk] reproductive organ

DON'T BE OUT TOO LATE, YOU TWO. SUPPER'S AT SIX, OKAY?
WHEN HAVE I EVER MISSED YOUR DELICIOUS FOOD! WE'LL BE BACK BEFORE YOU KNOW IT, BABE.
GISIGU GEWISING? IGENMUETU PLAMU.*
*ELDER, ARE YOU HUNGRY? I HAVE SALMON.
E'E, WELA'LIN.*
*YES, THANK YOU.

You are entering
Restigouche
MI'GMAQ
TERRITORY
Please Drive Safely
HOW MANY WOULD YOU LIKE?
SIX STEAKS SHOULD DO IT.
FIVE

DAD...
...WHY DON'T THEY WANT US TO FISH?
GWIS?
THEY WANT THIS RESOURCE FOR THEMSELVES. THEY'RE BLAMING US FOR THE LOW SALMON RUNS.
BUT WE'RE NOT THE ONES OVERFISHING.
WE'VE ALWAYS CAUGHT WHAT WE NEEDED. SOME YEARS ARE BETTER THAN OTHERS, BUT WE RESPECT THE CYCLE.
WE DID NOT CREATE THIS MESS.
YOU SEE OVER THERE? THEY ARE ALLOWED TO CATCH MORE THAN US BECAUSE THE GOVERNMENT SAID THEY COULD, AND FURTHER OUT, IN THE OCEAN, THEY CAN CATCH EVEN MORE.
WHY?

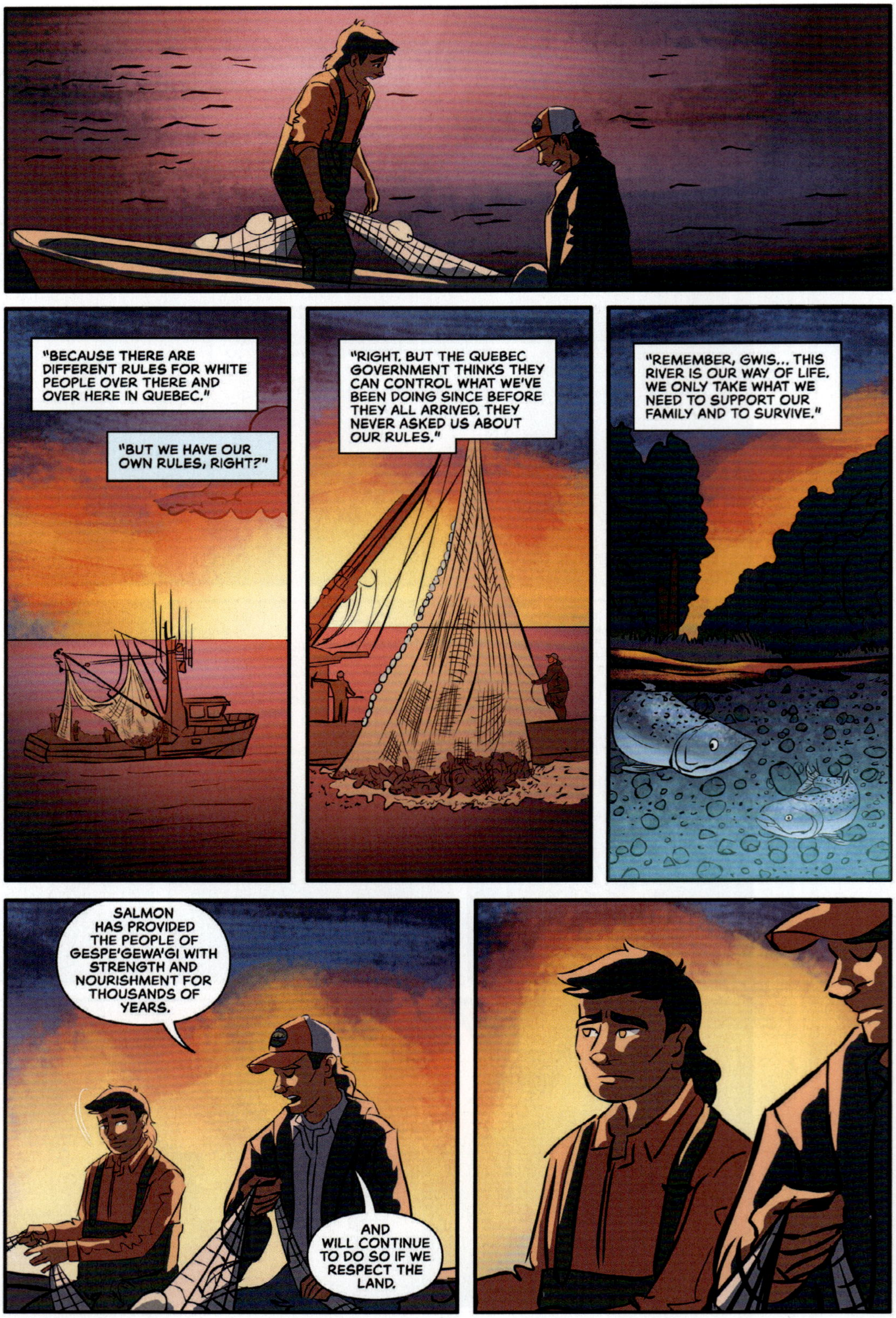

nourishment [ˈnʌrɪʃmənt] food that is needed to stay alive, grow and stay healthy

JUNE 11, 1981.
SCHOOL BUS
BE CAREFULL OUT THERE TODAY.
ALWAYS...I'LL BE BACK BEFORE YOU KNOW IT.
GWIS, AFTER SCHOOL YOU'RE GONNA HELP ME CLEAN THE CATCH AGAIN.

I DON'T THINK YOU SHOULD GO TO SCHOOL TODAY, GWIS.
IS EVERYTHING OK?
I JUST WANT YOU TO STAY HOME TODAY. YOU CAN FINISH YOUR SCHOOL WORK HERE.
WHAT'S THE MATTER, TUS*?
*NIECE/DAUGHTER-- SLANG FOR 'MY GIRL.'
WHAT'S GOING ON? SHOULDN'T DAD BE HOME BY NOW?
THIS IS NOT RIGHT...

a bunch of [əˌˈbʌnʃˌəv] lots of

THOSE ARE NOT OUR BOATS...
I KNOW.
I DON'T SEE DAD. WHERE IS DAD?
DON'T WORRY, GWIS. IT WILL BE OK.
DO YOU HEAR THAT?
YEAH... SOUNDS LIKE...
...BEES?

BZZZZZZZZZZZZZZZZZZZZZZ
TAP! TAP! TAP!

THAT'S DAD'S BOAT!

THEY CANCELLED SCHOOL NOT LONG AFTER WE GOT THERE. BUT THE BRIDGE WAS BLOCKED ON THE CAMPBELLTON SIDE... SO WE SNUCK OVER.
WHAT ARE THEY DOING?
THEY GOT MY DAD.
THEY GOT MINE TOO!

GET YOUR HANDS OFF OUR MEN.
TU N'ES PAS LE CHEF AUJOURD'HUI.*
FROM FRENCH: *YOU ARE NOT THE CHIEF TODAY.
I HAVE TO TELL MY MOM...

POLICE
NIN PESGUNATEG TE'SISGEGIPUNAI.*
TETT E⁻LIWS'TQAMUIAP.**
FROM MI'GMAQ: *I AM 90 YEARS OLD.
**I WAS BORN HERE.
MU EJIGLIWSIW UGJIT WEN PILUEI.*
*I'M NOT GOING TO MOVE FOR ANYBODY.
GI'MA' GISTLIMIWUN TA'N TUUJIW 'NP'T'S.*
*YOU ARE NOT THE PERSON WHO WILL TELL ME WHEN I'M GOING TO DIE.

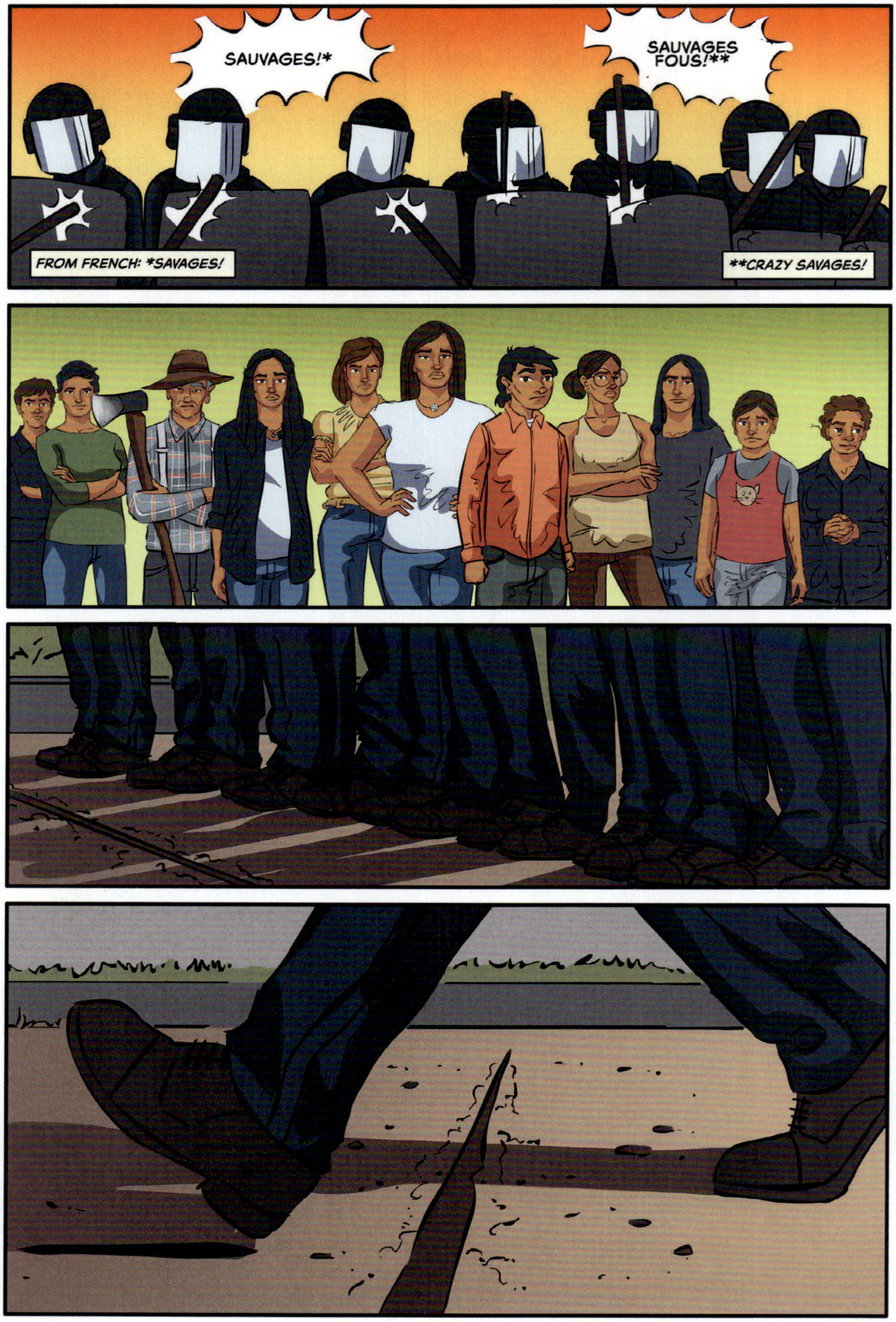
SAUVAGES!*
SAUVAGES FOUS!**
FROM FRENCH: *SAVAGES!
**CRAZY SAVAGES!

4 Your reaction → S3

READING

a) *What's your first reaction to the graphic novel? Write down your first impression.*

SPEAKING

b) *Read the skills box. Then compare the graphic novel to a comic and a 'normal' novel. Where are the similarities and differences? Think about theme, structure and tone.*

Reading skills

Typical elements of **graphic novels** are:
- **panels** = individual pictures
- **speech or thought bubbles** = what the characters are saying or thinking
- **captions** = sentences that explain what is happening
- **shots** = the distance between the reader and the subject; long, medium or close-up
- **sequences** = the order of the panels, e.g. consecutive, overlapping
- **onomatopoeia** = a word that suggests the sound it describes, comic sound effects, e.g. "SNAP!"
- **sound effect bubbles** = bubbles which suggest a sound, e.g. when a baton hits a shield

WRITING

5 Summing up the graphic novel → S23

Sum up the graphic novel. Give the title, year of publication and names of people who were involved in creating it. Then provide information about the setting, characters, theme, plot and conflict.

6 Analysing the graphic novel: Culture and characters → More help ○ 155/10, 11 → S7, S8

READING

a) *Collect details about the Mi'gmaq lifestyle, their culture and the importance of community.*

b) *Which languages are used in the graphic novel? Who uses which language and why? What effect does the author want to create? What do you think: Does it enrich the novel or not?*

WRITING

c) *Write a characterisation of the 90-year-old man. Compare his behaviour up to p. 105 to how he acts after p. 112. Why does he swap the walking stick for an axe? What causes this change?*

SPEAKING

d) *Read the quotation and discuss how the graphic novel contributes to changing the situation described.*

"While much of Canadian history is fascinating, most citizens have heard only a one-sided account. For many Canadians, there was (and sometimes still is) a disconnect between the 'facts' we're taught in school and the stories we're told at home or at gatherings. This is especially true for Indigenous Canadians who for many decades were legally prevented from telling their stories …"

READING

7 Analysing the graphic novel: Atmosphere and emotions → More help ○ 155/12 → S15

a) *Analyse the atmosphere on p. 96. What aspects contribute to creating it?*

b) *Analyse two panels where you think the colourist did an exceptional job of interpreting the scene.*

c) *Find panels that show close-ups of people. Analyse their facial expressions and emotions.*

WRITING

MK 8 What happens next? → S3, S15

What do you think happens after the police officer steps across the line on the ground? Using a storyboard tool or by hand, create the next three to five panels. Include the typical elements of graphic novels. Also think about body language and the use of colour to create an atmosphere.

WB 55–58/16–19

How to turn a literary text into an audio adaptation

In the unit task you're going to create an audio adaptation. On this page you will learn what is important to include in a script so the audio adaptation will be easy to follow.

1 Set the scene → S35

WB 59/20 a) *Read the skills box. Then look at the panels on pp. 96–118 and take notes about Listuguj (the town where the story is set) and its location. Then find the town on a map and look for photos of it online to verify or add to your findings. Using your notes write 2–4 sentences to describe Listuguj.*

Speaking skills

At the beginning of an audio adaptation, the **narrator sets the scene** by giving information on the time, place and some of the characters. This information helps listeners to picture the scene.

b) *Look at pp. 96–97. Then use the words and phrases below and the description of Listuguj you wrote in a) to write the beginning of the story which can be spoken by the narrator.*

summer of 1980 | early morning | light reflects on water | boats slide along the shoreline | silhouettes of people | a fisherman and a teenage boy have come to …

Start: Narrator: It's the summer of 1980 in Listuguj. …

2 Add information

WB 59/21 a) *Sometimes you need to add narration or a dialogue to a story. On pp. 96–97 there are no speech bubbles for the wardens of the Quebec Provincial Police. For wardens it's typical to inform and give instructions. Write a short dialogue.*

Get those nets … | The rest of you … | Put the salmon … | We're confiscating … | These people can't …

b) *When writing the script, you can change the order of events. Would you put the dialogue in a) before or after the information presented by the narrator? Give reasons for your choice.*

3 Include sound effects

To create an atmosphere or to make it clearer what is happening sound engineers add sound effects to a spoken text. Look at pp. 96–97. Collect ideas for sound effects that you would want to include.

4 Define the cast and write the script

WB 59/22 a) *To help the listeners to tell the characters apart, you need to define each character (except for the narrator). Make a grid like this and complete the information on the cast for pp. 96–97.*

character	sex and age of the speaker	language / accent
warden 1	male, about 45	Canadian English

b) *Use your results from this page and write a script with dialogue format. Include instructions for the speakers in italics, e.g. sounding shocked, speaking quietly, and sound effects in double brackets, e.g. ((sound of engine)).*

Create your own audio adaptation

D10 Word bank

Some people prefer listening to an audiobook to reading a book. To meet their preferences, turn the storyboard that you created in ex. 8 on p. 119 into an audio adaptation.

Step 1

Choose the panels. → WB 60/23

Get together in small groups. Compare the sets of panels for the graphic novel that you created in ex. 8 on p. 119. Choose the set you like most. You can also combine different ideas to make a new ending. → S32, S36

Step 2

Write the script.

Turn your ending into a script with a dialogue format. Note down who is speaking which parts. How many speakers do you need for the different characters and the narrator?

Step 3

Think of sound effects. → WB 60/24

Think of sound effects you could use. What sounds will set the scene or create an atmosphere? Which ones will make the action clearer? Mark the spots in your script where the different sounds should be.

Step 4

Find and save the sound effects.

Make and record sound effects yourself and/or find Creative Commons ones on the internet. Save them to your tablet or phone. → S35

Step 5

Practise the speaking parts. → WB 60/25

Assign the speaking parts: Who acts out each character and the narrator? Practise the speaking parts alone first and then in a group. Pay attention to pronunciation, intonation, speed and emphasis. Give constructive criticism that also offers a solution.

Step 6

Find a suitable tool. → WB 60/26

Find a tool to record and edit your story. Practise using the tool so you know how to add sound effects later.

Step 7

Record the story.

Record the story with your cast of speakers in a quiet place. You can record two or three takes to have a choice when editing later.

Step 8

Edit the recording.

Edit the recording and add the sound effects.

Step 9

Give and ask for feedback. → WB 60/27

Each group plays their recording for the class. The others take notes on what they especially liked about the other groups' audio adaptations, what was hard to understand, and what they could have done differently or better. They can also ask the other groups why they decided to do something in a particular way.

A 46–50 ◁))

Oil and Ivory[1]

1 Before you read → S2

SPEAKING

a) *Read the definition of solarpunk in the skills box and look at the title of the story. Then speculate on what the story could be about.*

READING

b) *Before reading the extract of the short story "Oil and Ivory", find out about the author Jennifer Lee Rossman on the internet. Present your findings in class.*

Reading skills

Solarpunk is a genre and art movement that focuses on the ecological and social consequences of technological progress. It expresses new hope for future societies. It's a philosophy and a lifestyle.

It's winter in the Arctic region. The pack ice extends from Greenland right across to Canada. It's the time of the annual narwhal migration. But as an oil spill[2] is threatening to poison[3] the ocean, and consequently the narwhals, this year brings a new challenge to Meri, her wife Qai and Zack, an oil rig[4] worker ...

A I'm just getting on the solar ski to head back when I hear the explosion.

Feel it, really. The sound comes a second later, a horrific blast that shakes the air itself.

Instinctively, I duck and cover my head. When I dare look, the fireball engulfing the oil platform is a stark orange flare amid the deep blue gloom of a winter where the sun never quite rises.

...

Poor fool was only wearing a down jacket. He almost succumbed to hypothermia[5], but my spare biomoss blanket[6] recognized the chill coming off of him and generated extra heat with a chemical reaction.

He wakes up later that evening, and blinks up at the glass panels of our geodesic igloo.

"What happened?" he murmurs, his hands exploring the layers of mossy blankets piled on him.

"What happened," I start, but Qai puts out her hand to stop me before I explode.

"You were in an accident," she says softly. "Part of your rig exploded and you were thrown into the sea. My wife Meri saved you. You're in our infirmary[7]."

Confusion crosses his pale, pointy face, soon replaced by dread. "The oil?"

"Poisoning the wildlife as we speak," I say, managing to keep a modicum of decorum[8] in my voice.

Qai starts to say something, but stops when her father, our head physician, enters the dome. "I'll leave you in the doctor's hands."

...

B "How bad is it?" she asks.

"The oil spill or the ice? Although the answer for both is really bad."

"I recognize the man. Zack something-or-other. He's come here before to trade. It's weird that no one has come to claim him."

"They don't care."

It sounds heartless, but that's what the company is. They just want to sweep the spill under the rug, ignore the whole thing. The press down south won't care about the opinion of a couple hundred Inuits – our protests over the rig have proven that much. We'll have to figure out another way.

...

Qai doesn't come to bed that night, and I know right where to find her.

1 **ivory** ['aɪvri] a hard substance that forms the tusks of elephants etc. | 2 **oil spill** ['ɔɪl spɪl] a large amount of oil in one place caused by an accident | 3 **to poison** ['pɔɪzn] to have a terrible effect on | 4 **rig** [rɪg] a large structure that is used to take oil out from under the sea | 5 **to succumb to hypothermia** [sə'kʌm tə ˌhaɪpə'θɜːmiə] to die from the cold | 6 **biomoss blanket** [ˌbaɪəʊ'mɒs 'blæŋkɪt] a cover to keep warm, made of small plants that grow in wet places | 7 **infirmary** [ɪn'fɜːmri] hospital | 8 **to keep a modicum of decorum** *(fml)* [kiːp ə 'mɒdɪkəm əv dɪ'kɔːrəm] to try to be polite

Every part of our glass igloo-domes are warm, thanks to the greenhouse effect storing what little sunlight we get during the winter, but Qai's lab is strip-down-to-a-tank-top warm, condensation streaking down the window panes.

"You're allowed to sleep," I say, coming up behind her and resting my chin on her headrest.

"Do you sleep when you're planning the narwhals' route?" she counters.

She has a point. With so few holes in the ice in recent years, I've taken it upon myself to map the most efficient path between them all, driving the whales in the right direction with submersible radio transmitters[9] that "hack" their echolocation and guide them.

This year, my sleepless nights are from helplessness rather than hyperfocus, and I envy Qai's ability to do something useful. The details of Qai's work usually go right over my head, but even I understand this project: modify a strain of bacteria at the genetic level, make it crave[10] oil the way I crave cloudberry[11] jam, and let it loose on the spill.

• • •

C I peek down the hall into the medical wing, where our patient has found some of my scarves, has tied them into loops, and is tossing[12] them over a sacred narwhal horn sculpture like it's some sort of game.

"They're talking about a bacterium that will eat the oil?"

I nod. "But even if we can grow enough, every day that we wait, the spill is just growing worse." I sigh and add, "And there's the narwhals to worry about."

"Narwhals." Zack frowns. "They're the ones with the horns, yeah?"

"Tusks, but yes. The ones you've been using for ring toss." On a whim, I say, "You want to see?"

I bring him to the computer where we track the pod. A hundred little dots blink off the coast, representing the transmitters we've attached to some of the whales, but it's only a fraction of their numbers.

"Tens of thousands of animals are coming, and they're not going to be able to break through the ice to breathe. Most of the species' entire population comes through here. We've been part of each other's lives for millennia, and it's going to end here. The day I saved your life, I was going to ask your people for some sort of drilling machine, but they have more important things to deal with now, like poisoning all of the ocean."

Zack is still under the impression that I care about what he's saying. "You guys have been protesting us forever, but you're hypocrites[13]. You don't get to criticize my people – look at how many animals you kill. Even your precious narwhals."

That's it.

I whirl around to face him. "We kill to survive, and we do it with compassion. It is our great shame that our diet is made of souls, so every life we take is honored. We're not like you because we don't pretend to be above the natural world – we're part of it. The Arctic is our home. We have survived here since before your ancestors decided to leave wherever you're from and mess with us. Could we leave? Yes. Will we? Never."

He stares at me, his eyes wide. "I think I'm strong enough to go back to the rig now," he says quietly.

I tell myself that I did the right thing, that he was never going to see things our way anyway, but I don't really believe it. In my heart, I know that I just made things worse, because now he's going to go back with stories about how hypocritical we are, and how vicious we get when we're called on it.

But I stood up for my people, and sometimes that's the only thing you can do.

"I think you're right."

• • •

D Qai's bacteria is ready, and hungry for oil. The next afternoon, the sun just a suggestion of warmth, on the horizon, we start loading up our solar skis for the first trip to the southern coast. Paltry[14] amount, just a few gallon

9 **submersible radio transmitter** [səb'mɜ:səbl 'reɪdiəʊ trænz'mɪtə] a device which produces radio waves for underwater use | 10 **to crave sth** [kreɪv] to have a strong desire for sth | 11 **cloudberry** ['klaʊdberi] a raspberry-like fruit, native to the Arctic and subarctic regions | 12 **to toss** [tɒs] to throw | 13 **hypocrite** ['hɪpəkrɪt] a person whose behaviour doesn't match the opinions that they claim to have | 14 **paltry** ['pɔ:ltri] very small

buckets each, and there'll be plenty more trips to transport all that we'll need.

I can't help but check the map as the whales approach, desperately trying to think of a way to turn them around or to break through the ice. But it's illogical to think that we could possibly cut large enough holes, even if we had the people to spare, and tricking their echolocation can only redirect them, not override their instincts to migrate.

The frigid air is still, filled only with the quiet murmur of voices muffled by the scarves pulled up over their faces. Then a rumbling comes over the ice.

One of the oil rig's machines, I realize, built like our amphibious skis but less elegant and sustainable. It chugs out exhaust as it burns gasoline.

I'm off in an instant, harpoon in hand. We expected them to resist us, but I'm not going down without a fight. Neither are my people; they follow suit[15], forming a line of bodies and spears.

A figure emerges from the top of the tank[16]. Zack. Of course.

"Wait!" He holds his hands up as if in surrender[17]. "Meri, I swear I mean you no harm[18]. When I got back, I told them about the whales ... They don't care."

If the food chain weren't collapsing around us as we speak, it'd almost be cute, how shocked he is about the things we've been saying for generations.

"I want to help you save the narwhals."

"The last thing we need is a white savior[19], swooping in to fix our problems," I inform him. With a reluctant smile, I add, "But I guess I need someone who knows how to drive that hulking machine."

• • •

E The drill cuts through the ice like a sharp knife through blubber[20], sending a thin spray of crystals into the air. In what seems like seconds, we have a perfectly round porthole to the deep blue ocean. But the machine drives so slowly and we have miles of ice to traverse. If we'd started a week ago like I'd wanted to ...

"Meri?" Zack prompts, leaning over from on top of the tank. "You want to direct me to the next spot?"

My phone beeps, signaling that the first narwhals have entered the area around the ice floe[21]. "There's no time." I shake my head slowly and squint up at him, the realization dulling my emotions for the moment and kicking me into survival mode. "Does anyone know you borrowed this machine? Because the last thing we need right now is them seeing us out here and storming the community to get it back –" I swivel to face the offshore rig. It's not far, not at all. A whale could make that distance in a single breath, no problem.

"Meri?" Zack prompts, but I wave my hand to quiet him while I think.

Math spins through my head. The surface area of the bay divided by the average size of a narwhal, multiplied by their population ... They'd fit. They'd fit, and we could use my echolocation hacking to corral[22] them in the bay temporarily while Zack drilled more holes ...

The rumble of approaching solar skis tells me the others are coming with the bacteria. But if the company wasn't already prepared for a fight, they are now that we tricked Zack into stealing a tank, as they'll probably phrase it. We can't just drive up to the spill and expect to pour bacteria in the sea without resistance. They'll call it a chemical attack and use it as an excuse to finally be rid of us.

But no one would suspect the narwhals.

I raise my radio to my mouth as the first whale erupts from the hole in the ice with a spray of water, his horn piercing the sky as he takes a deep breath of air. "Abort mission!" I yell. "Divert to Zack and the tank!"

I take off my biomass scarf, tie its ends together, and toss it up to Zack.

"When they get here, have them all do this with their scarves and dip them in the bacteria!" He looks at me in bewilderment. "And then what?"

15 **to follow suit** ['fɒləʊ su:t] to do the same thing | 16 **tank** [tæŋk] a military vehicle | 17 **to surrender** [sr'endə] to give up fighting | 18 **to mean no harm** [mi:n nəʊ hɑ:m] not to want to hurt sb/sth | 19 **savior** *(AE)* ['seɪvjə] sb who rescues sb/sth from a difficult situation | 20 **blubber** ['blʌbə] fat of whales | 21 **ice floe** [ˌaɪs 'fləʊ] a large area of ice floating in the sea | 22 **to corral** [kə'rɑ:l] to gather a group of animals and keep them in one place

I set my radio to click and chirp the way the whales do. "And then ring toss!" I say with a grin, and take off running. I stop at the edge of the ice, where the sea is sickly black, and pray to my ancestors that I did the right thing.

One by one, the whales streak into the bay, glimmering in the royal blue twilight. A good number of them carry scarves looped around their majestic, spiraling tusks.

Their horns may not be magic, but just like unicorns in the fairy tales, the narwhals purify their water with Qai's bacteria.

From: Jennifer Lee Rossman, *"Oil and Ivory"*, 2020 (abridged)

READING

2 Your reaction

a) *What's your first reaction to the short story extract? Is solarpunk a genre that you can relate to?*

b) *Can you recommend any similar stories, books or films to your classmates? If so, which ones?*

READING

3 Understanding the short story

→ More practice ○ 155/13 → More practice ● 155/14 → S1, S23

a) *Read the short story extract again. When and where is it set? What's its theme? Take notes.*

b) *Make a grid with the names of the main characters and write down what we find out about them.*

c) *Find examples of these types of conflict in the short story extract: human vs human, human vs nature, human vs self, human vs technology, human vs society.*

d) *Use your notes from a)–c) and write a summary of the short story.*

4 Appealing to the five senses

VOCABULARY

a) *To draw their readers into a story, authors try to appeal to the five senses: sight, hearing, touch, smell, taste. Read the short story again and find examples of things you can see, hear and feel.*

WRITING

b) *Add at least three sentences to the short story that appeal to the reader's sense of smell and touch.*

READING

5 Analysis: Narrative perspective, structure and genre

→ S6

a) *Define the narrative perspective in the story.*

b) *Read the skills box. In the story identify in medias res, rising action, climax, falling action and dénouement. Give line numbers.*

c) *What else hints at the fact that "Oil and Ivory" is a short story?*

d) *Find evidence to show that the story belongs to the genre 'solarpunk'.*

Reading skills

Stories, scenes and plays often follow this **structure**:

exposition – rising action – climax – falling action – dénouement

However, short stories start right in the middle of the action ('in medias res') and the elements follow one another quickly.

WRITING

6 Options

*Choose **one** of these options:*

A Write a characterisation of Zack, the oil rig worker, and outline his change of heart.

B Write an email from Zack to his family in which he explains what happened to him.

Can you ...

1. talk about Canada and its people?	The term 'mosaic' is often used to describe Canada because in some ways it is many nations in one.
2. use the past perfect progressive correctly?	Mom had been talking about Ottawa since the day they booked their flights.
3. express probability?	Oil extraction is said to pollute rivers.
4. create an audio adaptation?	To create an audio adaptation, you need a script, a cast of speakers and sound effects, for example.

LISTENING

1 School in Canada

A 51

Leon has done a podcast about schools in Canada for other future exchange students. You will hear the recording twice. Read the task. Then listen and choose the correct answer.

1. Students in Canada ...
   a) don't start school until they are six.
   b) have to pay for school when they are 18.
   c) are between the ages of five and 18.
2. Homeschooling in Canada ...
   a) is not controlled by the government.
   b) is well structured.
   c) has no required tests.
3. Parents who homeschool ...
   a) have a hard time finding materials.
   b) can get help from other parents.
   c) must teach every subject themselves.
4. Residential schools were ...
   a) voluntary.
   b) run by churches.
   c) in First Nations neighbourhoods.
5. The goal of the residential schools was to ...
   a) make Indigenous children forget their cultural heritage.
   b) teach children several languages.
   c) study Indigenous peoples.
6. Former students at residential schools have gotten ...
   a) money from Canada.
   b) new houses.
   c) an apology from the government.

MEDIATION

2 Life on a ranch in Canada

A 52

Ben is your pen pal in Coventry, England. His family is thinking about moving to a remote part of Canada. Ben is worried about what daily life will be like, such as school and free-time activities. Listen to the interview and take notes on these aspects. Then use your notes to write an email in English in which you react to Ben's worries.

SPEAKING

3 Canada, a huge country

About 29 of the 35 million Canadians live in cities near the US border. On average, there are only 3.7 people per sq. km. In contrast, Germany's population density is 229 people per sq. km. Canada is almost 28 times bigger than Germany and it takes five days to travel from east to west by train.

a) *Talk about the challenges and opportunities of living in such a huge country.*

b) *If you applied for a place on a student exchange in Canada, would you choose to stay in an urban or more rural area, in an English- or French-speaking part? Explain your choice.*

→ Solutions p. 282

READING

4 A travel blog from the Rockies

Cindy from London is on holiday with her parents. Read her travel blog.

CINDY FROM LONDON

23rd July / Here we go!

Yippie, we're on a road trip[1]! It's me again, Cindy. I really hope I'll get the chance to go online from time to time so I can keep in touch with you. We started our tour from Vancouver and headed for the Canadian Rocky Mountains. When we first saw them in the distance, the sun was already low so the mountains were a beautiful orange. I took so many pictures! We've spent the last two days driving through the Rockies in our motorhome[2]. Our engine has to work really hard when we go up the mountains. Sometimes we slow down so much that we would be faster walking.

Last night we camped in Banff National Park, and this morning we went to see Lake Louise. It's a very pretty, emerald[3] mountain lake. You wouldn't want to go swimming in it, though. That water is ice cold, let me tell you. But you can hire boats if you want to go on the water. There are also a few little shops there that look nice on the outside, but there's no time for shopping. But hey, who wants to go shopping with the whole family anyway?

28th July / Driving on the moon

We haven't had any internet for the last few days – and I haven't missed it either. But they have Wi-Fi here in our hotel, so it's time to write my blog again. We weren't planning to stay here in Jasper, but there was construction on Icefields Parkway. A person stood on the road holding a sign telling us to slow down. Never seen that before! It took forever, and then it started to rain. My dad was tired and didn't want to drive anymore, so we found this hotel on our way. Oh – this is crazy. On our way to Jasper we passed double-stack[4] container trains. Aren't they afraid they'll fall over?! They don't have those around London, that's for sure. The train was about as fast as we were so no need to race! Anyway, the Parkway is a spectacular road. It goes right through the heart of the Rockies, past mountains, waterfalls, glaciers and lakes. My personal favourite on the way was the Columbia Icefield. We walked to the foot of the glacier, and my brother even tried to walk on the ice. Not a chance, though. It's almost impossible to take a step without falling over. Don't try this at home, kids! 🙂
Instead, we jumped on a tundra buggy[5] – a bus that can drive on glaciers. And it was amazing. That's what driving on the moon must feel like.

30th July / Help! It's a bear!

Mum and I are sitting in a café. I'm still upset after what happened. So glad to be safe. We had stopped for a short break. When I walked towards the trees, I heard some noise. Suddenly a large brown bear was standing not far away from me. My heart almost stopped beating. I look at the bear, the bear looks at me. I look at the bear. Bear looks back at me. And then I remembered the advice: Make yourself B I G. So I did. And it worked! Thank God! The bear turned around and walked away … I was still standing there like that five minutes later when Mum came by to see if anything was wrong.
And that's the story of how I almost became bear dinner. We had even bought bear spray. But that isn't much help when it's still in your motorhome, is it?

1 **road trip** ['rəʊd ˌtrɪp] a long journey by car | 2 **motorhome** ['məʊtəˌhəʊm] a type of van in which sb can travel and sleep | 3 **emerald** ['emrld] deep green | 4 **double-stack** ['dʌblstæk] with two storeys | 5 **tundra buggy** ['tʌndrə ˌbʌgi] a type of bus that can drive on ice

READING

5 Understanding Cindy's blog

a) *Complete the sentences with the information from the blog.*

1. Cindy is on a tour through the Rockies with …
2. You can't go swimming in Lake Louise because …
3. On the Icefields Parkway there was …
4. They booked a hotel room because …
5. They got on a snow coach at Columbia Icefield because …
6. Cindy couldn't use the bear spray because …

b) *Are the following sentences true or false? Give evidence from the text by quoting 1–5 words from the blog.*

1. Cindy liked the colour of the mountains in the evening.
2. The engine of the motorhome wasn't powerful enough to get up mountains easily.
3. In London construction workers hold warning signs.
4. There were delays and bad weather on their way to Jasper.
5. Cindy's dad tried to walk on the ice.
6. A bear came quite close to Cindy.

c) *Look at the blog again and name three …*

1. places in the Rockies.
2. things Cindy liked.
3. kinds of weather Cindy mentions.
4. things they didn't do.

WRITING

6 Your choice

*Choose **one** of the options:*

A Write an essay in which you discuss the pros and cons of homeschooling.

B Add a comment on Cindy's travel blog. Which of the places she mentions would you like to visit? Which of the things would you like more information about? What doesn't interest you?

VOCABULARY

7 A huge country

Read the beginning of a travel guide text. Find suitable forms of the words from the same word family.

1. nature | 2. end | 3. life | 4. traveller | 5. fly | 6. settle | 7. danger | 8. cross

Canada is a land of huge distances and great 1 beauty. You can experience snow and ice in the cold north or see the 2 golden fields in central Canada. People often 3 and work in provinces which are thousands of kilometres away from their families. The best way to 4 is by air. A 5 takes about four hours from the east to the west coast. It was different when the first European 6 came to Canada. They used horses and the journey was long and 7 and took many months. 8 the country is a lot easier now.

→ Solutions p. 282

OCABULARY

8 Churchill – bears and ships

Choose the most suitable words to complete this information about Churchill.

The city of Churchill in Manitoba is located on the western shore of Hudson Bay. It is best known as the [1] (ice / polar / big) bear capital of the world since hundreds of the animals pass through in the fall. They are on their way to Hudson Bay, where they spend the [2] (spring / summer / winter) hunting seals on the ice. This bear [3] (migration / movement / walk) is good for Churchill's tourism [4] (society / aspect / industry). However, Churchill is also known as Canada's only Arctic shipping port. The shipping [5] (schedule / season / time) runs from the middle of July to the beginning of November. At other times of the year, Hudson Bay is frozen and ships can't pass through. Only the use of icebreakers could [6] (spread / extend / increase) the shipping season. Once the ships arrive in Churchill, their [7] (products have / things have / cargo has) to be unloaded onto trains for further [8] (movement / transport / shipping) because there are no roads that lead to Churchill. Using trains is still more [9] (professional / efficient / useful) and cheaper than sending ships through the Great Lakes and the St. Lawrence Seaway.

GRAMMAR

9 < Disaster hits Churchill >

Complete the news report extract. Use the ***simple past, present perfect progressive*** *or* ***past perfect progressive.***

The people of Churchill [1] (already / to worry) about climate change for years when two storms [2] (to hit) and [3] (to flood) the rail tracks in and around Churchill last month. Before disaster [4] (to strike), the inhabitants of the town [5] (to expect) the best tourist season ever. But the flooding [6] (to destroy) the rail track and [7] (to cut off) Churchill and other communities along the line. One man said, "Since the trains [8] (to stop) running, we [9] (to fly) in food by plane." He continued, "We [10] (to pay) more than twice as much for a gallon of milk, seven dollars for a loaf of bread and eight dollars for a head of broccoli since the disruption of the land link." Researchers who [11] (to plan) to finish building a centre to study the effects of oil spills on sea ice were also affected because they [12] (can't) get any new supplies.

GRAMMAR

10 < What will happen to Churchill? >

Rewrite the text. Use these phrases to express probability: ***to happen to, to be said to, to be supposed to, to be likely to*** *and* ***to be certain to****. The words in* ***bold*** *indicate where changes are possible.*

Churchill **coincidentally stands** on a very fragile kind of landscape called permafrost. **Experts say that** the infrastructure there **depends** on the frozen ground to support it. However, Churchill **will probably lose** up to 70% of this permafrost by the year 2100 because of global warming and increased precipitation. The 900 people who live there year round and their income **are definitely going to be affected**. Beluga whale and polar bear tourism make up about 60% of its economy, but forecasts predict that these animals and the tourists **will stay away** if temperatures continue to rise. The tundra buggies that **are meant to transport** tourists across the permafrost ground to see the polar bears may not have any ground to drive on. There may be small lakes instead. But it's not only about tourism. About 51% of the population identifies as Indigenous. According to studies, at least one quarter of these people **hunt** for their meat. But as the ground changes, so too will the wildlife. Some animals that are traditionally hunted **will definitely disappear**.

Check-in

Text and media smart 3

Dealing with plays

On these Text and media smart pages, you are going to learn how to understand and analyse play-scripts. You will also write a scene and perform scenes live on stage or do an online version of them.

SPEAKING

1 Warm-up: Staging a play → More practice ○ 156/1 → More practice ● 156/2

WB 61/1

Have you ever been part of a theatre performance? If you have, talk about the title of the play, who wrote it, the genre and the plot. On what occasion did you stage it? Did you act in it or did you help in some other way? Did you enjoy rehearsing and staging the play?

to write / to edit the playscript | to organise props and costumes | to help with make-up and hair | to help with lighting / sound | to direct the play | to design / print flyers | to paint / build the set | to sell tickets | to organise the seating | to prepare and decorate the room | …

Useful phrases

I played … | I was in charge of … | I was responsible for … | I helped with …

Genres:
drama | comedy | musical | cabaret | radio play | dance | nativity play | pantomime | film / book / stage / audio adaptation

VOCABULARY

2 At the theatre → S11, S37 → <G17>

WB 61/2

a) *Match the words to letters A–G in the photo of a theatre. Then describe the photo.*

auditorium | stage | curtain | seat | dress circle | upper circle | aisle

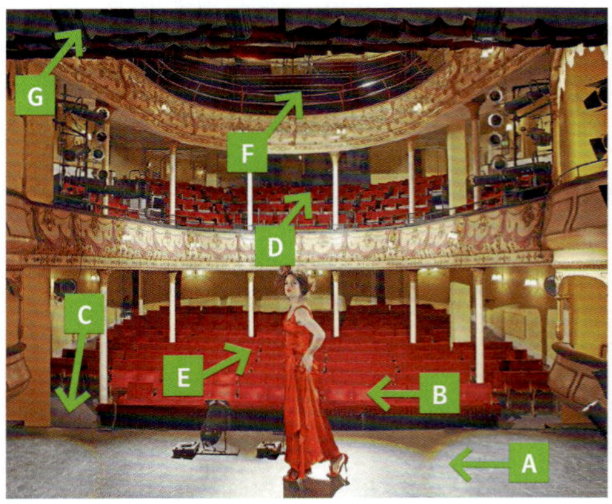

b) *Complete the text below with the correct forms of the verbs. Sometimes you need the passive voice.*

to be based on | to close | to compose | to open | to play | to run | to sell out | to be set in | to star | to write

One of the most successful stage musicals of all time is *Phantom of the Opera*. It **1** in London in 1986 and **2** for more than 13,000 performances. It was extremely popular and many performances **3**. The London show finally **4** in March 2020 due to the COVID-19 pandemic. There have been many other productions of the show around the world, including touring productions. The musical **5** the novel of the same name by Gaston Leroux and it **6** Paris in 1919. The music **7** by Andrew Lloyd Webber and the lyrics **8** by Charles Hart. The original cast production **9** Sarah Brightman, Lloyd Webber's wife at that time. She **10** the central character Christine.

Help desk

1 Calling a help desk → S29

LISTENING A 53

a) *Listen to a customer who is calling the help desk at the local theatre and answer these questions: What problem does the customer have and what does she want the box office assistant to do? Why can't the assistant do this? What does he offer to do instead?*

SPEAKING

b) *Your turn: Have you ever called a help desk? What was the problem? Was the person able to help you? Did you both stay polite? If you haven't, what kind of problem would you call a help desk about? How would you expect the person to react?*

READING

2 Help Desk by Don Zolidis → S2

WB 62/3

Read three scenes from the play Help Desk. *The scenes are based on different situations in which characters call a help desk. What's your first reaction? Do you find them funny?*

cast		
Scene 1	**Scene 2**	**Scene 3**
JERALYN	CHASE	VINNY
ANGEL	YAMIRA	WATKINS

VIP File

Don Zolidis is an American playwright and novelist. He has published more than 125 plays, which have been performed all around the world. His plays are especially popular for school performances. Some of them can be adapted for online performances.

Scene 1

(JERALYN is at the Help Desk, with headphones on. She is scrolling through her phone.)

(Lights up on ANGEL, calling in.)

(JERALYN lets it ring for a moment, calls out.)

JERALYN: Anyone else gonna get that? *(No response from anyone else. The phone keeps ringing.)* Oh okay I guess I got it then. I guess I'll take this one. Whatever. It's cool. *(The phone keeps ringing.)* Y'all disappointing. *(She answers it.)* Help Desk, this is Jeralyn. What seems to be the nature of your problem?

ANGEL: Hey – so I'm trying to log in to the network and I can't seem to make it work.

JERALYN: Oh okay. Boy that's a challenge. Glad I picked up this call.

ANGEL: I'm sorry?

JERALYN: No go ahead. Walk me through how terribly difficult this is.

ANGEL: Um … so – I put in my ID and password –

JERALYN: Uh-huh.

ANGEL: And then it says it can't log me in.

JERALYN: Right. Mystery. What could it possibly be?

ANGEL: Well, this is super weird, 'cause normally I don't have any trouble.

JERALYN: Oh you never have trouble. This is your first time encountering an insurmountable difficulty. So difficult, in fact, that it prompted you to call the Help Desk.

ANGEL: Yeah.

JERALYN: You feel like this problem is so hard that it demands assistance from a paid professional. You can't crack this nugget. Impossible to figure out.

ANGEL: Um … did I catch you on a bad day?

JERALYN: Why would you say that?

ANGEL: It just seems you kinda have an attitude.

JERALYN: WHOA. *I* have an attitude? I'm just sitting here, minding my own business, I'm not the person who can't figure out how to log in to the network. I'm in the network just fine. I got no problems.

ANGEL: Right, but you work at the Help Desk.

JERALYN: Oh, you know ALL ABOUT me, don't you? ALL ABOUT ME.

ANGEL: Can you just help me, please?

JERALYN: Oh now you need help. Just a minute ago you were saying I had an attitude, and now all of a sudden you're desperate for my assistance. I don't know, maybe you think it's cool to insult someone and then demand they help you. That's how it works where you live. You do you, I guess.

ANGEL: So … with my password? Please.

(JERALYN sighs.)

JERALYN: All right – have you tried turning off your computer and turning it back on?

ANGEL: Does that work?

JERALYN: No, I'm just saying stupid stuff to keep you occupied. I'm just making stuff up over here because that's what I like to do with my time. Turn off your computer, then turn it back on again. Do it. DO IT.

ANGEL: Okay, okay! *(ANGEL turns off her computer.)* Um … so now I turn it back on?

JERALYN: No, we just leave it off.

ANGEL: Oh.

JERALYN: *Of course you turn it back on!* What part of "turn your computer off, then turn it back on again" didn't you understand?! Did your brain just cut out after the first part of my instructions?

ANGEL: Sorry I –

JERALYN: How are you gonna log in to a network with a computer turned OFF? How are you gonna do that? Are you magic? Do you have magic? Are you a wizard? Are you gonna get your wizard wand and abracadabra yourself into the network, is that what you're planning on doing?!

ANGEL: No! I don't know! Maybe!

JERALYN: Is your computer back on yet?

ANGEL: It's booting up.

JERALYN: Uh-huh. All right – well I guess we wait for that then.

ANGEL: I'm doing what you asked me to do!

JERALYN: Not fast enough! I got other people to help, all right? I got people who got real problems calling in – and what are they gonna do if the line is busy?

ANGEL: *(Near tears:)* I don't know. I just can't log in to the network.

JERALYN: And it's my problem that you FAILED? Take some responsibility for your actions.

ANGEL: I'm trying to! I'm having a hard day!

JERALYN: I bet you are! It's about to get harder!

ANGEL: No!

JERALYN: Did you remember your password correctly?!

ANGEL: Yes.

JERALYN: Did you?!

ANGEL: Yes!

JERALYN: Stop lying to me! I know you're lying! Did you enter your password correctly?!

ANGEL: I think so!

JERALYN: Before you were sure and now you just think so?! Which is it?

ANGEL: I don't know! I don't even know who I am anymore! I tried to do the captcha thing and it asked if I was a robot and I started thinking about it, and I was like, am I a robot? If I was a robot would I even know? Maybe I'm a robot that's programmed to think it's a human being! And all of a sudden I didn't even know if I deserved to get into the network if I couldn't even prove that I was a human! I mean, maybe I'm just a brain in a vat and this is a computer simulation and – *(Types something into the computer.)* Oh. Hold on. I think I got in. *(She exhales.)* Oh I made it in. Thank you. I think I learned something today.

JERALYN: I think you did, lady. I think you did.

ANGEL: You saved me.

JERALYN: Just doing my job. Next time … you're a human being. Remember that.

ANGEL: Thank you.

JERALYN: 'Cause a robot never woulda made that kind of dumb mistake.

(Lights change.)

Scene 2

(Lights up on CHASE and YAMIRA.)

(YAMIRA is wearing as much of a beekeeper's outfit as she can manage. Heavy gloves, a hood or helmet if possible.)

CHASE: Help Desk, this is –

YAMIRA: Bees! There are bees!
(YAMIRA ducks.)
They're everywhere! They're inside my house! BEES!

CHASE: This is Chase, how can I help you?

YAMIRA: I'm telling you there are bees!

CHASE: Oh so I'm talking to an amateur beekeeper, am I? Fantastic. Do you know the word apiary? I do.

YAMIRA: Help me!

CHASE: Absolutely! The key to beekeeping is to make sure that your queen is happy.

YAMIRA: She's sending her minions after me! They are inside the house! Aaaaah!

CHASE: Right. Don't keep bees inside the house.

YAMIRA: How do I kill them?!

CHASE: Bees are actually endangered.

YAMIRA: I want them MORE endangered!

CHASE: Bees and other pollinators are responsible for quite a lot of our food. Instead of fearing them, we should be thanking them. But don't shake hands with a bee, though.
(YAMIRA gets stung.)

YAMIRA: Ah!

CHASE: I said don't shake hands with them.

YAMIRA: They're shaking hands with me!

CHASE: They must like you.
(He chuckles.)
Just kidding, they see you as a threat that must be eliminated.

YAMIRA: How do I eliminate them?

CHASE: Maybe it would help if I understood how the bees got in your house.

YAMIRA: I wanted honey.

CHASE: Classic mistake.

YAMIRA: And I thought it would be fun to keep bees. Aaaah!
(She dives to avoid one.)
So I got a hive, and I got a queen, and I got a whole bunch of bees. And they were fine for a while – aaaahhh – but I thought it was going to rain, and I was worried about my hive, and they seemed super nice … I brought them into the house.

CHASE: You brought the entire hive into the house?

YAMIRA: I was worried about them!
(She dives again.)
I shouldn't have been, because they're MEAN!
(She gets stung again.)
Ah!

CHASE: Where's the hive now?

YAMIRA: On the kitchen table. But I can't get near it because there are A LOT OF BEES.

CHASE: All right, listen to me, you need to calm down. Bees can smell fear.

YAMIRA: Can they?

CHASE: Yes. They smell it and they love it. So stand up. And don't be frightened!
(YAMIRA stands up.)
(She gets stung. Tries not to react.)

YAMIRA: … Ow.
(She gets stung again. Tries not to react again.)
… Ooooow.
(She lets out a high-pitched whimper as she gets stung again.)

CHASE: You're doing great.

YAMIRA: … They … keep … stinging … me.

CHASE: Oh are these honeybees?

YAMIRA: Yes?

CHASE: Okay, they can't smell fear then. I was wrong. They smell weakness.
YAMIRA: I am very weak.
CHASE: I know. There's only one thing you can do.
YAMIRA: What's that?
CHASE: You must do battle with the queen.
YAMIRA: I have to … do battle with the queen?
CHASE: Absolutely. That's the only way they're going to respect you. You have to assert dominance.
YAMIRA: Are you sure you know a lot about bees?
CHASE: It's pretty clear that I know more about bees than you.
YAMIRA: Good point.
CHASE: You must defeat the queen in one-on-one combat. Then you need to extrude a fragrant odor. Bees actually navigate by smell. Amazing.
YAMIRA: How do I extrude an odor?
CHASE: Believe in yourself. And a high fiber diet. Once you've entranced the bees with your scent, you need to lead them outside, pied-piper style.
YAMIRA: Okay.
CHASE: Good luck. On the count of three – charge …
YAMIRA: I'm scared.
CHASE: You should be. One … Two … Three … CHARGE!
YAMIRA: AAAAAAAAAAAH!
(YAMIRA charges offscreen [or offstage].)
Aaaah! Oh now. Ow! Ow! This was a terrible idea! Ow! Oww! Oh no! Oh! Ouch! Ouch! Oh it hurts so much!
(Chase picks up some reading material.)
Oh no! AAAAAAAH! Aaaaah!
(YAMIRA crawls back onto the screen.)
I've got a new plan: This is the bees' house now. I'm gonna move.
CHASE: Good idea.
(Lights down on them.)

Scene 3

(Lights up on VINNY and WATKINS.)
(VINNY answers the phone.)

VINNY: What?
WATKINS: Is this the Help Desk?
VINNY: Yeah.
WATKINS: I'm calling to complain about a delivery.
VINNY: You're calling to complain about a delivery.
WATKINS: Right.
VINNY: Great. Sure. Go ahead.
WATKINS: So I got a delivery today of a very important package.
VINNY: I'm thrilled for you.
WATKINS: It was a disaster! At first I heard a loud honk, like someone was laying on the horn, and then I saw your delivery vehicle careening down my street – I don't even think it slowed down – but with a screech of tires my package hurled from the open door. The truck didn't even slow down.
VINNY: It's phenomenal what drivers can do these days.
WATKINS: He HURLED it from a moving vehicle.
VINNY: Did you get the package or not? It sounds like you got it in the most awesome way possible.
WATKINS: It struck the hood of my car, ricocheted into the air – then bounced off my garage door, before landing on my front stoop.
VINNY: So you got the package.
WATKINS: At the same time that the driver hurled the package, I heard him yell, "Here's your package loser!" and he laughed maniacally, before gunning the engine and speeding off.
VINNY: Sounds like he was pretty busy. But did you get your package?
WATKINS: I got the package.
(WATKINS sets the most battered box imaginable on the table.)
VINNY: Then there's no problem.
WATKINS: Inside the package was a crystal vase.
VINNY: Okay.

WATKINS: Shards of a crystal vase.

VINNY: Why would you order shards of a crystal vase? That's on you.

WATKINS: It was a WHOLE crystal vase before it was hurled from the truck.

VINNY: I don't see how you can prove that. Were you inside the box? No. So who knows how it got broken.

WATKINS: I know how it got broken!

VINNY: Whoah whoah whoah calm down. You ever tried Gorilla glue? That stuff works great.

WATKINS: My vase is shattered.

VINNY: How about instead of looking at negatives, you look at positives.

WATKINS: What are the positives?

VINNY: You got your package! Maybe you should be thankful for that.

WATKINS: I paid for delivery!

VINNY: You know what? I got a beautiful daughter –

WATKINS: I don't care, I don't care –

VINNY: And I have to spend time away from her in order to deal with you whiners.

WATKINS: Does this look like it was properly delivered?!

VINNY: She looks at me and says, "Daddy, where are you goin'?" and I say, "I'm going to work, Pumpkin, 'cause there's a lot of people out there who don't know nothing."

WATKINS: What don't I know?!

VINNY: How to put your vase back together with Gorilla glue! You think you're the only person who ever broke something?!

WATKINS: I didn't break it!

VINNY: This is the REAL WORLD. Things break!

WATKINS: When they are HURLED from a speeding truck!

VINNY: How was my driver supposed to know that? Huh?

WATKINS: It says FRAGILE on the box! That means FRAGILE!

VINNY: Maybe you should stop being so fragile! All I hear from you – this whole call – "I got problems help me help me help me," do you care about my problems? No?

WATKINS: You're the person who is supposed to help me!

VINNY: I wish I could help you, but I can't. Did you accept the terms and conditions of delivery?

WATKINS: Yes.

VINNY: Did you read them?

WATKINS: Did it say that my package would be launched from a moving vehicle?

VINNY: So you didn't read them?

WATKINS: Did it say that?

VINNY: You would know that if you read it. You checked a box without reading the fine print. This is your fault.

WATKINS: What was in the fine print?

VINNY: It states that you are required to provide a safe landing space for the item.

WATKINS: What?

VINNY: You're supposed to provide a bouncy castle on your front lawn for the driver to hit. He drives by, he fires the object out of a slingshot, and it goes straight into your bouncy castle. You endangered my driver by not providing a bouncy castle. I should be suing you.

WATKINS: I don't own a bouncy castle!

VINNY: Your irresponsibility is not my problem.

WATKINS: How am I supposed to even get a bouncy castle?

VINNY: You're in luck, I sell them. Tell you what: I will let you buy a bouncy castle from me for a ten percent discount.

WATKINS: I could actually use a bouncy castle.

VINNY: Do it. Do it. Buy it now.

WATKINS: Okay.
(He clicks on something on the computer.)

VINNY: Do you accept the terms and conditions?

WATKINS: Sure.

VINNY: Sweet. You better get to your roof.

WATKINS: What's going to happen there?

VINNY: Make sure you take the jello.

(Lights down on them.)

READING

3 Understanding and analysing the scenes → S4, S5, S8

WB 63/4

Get together in six groups, two groups for each scene. Read your scene again and do tasks a) to c). When you have finished, compare your results with the group which chose the same scene. Correct and add to your notes if necessary. Each pair of groups then presents their results to the class.

a) *Take notes to answer these questions. Then use your notes to sum up the scene.*

1. What is the theme of the scene?
2. Where are the different characters?
3. What is the caller's problem?
4. How does the assistant react at first?
5. What instructions does the assistant give to the caller?
6. What mistake did the caller make?
7. What is the result of the conversation?

b) *Analyse the scene.*

1. Explain how the situation is unusual or unexpected.
2. Explain the conflict between the characters.
3. Examine how the relationship between the characters changes during the call.
4. Identify the exposition, rising action, climax, falling action and dénouement. Give line numbers.

c) *Analyse the language.*

1. Identify the register used by each character, e.g. quite formal, neutral, very informal.
2. Identify the tone used by each character, e.g. ironic, sarcastic, emotional, confused.
3. The scene uses phrases that you wouldn't normally expect to hear from a help desk assistant. Point out examples (e.g. unexpected responses, exaggeration) and say what effect they have on the reader.

SPEAKING

4 Role-playing a help desk call

WB 63/5

a) *Choose **one** of the scenes on pp. 131–135. Decide who will play each character. Then read the skills box and think about how to use your voice. Practise your role.*

b) *Practise acting out the help desk call and record yourselves.*

c) *Listen to your recording and assess yourselves. What worked well and what can be improved next time? Then record a final version to play in class.*

Speaking skills

When **stepping into character**, consider the character's personality, the setting and the topic. Try to create humour with the tone and the register you use.
Think about …
- voice level (quiet, normal, loud)
- speed of delivery (fast, moderate, slow)
- use of pauses
- stressing key words and phrases.

READING MK

5 Playscript layouts → More practice ● 156/3

Look at the playscript on pp. 131–135. What layout and format are used for the characters, dialogue, stage directions, sound and lighting effects and directions for costumes and props? Make notes about the layout of each element.

capital letters | italics | quotation marks | colon | brackets | parenthesis | indented | centred | right-aligned | left-aligned

A humorous scene

WRITING

1 Write a scene → More practice ○ 157/4 → More practice ● 157/5 → More help ○ 157/6 → ‹G18› → S5, S8

WB 64/6

You are going to write a short humorous scene that features a help desk call.

Step 1: Brainstorming ideas
Brainstorm ideas for a help desk situation, e.g. in a mind map. You can use the photos below to help you or choose your own idea.

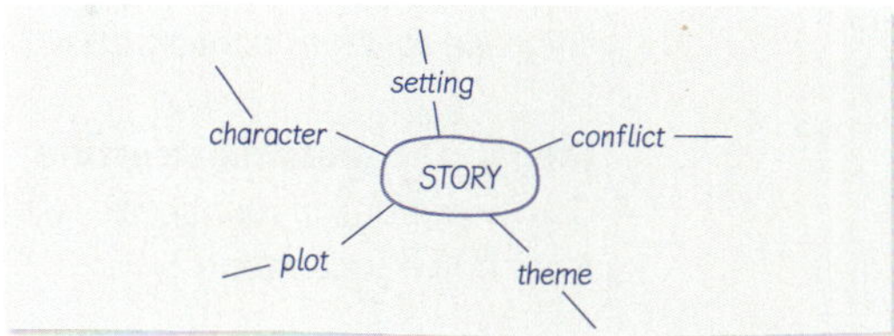

A
Incorrect deliveries

B
Finding out about a product

C
Using filters on social media

D
Dealing with computer problems

E
Encountering problems while booking a ticket

F
A class trip adventure

Step 2: The characters
Decide on details about the characters. Where are the caller and the help desk assistant exactly? How old are they? What are their personalities like? What register and tone will they use for their conversation?

Tip

Remember to make the characters' personalities, behaviour and / or the way they speak humorous in some way.

Step 3: The plot and structure
Create a plot for your scene with an exposition, rising action, climax, falling action and dénouement. Note down your ideas.

- *At what points will key information about the characters and past events be introduced?*
- *How does the relationship between the characters develop?*

Tip

To create suspense, don't introduce too much information all at the same time.

Step 4: A rough draft
Write a rough draft of your playscript. Don't worry about getting everything just right. The important thing is to write down your ideas in dialogue form. You can start using a playscript layout now, or leave it until later.

Useful phrases

Help Desk, this is … | This is …, how can I help you? | What seems to be the problem? | What is the nature of your problem? | I'm calling to complain about … | Can you describe …? | What's wrong with …? | Did you accept …?

Step 5: Improving the scene
Look for ways to improve your scene, e.g.:

- *Does it contain all the information that the audience will need to understand the action?*
- *Is there any unnecessary dialogue that you could cut?*
- *Are the characterisations consistent?*
- *Can you think of ways to add more humour, e.g. unexpected responses, exaggeration?*

Tip

Sometimes it helps to put a text aside and read through it another day. You can also ask another group to read your text and give feedback.

Step 6: Adding information
If you haven't already, add stage directions, information on sound and lighting effects as well as directions for props to your playscript.

Step 7: The final draft
Write your final draft. If you haven't already, use the correct layout features for a playscript.

Step 8: A read-through
Do a read-through of your playscript (acting while reading the script). How well does it work when it is acted out? Do you need to make any further changes to your playscript?

VIEWING MK **1**

Watch a play → S15

Find video versions of Don Zolidis' Help Desk *online. Choose* **one** *version and watch it. Were voice and body language used successfully? Did the scene come across as being humorous? Was there anything that struck you as being particularly creative? Discuss your reaction.*

SPEAKING **2**

Rehearse your scene

a) *In class, decide whether you want to stage the scenes, e.g. in school, or do an online version of them.*

b) *Work in small groups. Choose* **one** *of the scenes in Option A, B, C or D. Decide who is going to play which character or do a job in the production of the scenes. While working on the task, also remember what you liked about the video version you watched in ex. 1.*

Option A
Choose **one** *of the scenes from Station 1. Rehearse your scene. Add stage directions if necessary.*

Option B
Choose **one** *of the scenes from Station 1. Rewrite the scene with a key difference in the characterisations, e.g. Jeralyn is very polite or Yamira is very calm. You might have to change the storyline at times too. Then rehearse your scene.*

Option C
Choose and rehearse **one** *of the scenes you wrote for Station 2.*

Option D
Ask the other groups for their playscripts. Organise everything to stage the play live or to record an online version of it, e.g. make-up, hair, props, costumes, set. Also create tickets and flyers or think of online tools.

Tip

- Think about useful strategies for learning your lines, e.g. strategies you use to learn poems by heart.
- If you feel nervous before going on stage, take some deep breaths or take a short walk through the building.
- Remember to use your voice and body language.
- If you're performing live, choose a point at the back of the room to focus on. The audience will think you're looking at them.
- Become familiar with sound and lighting tools.
- If you're doing an online version, learn how to use conference and editing tools.

SPEAKING **3**

Do a dress rehearsal

a) *As a class, decide on the order you would like to present your scenes in.*

b) *Act out the scenes live or online. After each scene ask your classmates for feedback on your performance.*

Tip

You may need to do several test runs until you feel confident.

SPEAKING MK **4**

Stage or present your play

a) *Depending on your decision in ex. 2a), stage your play or present your video version.*

b) *Your turn: Talk about your experience. What went well or not so well? How did you feel before and while performing it? Did you or your classmates discover any strengths / skills / talents you weren't aware of?*

Key

These symbols and explanations show you how to work with the tasks in the Diff pool. You should do the first exercise in the Diff pool while you are working through the unit. You can check the solutions at the back of your book (pp. 276–285).

More help	○ p. 141/4	You can use this exercise to do the exercise in the unit.
More practice	○ p. 140/2	You can do this exercise if you want to practise the material in the unit again.
More practice	● p. 140/3	You can do this exercise if you would like a challenge.

Unit 1

● 1 Negative aspects and solutions → More practice Check-in, p. 14/1

a) *As you go through the unit, make a list of vocabulary that is useful for talking about the environment and consumerism. Write definitions of the words you find in English.*

b) *Take notes on the negative aspects of consumerism and solutions to avoid them.*

c) *When you have finished the unit, think about ways that you and your class could consume in a more sustainable way. Use your notes in a) and b) to make a (digital) poster for a gallery walk.*

○ 2 Young activists → More practice Check-in, p. 15/3

A2 🔊 *Read the tasks. Then listen to the radio interview and choose the correct answer.*

1. Fridays for Future uses social media …
   a) to create hashtags.
   b) to organise protests.
   c) to reach teachers and politicians.
2. Fridays for Future has shown adults that they are …
   a) able to protest.
   b) responsible for the problems with the climate.
   c) not interested in the climate.
3. K-Pop's strength is that its members have …
   a) good computer and social media skills.
   b) good IT and communication skills.
   c) good writing and social media skills.
4. The Lobby for Animals website includes useful materials such as …
   a) examples of emails.
   b) tutorials about political science.
   c) information about planned laws and lobbying[1].

● 3 Meet some young activists → More practice Check-in, p. 15/3

A2 🔊 *Read the sentences. Then listen to the radio interview and complete the sentences.*

1. Fridays for Future uses social media to …
2. Fridays for Future has shown adults that they are …
3. K-Pop's strength is that its members have …
4. The Lobby for Animals website includes useful materials such as …

1 **lobbying** ['lɒbiɪŋ] ways of persuading politicians to change a law

4 An online survey → More help Station 1, p. 16/1

Use an online survey tool to prepare a survey. You can use these questions:

1. Where do you get your clothes?
   a) in second-hand and vintage shops
   b) mainly from clothing swaps
   c) on the high street
   d) other
2. How do you decide what you need?
   a) When I see something nice, I buy it.
   b) When clothes are torn, I replace them.
   c) When the latest fashions are in the shops, I like to buy something new.
   d) other
3. On average, how long do you keep your clothes?
   a) less than 6 months
   b) less than one year
   c) more than two years
   d) a long time
4. How do you dispose of clothes you don't wear any longer?
   a) I donate them to a charity shop.
   b) I sell them online.
   c) I put them in the bin.
   d) other

5 What we could do better → More help Station 1, p. 18/6

Match the two parts of each sentence to make good advice about reducing our ecological footprint.

1. Wash your clothes less often
2. Take broken things to a repair café
3. Only buy what you actually need
4. Treat even your cheapest clothes
5. Keep using every old item
6. Share tools with your neighbours
7. Try to reduce your ecological footprint

a) as if people from the future were watching you.
b) as local communities did in the past.
c) as though they were expensive.
d) in case it's possible to fix them.
e) in order to save electricity.
f) like you would if you couldn't buy a new one.
g) so that you don't waste resources.

6 How to: Understand a formal letter → More help Station 1, p. 19/9a)

You are doing work experience with a company in your town that imports clothes from Ireland. Match the abbreviations in a formal letter with their meanings 1–6.

Re | Attn | pp. | Ref. | Enc. / Encl. | c/o

1. used when signing a letter for somebody else
2. a person who will pass the letter to its recipient
3. the topic of the letter
4. for the attention of
5. a document which the recipient will find in the envelope
6. a number which refers to a specific order

7 Talking about figures → More help Station 2, p. 21/1b)

Explain what the figures in the text on p. 20 refer to. You can use the phrases on the right for help.

29 | 40 | 50 | 17

1,300,000,000 | $^1/_3$

Word bank

the percentage by which we need to … | the number of days by which … | the date in … on which … | the amount of the total production of food that … | the amount of food in tonnes that … | the number of kilos of carbon dioxide that …

○ 8 Words to talk about environmental issues → More help Station 2, p. 21/2

Match the words from the text on p. 20 with the definitions.

1. consumption (l. 2)
2. regenerate (l. 12)
3. calculating (l. 24)
4. generates (l. 26)
5. reducing (l. 30)
6. diet (l. 34)
7. greenhouses (l. 60)
8. fertilisers (l. 61)

a) making something less
b) substances that help plants to grow
c) the act of using sth
d) finding out a figure
e) make something grow again
f) buildings for growing plants
g) what is regularly eaten
h) produces or causes production of

○ 9 Talking about the environment → More practice Station 2, p. 21/4

Complete the sentences about the environment. You can use ideas in the Word bank or your own ideas.

1. In order to waste less food, we ought to …
2. … would reduce my ecological footprint.
3. If we don't stop wasting resources, we might …
4. As a species we must ask ourselves, "Shall we … or shall we …?"
5. Governments and big companies ought to …
6. … would be better than …

Word bank

to cycle or walk | to destroy our planet | to take care of sth | to plan meals | to repair things | to protect the environment | to have serious shortages of … | to throw things away

● 10 What shall we do? → More practice Station 2, p. 21/4

Complete the sentences with your ideas. Use the modals ***shall, might, ought to*** *and* ***would*** *at least once.*

1. In order to waste less food, …
2. … reduce my ecological footprint.
3. If we don't stop wasting resources, …
4. As a species we must ask ourselves, "…?"
5. Governments and big companies …
6. … be better than …

○ 11 Why greenwashing matters → More practice Action!, p. 23/3

Match the products with the claims and the reasons why the claims may be examples of greenwashing.

product	claim	reason
can of lemonade	Energy-saving LED	The other 80% is probably new plastic.
children's toy	All the products in our fridges come in eco-friendly packaging	It doesn't say what the standards are, or if they are checked by another organisation.
supermarket dessert	Meets our Green Label farm quality standards[1]	Some LED light bulbs are more energy-saving than others.
packet of sausages	100% recyclable aluminium container	It doesn't say why it is 'eco-friendly'.
light bulb	Made with 20% recycled plastic	It takes a lot of energy to recycle metal.

1 **to meet a standard** [ˌmiːt ə ˈstændəd] einem Standard entsprechen

12 The problem with greenwashing → More practice Action!, p. 23/3

Match the products with these claims. Then explain how they may be examples of greenwashing. Think about raw materials, transport, recycling and evidence given to support the claims.

light bulb | supermarket dessert | can of lemonade | packet of sausages | children's toy

1. 100% recyclable aluminium container
2. Made with 20% recycled plastic
3. All the products in our fridges come in eco-friendly packaging
4. Energy-saving LED
5. Meets our Green Label farm quality standards

13 What is the story about? → More practice Story 1, p. 26/2

Look at the headings and match them to parts A–E of the novel extract on pp. 24–26.

1. James fails to make an impression on the new guy
2. The new guy makes an impression on Sadie
3. The new guy makes an impression on the school
4. All eyes on the new guy in action
5. James is jealous of the new guy

14 Create headings → More practice Story 1, p. 26/2

Read the novel extract on pp. 24–26 again and think of headings for each part of the extract A–E.

15 Yearbook article about the new guy → More help Story 1, p. 26/5

Choose the facts / events you think should go into the yearbook article about Jedediah Strock and put them in a good order. The article should be short and humorous.

- how he takes food that people are going to throw away in the cafeteria
- his physical appearance
- the impression he makes on students
- his singing and guitar playing
- James' opinion of him
- his life with his parents in India
- how everyone claps when Mr. Greco takes him to the principal's office
- Sadie's opinion of him
- his interview with the school paper
- his parents' visit to the school

16 Formal and informal letters → More help Skills, p. 27/1b)

Read the phrases from letters A and B on p. 27. Match each formal phrase with an informal one.

In fact, | Did you know that …? | The actions he took … were completely harmless. | We think the teachers ought to show … | The reason given for expelling Mr. Strock was … | They would like to point out … | Jedediah was expelled because … | Furthermore, | We've checked all the school rules | Thank you in advance | Having examined the school rules, … | They respectfully ask the school authorities to produce … | Moreover, | On top of that, | What he did in the cafeteria did no harm … | Thanks,

Text and media smart 1

○ 1 The vocabulary of advertising → More practice Check-in, p. 38/1a)

Read the definitions 1–8 and match them with the advertising words.

advertisement | bargain | to catch sb's attention | celebrity | claim | customer | to exaggerate | to persuade sb

1. text or picture that tells people about a product
2. someone who is famous
3. something that is cheaper than normal
4. person who buys something
5. to get someone to notice something
6. to try to make someone do something
7. to make something seem bigger, better etc. than it really is
8. a short statement about the advantages of a product

● 2 Talking about advertising → More practice Check-in, p. 38/1a)

These words and phrases all have something to do with ads. Write definitions to explain them.

advertisement | bargain | to catch sb's attention | celebrity | claim | customer | to exaggerate | to persuade sb

○ 3 Buy it now! → More help Station 1, p. 40/2c)

Complete the ad copies for the products on p. 40 with these words:

electric toothbrush | ingredients | mouth | muesli bar | phone battery | power | sugar | toothbrushes | video

● 4 Understand and analyse a commercial → More practice Station 1, 41/4

*Find an English language commercial on the internet, e.g. on a company website, social network, video platform. Choose **one** commercial that you like or that you find bad or provocative. Write a description and analysis of the commercial. What is it selling? Who is it aimed at? What techniques does it use? What does it try to get people to do? How effective is it? Does it follow the AIDA formula on p. 39? You can use these ideas to help you:*

name and type of product | slogan | language, e.g. personal, factual, informal | tone, e.g. serious, humorous, ironic | target group | setting and characters | plot or storyline | dialogue | voiceover | camera work | atmosphere | use of music | effect on the viewer

○ 5 What does it really mean? → More help Station 2, p. 42/1b)

Look at your answers to ex. 1a) on p. 42 and explain why the claims on p. 42 could be misleading. You can use these phrases:

Useful phrases

it may not be good for you | large amounts of … are unhealthy | the product may / could still contain … | some unhealthy products can contain … | … but they still aren't good for you | the product could (still) have a lot of / too much sugar / fat | the claim doesn't mean anything | … doesn't have to be good for you

○ 6 Food advertising → More practice Station 2, p. 42/2

V4 ▷ *Read the questions. Then watch the film on food advertising and answer the questions:*

1. The number of ads children and teens see each day is between …
   a) 2 and 12.
   b) 12 and 21.
   c) 21 and 35.
2. The types of food that are advertised the most to children and teens are …
   a) healthy snack foods.
   b) bread and cake.
   c) fast food and drinks with sugar.
3. Food advertisers make their products look attractive …
   a) by using tricks and food stylists.
   b) by using special cameras.
   c) by using photo-editing techniques.
4. Advertisers also use older children …
   a) to explain how products work.
   b) to make products seem cool to younger viewers.
   c) to give a serious impression.
5. Food advertisers use misleading phrases in order to …
   a) list the exact ingredients.
   b) suggest the product is healthy.
   c) describe how the product tastes.
6. You can avoid advertisers' tricks …
   a) by only buying vegetables.
   b) by checking the company's website.
   c) by checking the labels on food products.

● 7 The problem with food advertising → More practice Station 2, p. 42/2

V4 ▷ *Read the questions. Then watch the film on food advertising and answer the questions:*

1. What statistic is given about the amount of food advertising children and teens see?
2. What types of food are advertised the most to children and teens?
3. How do food advertisers make their products look attractive?
4. What strategy do advertisers use to make products seem cool to younger viewers?
5. Why do food advertisers use misleading phrases?
6. How can you avoid advertisers' tricks?

○ 8 Sum up the problems → More help Station 2, p. 44/5c)

Complete these sentences to sum up the three problems that the article on p. 43 identifies.

1. Some influencers do not acknowledge that they are paid …
2. Children who become kidfluencers are used by adults to …
3. Some influencers accept money to promote a product or company which …

Unit 2

1 What I want you to know → More practice Check-in, p. 50/1

As you are going through the unit, think about the following questions:

- *What things don't adults understand about teenagers' interest in technology and social media?*
- *What do you want them to know about the digital lives of teenagers? Why?*
- *What would be different if adults understood this aspect of teenagers' lives better?*

Collect your ideas, ideally in a digital document that you can easily edit. Think about different aspects of digital life and technology, e.g. social media, gaming and cyberbullying. How do your parents, teachers and other adults handle these topics? How does this affect you?

After you have completed the unit, present your results in ***one*** *of these formats: a poem for a poetry slam, blog entry, comment, video or a comic strip.*

2 Describing music → More help Check-in, p. 51/2b)

A 20

Use some of the words and phrases below to describe the music of "Look on up" by Relient K.

Word bank

genres:	pop | hip-hop | dance/electronica | folk | electro pop | indie | jazz | rock | soul | metal | classical music | reggae | country
instruments:	(electric) guitar | drums | piano | keyboard | bass | saxophone | violin | vocals
rhythms:	slow / fast | catchy | calm | exciting | regular / irregular beat
effects on the listener:	relaxing | moody | sad | depressing | hopeful | exciting | happy | emotional | optimistic

3 Future forms → More help Station 1, p. 53/3a)

Use the visuals to help you to match the uses of the ***will-future progressive*** *and the* ***will-future perfect*** *A–D in ex. 3 on p. 53 to the sentences 1–4 from the text. Which uses belong to which tense?*

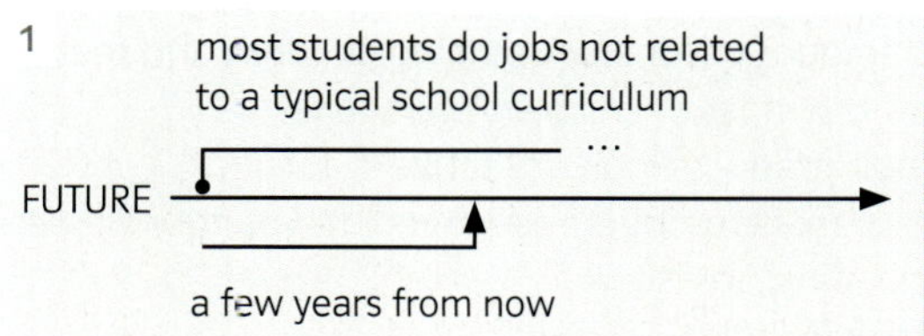

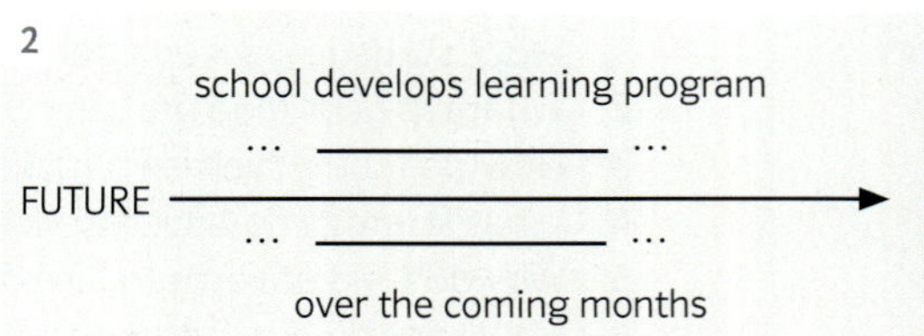

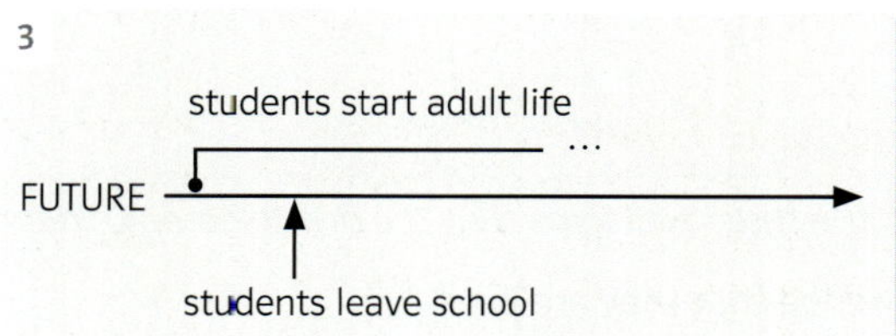

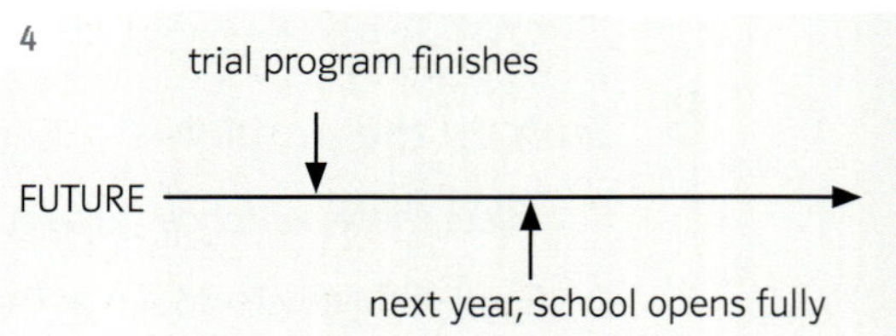

4 Alexis' day at NewSchoolUS → More practice Station 1, p. 53/5

Alexis goes to NewSchoolUS. Look at her planner. Complete what she says about her day. Use the verbs in the correct tense.

"From 8-8:20 I **1** (ride, future progressive) the bus. By 8:50 I **2** (plan, future perfect) the day together with my class teacher. At 8:50 I **3** (walk, future progressive) to the gym for physical education. From 10:30-12 I **4** (finish, future progressive) my biology group project. By 12:45 I **5** (not prepare, future perfect) for my online maths exam yet. But I **6** (have, future perfect) lunch. At 4:30 I **7** (catch, future progressive) the bus home. I **8** (talk, future perfect) to my class teacher about my day by then."

8:00–8:20	ride bus to school
8:30	plan day together with class teacher
8:50	walk to gym for physical education
10:30–12:00	finish biology group project
12:15–12:45	have lunch
1:00–2:45	prepare for online maths exam
3:00	take exam
4:00–4:15	talk to class teacher about the day
4:30	catch bus home

5 Alexis' plans for tomorrow → More practice Station 1, p. 53/5

Alexis goes to NewSchoolUS. Look at her planner in ex. 4. Complete what she says about her day. Use the ***will-future progressive*** *and the* ***will-future perfect****.*

1. From 8-8:20 I …
2. By 8:50 I …
3. At 8:50 I …
4. From 10:30-12 I …
5. By 12:45 I won't … yet.
6. But I will …
7. At 4:30 I …
8. I … to my class teacher about my day by then.

6 Selfie Harm → More practice Station 2, p. 56/2

Go online to find more photos from the series 'Selfie Harm' by British photographer Rankin. Describe the photos and discuss the meaning of the name of the series.

7 Holiday posts → More help Station 2, p. 57/7

Ryan and Ellie are talking about their last holiday. Choose the correct relative adverb ***where*** *or* ***when****. Then decide whether the relative clause is defining (= necessary information) or non-defining (= unnecessary information) and add a comma where needed.*

Ryan: That was the beach next to our hotel **1** (when / where) you took a really nice photo of me.
Ellie: Oh, I remember. The day **2** (when / where) I took this photo was very cloudy.
Ryan: Do you think I should post it? I don't usually put photos of myself on social media **3** (when / where) there's always a risk of getting negative comments.
Ellie: That's true. I'd really like to live in a perfect world **4** (when / where) everybody is polite on social media.
Ryan: Do you remember this time last year **5** (when / where) you first started posting content?
Ellie: I do. Fortunately, I haven't had any negative experiences so far. But at my school **6** (when / where) cyberbullying has become very common they've decided to ban mobile phones.
Ryan: That's so sad. I don't know. Maybe I shouldn't post it.
Ellie: It's your choice. Sometimes I wish I hadn't started using social media last year **7** (when / where) I didn't care that much about my online image.

8 Video games → More help Station 2, p. 58/9

Complete the description of the cartoons with the words and phrases below.

boring | video game | female | hanging | horns | informs | inventive | irony | looking | making fun of | reflects | terrified | typing | uninteresting | violent | wide open | wings | avatar | criticises | skulls

The cartoon on the left deals with creating an **1**. It shows two fantasy creatures in a stone castle. One is a creature with sharp teeth, a pig-like face and **2** on his head. He is sitting on a chair with **3** and with animal feet. He is **4** on a keyboard and **5** at a computer screen. A green **6** figure with long blond hair is standing behind him. She has two very large white **7**. The creature with horns is creating an avatar which is not very **8**. He chooses what we would call a very normal person, in an **9** job in an unspectacular city in the UK. The cartoon is **10** the idea that people create fantasy avatars in fantasy worlds to escape from their own lives, which they might find **11**. The **12** for us is that the roles are turned around.

The cartoon on the right deals with **13** video games. A small child is sitting on a large sofa watching a screen which is **14** from the ceiling. The child looks **15**: His eyes are **16**. His parents are standing behind the sofa, watching the screen too. The father is holding a cup. He thinks his son is playing a **17** and he is saying that they are too violent. The mother **18** him that it is the evening news. The cartoon reminds us that we live in a violent world and that violence in video games **19** this. It also **20** the typical argument that video games are too violent and that's why they shouldn't be played by children by highlighting that there is no such criticism of the news, which is also violent.

9 Help with cyberbullies → More help Action!, p. 59/4a)

Match the words and phrases to find ideas about ways of dealing with cyberbullying.

how to protect yourself	
1. tell the bully	a) offline for a while
2. block and report	b) nasty posts / embarrassing images
3. keep	c) evidence so that you can show it to parents / teachers / the police
4. go	d) it's not OK
how to help victims	
5. ask the cyberbully	e) to the victim of cyberbullying
6. ask the victim of cyberbullying	f) the group / conversation
7. don't forward/share	g) the cyberbully's messages
8. don't take part	h) in the cyberbullying
9. leave	i) to stop
10. say sth nice	j) if they need help
where to get help, who to talk to	
11. call	k) a counselling[1] centre for cyberbullying
12. go to	l) online counselling for teens
13. talk to someone you trust, e.g.	m) a helpline
14. use	n) parents, teachers and friends

1 **counselling** [ˈkaʊnsəlɪŋ] when a professional listens to sb who has a problem and gives advice

○ 10 SLAY → More help Story 1, p. 62/3c)

Read information from the extract about the effect of video games on developers and on users. Then copy the notes in a grid like the one in ex. 3c) on p. 62.

- video games can be a form of art / creative expression (ll. 5–6)
- they are responsible for the negative effects of games on users (ll. 6–8)
- video game characters can be seen and used as an extension of one's own personality (ll. 8–9)
- playing a video game for too long can have negative effects on one's health (ll. 15–18)
- video games can be taken too seriously (ll. 18–21)
- people can make money by doing something they love: playing video games (l. 36)
- they might meet dangerous people online (ll. 40–43)
- people can be whoever they want to be (ll. 62–64, ll. 85–87)
- people don't always respect the rules of a game (ll. 67–70)
- games are not always designed to be inclusive and can therefore be discriminating towards minorities (ll. 74–81)
- people are free to do whatever they want within the limits of the games without risking anything (ll. 85–89)
- harmful actions don't have any consequences in real life; anonymity of games can be abused (ll. 90–94)
- they can create a new world for people who need one (ll. 100–102)

○ 11 <The narrator's language> → More help <Story 2> p. 67/4b)

Complete this analysis of the narrator's language by choosing the correct words.

The narrator's language is rather **1** (formal / informal). She creates a **2** (serious / relaxed) atmosphere by using informal words and expressions like "sneak a look" (l. 3), "ugh" (l. 5), "rubbish" (l. 5), "sort of" (l. 7), and "going on at me" (l. 73). She also uses **3** (long / short) forms, **4** (complex / simple) sentences (e.g. ll. 12–14, l. 27), and even sentences with just one or two words (ll. 43–45). This creates the impression that the narrator is talking to us as if we **5** (knew / didn't know) her, which makes it **6** (easier / harder) for the reader to identify with her and her experience.

The narrator gives the story a **7** (serious / humorous) tone, for example when she makes fun of her head teacher's argument that taking part in the challenge might make them happier. The narrator reacts by saying that she doesn't know what he is talking about since everyone knows that "schools only care about exam results" (ll. 54–56). In a similar way, she uses **8** (criticism / humour) when she compares Dame Irene's time at school to a history lesson (ll. 67–70). The narrator's **9** (neutral / exaggerated) language adds to that **10** (tone / register), e.g. when she says that knowing someone who grew up without a phone is "like knowing someone who remembers Henry VIII beheading his second wife" (ll. 84–85), or that her "head splits into two, like it's a watermelon" (ll. 148–149) when she hears about the prize money.

Text and media smart 2

1 Analysing a text → More practice Check-in, p. 72/2

Look through newspapers and magazines or go online to find a text, e.g. a news report, an article, an interview, a film or book review, and answer these questions: What's the author's intention? Does the author give their personal opinion? What kind of tone and register does the author use?

Word bank

author's intention: to persuade | to inform | to entertain | to explain | to describe
personal opinion: to be subjective | to be objective | to comment on | to give one's point of view
tone and register: serious | ironic | humorous | entertaining | respectful | formal | informal

2 Your checklist for summary writing → More help Station 1, p. 74/3a)

D5 Checklist

Compare this checklist for summary writing with the model summary in ex. 2 on p. 74. Correct the mistakes which have been highlighted and write the correct checklist in your exercise book.

- *reduce the text to 30–40% of the original / one to three pages for longer texts*
- *introduction: state **title and main point** (plus source and publication date if it's an article)*
- *main part: structured in paragraphs; **not every** new point needs a new paragraph*
- *conclusion: not needed*
- *order of points: either **chronologically** (combined in a new, logical way) or **thematically** (as in the original)*
- ***include** details, examples, quotations and your own opinion*
- ***copy** original lines word for word*
- *use an **informal** register*
- *use the **past tense** if you describe the actions of the author, e.g. "The author concludes …"*

3 Judging an analysis → More help Station 1, p. 77/7b)

These aspects of texts can help you to judge which analysis is more successful:

A **well-written analysis** …
is easy to understand | doesn't contain too many long / very short sentences | is written in more formal, serious language | is well-structured in paragraphs for different ideas and arguments

A **convincing analysis** …
presents arguments | contains facts and figures | includes quotations to support the arguments | makes sense to the reader | convinces with factual language, information, and sometimes quotations from experts, but not with emotional language and feelings

An **interesting analysis** …
focuses on what would interest the reader | presents clear examples | contains humour / suspense / surprising information to grab / keep the reader's attention | avoids a boring style

4 Making a difference → More practice Station 2, p. 79/2

*Some media producers try to make a difference by showing realistic and authentic images of people. Find examples of movies, series, books, magazines or social media accounts that – in your opinion – (try to) make a difference. Choose **one** example and write a short description in which you present that media. How do they present people? How does that affect the reader or the audience?*

5 Smartphones at school → More help Station 2, p. 80/4

a) *As a member of the student council, Vanessa is part of a group that is examining the regulations on smartphone use at her school. Another student submits a petition to include the following change to the regulations:*

From Year 11 (age 15/16), all students should be allowed to use their smartphones as much as they like at school.

The head teacher asks Vanessa to discuss the change with the members of the student council and comment on the rule from their point of view. Read the arguments and sort them into pros and cons. Order each side's arguments from weakest to strongest.

students without smartphones feel left out | useful for research in lessons | most students aged 15/16 can be trusted to behave responsibly | stops students joining in with face-to-face school life | normal now to have a smartphone at all times | rude posts about other students, cyberbullying etc. cause disruption | very helpful in an emergency | distracts students from lessons | many classrooms have computers, tablets etc. | makes it easier to meet friends in breaks etc. | emergencies in which you need a smartphone are very unusual

b) *Decide if you are for or against the new rule. Then use three of the pros and cons in a) to write Vanessa's comment. Use the example and information on p. 79, ex. 3 for help.*

6 Structuring an argumentative essay → More help Station 2, p. 80/5

*Look at the arguments and decide which ones you could use to argue **for** a minimum age for social media use and which ones **against**. Make a grid in your exercise book. Use the ideas for your essay.*

social media help them to connect with or make new friends | makes it illegal for social media platforms to collect the personal data of kids for advertising | more time to teach kids about online safety, cyberbullies and the dangers of meeting strangers online | kids have already learned about online safety, cyberbullies and the dangers of meeting strangers online by the age of 13 | older teens are more likely to spot misinformation and fake news | one age limit for all ignores the fact that every kid is different | easier for parents to argue against social media | social media are an important part of the everyday life of kids aged 13–15 too | without social media kids have more time for meaningful activities like being creative or doing sport | impossible to make sure kids respect the age limit | the current age limits are ignored, and any other age limit will be too

Unit 3

1 The Canadian mosaic → More practice Check-in, p. 86/1

An individual piece of a mosaic is called a tessera[1]. As you are going through the unit, collect different tesserae that you believe are part of the Canadian mosaic. Think about different aspects of living side by side in Canada. You can also look back at the information presented in Across cultures 3. It's probably best to note down information in a digital document so you can rearrange information more easily if necessary.

After you have completed the unit, comment on whether the unit has convinced you that Canada is indeed a mosaic. You can also do some online research to find more examples of Canadian tesserae to make your mosaic more complete.

2 First impressions → More practice Check-in, p. 86/1

Find photos for two other aspects that are mentioned in texts A–D on pp. 86–87.

3 < Find the rule > → More help Station 1, p. 89/2c)

a) *Match the sentence parts. Then compare the use of the* ***present perfect progressive*** *and the* ***past perfect progressive*** *to help you write the rule for the past perfect progressive.*

1. We've been looking for the entrance to the hotel for 15 minutes …
2. The bus driver had already been driving for an hour …
3. She's been talking to a retired[2] police officer at the museum for 20 minutes …
4. They looked tired …
5. Although Leon has been learning French since he was twelve, …
6. He'd been giving guided tours for six years …

a) when he realised he was going the wrong way.
b) but hasn't finished yet.
c) he still doesn't speak it perfectly.
d) and we still haven't found it.
e) before the first question came that he couldn't answer.
f) because they'd been kayaking since two o'clock.

b) *Put these sentence parts in the correct order to write two rules for using the* ***past perfect progressive****.*

1. to stress | had continued | you use | in the past happened | an activity | the past perfect progressive | how long | before another event
2. had happened | up to a point in the past | an activity | it emphasises that | several times

c) *Look at the sentences you found on p. 89, ex. 2b) and decide which rule in b) applies.*

1 **tessera, tesserae** ['tesərə, 'tesəri] a small piece used in mosaic work | 2 **retired** [rɪ'taɪəd] no longer working because of old age

4 < Working in the forestry industry > → More help Station 1, p. 90/4

Complete what Leon says about his host dad. Use the verbs in the correct tense.

"Since I **1** (to arrive, simple past) here, I **2** (to try, present perfect progressive) to learn all about unique jobs in Canada so that I can write about them in my blog. My host dad **3** (to work, present perfect progressive) as a field crew supervisor in the forest industry for more than 20 years. He **4** (to plan, past perfect progressive) to study Forestry at university but then his father **5** (to lose, simple past) his job and they **6** (not to have, simple past) enough money. He **7** (not to give up, simple past) though and eventually **8** (to find, simple past) a job that was suited to his interests. He **9** (to be, present perfect simple) in charge of his crew for ten years. He's responsible for forest development and harvesting, wildfire protection and road system layouts. He **10** (to work, present perfect progressive) on developing a new GPS system for a few years now."

5 The interview → More help Station 1, p. 90/7a)

a) *After you have sent your application email, you are invited to an interview and want to prepare for it. Look at the topics the interviewer might ask about and match the questions to the topics.*

1. your background
2. your characteristics
3. what you know about the programme
4. resilience and judgment
5. school life
6. host country

A What do you know about the exchange organisation you're applying to?
B Have you been or even lived abroad before?
C In 2018 Canada legalized the use of cannabis. If your host brother or host sister offered you a joint, would you try it?
D What are your personal strengths and weaknesses?
E What do you hope to get out of[1] being an exchange student?
F What do you think you can expect from the exchange organisation during your stay[2] abroad?
G What is the currency of Canada?
H If you had a problem with your host family, what could you do to find a solution?
I What is the capital of Canada?
J What are your grades like?
K As an exchange student, do you think you'd be a good ambassador[3] for your home country? If yes, why?
L Are you involved in any after-school activities?

b) *Find two more questions for each topic in a).*

1 **to get out (of)** [ˌget ˈaʊt (əv)] to gain; to win | 2 **stay** [steɪ] a period of staying; a visit | 3 **ambassador** [æmˈbæsədə] a representative of one's own country

○ **6** **< Find the rule >** → More help Station 2, p. 92/3b)

Copy the grid into your exercise book. Then put the words from the new phrases in ex. 3a) on p. 92 into the right column.

form of to be	form of verb	past participle	adjective	infinitive
is		supposed		to be
…	…	…	…	…

○ **7** **A cartoon** → More help Station 2, p. 93/6

Complete the description and analysis of the cartoon on p. 93. Use the verbs in the correct tense. There are three more verbs than you need.

to rain | to wear | to cover | to throw | to shine | to stand | to rain | to try | to snow | to swim | to feed

In the cartoon you can see that the water is unusually high and 1 cars and houses. The area is flooded and it 2 (still). A woman 3 in the door of her house. She 4 rubber boots[1] and a rain hat. She 5 food to salmon in her backyard. In the background you can see snow-covered mountains and pine trees[2].
I think that the cartoon 6 to show that climate change causes extreme weather conditions. In this case, there is too much rain. It probably usually 7 in Vancouver instead of 8. Because of all the water, the salmon are closer to the people and the woman can feed them in her backyard.

● **8** **Your own backyard** → More practice Station 2, p. 93/6

Think about environmental problems which could show up at your 'back door'. Desertification? Storms? Wild animals? Water shortages? Draw or describe a cartoon of your backyard with the consequences of the environmental problem.

● **9** **Could you write the subtitles, please?** → More practice Action!, p. 94/4

D11 Film script

a) *You are doing work experience with a news website provider. The boss of your department asks you to write German subtitles for the film* Ice fishing in the Yukon. *Write the subtitles.*

b) *With another pair, discuss the difficulties which you experienced while writing the subtitles. Here are some ideas:*

to find the appropriate translation | to have trouble with space (when sentences / words are long) | to make it sound like proper German | to find the right timing (speed of spoken language / enough time to read the subtitles) | …

Media skills

Subtitling a film means showing the words that are being said at the bottom of a film or television picture. **Dubbing** a film means replacing the original speech in a film or TV programme with words in another language.
What reasons might there be for subtitling or dubbing a film? What are the advantages and disadvantages of each method? How are these methods different from mediation?

1 **rubber boots** *(AE)* [ˈrʌbə ˌbuːts] waterproof boots that almost reach up to your knee | 2 **pine tree** [paɪn triː] an evergreen forest tree with leaves like needles

○ 10 Mi'gmaq culture → More help Story 1, p. 119/6a)

Explain which aspects of Mi'gmaq lifestyle, culture and importance of the community are emphasised by these terms.

gwis | farming tools | to clean fish | to repair nets | elder | thousands of years | salmon run[1] | to respect the cycle | government | to ring the church bells | rules and laws

○ 11 Writing a characterisation → More help Story 1, p. 119/6c)

These steps and phrases will help you when writing the characterisation of the 90-year-old man.

1. Start your characterisation by describing the man's appearance.
   He is wearing… | His skin is … | His hair is … | It looks like he can't … | He uses …
2. Next, describe his relationship to the other characters and his behaviour.
   He seems very independent … | He refuses … | He is pleased when … | He stands with … | At the end, he acts like …
3. Finally, talk about his feelings or thoughts.
   I think that he feels strongly about … | He seems to be worried … |
   He probably thinks that the situation is/will … | He is determined not to let …

○ 12 Emotions → More help Story 1, p. 119/7c)

a) *Choose six of these emotions and find panels in the graphic novel that show the emotion.*

disgust | anger | confusion | surprise | dismay[2] | fear | sadness | anxiety | relief | pride[3] | happiness | excitement

b) *Choose three of the emotions in a). Give the page number and a short description of who is in the scene and what caused the emotion.*

○ 13 ‹ Dividing the short story "Oil and Ivory" into sections › → More practice ‹ Story 2 ›, p. 125/3

a) *Divide the short story into sections (not necessarily the ones labelled A–E) and find a suitable heading for each one.*

b) *Choose **one** section and make a drawing to go with it.*

● 14 ‹ Conflict in "Oil and Ivory" › → More practice ‹ Story 2 ›, p. 125/3c)

Which conflict do you think is most important in the story? Explain why.

1 **salmon run** ['sæmən ˌrʌn] the migration of salmon up a river | 2 **dismay** [dɪ'smeɪ] a feeling of unhappiness, disappointment or shock | 3 **pride** [praɪd] the feeling of being proud

Text and media smart 3

○ 1 Jobs in the theatre → More practice Check-in, p. 130/1

a) *You already know jobs in the theatre like actor/actress, singer, (ballet) dancer and musician. Look at some more jobs there and work out their meaning. Write a short job description for each one.*

playwright | director | choreographer | set designer | lighting technician | prop maker | costume maker | make-up artist | sound technician

Start: As a playwright, you are supposed to be good with / at …
Playwrights are expected to be … and they are supposed to have …

b) *When you have finished writing the descriptions, present the jobs in the theatre to the students who did ex. 2 below.*

● 2 Jobs in the theatre → More practice Check-in, p. 130/1

a) *You already know jobs in the theatre like actor/actress, singer, (ballet) dancer and musician. But there are also names for jobs that don't tell you what the people do exactly. Use a dictionary or do some online research to find out what the people do in their jobs. Then write a short job description for each one.*

stage manager | head of wardrobe | stage crew | prompter | usher | box office assistant | understudy

Start: As stage manager, you are supposed to be good with / at …
A stage manager is expected to be … and they are supposed to have …

b) *When you have finished writing the descriptions, present the jobs in the theatre to the students who did ex. 1 above.*

● 3 It's your decision! → More practice Station 1, p. 136/5

You are a director. Choose ***one*** *of the scenes on pp. 131–135 and decide on the following:*

1. the age and appearance of each character
2. the set behind each character
3. adjectives to describe how each character behaves and the way that they speak during the phone call
4. any sound and lighting effects that are needed

4 Formal vs informal → More practice Station 2, p. 137/1

a) *Complete the phrases from the listening text on p. 131, ex. 1 and the scenes on pp. 131–135.*

Assistants:

1. What seems to be the ___ of your problem?
2. How can I ___ you?
3. What could it ___ be?
4. I'm ___ to hear that. I'll see what I can do.
5. Maybe it would help if I ___ how the bees got in your house.
6. Could you come that evening ___?
7. This is your first time encountering an ___ difficulty. So difficult, in fact, that it ___ you to call the Help Desk.
8. You feel like this problem is so hard that it ___ assistance from a paid professional.
9. You can't crack this ___. ___ to figure out.
10. Just a minute ago you were saying I had an ___, and now all of a sudden you're ___ for my assistance.
11. I'll have a ___.
12. How ___ this?
13. Just ___ my job.
14. You're very ___. I'm ___ I could help.

Customers:

1. Can you ___ help me please?
2. I've got a problem, and I ___ if you can help me with it.
3. I'm calling to ___ about a delivery.
4. Would it be possible to ___ our seats?
5. You ___ me.
6. That would be ___. Thank you very much ___.

D12 Script

b) *Refer to the audio script and the scenes on pp. 131–135 to check your answers in a).*

c) *Look at your answers in a) and decide which of the phrases are less polite and informal (-) and which ones are more polite and formal (+).*

5 Formal vs informal → More practice Station 2, p. 137/1

D12 Script

Read the scenes on pp. 131–135 and the audio script for ex. 1 on p. 131. Note down phrases that the customers and the assistants say. Then mark the polite and formal phrases to differentiate them from the less polite and informal ones.

6 Write your scene → More help Station 2, p. 137/1

Here are prompts for three of the photos on p. 137. You can also use phrases from ex. 4.

B to be hard to read | to harm | to be allergic to sth | to be tested on animals | the fine print | ecological footprint[1] | chemicals | ingredients | magnifying glass

D to work | instructions | to repair | tool | to cause | to connect | power cut | tutorial | DIY[2] | to avoid | to check | spare part | explosion | wire | mistake |

F to break | to swing | to attack | to push (sb off) | to climb | to get lost | to be injured | rope | emergency call | boardwalk | wild animal | GPS device | ranger

1 **ecological footprint** [ˌiːkəˈlɒdʒɪkl ˌfʊtprɪnt] damage sb does to the environment | 2 **DIY** [ˌdiːaɪˈwaɪ] do-it-yourself

Reading

S1 Skimming and scanning

The reading techniques skimming and scanning are helpful when you need to find the main points in a text, answer questions about a text or do a mediation exercise. With both techniques you don't read every word in the text. Then you can mark the relevant words and phrases in the text, if possible, or take notes.

Skimming	Scanning
When you skim a text, you read it quickly to get the general idea (gist). Read the title, any headings, the first sentence of each paragraph and the last paragraph as they often sum up the text. Concentrate on looking for the main information.	When you scan a text, you look for specific information (details). When you find a key word, read that part of the text carefully and answer the questions about the text.

S2 Guessing new words

The following techniques can help you to guess the meaning of new words:

1. **The unknown word is similar to another word you already know**
   You can guess the meaning of a word with a prefix (before it) or a suffix (after it) if you recognise the root (main part of the word). For example, you can work out the meaning of 'disappear' and 'invention' if you understand the roots 'appear' and 'invent'. Sometimes the same word is used as different parts of speech, e.g. waste – to waste. If you understand the noun, you will certainly understand the verb.

How words can start or end

By putting a prefix before a word or a suffix after it, you can form new words in that word family.

adjectives

dis-	honest	help, hope, thank, use	**-ful**
in-	appropriate, dependent, direct, secure	help, end, use, meaning	**-less**
im-	possible	health, luck, cloud	**-y**
ir-	regular, relevant, responsible	alternat(ive), attract(ive), imaginat(ive), innovat(ive), informat(ive), creat(ive)	**-ive**
non-	native		
re-	told, written		
un-	expected, developed, realistic, restricted		

How words can start or end

verbs

dis-	appear, agree
en-	danger
mis-	behave, lead, understand
re-	build, create, read, tell, write
un-	wrap, pack

! Be careful with the pronunciation:
In English you don't put the stress on the prefix.
honest – dishonest

nouns

re-	action, discovery, instatement
ex-	change
in-	dependence, equality

interview, report, sing	**-er**
champion, friend, relation	**-ship**
surf, kayak	**-ing**
invent, narrat(e), surviv(e)	**-or**
demonstrat(e), organis(e)	**-ion/-ation**
settle, improve	**-ment**
dark, aware, good, ill, open	**-ness**
child, boy, neighbour	**-hood**
activ(e), secur(e), divers(e), personal, similar	**-ity**
import(ant), dist(ant), differ(ent), sil(ent), conveni(ent)	**-ance/-ence**

2. **The unknown word is similar to a word you know in other languages**
   Many English words are to similar or even the same as German words, e.g. 'product', 'protest', 'opera' or 'ignore'. Words you know from other languages (French, Latin, …) can also help you to understand words in English when they look or sound similar. You should be careful of false friends: words that are written in (almost) the same way in German and English, but have a different meaning, e.g. 'actual' means *tatsächlich, wirklich, eigentlich* and not *aktuell*.

3. **The meaning of the word is clear from the context**
   Sometimes you can guess the meaning of a word by looking at a picture or a heading that goes with the text. Or maybe you can guess its meaning from the context. For example, if the word 'abandon' is unknown in the sentence, We passed some furniture on the side of the road, which someone had abandoned, then 'abandon' must mean something like 'left there' because you don't normally see furniture on the side of the road.

4. **The unknown word is a compound word**
   When a compound word is made up of words you already know (e.g. countdown, hairdryer), you can usually work out its meaning.

S3 Identifying the features of different text types

Texts usually belong to one of these two categories:

1. Fictional texts

These text types include novels, short stories, plays, poems and graphic novels. Fictional texts can also be described by genre, e.g. thriller, young adult fiction, solarpunk (a type of science fiction). Some of the main features of the different text types are as follows:

novel	A long fictional text that often includes a large number of characters, different settings (i.e. the time and place) and a complex plot (storyline).
play	A play is a story which is performed on stage. The characters speak to each other in dialogues, or they sometimes speak directly to the audience. A play is divided into acts and scenes.
poem	A text which may or may not rhyme and which is often divided into verses (stanzas). The words usually create images in the reader's mind.
short story	A short fictional text that usually focuses on a single event (i.e. plot, theme and conflict) and has one setting. There are often only one or two main characters. A short story often starts in the middle of the action (in medias res), and there is often a turning point and a surprise ending.
graphic novel	A story that is told with words and pictures. Not only is it important that you pay attention to the speech bubbles, thought bubbles and captions, but also to the design and order of the panels (see examples below). As is the case in films, the images can be close-ups, medium shots or long shots (→ S15).

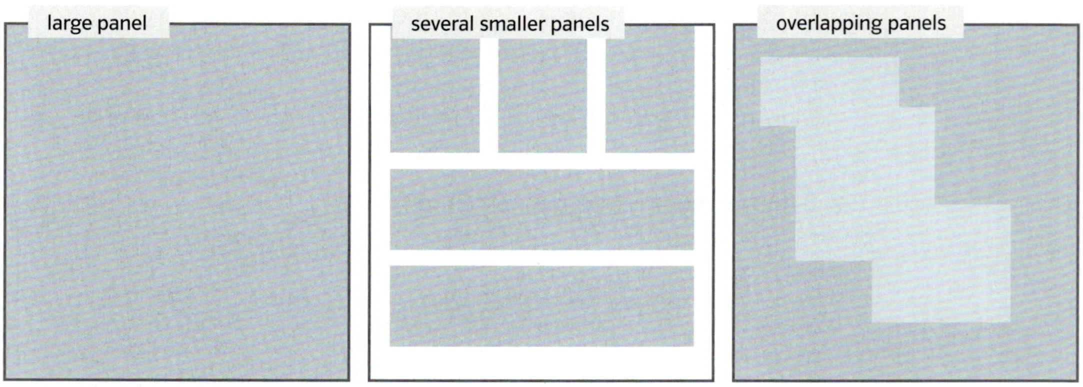

to introduce the setting | to create a distance / a quiet atmosphere	to show action in the story | to show reactions / feelings of characters	to introduce fast action / speed | to create suspense | to make the reader experience the story

2. Non-fictional texts

These text types include news reports, comments, argumentative texts, book reviews, formal letters and emails, letters to the editor, instructions, advertisements and travel blogs. Non-fictional texts may provide information and facts. They can also give the writer's opinion or try to persuade the reader. Non-fictional texts have a clear structure and are written in clear, direct language.

S4 Analysing texts

Before you analyse a text, you should identify the type of text it is (→ S3).

No matter which type of text it is, in the analysis you should:
- Choose one or more aspects that you want to describe and explain in detail.
- Write an outline which includes an introduction, a main body and a conclusion.
- Introduce each new aspect in a new paragraph.
- Describe and explain each aspect. Give examples from the text to support your ideas.
- Use a formal register (i.e. no short forms).
- Do not give your own feelings about the information in the text.

The checklist can help you to focus and take notes on the relevant aspects:

for all texts:
- author (e.g. journalist, private person)
- name and date of publication (e.g. published in [name] on June 4 2023)
- author's intention (e.g. to provide information, to entertain, to argue a point)
- structure (Is the text divided into chapters, acts / scenes, paragraphs, verses?)
- content (Which topics are mentioned? Are they discussed in a neutral / subjective / balanced way?)
- language and register (e.g. formal / informal, long/short forms, long / short sentences)
- stylistic devices (e.g. similes, metaphors, personification, rhetorical questions)
- tone (e.g. friendly, positive, funny, ironic)
- how the content affects the style used
- atmosphere (e.g. dark, optimistic, hopeful)
- effect on reader (e.g. makes sb think)

for fictional texts:
- genre (e.g. science fiction, solarpunk, thriller)
- narrative techniques and narrative perspective (e.g. first-person narrator, third-person narrator)
- setting (Where and when does the action happen?)
- characters (Who are the main characters? What do we get to know about their character traits; How do their feelings change?)
- plot (What happens in the story?)
- conflict (What is the main character's dilemma?)
- theme (What issues does the author raise?)

S5 Narrative techniques

When you analyse a fictional text, you shouldn't only think about the plot, but also about the way in which the story is told, i.e. the narrative techniques that are used.

atmosphere / mood	**Atmosphere** refers to a feeling that is created in a setting or among a group of characters. The writer can produce an atmosphere by using imagery, descriptions of a place and time as well as references to what the characters see, hear, smell, taste and feel.
exposition, rising action, turning point, climax, falling action, dénouement	The **exposition** is the first part of a fictional text. It gives information about the setting, the characters and the plot. In the main part of the text, the conflict begins and characters react to it (**rising action**). The **turning point** is the moment when the action begins to move towards the **climax** (= the most important or exciting part). The part of the text in which characters deal with the results of the climax is called **falling action**. The concluding part can bring a solution or **dénouement** (which may be missing in the case of a surprise ending).
exaggerated storyline	An **exaggerated storyline** can help to create suspense. This may involve coincidences, unrealistic situations, out-of-character actions, extreme actions and reactions.
flashback	A **flashback** is a short scene that happened at a time before the main story, e.g. one character remembers a past event.
foreshadowing	A writer uses **foreshadowing** to give the reader clues about what is going to happen later in the novel.
suspense	**Suspense** draws the reader into the story. It's the feeling of excitement or anxiety while waiting for something (uncertain) to happen. Suspense can be built up in the first lines or in the course of the story. It's created by using dramatic language or by not giving certain information.

S6 Narrative perspective

The effect that a story has on the reader or listener is influenced by the narrative perspective or point of view from which it is told.

! The author and the narrator are not the same person.

There are two main types of narrative perspective:

1. Third-person narrator
This type of narrator tells the story from the outside but knows about the characters' thoughts and feelings as well as the background of the story.

Everybody in the crowded restaurant stared when the young woman suddenly threw a glass of wine in the face of the older man sitting opposite her at a table near the window. The young woman was attractive and well dressed. The man was at least twenty years older than she was. He looked shocked. From: Robert O' Neill, *Laura*

2. First-person narrator

This type of narrator brings the reader close to the feelings and opinions of a particular character in the story because the narrator is identical with this character. You only get to know what this character knows.

So I'm sitting in the lounge with Jessica and some other people, and Rich Herrington comes over and starts talking about this new guy and something he did in the cafeteria. I don't know what he's talking about, but he's very excited. So is everyone else. They've all heard about this new guy. Other people join in the conversation. *Did you hear what he did? Did you hear what he said? What's his name, anyway? Where's he from?* I've never seen people at my high school get like this.

People in my high school usually don't care about anything.

From: Blake Nelson, *Destroy all cars*, 2009 (abridged)

S7 Characterisation

When you analyse the characters in a novel, film, play etc., it is important to examine their appearance and character traits, their social background, their feelings, thoughts and behaviour and their relationships with other characters. You should also mention if the characters change in the course of a story.

The main character is also called the **protagonist**. If there is a conflict with a secondary character, that character is called the **antagonist**.
The main character may be characterised directly or indirectly. In a **direct characterisation**, the narrator or another character tells the reader what a character is like. In an **indirect characterisation**, the reader learns what a character is like by examining and interpreting the character, i.e. by reading between the lines.

Useful phrases

General phrases: In line(s) … the protagonist tells us … | It becomes obvious / clear in line(s) … that he / she … | His / Her feelings / attitude towards … changes … | He / She also thinks / wonders about … | He / She is critical of …

Personal data: young | middle-aged | elderly | old | …-year-old | male | female | gay | lesbian | straight | same-sex | married | single | divorced | outsider | mainstream | of … origin | rich / wealthy | poor | middle-class

Appearance: tall | small | pretty | attractive | good-looking | beautiful | ugly | fat | thin | healthy | round face | long / flat nose | bright eyes | long / short hair | bald | tattooed / smooth / (un)healthy skin | loud / soft / quiet voice

Positive characteristics: brave | clever | confident | creative | gentle | honest | open-minded | optimistic | patient | reliable | smart | sensitive

Negative characteristics: aggressive | dishonest | insensitive | jealous | rude | violent | unreliable

S8 Style, tone, register

When analysing the language in a fictional or non-fictional text, you are often asked to comment on the style, tone and register.

- The **style** of writing refers to the language used and it can be objective, subjective, biased, balanced etc.
- The **tone** refers to the mood and feelings that are expressed by the author. A text can be humorous, critical, serious, sarcastic etc.
- The **register** refers to whether a text is formal or informal. The register used depends on the context, e.g. a letter of application is formal; an email to an exchange partner is informal. In an informal text, short forms are often used; in a formal text long forms are more common.

! When writing a text, the style, tone and register you use depends on the reader. For example, a chat with a company or a hotline requires a formal style and register. The same is true for a blog entry which is read by your teachers or people you don't know. The reader is more likely to take a formal chat or blog entry seriously.

Useful phrases

to examine both sides of an issue | to have a humorous / ironic / sarcastic / serious / critical / friendly / positive tone | to address sb politely / rudely | to create a certain atmosphere by using informal / formal language | to use mainly complex / simple sentences | to include imagery / exaggerated language | to give the text a humorous/critical tone

S9 Analysing poetry

A poem is often divided into verses (stanzas). It produces rhythm, sounds, pictures and meanings in a few words.

The following steps can help you to analyse a poem:

- Look at the structure of the poem. Is it divided into verses? Free verse poems don't have a clear structure or stanzas.
- Read the poem. Look up any new words or phrases as every word is important.
- Read the poem again. Does it tell a story, create an atmosphere or describe a feeling or a situation? Who is the narrator (lyrical speaker) in the poem? What does the reader learn about the narrator and his / her thoughts and feelings? Try to sum up these aspects in your own words.
- Read the poem out loud to get a feeling for its theme, the rhythm, the language and the emotions it creates. These emotions are supposed to have an effect on the reader.

Together we are Canada

My name is British Columbia
The jewel of the West Coast.
Forestry and fishing are
The things that I do

From: Leanne Guenther, "Together we are Canada"

Other stylistic devices that you can look for in a poem include:

imagery / symbols / similes / metaphors	Imagery is used to create pictures in the reader's mind and evoke emotions. Imagery takes different forms, e.g. – A **symbol** is an image or an object that stands for a feeling, idea, belief or action. For example, a heart shape can be a symbol of love. – In a **simile** two things are compared using 'like' or 'as', e.g. My love is like a fire burning in my heart. – In a **metaphor** one thing is described by referring to something else but without using 'like' or 'as' e.g. "We are Atlantic Provinces, the three musketeers of the sea").
personification	Animals, plants or objects are given human characteristics, e.g. The clock in the hall watched the children change over the years.
rhyme scheme	Typical rhyme schemes are end rhymes (e.g. AABB or ABAB). Free verse poems don't rhyme (e.g. shape poems, haikus and acrostic poems).
rhythm / stress	A poem only works with the right **rhythm**. It decides which part of each line is emphasised. The **stress** is always in the same place. With free verse poems, you should decide where to put the stress or make a pause.

S10 Analysing songs and music videos

Song lyrics are similar to poems (→ S9), but the music is important too as it creates a certain atmosphere and makes the song memorable. A music video uses visual elements to represent what an artist wants to say in a song.

The following questions can help you to analyse songs and music videos:

1. Music
- What musical genre is it? (e.g. pop, hip-hop)
- What instruments are used? (e.g. drums, guitar, piano)
- What is the music like? Does it get faster, slower?
- Are any rhythms repeated? Is the rhythm slow / fast?
- What emotions are created by the music?

2. Lyrics
- What is the structure of the song (stanzas and chorus)? What is the function of the chorus?
- What is the narrative perspective? What does the reader learn about the narrator?
- What imagery and other stylistic devices are used? (→ S9)
- What atmosphere is created? What emotions are produced by the lyrics? What effect do these elements have on the listener?
- What is the message of the song?

3. Music videos

- What is the message of the lyrics? (See above)
- What musical genre is it? Who is the artist? What is more important in the video: the artist or the song?
- What is the storyline of the video (if it has one)? How does the storyline add to the message of the song?
- What camera shots and movements are used? (→ S15) What atmosphere do they create? What effect do they have on the viewer? (→ S15)

Useful phrases

The lyrics are sad / happy / optimistic. | The music is simple / catchy / memorable / loud. | It has a complex / simple rhythm. | The chorus is repeated. | You can't keep your feet or hands still. | You can dance to it. | It's easy to sing along to. | The first / second / … verse makes you feel happy / sad / … | You can't get it out of your head. | I like the atmosphere / language … | The … reminds me of … | When I hear …, I think of … | The … sounds like / as if …

Dealing with visuals

S11 Working with pictures

If you want to describe and analyse a picture (e.g. a painting, graffiti, a photo, an illustration, panels in a graphic novel, a cartoon), the following steps can help you:

1. Background information

Give the title of the visual and the name of the artist. Say what type of visual it is, the subject and when it was made/taken.

2. Description

Describe any people and their actions, places, objects, buildings etc. Use the present progressive. Also include the shape, size and colour of things, people's facial expressions and their relationships with each other. Describe how light and colours are used.

Tip

Try these techniques:

- Divide the picture into four sections.
- Circle any unusual elements.
- Describe the sections in a certain order, e.g. left to right, top to bottom.

3. Analysis

Try to answer these questions in your analysis:

- What message is conveyed by the visual? What is the function of the elements in it?
- What impression does the artist want to create?
- What effect did the artist probably want the visual to have on the viewer? How is this achieved? If it is a historical visual, what do you know about the situation / events at the time it was made?

Useful phrases

Background information: The picture was painted by … in … | The photo was probably taken in/at … | It is a portrait / a still life / a landscape / an oil painting / a watercolour / a panel. | The subject … | It is a photo of an individual / a group photo | old | recent | in colour | black and white | sharp | blurry | a silly / serious / natural / posed photo | to print / publish a photo in …

Description: The illustration / photo / painting shows … | In the picture a person is (+ verb + ing) … | In the background / foreground of the … | In the middle / centre of the … there is … | At the top / bottom … | On the left / right … | In the top left-hand / bottom right-hand corner … | There is a contrast between … | The focus in the picture is on … | The colours are bright / dark | … is seen from above / below / the front / the back.

Analysis: The photo shows / represents / symbolises / suggests / refers to … | The artist is trying to show … | The photo is boring / exciting / convincing … because … | It conveys the impression that … | This creates a / an … atmosphere.

S12 Working with statistics

Diagrams sum up a lot of information in a little space.

1. Types of diagrams

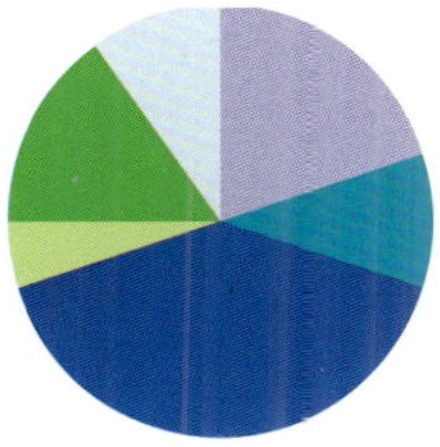

The circle in a **pie chart** represents 100%. Each segment shows a percentage.

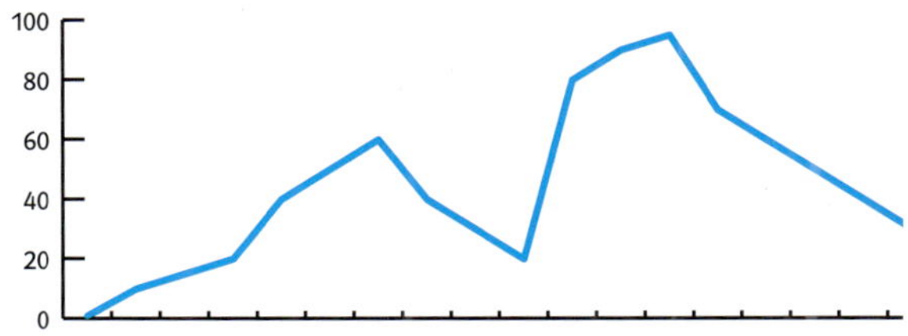

A **line graph** shows a development over a certain period of time.

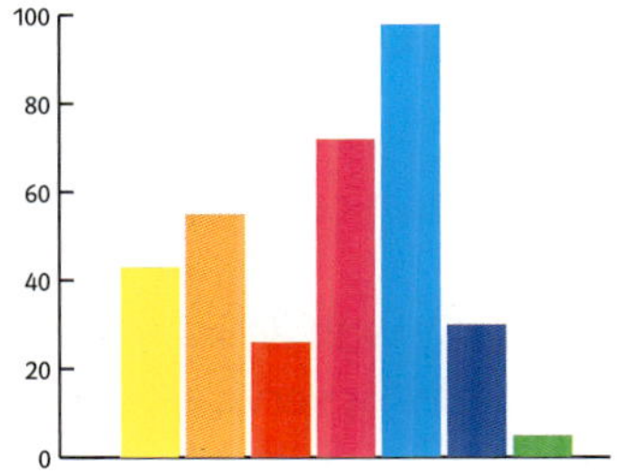

A **bar chart** compares figures directly.

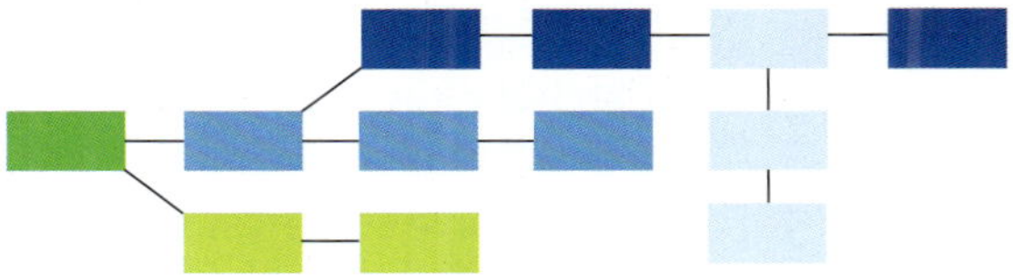

A **flow chart** describes processes that involve decisions at certain points and shows alternatives.

2. Analysing statistics

- Give the topic and type of diagram, the source and year of publication.
- Summarise the most important information in the diagram.
- Try to give reasons for the figures and how they develop.

Useful phrases

Talking about statistics: The table / bar chart / line graph / pie chart / … was published by … in … | It is about … / deals with / shows / illustrates the number / size of … | The figures show / indicate / suggest that … | The number of … has gone up / has increased by … | The number of … has dropped / has decreased by … | The latest figures / data … | We can draw the conclusion that … | … could / might explain these figures / developments. | It proves that … | To make it clear that … | … lead to … | … is / are due to … | … result in … | to rise / increase | to decline / drop / fall / decrease

Qualifiers: The (second) largest group of … | The majority / minority of … | Only a small minority … | Half of its volume … | Most of … | About / Just over / Under 30 percent of the people come from … / are … | A high / low percentage of … | A significant number of … | A total of … | approximately | exactly | on average | to rise / to fall slowly / steadily / sharply

Comparing and contrasting: The number of … hasn't changed / has stayed the same. | Compared to / In comparison with … | twice / three times as many … | more / less / fewer than …

S13 Working with cartoons

Cartoons usually combine a drawing with some text. They often focus on a current issue and criticise people, institutions etc. by making fun of them. The text can be a caption (a statement below the drawing); one or more speech or thought bubbles; a sign or a poster.

When you analyse a cartoon, you should look for symbols, exaggeration or irony, which cartoonists use to make a point. You should also consider its context (e.g. when it was drawn and events at the time, where it was published). (→ S11) Say what effect the cartoon has on the reader.

S14 Working with advertising

Advertisers aim to make products and services attractive so that the target group will buy them. They use print and online ads, commercials and influencer ads to introduce new products and get a message across to the target group. The AIDA formula is useful when creating or analysing adverts:

- Catch the target group's **attention** by means of an eye-catching visual, a clever slogan, an unusual layout etc.
- Hold people's **interest** so that they read the ad copy with an interesting text or a situation in which someone is using the product or service.
- Create a **desire** for a product or service by showing its unique features.
- Get the target group to take **action** (e.g. buy a product, visit a website to get more information).

Useful phrases

General phrases: The advertisement / commercial / influencer ad is entertaining / memorable / surprising. | The visual / slogan / ad copy makes me / the reader / the viewer … | It tries to persuade / convince … | It compares … with … | It catches the attention of … by …

Target groups: children | teenagers | parents | adults | women / men between the ages of … and … | people who enjoy / need / want to / are interested in …

Language: strong adjectives / adverbs | double meanings | persuasive language | facts and figures

Effects: sound effects | music | light | camera shots | camera movements | special effects

Viewing

S15 Working with films

1. Identifying the genre

The following descriptions can help you to work out the genre of a film:

action film	Action films are usually about a hero or heroine who fights bad people. The action often includes stunts, car chases and violent scenes.
animated film	An animated film is made up of a series of drawings which are shown quickly one after the other so that the characters seem to move.
comedy	Comedies have a humorous plot that makes viewers laugh. Often the characters are exaggerated, and the language plays an important role.
detective film	The focus is on a crime that is usually solved in the course of the film.
documentary	A documentary is a film about a non-fictional topic (e.g. a true event, a social issue, another culture). It can teach, persuade, criticise or just show real life.
fantasy film	Fantasy films are about magic or supernatural powers. There is often a hero or heroine at the centre of the plot.
historical drama	Historical dramas are often based on true events in a specific historical period, but they are not completely true.
musical	A musical is a play for the theatre or a film. The plot is mainly represented by song and dance.
re-enactment	Historical events are re-enacted in a way that seems true to detail.
romantic film	Romantic films focus on the relationship between two characters. They usually have a happy ending.
science-fiction film	These films deal with inventions in science and technology, time travel or aliens, for example. The setting is often in the future.

2. Analysing a film

A film usually tells a story. When you analyse a film, you should sum up and analyse the plot, setting, characters and narrative techniques as you do with a fictional text (→ S4). You can also choose specific camera shots and movements and say how they add to the plot and the action, what they tell the viewer about the characters etc.

The following points can help you to analyse a film:

- Make a list of interesting camera shots and movements (see 3. below). Take screenshots and note down the time codes. Say what effect each shot creates, e.g. it shows a character's emotions; it includes the viewer in the scene; it shows where the action is taking place.
- If the film is based on a novel, short story or play, how much of the original plot has been re-used? Have characters been cut out / added in? Why? Compare the message of the film with the original version. Do you prefer the book or the film? Why?
- Is the music memorable? Does it create an atmosphere? What effect does it have on the viewer, e.g. it increases suspense, it makes the viewer cry / laugh / …
- Compare the film script to one or two scenes in the film. What changes have been made?
- Describe the film poster and / or film trailer. What aspects of the film does it emphasise?
- Check the internet for online reviews and comments. Compare them with your opinion.

3. Describing camera movements and camera shots

static shot: camera does not move

to pan left / right
to tilt up / down

to zoom in on / out of sth

tracking shot: camera is moving on a vehicle

long shot: people / objects shown from a distance

full shot: shot of the whole body / object

medium shot: upper body / part of an object

close-up: head and shoulders

extreme close-up: face only, detailed shot

Useful phrases

In the foreground / background there is / are … | The camera takes a long shot / medium shot / a close-up of … | This brings the viewer closer to the action / the character and his / her feelings / … | This creates a distance between … and … | The viewer sees … from the front / from above / from below / from behind. | The camera zooms in / out … | The movement of … is followed in a tracking shot. | The viewer sees a close-up of … | The camera pans from (left) to (right). | The shots follow each other quickly. | There are very few cuts (at the beginning). | … is shown in slow / fast motion.

S16 Making a film with a tablet

MK

1. Writing a film script

❶ First, write the script for each scene. You should include stage directions so that the film crew and the actors know where and when the scene takes place. INT. stands for 'interior' and EXT. for 'exterior'.

❷ When a character appears for the first time in the film, they are written in capital letters with their age in round brackets. Facial expressions, movements and props are also included for each scene. All of this information is left-aligned *(linksbündig)*.

❸ Each character and their role is centred on the page. You should use spoken English, e.g. short forms and question tags.

❶ EXT. CAFÉ – DAY

❷ BOY 1 (20) and PENNY (20) outside getting coffee. Boy at front of queue; Penny arrives at back of queue, gives Boy 1 big smile.

❸ BOY 1
Coffee?

PENNY
I'm Penny.

It is also useful to turn the script into a storyboard with details about the scenes, a timeline, the characters, the dialogue and action. Draw the parts of the scene or use an online storyboard.

2. Before filming

- Put the tablet on a **tripod** *(Stativ)* to stop it from shaking.
- Press 'record' and wait for three seconds before you start. The same applies to the end when you stop recording. This will help when cutting the film later.

3. While filming

- Use a clapperboard *(Filmklappe)* to mark the beginning and end of each scene.
- Use a **16:9 format** for all takes and scenes. This is the most popular format.
- Avoid using a backlight *(Gegenlicht)* or changing lights so that the light doesn't flicker.
- Sit on a swivel chair *(Drehstuhl)* to move forward or backward, or to the right and left.
- Zoom in to focus on details, zoom out to show the "bigger picture" / more of the setting.
- Write a cutter's report *(Cutterbericht)*, i.e. make notes in the script about good and bad cuts. This will help you to find good material during post-production.
- Remember not to put your finger in front of the lens while filming.

4. Post-production
- View the material and decide which scenes you want. The cutter's report will help you with this step.
- Only save the best scenes to reduce the amount of material and the time needed for cutting.
- Arrange the scenes in your tool based on the timeline in your storyboard or film script.
- Decide what speed you want to use (a fast or slow sequence of images). The beginning and the end of the individual shots can be changed a little so the scenes flow smoothly.
- Look at all of the scenes again. If necessary, change individual shots and transitions, and move scenes around. Add sound effects and music from Creative Commons licence sources.
- Save the final version. You can share it by uploading it to a cloud and then sending a link.

Writing

S17 Checking written texts

When you have written a text, you should ask yourself the following questions, which can help you to check and improve the text:

1. Content
- Have you included all of the aspects required by the exercise?
- Have you used a good structure for the text (introduction, main body, conclusion)? Have you started a new paragraph for each new idea?
- Have you connected your ideas logically with linking adverbs? (→ S18)
- Have you used a style, tone and register that fit the text type / situation / character / reader of the text? (→ S8)

2. Spelling
- Have you spelled everything correctly? Have you checked your text with a spelling checker?
- Have you used a capital letter at the beginning of each sentence?
- If you are unsure of the spelling of a word, have you looked it up in a dictionary?

3. Grammar
- Have you used the correct tenses? Have you used the correct form of the tenses?
- Have you checked that the word order in your sentences is correct?
- Have you checked any grammar points you are unsure about?

4. Punctuation
- Have you used apostrophes, commas, single and double quotation marks and periods in the correct places?

The following points can help you to use punctuation correctly:

apostrophes	– show that letters have been left out, e.g. short forms and negative forms – they've got = they have got; we aren't = we are not. – indicate the genitive, e.g. Sally's brother, James' book.
commas	– are used in lists, e.g. We took food, a map, a compass and a torch. – are used after the salutation or the standard ending in a letter or an email, e.g. Dear …, Hello …, All the best, See you soon, – separate the main and subordinate clauses if the conditional clause is at the beginning of the sentence, e.g. If we change the way we shop, it will make a big difference. – separate a non-defining relative clause, including a commenting relative clause, from the sentence, e.g. I brought my Canadian host mom some wooden Christmas decorations, which she loved me for. – are used after most sentence adverbs at the beginning of the sentence, e.g. Hopefully, the changes to the menu will make the cafeteria a more environmentally friendly. – are used for numbers of a thousand or more, e.g. 7,460.
double quotation marks	– are used for titles of books, films, songs, poems and short stories, e.g. "Destroy all cars". – are used in direct speech, e.g. "Anybody can do it," he said. Note: The comma is before the closing quotation mark.
hyphens	– are used when two or more words act as a single idea (compound adjectives) and come before the noun they describe, e.g. non-native insects, second-hand shop, black-and-white graffiti, eco-conscious shopping, the world-famous dish. – are put between the numbers in a fraction, e.g. one-fifth, one-third. – are used to divide a word at the end of a line. You can only do this between syllables. A one-syllable word cannot be divided with a hyphen.
full stops / periods *(AE)*	– are put at the end of sentences. – are used for decimal numbers, e.g. 6.5 miles, 7.8%. – are used for abbreviations such as e.g. and etc. both in British and American English. – are put after titles in American English, e.g. Mr., Mrs., Dr., but not normally in British English. – ! If you aren't sure of the use of full stops, use a British-English or an American-English dictionary for help.
single quotation marks	– are used for thoughts, e.g. Do you often think, 'What impact will the food I buy have on the environment?'

! Canadian English usually follows the rules of punctuation used in American English.

MK If you use the spell and grammar check to check your text, you can choose which type of English (e.g. Canadian English) it uses. Look carefully at any suggested corrections before accepting them.

S18 Writing a formal letter

You can write a formal letter to ask an organisation or company for information, to inform somebody about a change in arrangements, to apply for a job etc.

1. General aspects
- Make notes about the most important points and put them in a logical order.
- Write in a polite and factual manner and be aware of the formal aspects (see below).
- At the beginning of your letter say why you are writing.
- Finish your letter by summing up the most important point.
- Check if your letter has a clear structure and then check your grammar, spelling and punctuation. (→ S17)

2. Formal aspects
- You can use the phrase 'Dear Sir or Madam' if you don't know the recipient's name.
- Start the first sentence with a capital letter, e.g. Thank you for …
- Don't use short forms (e.g. don't) or question tags (e.g. do you?).
- Finish with a suitable ending. Best regards, / Kind regards, are acceptable; Sincerely, / Yours sincerely, are very formal.
- You should always sign your letter and type your full name under it.
- In the UK commas are not always used after Dear and Yours sincerely. In the US you must use commas. Canadian English usually follows the rules of punctuation used in American English.
- If you enclose a document, write Enclosure(s) or Enc. / Encl. under your name.

Useful phrases

Starting the letter: I am writing to ask you about … | With reference to your letter of … | Thank you for your letter of …

Main body: I apologise for … | I am sorry to have to tell you that … | Please send me …

Linking adverbs to connect ideas: Furthermore, … | However, … | In fact, … | Therefore, … | Moreover, … | Nevertheless, … | Additionally, …

Conclusion: I look forward to hearing from you. | Please do not hesitate to contact me if you need any more information. | Thank you very much for your help. | I have enclosed …

3. A letter to the editor
A letter to the editor is a formal letter in which you give your opinion about some aspect(s) of an article or about a comment from another reader. The letter is addressed to the editor and not to the writer of the article or the person who wrote the comment.

The following points can help you to write a letter to the editor:
- In the introduction you refer to the original article and its date of publication.
- In the main body you give the reasons why you are writing the letter and any facts, statistics etc. which support your point of view.
- In the conclusion you can sum up your opinion, suggest a solution or call on other readers to act.
- Only give one argument per paragraph.
- Try to use personal pronouns (I, my, me) to make the letter more personal.
- Use a serious tone and formal language.

Useful phrases

Starting the letter: Dear Editor, … | I would like to add my views to the comments in your report from (date) on (theme of the report)

Main body: Firstly, I do not think that the comments about … were appropriate / correct / helpful as … | Secondly, I feel the report did not look at / discuss / mention / really explain … | Finally, the report was one-sided / incomplete / incorrect …

Supporting an opinion: In my opinion, … | As far as I know, … | I am sure that … | My point is that … | The fact / truth is that … | It is obvious that … | Some people might say that … | Although … | It is a typical mistake to say / think/claim that …

Conclusion: I think the (online) newspaper has a responsibility to … | I am sure that other readers feel the same way that I do.

S19 Writing an email

Emails can be formal (e.g. a job application email), semiformal (e.g. the first email to a host family) or informal (e.g. an email to a student at a partner school).

The following tips can help you to write an email:
- Write a subject line so that the recipient knows what the email is about.
- Give the most important information first.
- Use one paragraph for each idea.
- Write short, simple sentences. Follow the **KISS** rule – Keep **I**t **S**hort and **S**imple.
- Never use abbreviations, smileys etc. in formal emails.
- Writing words in capital letters is not polite: It is like shouting at somebody.
- When you have finished the email, check your grammar, spelling and punctuation. (→ S17)

Useful phrases

formal: Dear Mr / Mrs / Ms / Miss …, | Dear Sir or Madam, | Best wishes, | Best / Kind regards,

semiformal: Dear all, | Dear host family, | All the best,

informal: Hello …, | Hi! | See you soon, | Bye, | Love, | XOXO

S20 Writing a letter of application (cover letter)

A letter of application follows the same rules as a formal letter. (→ S18)
However, the main body of the letter should contain the following information:

- **Opening paragraph:** Introduce yourself and say why you are writing the letter. Add where you found out about the job.
- **Second paragraph**: Give your relevant qualifications and experience as well as the personal qualities that make you a suitable candidate.

- **Third paragraph:** Say why you are interested in the job and the company. Also say why you think you can do the job.
- **Closing paragraph:** Express interest in receiving an answer and/or in doing an interview.

! A job application email has the same content and structure as a letter of application.

Hauptstr. 1
70183 Stuttgart
Germany
00 49/(0)711/123456
Email: pbraun@online.de

8 May 2023

Personnel Manager
Creative Concepts
Denmark Street
London WC5 10B
England

Re: Your advertisement of 2 May 2023

Dear Sir or Madam,

My name is Petra Braun and I am a 17-year-old student at a grammar school in Stuttgart, Germany. With reference to your advertisement in the *Daily Times* (2 May), I am writing to apply for a summer job with your company.

As you will see from the enclosed CV, I have been learning English at school for eight years and I have done an online school exchange with our partner school in Leeds. In September, I will be starting Year 11. Hopefully, I will get a place at university to study IT when I finish school.

I am interested in working in London as it is one of the most creative centres for web design. I would like to get practical experience and learn more about the services that your company offers. My computer skills are very good, and I would be able to carry out the tasks mentioned in the advertisement.

Please do not hesitate to contact me if you need any more information.
I look forward to hearing from you.

Yours sincerely,

Petra Braun
Petra Braun

Enc. CV

S21 Writing a CV

CV is short for 'curriculum vitae'. In the US and in Canada, it is also called a 'résumé'. Your CV should be well-structured and clearly arranged on the page. You should also make sure that the information in it is true and correct.

The following points can help you to write a CV:
- Include skills and interests that are relevant for the job.
- Explain any German terms (e.g. *Gymnasium*) in English.
- Don't write more than one page.
- Don't sign your name at the end of the CV.
- Check your CV for mistakes and ask someone else to read it before you send it.

The following example can help you to structure your CV:

Curriculum vitae

Personal details:

Name:	Petra Braun
Address:	Hauptstr. 1 70183 Stuttgart Germany
Tel:	0049 (0)711 123456
Email:	pbraun@online.de
Nationality:	German
Date of birth:	17 September 2008

Education:

Since 2018	Geschwister Scholl Gymnasium (grammar school) in Stuttgart, Germany
2014–2018	Grundschule (primary school)

Work experience:

August 2023	Work experience at ScreenDesign (a computer programming firm) in Stuttgart, Germany
August 2022	Volunteer work for Staatsgalerie Stuttgart (an art gallery) in Stuttgart, Germany

Personal profile:
I am creative and reliable and have very good computer skills. My English is good as I have done an online student exchange programme with our partner school in Leeds. I love travelling and meeting new people. My main hobbies are modern art and computer games. In my free time I also play volleyball, which has helped me to develop good teamwork skills.

References available on request

MK

You can also look online for a template for your CV. The template can help you to structure your ideas and make your CV easier to read. It can also help you to remember all of the important information you should include.

Useful phrases

I have good computer / communication / teamwork skills | My main strength is that I am hard-working / well-organised / interested in … | I have a lot of experience in organising … | I enjoy …

S22 Writing a news report

News reports inform readers about interesting and important events. A news report in a quality newspaper is likely to be factual and use formal language. In comparison, a news report in a popular newspaper is usually subjective and emotional, and it uses informal language. It may also use larger, more controversial photos.

The following points and the example below can help you to write a news report:
- Think of a headline that will attract the reader's attention.
  You can use a participle instead of the passive to make the headline more interesting.
- Put the most interesting point in the first sentence / paragraph so that the reader continues reading.
- Use the passive (→ G17) to emphasise actions rather than who did them.
- Use participle constructions to express reason or time, for example.
- Divide the report into an introduction, main body and conclusion.
- Follow the **three Cs** of news writing: be clear, concise and correct.
- Try to answer the **five Ws**: Who? What? When? Where? Why? and sometimes How?

Canada forced to use emergency reserve amid maple syrup shortage

A shorter and warmer harvest has caused problems for production in Canada as suppliers struggle to keep up with rising global demand.

A surge in demand for maple syrup has forced The Federation of Quebec Maple Syrup Producers (QMSP) to use their strategic reserve for the first time in three years.

The QMSP, which helps regulate and oversee production of maple syrup in the region, has been forced to respond over fears of supplies running low.

They have released approximately half of its emergency reserve – roughly 22 million kilograms of syrup.

But despite the move, Helene Normandin of QMSP tried to calm fears there could be a shortage for customers.

Speaking to US radio, she said: "That's why the reserve is made, to never miss maple syrup. And we won't miss maple syrup!"

Quebec produces approximately three-quarters of the world's maple syrup.

The combination of soaring global sales – a jump of more than 36% between 2020 and 2021, according to QMSP – and output falling following a warmer and shorter harvest, has created the problem.

Maple trees can only be tapped when temperatures fall below 0°C at night but remain above freezing during the day.

Commenting on the move to tap into the reserves, Ms Normandin added: "This system prevents practically all stock shortages and ensures the market is adequately supplied."

The QMSP have predicted that a further seven million trees will be required to avoid shortages next year.

From: Casey Magloire, Sky News, 7 December 2021

S23 Writing a summary

In a summary you give the author's main ideas (non-fictional texts) or sum up a story in your own words (fictional texts). Your summary should be much shorter than the original.

1. Summary of a non-fictional text
- Read the text. Mark / write down the sentences which express the main idea or argument.
- Mark/write down the facts or arguments that support the main idea or argument.
- Start your summary with an introduction; then add the main idea or argument in the main body and write a conclusion.
- Write short paragraphs. Use your own words. Use the present tense when discussing the text, e.g. The writer begins by / discusses / goes on to … / concludes by …. (→ G12)
- Don't include any information that is not essential, e.g. examples, descriptive details, direct quotations or interpretations.

2. Summary of a fictional text
- Read the text and mark / write down the names of the main characters and details about the setting, plot, important themes and conflict.
- Divide the text into sections if the author hasn't already done this. Mark / write down the key words and main points in each section as well as the turning point.
- Using the present tense to write short paragraphs which sum up the plot, characters, setting, conflict and important themes.
- Use linking adverbs to connect ideas. (→ S18)

S24 Writing a comment

In a comment you express a personal opinion on a topic or a statement. You should also give facts and examples to support your view.

1. Getting started
- If the task lets you decide, choose the opinion you want to present.
- Do research on the topic and make notes about any facts and examples that support your opinion. Also make notes about your sources or use bookmarks to create links to the sources. Use more than one source so that you can compare information. (→ S35)
- Make an outline of your comment. Start with the weakest argument and finish with the strongest one. In the main body, you should put a topic sentence at the beginning of each paragraph.
- You can use these phrases to express a probability: to be supposed to, to be likely to, to happen to, to be certain to and to be said to + infinitive. (→ G16)

2. Structuring ideas
The following structure can help you to organise your ideas logically:

introduction	make the readers interested in the topic
▽	
main body	explain your opinion; give arguments and examples to support it
▽	
conclusion	give a summary of your opinion

S25 Writing an essay

An essay deals with a topic from opposite points of view. After giving the arguments for something (pros) and the arguments against something (cons), you should come to a conclusion. An essay doesn't usually give your personal opinion.

1. Collecting information

- Note down everything that comes to mind about the topic. Include any pros and cons you can think of.
- Do research on the topic to find facts, statistics, examples and quotations. Match them with the pros and cons in your notes.

2. Choosing a structure

Use **one** of the following structures for your essay:

introduction
▽
pro → con (1 paragraph)
▽
pro → con (1 paragraph)
▽
pro → con (1 paragraph)
▽
conclusion

introduction
▽
pros (1 per paragraph)
▽
cons (1 per paragraph)
▽
conclusion

3. Writing an argumentative text

The following points can help you to write the introduction, main body and conclusion of the argumentative text:

- Present the issue briefly in the **introduction**. To attract the reader's attention, you can:
  - Include facts about the history / background of the problem.
  - Give information about its importance today.
  - Use a relevant quotation.
  - Ask questions that you promise to give answers to.
- When you write the **main body**, you should:
  - Present each pro or con in a separate paragraph.
  - Sum up each of the pros / cons in a topic sentence.
  - Support this point in the rest of the paragraph with examples, statistics etc.
- In the **conclusion** you shouldn't mention any new points. However, you can:
  - Give a summary of what you have found out.
  - Point out the consequences of something.
  - State your own opinion in the case of a comment.
  - Ask readers to reach their own conclusion.

4. Checking the text

Read your text again and check your grammar, spelling and punctuation. (→ S17)

Useful phrases

Introducing a topic: In the past this issue was … | The topic of … is very important / controversial / relevant today because … | As … once said, "…" | The question that needs to be answered is …

Putting ideas in order: First of all … | Firstly / Secondly / Thirdly … | My main argument is … | In addition (to) … | Finally … | To sum up …

Linking adverbs: additionally | furthermore | however | in fact | moreover | nevertheless | therefore | hence

Adverbs of comment: certainly | fortunately | hopefully | luckily | of course | personally | probably | surely | unfortunately

Adverbs of purpose and manner: as if | as though | in case | in order to | (just) as | like | so | so that

Comparing and contrasting: as well as | in contrast to | on the one hand | on the other hand

Giving examples: for example | for instance | such as

Giving a conclusion / summary: To sum up, … | In conclusion, … | I would conclude that … | Having examined the pros and cons, I would suggest / recommend … | At the end of the day everybody has to decide …

S26 Creating an infographic

MK

In an infographic you can present information, facts and statistics in a way that is easy to read.

The following points can help you to make an infographic:
- Decide on the topic or aspect of the topic you want to present.
- Do research on the topic, find interesting statistics and make notes. (→ S35)
- Choose the points you want to include and write a short text for each one. Also think of a catchy title or caption for each point and for the infographic itself.
- Find Creative Commons visuals (e.g. drawings, symbols and icons) to go with each text.
- Put the information in a logical order.
- Find a suitable template *(Vorlage)* online to present the information.
- Make a note of your sources and include them at the end of your infographic.

S27 Writing a review

A review presents a book or film, for example, in a way that helps the reader to decide whether to read, watch or buy it. After describing the story or content, the reviewer may give the pros and cons, and finally recommend or warn against the book, film etc. (often presented as a rating, such as four stars out of five). Another type of review may discuss a past event, such as a concert, a virtual tour etc. In this case, the reviewer gives his / her thoughts and feelings about the event.

Film review (→ S15)
The following points can help you to write a film review:
- the genre: Is it a comedy, a romance, a thriller, an animated film etc.?
- the film series: Is it a sequel to another film? Is it one of a series?
- the director: Who is the director? What has he / she directed before?
- the plot: What happens at the beginning of the film and how does the plot develop? Are there any unexpected twists?
- the source of the film: Is the film based on a novel? Is it a new version of an old film? How is the film different to the original / the old film?
- the actors: Who was really good / convincing / suitable for the part?
- the soundtrack (music): What type of atmosphere does the soundtrack create? Which of the characters' emotions does it convey? Which time period does the music refer to?
- the special effects: Were they exciting / impressive / appropriate / too much? What effect do they have on the viewer?

Book review (→ S4–7)
The following points can help you to write a book review:
- the storyline: the plot, the themes, the setting, the main characters and the conflict.
- the author: Who is he / she? What has he / she written before?
- the genre: Is it a thriller, a science fiction novel, a collection of poems etc.?
- the analysis: characterisation, protagonists, language, style and point of view.

Useful phrases

General phrases: I feel that … | In my opinion … | I (can't) believe … | I'd (only) give it … out of five stars.

Positive: I couldn't put the book down. | We came out of the cinema feeling … | What is really clever about … is that … | It's amazing that … | It made my laugh/cry when … | I had been looking forward to watching … and I was / wasn't …

Negative: … gave me a headache. | I didn't like/enjoy … much. | The story doesn't flow. | … makes it difficult to read / watch / understand …

Adverbs of degree: very | terribly | really | extremely | completely | quite | almost | too | enough | slightly

Strong adjectives: amazing | awful | beautiful | clever | delicious | disgusting | exciting | fantastic | fascinating | huge | interesting | pretty | spectacular | terrible | wonderful | wide

S28 Doing a survey

You can do a survey to get a general idea of what people think or do, or to compare the opinions or behaviour of different target groups. If your survey is based on an assumption (e.g. "People don't think about environmental issues when they go shopping for clothes") the questions in the survey should help you to prove or disprove this assumption.

1. Getting started
- Choose a topic and define the aims of your survey.
- Decide who your target group is.

2. Preparing the questions
- The type of questions you use in the survey depends on the results you are hoping to get and how you want to present them.
  a) Open-ended questions let people give any kind of answer, which is good when you cannot think of all possible answers or you want a creative solution to a problem. However, summarising and comparing the results is a lot of work.
  b) Yes / no questions are only useful if the question is absolutely clear and there is no third option. The questions are easy to answer, and the results are easy to present and compare.
  c) Multiple choice questions are easy to answer, and the results are easy to present and compare.
  d) Ratings are a good way of getting a little more information about people's opinions rather than by just asking yes / no questions.

> **a)** What could be done to stop the negative effects of globalisation?
>
> Answer: ____________________
>
> **b)** Do you use public transport to get to school?
> - ☐ Yes
> - ☐ No
>
> **c)** Which products do you buy at least once a week?
> - ☐ Meat
> - ☐ Fruit
> - ☐ Vegetables
> - ☐ Sweets
>
> **d)** How would you rate the quality of your school lunch?
>
> ☐ ☐ ☐ ☐ ☐ ☐ ☐ ☐ ☐ ☐
>
> poor … great

- Include questions about the person who is doing the survey, e.g. their age, gender, profession, where they live etc.
- Tell the people who are taking part in the survey exactly what to do and give them enough time to answer the questions.

3. Analysing the survey

Once you have carried out the survey, you should decide how you want to analyse and present the results:
- Do you want to present only the most surprising / interesting results?
- Do you want to show how your assumption was proved right or wrong?
- Do you want to compare the answers of different groups (e.g. male / female, people living in an urban / a rural area)?
- Do you want to give the opinion of the majority of the people who did the survrey?

MK

4. **Presenting the results**
- Depending on the aims of your survey, sum up and present your results in a table or a diagram. (→ S12) You can use digital tools to create bar charts, graphs and tables. You might need to sum up and interpret the results of ratings and open-ended questions.
- Say how many people took part in the survey and what kind of people they are, e.g. ages: between … and … years old; profession: teacher, student etc.; what they have in common: all students in Year 10, families and friends of Year 10 students …

Listening

S29 Dealing with listening exercises

The best way to improve your listening skills is to vary the types of authentic recordings you listen to. Podcasts and audiobooks, for example, are a good way of practising as they often contain different types of English accents and vocabulary. In viewing and listening situations (e.g. documentaries, films and commercials), the pictures, the context and the speakers' body language and gestures will help you to understand what they are saying. However, in listening situations (e.g. radio interviews, conversations, speeches, phone calls and podcasts), no visual help is offered, so you have to listen carefully to what the speakers are saying.

1. **Before you listen**
- Read the listening exercise carefully: It often gives you information about the type of listening situation, the speakers and the topic. Photos can also give you information about the situation, the topic or the speakers.
- If you have to listen for pros and cons, you can make a grid with two columns for your notes. If you have to find specific information (as given in the exercise), make a checklist with the key words so that you can take notes while you listen.

2. **Listening for gist and detail**
- If you have to sum up a topic in the listening text or answer questions, for example, take notes while you listen. Then you can write complete sentences later.

- If you need to listen for detail (e.g. to complete sentences, to tick answers true / false, to tick boxes in a multiple choice exercise), you can do this step while you listen. The second time you listen, you can check and correct your answers.
- When you practise doing listening comprehension exercises, listening in stages can be helpful. You can concentrate on particular sections and you will have enough time to take notes (see 3. below). In an exam situation, however, you will only hear the text twice.

3. Taking notes while listening

- Only write down the most important information – you will not have time for everything.
- Take notes in the order you hear the information. Leave space between your notes so that you can add information the second time you listen.
- Use symbols or abbreviations when taking notes, if possible.

Speaking

S30 Giving a presentation

The type of presentation you give can vary from a one-minute presentation on your own to a longer group presentation in which you use presentation software.

1. Getting started

- Choose one aspect of the topic, which you can cover easily in the time you have.
- Think about the audience, what they probably know about the topic and what other aspects they would find interesting.

2. Finding and choosing materials

- Collect information from reliable sources. (→ S35) Try to include interesting, surprising, provocative or funny details to keep your audience interested.
- Make notes about the sources or use bookmarks to create links to the sources.

MK

3. Planning the presentation

When you plan your presentation, you should divide it as follows:

- **Introduction:** Give an outline of your presentation so that everybody knows what to expect. This makes it easier for your audience to follow what you are saying.
- **Main body:** Develop your ideas / arguments. If you are presenting the pros and cons of a topic, you can give a pro followed by a con followed by another pro and so on. Alternatively, you can give all the pros together and all the cons together. If your topic is a problem, present possible solutions one after the other and examine them.
- **Conclusion:** Sum up your points briefly and state the conclusion you have come to. You should also name your sources or show a slide where they are listed.

4. Collecting and organising information

- Support your ideas with background information, visuals and examples.
- Link each section of your presentation. You can use the useful phrases below.
- Repeat and emphasise important ideas.
- Don't write a script. Prepare prompt cards with key words, comments, facts and figures. Put the cards in a logical order and number them.

MK
- You can make the presentation or slide show with a software programme or an online app. Decide which visuals you want to use, e.g. maps, photos or diagrams. Add them to the app or slides. The slides should not be too full. Any visuals and text should be clear enough to read, even from the back of the classroom.

5. Preparing a handout for the audience

- Include a summary of the main points in the presentation, any relevant statistics and visuals and the sources of any material.
- Don't make the handout too long - one page is enough - and it should have the same structure as your presentation. If you use a presentation programme, you can print a number of slides on one page.
- Create a QR code in order to share the handout online.
- If you want to hand out copies of the handout, do this after you finish speaking, not before you start.

6. Preparing yourself (and your group)

- Practise your presentation. Use your prompt cards to help you remember the points.
- Check the time to make sure you stay within the given limits.
- Adverbs of purpose and manner will make your presentation more interesting. (→ G2).
- When you do a group presentation, decide who is going to do the introduction and conclusion, present the main body, answer any questions, look after the technical side of the presentation etc.

7. Doing the presentation

- Greet the audience politely.
- Speak loudly and clearly and not too fast. Use short sentences. Also vary your voice so that it doesn't sound boring.
- Keep your body language positive, e.g. use your hands to stress a point, keep eye-contact with the audience, stand up straight and smile. You shouldn't cross your arms or turn your back to the audience.
- Stress certain words to emphasise key points or pause at the end of an important sentence.
- Use words that you are comfortable with. Don't use new words you don't understand or can't pronounce!

8. At the end of your presentation

Once you've finished your presentation, you could:
- explain which sources you used and say which websites were better than others;
- explain how you decided on the format of your presentation;
- outline any problems you had and how you solved them;
- ask the audience if they have any questions.

Useful phrases

Introduction: Good morning. | Hello everybody. | My name is …, and today I'd like to talk to you about … | My presentation is about … | My topic today is … | As … once said, "…" | Have you ever …? | Today we would like to present / show / explain … | Our project focuses on the following aspects: … | (name) will take you through … | We did a survey / some interviews with … | We discussed … and we decided to …

Main part: Firstly / Secondly / Thirdly | After that/Next … | Finally … | The reason is … | Let me give you an example. | Now / Next let's take a look at … | It's really interesting because … | Another interesting point is … | Here's a new word. It's … in German. | On my poster you can see … | The mind map shows … | I can see you're surprised. | Let's ask ourselves …

Smooth transitions: I'd like to hand over to (name), who will tell you … | (Name) would now like to present the results of our … | As (name) just said …

Conclusion: So, what we've learned today is … | To sum up, … | We hope that our presentation has shown you … | In fact, we are sure that … | Do you have any questions? | Thank you for listening. | We'd like to thank you for your attention. | I've prepared a handout for you.

S31 Taking part in a conversation

Depending on the type of conversation, the other speaker(s) and the topic, you need to use appropriate language and the correct register. For example, when you do an interview for a student exchange programme or talk to the teachers at your partner school, the language you use should be more formal and polite than the language in a conversation with your exchange partner.

The following tips can help you to have a conversation in English:
- If you don't know which register to use, it is better to be more formal / polite, especially with older people you haven't met before.
- Respect is also shown by body language, e.g. try not to stand with your hands in your pockets while talking to someone.
- Listen to the kind of vocabulary the other person is using. If you don't understand a phrase or word (e.g. you might not know Canadian terms such as 'poutine' or 'washroom'), ask politely what it means. If you are living in an exchange family, use the new words to show that they are helping you to learn.
- Try to show cultural awareness when talking with people from other countries. Never talk about sensitive topics (e.g. when talking about Canada, you shouldn't suggest that Canada and the US are the same).

Useful phrases

Polite phrases: please | thank you | you're welcome | don't worry | not at all

Short answers: (instead of just saying yes or no): Yes, I will. | No, I don't.

Polite modals: Could I/you …? | Would you …? | May I …? | I'd like …

Agreeing / Disagreeing: Yes, that's true, but … | I agree, but …

Reacting to a suggestion: I'd love to … | That's a good idea!

Showing interest: Of course. | I see. | Really? | Are you sure? | That's interesting.

Question tags: (good for small talk and to keep conversations going): …, are you? | …, can I? | …, isn't it? | …, shouldn't I?

S32 Having a discussion

Discussions in class can take different forms, from an informal exchange of ideas to more formal situations, e.g. a talk show or a formal debate (see below).

1. Hosting a formal (online) discussion

- Prepare a short introduction in which you give the topic and point out its importance. Don't express your own opinion!
- Prepare prompt cards with key words on the main aspects of the topic. Ask open or provocative questions to keep the discussion going.
- Greet the audience and introduce the participants.
- Keep a list of the people waiting to speak and give everybody a chance to say something.

- Ask participants who have said nothing to speak. If you feel that someone has been speaking for too long, politely interrupt them.
- Take notes on what has been said or ask someone else to do so. If you finish the discussion a few minutes before the end, you can use the notes to sum up the main arguments.

Useful phrases

Introducing the topic: Hello and welcome to our discussion / talk show. | Today we're going to discuss … / present the pros and cons of … / examine the topic: …

Asking speakers to speak: (Name), how do you feel about …? | What do you think about …? | I'd like to call on … who's been waiting for … minutes.

Interrupting / Including speakers: (Name), may I stop you there? | Thank you (name) for that and now let's hear from the other side. | (Name), would you like to make a comment? | Now let's hear from someone else.

Concluding: I'm afraid we've run out of time. | I'd like to use the last few minutes to sum up … / thank our speakers / take questions from the audience.

2. Taking part in a formal discussion
The following tips can help you to take part in a formal discussion:
- Try to remember everything you know about the issue and decide what your opinion is.
- If you have time, note down arguments for both sides of the discussion. Arrange your ideas in a logical order. Support your arguments with examples.
- Speak clearly and keep to the point. Don't repeat what other people have said. Wait until you have a real point. This is much more effective.
- Be polite and don't interrupt other speakers. Disagree with arguments not with people.

3. Having a debate
The following points can help you to have a debate in class:
- Get into two teams: One team is for and one is against a statement (also called the 'motion').
- The chairperson presents the motion to the audience.
- In the first round, six speakers (three from each team) speak for or against the motion. Each speaker gives a speech which is not interrupted.
- Now the debating begins. Based on what was said in the first round, the two teams exchange arguments.
- The audience may ask questions or make comments. To do this, they raise their hands and wait to be called on by the chairperson. At this stage the teams don't reply to the questions.
- One speaker from each team gives a summary of their arguments and answers any questions that the audience has raised.
- The chairperson asks the audience to vote for or against the motion by raising their hands.

Useful phrases

Introducing arguments: I'd like to begin by … | First of all … | Next … | I think … | I believe … | It's important to remember that … | Another point I'd like to make is … | I'd also like to say that … | Finally …

Supporting arguments: If you think about …, then … | A really good example of this is … | I'm sure that we have all heard about …

Disagreeing with others: It's true that …, but … | I agree, but … | I admit that …, but … | But don't forget … | I'm afraid I don't agree with … | Surely you have to admit that … | You might think differently if … | I think it's wrong to say … because …

S33 Preparing for and doing an interview

When you are interviewed for a job or a place on a student exchange programme, the interviewers want to find out more about you and whether you are suitable for the job or exchange programme.

1. Preparation for an interview
The following points will help you to prepare for:

a job interview
- Find out about the company and be prepared to say why you want to work for them.
- Know what is on your CV and be prepared to talk about your education, work experience, skills and interests.
- Look at the criteria in the job advert. Prepare a list of reasons why you have applied for the job and why you are the right person for it.
- Prepare questions that you can ask the interviewer about the company or the job.

an interview for a place on a student exchange programme
- Find out about the exchange programme.
- Know what is on your CV and be prepared to talk about your education and interests.
- Prepare a list of reasons why you want to go abroad and how it will help you in the future, e.g. at school, in your career.
- Look carefully at the criteria for taking part in the programme. Prepare questions that you can ask the interviewer.

2. At the interview
- Stay calm and confident.
- Use positive body language and don't answer questions with just 'yes' or 'no'.
- If you don't understand a question, say so and ask the interviewer to repeat / explain it.

Useful phrases

What the interviewer can say: What makes you want to work in …? | How would you describe your strengths? | What's your biggest weakness? | How would your friends describe you? | What do you know about the exchange programme/Canada? | Why are you interested in an exchange with a school in Canada? | Would you mind being so far from home for … months? | Do you have any questions about …?

What the candidate can say: I'll be leaving school in … | During my time at school, I did work experience with … | I already have some experience in … | I'm a … person. | I have excellent … skills. | I'm quite good at … | I might be less good at … | As you can see from my CV, … | There are a couple of reasons why I'm interested in an exchange. Firstly / Secondly / Thirdly / Finally, … | One thing that really interests me about Canada is … | That's a good / an interesting question. | Let me see … | I've been told I'm good at … | I like to think that … is my biggest strength.

Mediation

S34 Doing mediation exercises

In mediation exercises you convey specific information from a written or spoken text in another language. The result is a summary of the gist of the original text. It is **not** a translation.

1. Getting started

The answers to the following questions can help you to do a mediation exercise:

- Who are you producing the target text for, e.g. a special interest group or an employer?
- What kind of target text should you produce, e.g. an email, a comment or a role play?
- What style of language and register should you use in the target text, e.g. formal or informal language?
- What information do you need to include?
- Which aspects of German, British, American or Canadian culture must you explain?

Tip

Look carefully at the instructions in the exercise.

2. Producing the target text

- If the original text is a written text, use **skimming and scanning** to find key words and phrases, names, numbers, dates, places and words that are often repeated. (→ S1)
- The context, the word family or similar words will help you **to guess new words** in a written text. (→ S2) For a spoken text, body language and pictures can help you.
- If you don't know the exact translation of a word or phrase (e.g. *Bundeskanzler/-in*, *Bundesrat*), use other words to paraphrase it.
- Remember how to deal with grammar topics like gerunds or participle constructions (→ G9) as you can't translate them directly from English into German.
- Be careful with the order of words in your sentences.
- When you have finished writing, check your grammar, spelling and punctuation. (→ S17)

Useful phrases

It's somebody / a person who … | It's something that you use to … | It's a place that / where … | It's the same as … | It's the opposite of …

MK

3. Using a translation tool

You might sometimes like to have a quick translation of a text while doing online research. In this case, you can use an online translation tool. However, you have to be careful that the tool hasn't translated some things incorrectly.

The following criteria can help you to check a translation by a translation tool:

- Does the tool translate phrases word for word or does the translation sound natural?
- Many words have more than one meaning, depending on the context. Does the translation tool find the correct meaning each time?
- Does the style of the translation match the original text type? For example, a legend should not sound like a news report.
- What does the tool do with proper nouns (= the names of people or things)?

Study skills

S35 Doing research

You normally have to do research before you can talk or write about a topic.

1. Looking for information
- Look in books, newspapers and magazines (print or online) in your school library or local library.
- Talk to someone who knows about the subject, e.g. English / American / Canadian exchange students at your school or at your partner school.
- Write to organisations or agencies (e.g. tourist offices, museums, government agencies, non-governmental organisations NGOs and political parties) that might send you brochures, posters or leaflets.

MK **2. Doing online research**
- Use a search engine and enter the topic you are looking for (e.g. 'solar energy projects in Germany'). Be as specific as possible.
- If you are looking for a particular phrase, use inverted commas (e.g. 'Martin Luther King's speeches').
- You can use + or the word 'and' to find two key words together, and use – (minus) when you don't want to include a particular topic.
- If you get too many / the wrong results, try changing the key words.
- If you don't get the results that you are looking for, try a different key word or use the help function of the search engine you are using.
- Use bookmarks to create links to the sources so that you can find them again.

3. Finding information quickly and using it
- Many websites have a search function to find a word or phrase on a page quickly. You can also use Command + F or Control + F.
- Note down important points so that you can sum them up later in your own words. Don't copy complete sentences or the whole article.
- Make a note of the sources you have used so that you can find them again.

4. Checking results
- Ask yourself how reliable the website is. Is it the website of an institution, a government agency, an online newspaper or a museum? Or did a hobby historian with a personal opinion upload the information? When was the information last updated?
- Compare the information you find with at least one other source.
- Find out where any pictures were first published and in which context by doing a reverse image search on a search engine. Are some parts blurry?
- When you find videos, you should check them carefully: Are the transitions between scenes smooth or not? Are people's faces or mouths unclear? In fake videos the light and colours may not match, and the background may be blurry. Also pay attention to the direction that people are looking as well as their eye movements.

S36 Doing project work online and offline in a group

Working on a group project is more complex than doing a presentation by yourself. The results can be presented orally or in a written form.

1. Organising group work

- The group should not be too large (3–5 people).
- Think about how much time you have and decide what you want to do in that time. Then divide the work into tasks and decide who will do what, e.g. task manager, time keeper, secretary, …
- Agree on dates for when each part of the project should be finished.
- Choose a suitable format to present your results, e.g. a five-minute talk or a poster.
- Make rules for working together and decide who is going to make sure that everyone follows them.
- Decide who is going to keep track of dates, make notes at meetings, prepare visuals on a computer and do each part of the oral presentation.

MK

2. Using digital and non-digital tools

Depending on the devices that are available, the following table can help you to structure group work:

part of group work	digital tools	non-digital tools
organising meetings, distributing tasks, setting milestones for when tasks should be done	video conferencing tools / chat apps / checklist apps which remind group members to hand in work / timeline app with milestones	your group arranges a time and place to meet; make a list of tasks, group members who should do them, and deadlines; make a note of dates in a planner
collecting ideas	digital noticeboards / mind mapping tool	use large sheets of paper to write down ideas
doing research	search engines	books / newspapers in your school / local library
writing and editing texts	word processing programmes / collaborative writing tools / storytelling tools; grammar websites; online dictionaries	each part is written by one and checked by another group member
choosing a tool for the presentation	presentation programmes / interactive boards / projectors	transparencies / posters / flip charts
preparing information to give to the audience	communication platforms / QR codes to give access to a document	photocopy a handout

Useful phrases

Alright, we've got two weeks till we have to hand in … | present … | Who wants to …? | Do you think it's realistic to do … by next Thursday? | Let's meet again on … | Would you have time to check …? | Could you print out … handouts?

S37 Working with a dictionary

1. Using a printed dictionary

Both English-English and German-English / English-German dictionaries contain similar information:

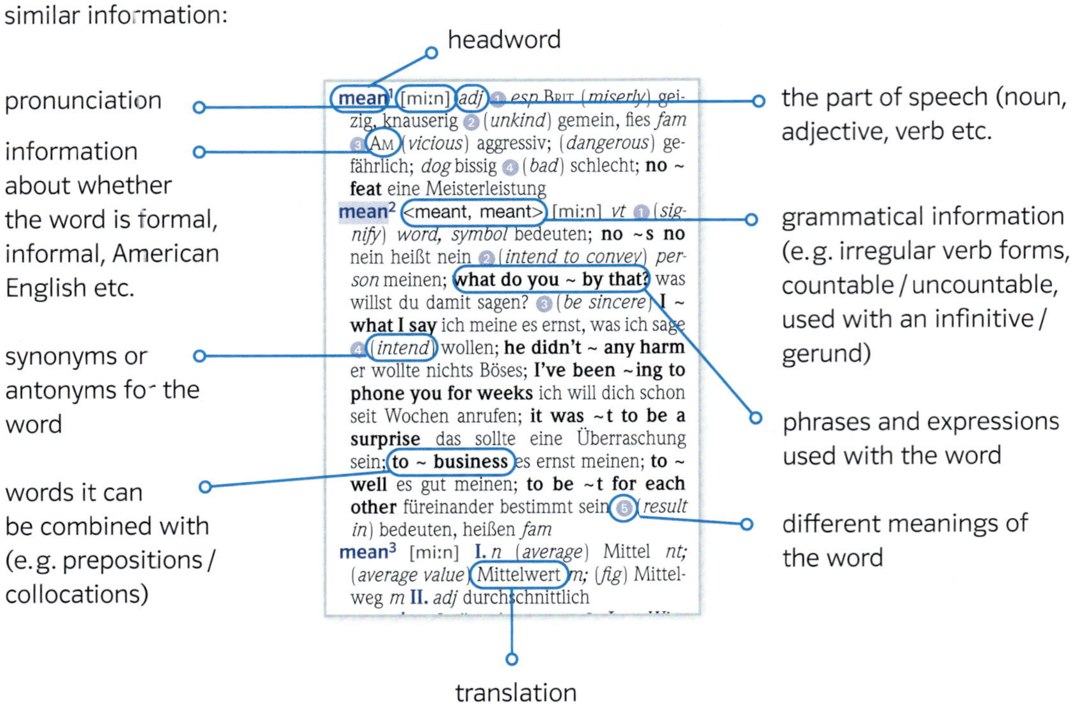

2. Using an online dictionary

An online dictionary can be quicker to use than a printed version as you just type in the unknown word. You can also listen to its pronunciation in British English and American English.

mean
verb [mi:n] PAST TENSE AND PAST PARTICIPLE meant

to have a particular meaning *(used in simple tenses only)*
1 when a word has a particular meaning in that language or in another language
What does this word in the news report mean?
The German word Eis means ice cream in English.
2 when a word represents something
to mean something to somebody
This tradition means a lot to the Inuit people.
'Eco-conscious' shopping means different things to different people.
to mean something by something
What is meant by the term 'activism'?

to want to say something *(used in simple tenses only)*
He didn't mean anything by what he said.

3. Getting a good translation

- Before you look up a word, check what part of speech it is, e.g. a noun, a verb, …
- The first translation may not always be the one you need, e.g. The word nerve means *Nerv*, but it also means *Unverschämtheit, Frechheit* in 'The nerve of that guy!' = *Der Typ da ist unverschämt!*
- Always read the expressions as the word might be part of an expression, e.g. 'to break the law' does not mean … *brechen*; it means *gegen das Gesetz verstoßen*.

Grammar

You can refer to this grammar section for new grammar points, to revise texts or for tests. The grammar section covers the most important grammar points that you have dealt with so far. It is designed to help your self-evaluation, i.e. every section (**G**) includes an explanation of the rule and its exceptions (**!**) followed by one or two exercises. There is one exercise for new grammar points that are also covered in one of the units in this book, and two exercises for grammar points that are reviewed. You can look up the answers to all exercises on pp. 277–285. The chapter (Unit, Text and media smart) and page number next to each heading indicate where it might be particularly useful to practise this grammar point.
The brackets (**〈G〉**) indicate that a grammar point is being reviewed or an additional, non-compulsory grammar point is being presented (this applies to **G14** and **G16** in the state of North Rhine-Westphalia).

Grammatical terms

grammar point		example
Adverbial clauses of time, reason, concession, contrast, comparison, place and direction	**〈G1〉**	**Everywhere** Kim goes, she discovers products that claim to be environmentally friendly.
Adverbial clauses of purpose and manner	**G2**	A lot of farmers use pesticides **in order to** make their cotton fields more profitable.
Modals and their substitute forms: *can / can't, must / needn't, may / mustn't*	**〈G3〉**	The inhabitants of the town **won't be allowed to drive** their cars on Sundays any longer.
More modals: *shall, should, ought to, might, would, used to*	**G4**	What **shall** I **cook** for dinner?
Adjectives and adverbs	**〈G5〉**	The muesli bar has a **great** taste but comes at a **small** price. It fits **comfortably** in your pocket.
Tenses referring to the future: – The will future – The going-to future – The simple present – The present progressive	**〈G6〉**	 I**'ll help** you to set up your new phone. I**'m going to study** Computer Science. The first lesson **starts** at 8 a.m. We**'re meeting** at 3:30 p.m. tomorrow to carry on with our project.
The will-future perfect	**G7**	Let's do the interview at 2 p.m. I**'ll have had** lunch by then.
The will-future progressive	**G8**	Over the coming months, we **will be developing** an exciting VR-based collaborative learning programme.

grammar point		example
Relative clauses: – Defining relative clauses and contact clauses – Participles in place of defining relative clauses – Non-defining relative clauses	〈G9〉	Samuel follows a way of life **which / that** is based on training every day. Each gamer has a badge **stating** their full names. Photo-editing apps, **which** you can download for free, are quite easy to use.
The relative pronoun *which* to comment on the main clause	G10	There are lots of free apps available, **which** is good news if you don't have much money.
Relative clauses with *where* and *when*	G11	I can't remember the date **when** the gaming competition starts.
Tenses referring to the present: – The simple present – The present progressive	〈G12〉	Devices like computers and smartphones **don't work** without electricity. According to recent surveys, the number of parents who track the location of their children **is increasing**.
Tenses referring to the past: – The present perfect simple – The present perfect progressive – The simple past – The past progressive – The past perfect simple	〈G13〉	**Have** you **paid** for the tickets for the flight yet? Leon **has been living** in Toronto for almost eight months now. My parents and I **travelled** more than 600 miles while they were in Canada. Lots of people **were watching** us while we **were doing** the Edge Walk. Leon was shown around on the first day at his new school after he **had met** the principal.
The past perfect progressive	〈G14〉	I went to the doctor's because I **hadn't been feeling** well since I got back from my holiday.
Indirect speech	〈G15〉	Mom: I**'ve** never **been** to Toronto before. → She explained that she **had** never **been** to Toronto before.
Expressing probability: *to be supposed to, to be likely to, to be said to, to be certain to, to happen to*	〈G16〉	The resort town of Whistler **is supposed to be** environmentally friendly.
The passive	〈G17〉	The music **was composed** by Andrew Lloyd Webber.
Conditional sentences	〈G18〉	If you **give** the wrong answer to a CAPTCHA, the system **will generate** a new one and ask you to try again.

⟨G1⟩ Revision: Adverbial clauses of time, reason, concession, contrast, comparison, place and direction

→ Unit 1, p. 17

An adverbial clause is a subordinate clause which is connected to the main clause by a conjunction (often called 'linking word'). You use an adverbial clause to add information to what is said in the main clause. Adverbial clauses help you to create longer sentences and make your text flow better. There are adverbial clauses of time, reason, comparison, concession or contrast and place or direction:

time: after, as *(als)*, as soon as, before, since *(seit, seitdem)*, until/till, when, whenever, while *(während)*	Kim was looking online for clothes with a low ecological footprint **when** she found an interesting article about the environmental impact of the production of T-shirts.
reason: as *(da, weil)*, because, since *(da, weil)*	Nowadays people buy more environmentally friendly clothes **because** they are more easily available in shops or online stores. **As** there are special labels for them, they can also be identified more easily.
comparison: than	She knows that workers in the textile industry in Bangladesh or India have to work longer hours **than** workers in England, for example.
concession or contrast: although, (even) though, whereas, while *(obwohl)*	People buy environmentally friendly clothes **even though** they are sometimes slightly more expensive. **While** customers are paying more money, many people who produce these clothes still have poor working conditions.
place or direction: everywhere, where, wherever	**Everywhere** Kim goes, she discovers products that claim to be environmentally friendly. She often doesn't know **where** she can find reliable information on products.

! You can often place the adverbial clause before or after the main clause. If the adverbial clause comes first, you need to put a comma between the adverbial clause and the main clause, e.g. **While** Kim was looking online for clothes with a low ecological footprint, she noticed an interesting article about the environmental impact of the production of T-shirts.

Test yourself

Exercise 1

Choose the correct conjunction to complete the text from a campaign group's website.

1 (Everywhere/Wherever) we go in this city, we see advertising in different forms. 2 (After/As soon as) we leave our homes, we are told to buy things we didn't know we needed. 3 (Since/While) most people accept this as part of everyday life, many of these endless messages to consume are inviting us to harm the planet. They also damage the atmosphere of the city 4 (because/where) they distract us from the beautiful buildings of our wonderful historic centre. Older residents may remember how the city looked 5 (before/than) it became a big space for advertisers to use. The amount of street advertising has been steadily increasing 6 (since/after) more people started to make their homes in the cities, and now we are seeing more of it 7 (than/when) we have ever before. The situation recently got significantly worse 8 (than/when) most of our bus stops suddenly became multimedia advertising platforms! Ad-free Streets is asking the council not to allow any new street advertising 9 (until/as) this issue has been properly debated. We believe that everyone should live 10 (where/while) they can enjoy an ad-free environment.

Exercise 2

Use conjunctions from the table on p. 197 to complete the post about using an online carbon footprint calculator. Sometimes more than one answer can be correct.

To calculate your footprint properly, I recommend using an online calculator **1** your carbon footprint may actually be higher than you think it is. **2** I was putting in my information, I realised there were lots of things I hadn't given much thought to. For example, I hadn't considered the environmental impact of my shopping **3** I read the questions asked by the calculator. But it's not just the impact of making things. Shopping has a big environmental impact **4** I live too. I buy junk I don't need **5** I know that energy is needed to make things. So my footprint from shopping looks terrible **6** my footprint from travelling seems quite small.

G2 Adverbial clauses of purpose and manner

→ Unit 1, pp. 17–18

You already know various types of adverbial clauses (→ G1). Two more types are adverbial clauses of purpose and manner. While you use an adverbial clause of **purpose** to describe **why** something is happening in the main clause, you use an adverbial clause of **manner** to describe **how** something is happening.

purpose: so, so that, in order to, in case	What can you do with your clothes and other products **so that** they have a longer life cycle? A lot of farmers use pesticides **in order to** make their cotton fields more profitable.
manner: like, as *(wie)*, as if, as though, just as	Many people treat clothes **as though** they are disposable. According to some sources, it looks **as if** at least one-fifth of clothing in the US is never actually worn. Studies found that the last two stages in the life cycle of a T-shirt also have a large ecological footprint **just as** environmentalists had expected.

Test yourself

Exercise 1

a) *Complete these statements on sustainable living with adverbials of manner from the table above. Sometimes more than one answer can be correct.*

1. We can't consume, consume, consume ___ some people in our parents' generation did.
2. Recycle as much of your rubbish ___ you can.
3. Even if you are rich, consume ___ you were poor.
4. Don't say you care about the environment and then behave ___ somebody who doesn't.

b) *Use your own ideas to complete these statements on sustainable living. Use different adverbials of purpose each time.*

1. We should try to live more sustainably …
2. Learn the environmental impacts of different things …
3. Check where things you plan to buy come from …
4. It's a good idea to collect rainwater …

⟨G3⟩ Revision: Modals and their substitute forms

→ Unit 1, p. 21

Can, **can't**, **must**, **mustn't**, **needn't** and **may** are the most common **modals**. You use them to add additional meaning to the **main verb** (= infinitive without to) of a sentence, i.e. ability *(Fähigkeit)*, obligation *(Verpflichtung)*, permission *(Erlaubnis)* or possibility *(Möglichkeit)*. Modals are usually used in the present tense and for all other tenses you need a substitute form. (Note: You can also use the substitute forms in the present tense.)

modal	substitute form	example
(in)ability		
can ↔ cannot / can't *(können ↔ nicht können)*	to be able to	Kim **is able to reduce** her ecological footprint by buying local produce regularly. Her family **weren't able to find** locally grown pears, so they bought apples instead. They **will be able to buy** their food from a zero-waste shop when it opens next month.
(no) obligation		
must ↔ needn't *(müssen ↔ nicht brauchen)*	to have to	Companies **have to do** more to reduce their carbon emissions. He **had to take** his phone to the repair café. They **won't have to use** their car. It's not that far so they can walk.
(no) permission, possibility		
can, could, may ↔ cannot / can't, may not, mustn't *(könnte/n; dürfen ↔ nicht dürfen)*	to be allowed to	Kim **is allowed to use** her dad's car when he doesn't need it himself. In previous years they **weren't allowed to use** the computer room without a teacher. The inhabitants of the town **won't be allowed to drive** their cars on Sundays any longer.

! There are two meanings of **could**:
- You use **could** as the simple past form of **can** to express an ability, e.g.
  Kim **could reduce** her ecological footprint by buying local produce.
  (= was able to reduce)
  Her family **couldn't find** locally grown pears, so they bought apples instead.
  (= wasn't able to find)
- You use **could** instead of **may I / we** in polite questions, e.g.
  Could I **have** three apples, please? (= May I …?)

! There is a slight difference in meaning between **must** and **to have to**:
- You use **must** if the speaker thinks that an action is important, e.g.
  "I **must tidy** my room today."
- You use **to have to** to show that the action is important for someone else (i.e. other than the speaker), e.g.
  Daughter: I **have to tidy** my room every Saturday.
  (because my mum told me to – action is important to her mother, not her)

Test yourself **Exercise 1**

*The owner of a zero-waste shop is giving some information to a new member of staff. Rewrite the sentences using **substitute forms** instead of the **modals**. Be careful with the tenses in number 6!*

1. You **must** wash your hands before touching the food.
2. Customers **can't** touch the food at all.
3. Customers **can** taste something before they buy it, but it **must** be given to them on a plate. They **mustn't** just take things.
4. You **may** chat with customers to make them feel welcome, but only if you **can** do all your other work too.
5. You **needn't** ask me if you need to take a toilet break.
6. Starting next month, we **can't** offer our customers any coffee. This is because we **couldn't** get any more coffee without packaging, so we **couldn't** say it's zero waste.

Exercise 2

a) *Partner A completes this comment on the article on p. 20 with modals. Partner B completes this comment with substitute forms.*

We **1** remember that Overshoot Day refers to the date for the entire world. You **2** be an environmental expert to realise that the date is different in different countries. I think it's a pity that the writer **3** find enough space to include that point in the article. I believe that very soon we **4** agree on strict environmental rules for every country. However, I don't think we **5** agree on those rules until we know what works for each country. We simply can't say that every country **6** follow the same rules. In the future rich countries with higher ecological footprints **7** do much more to improve their impact on the planet while poor countries with much lower ecological footprints **8** continue developing their economies.

b) *Exchange your versions of the comment and correct them.*

G4 More modals

→ Unit 1, pp. 21–22

You already know various modals and their meanings (→ G3). Here are some more:

a) **should and ought to *(sollen)***

	modal	example
To ask for instruction or advice you use …	shall (I / we) should	**Shall** we **have** lasagne tonight? What **shall** I **cook** for dinner? What **should** he / she / they **do**?
To express an obligation you use …	should	I **should work** on my presentation after dinner.
To express advice, an opinion / criticism or an expectation for the future you use …	should ought to	I think we **should / ought to do** more to protect the environment. That **shouldn't / ought not to be** difficult to arrange.

❗ **Shall / shan't (= shall not)** is sometimes used for talking about the future instead of 'I/we will' or 'I/we won't'. However, it sounds very formal, e.g.
I **shan't** be able to attend the meeting.
We **shall** inform you of our decision next week.

In the past **shall** and **shan't** were more widely used. You can still find them in books (e.g. in novels dating back to the 18th and 19th centuries), expressions, sayings, quotations and legal English, e.g.
Somebody who **shall** remain nameless …
As you sow, so **shall** you reap.
The vendor **shall** supply documentary evidence of …

b) **might and might not *(vielleicht, eventuell, möglicherweise, unter Umständen)***

You use **might** and **might not (= mightn't)** …

	example
– to express a slight possibility in the future.	After my A-levels I **might spend** a year working abroad. The government **might introduce** stricter laws later on this year.
– to ask for permission (formal, not used very often).	**Might** I **ask** you for your phone number? – Yes. It's 0123 4567889.
– to express advice or to make a polite and less direct suggestion.	Server: You **might like** to try our meal of the day. (instead of: Would you like to try …?)

❗ **Might** is also used as the past form of **may** in indirect speech, e.g.
"That **may be** a problem," said Nora. → Nora said that it **might be** a problem.

❗ Often **might have + past participle** is used to express disapproval or criticism of an action in the past, e.g. You **might have told** me you were going to be late.

c) **would and would not *(würden)***

You use **would** and **would not (= wouldn't)** …

	example
– to express a polite and formal request.	**Would** you **make** me a couple of sandwiches for lunch? (instead of: Will you make …?)
– to express an imagined situation in a conditional sentence type 2.	If we went to London by plane, we **would produce** a lot of carbon emissions.
– to express frequent actions in the past (often used in stories).	When I was young, we **would travel** to Scotland by car every summer. When my grandfather was a child, he **would help** his dad on the farm almost every day.
– to add emphasis or in a formal context.	My parents **would not approve** of the kind of stunts that some activists do. (instead of: My parents don't …)
– to talk about the future in the past.	I thought it **would rain**, so I brought my umbrella.

❗ **Would** is also used as the past form of **will** in indirect speech:
"That **will be** a problem," said Joanna. → Joanna said that it **would be** a problem.
"I'**ll pay** for the ice cream," said Jack. → He said that he **would pay** for the ice cream.

❗ To make statements sound less direct you can also use **would** with verbs such as …

to advise	I'**d advise** you to use public transport more often.
to imagine	I've never tried to be vegetarian, but I'**d imagine** it's difficult to stop eating meat.
to recommend	I'**d recommend** that you correct and rewrite the letter. (formal)
to say	I'**d say** there is a lot more we can do to save electricity.
to suggest	We'**d suggest** that you take this route. It's much shorter. (formal)
to think	I've heard that restaurant is really popular. I'**d think** you would need to call ahead and book a table.

d) used to *(früher, damals)*

You use **used to / didn't use to + infinitive** to talk about …

	example
– an action in the past that no longer happens now or a state / situation in the past that is no longer true.	Emma **used to buy** new T-shirts every month when she was younger. They **didn't use to have** good working conditions.

❗ **Used to** can only be used in the simple past, e.g.
Emma **used to buy** new T-shirts every month when she was younger.
= Emma **bought** new T-shirts every month when she was younger.

Test yourself **Exercise 1**

Complete the conversation between a member of the student council and the head chef of the school cafeteria with ***modals*** *from sections a), b) and c). Sometimes more than one answer can be correct.*

Student: 1 I speak to you for a moment?
Chef: Sure. You said in your email that you 2 come today, so I was half-expecting you. What 3 you like to discuss?
Student: We think that the cafeteria 4 offer more than one vegan option each day. Vegans 5 have a choice just like everyone else. At my last school, the cafeteria 6 usually offer at least two vegan dishes. You agreed that you 7 do that last term and we thought the menu 8 change, but it hasn't happened yet.
Chef: Our worry was that there 9 be enough demand for them. We thought that if we produced more vegan dishes, there 10 be enough vegan customers to buy them.
Student: I 11 suggest making vegan dishes which are so tasty that everyone wants to eat them, not just vegans.
Chef: That's a fair point. 12 you give me a few days to think about it?
Student: Of course. 13 we meet again at this time on Friday next week?
Chef: That 14 be a problem for me, but I'll check my diary to be sure.

Exercise 2

An elderly man remembers supermarkets in the 1970s. Complete what he says with ***used to / didn't use to*** *and the verbs below.*

to stock | to be | to throw away | to use | to sell | to offer

I think supermarkets back then **1** a bit more environmentally friendly. I'm sure they **2** as much food packaging as they do now. They **3** more food by weight and they **4** so many different options. For example, my local supermarket **5** three or four types of yoghurt, not 30 or 40. I'd imagine they **6** a lot less food than they do today.

〈G5〉 Revision: Adjectives and adverbs

→ Text and media smart 1, p. 40

You use **adjectives** to give more information about a noun or pronoun, i.e. adjectives tell the readers or listeners what people or things are like. You use adverbs to refer to a verb, i.e. **adverbs** describe how you do something or how something happens.

adjective	adverb
The muesli bar has a **great** taste but comes at a **small** price.	The bar fits **comfortably** in your pocket.
It is **healthy**.	You should chew the bar **slowly** to enjoy its taste.

! You also use **adjectives** after …

	example
– verbs describing the state or quality of a noun: to be, to keep, to remain, to seem, to stay.	A power bank can **be** **useful**.
– verbs referring to a future state (*werden*): to become, to get, to go, to grow, to turn.	By using our electric toothbrush, your teeth will **turn** **white** again.
– verbs of perception: to feel, to look, to smell, to sound, to taste.	The orange juice **smells** **delicious**.
– certain verbs used with an object + adjective: to call, to find, to keep, to like, to make, to see.	This toothpaste will **keep** your breath **fresh** all day.

a) **Comparison of adjectives**

	adjective	comparative	superlative	spelling rule
	adjectives of one syllable or adjectives of two syllables ending in -y			
comparison with -er/-est	small	smaller	the smallest	
	big	bigger	the biggest	end consonant doubles after a short vowel
	nice	nicer	the nicest	no silent -e
	easy	easier	the easiest	-y turns to i if the adjective ends with a consonant + -y (except: shy)
	healthy	healthier	the healthiest	
	adjectives of two or more syllables			
comparison with more / most	attractive	more attractive	the most attractive	
	delicious	more delicious	the most delicious	
	useful	more useful	the most useful	

❗ With **adjectives of two syllables ending in -le**, **-ow** or **-er** and some others (quiet, polite, stupid etc.) two forms are possible:
clever → cleverer / the cleverest; more clever / the most clever
gentle → gentler / the gentlest; more gentle / the most gentle
narrow → narrower / the narrowest; more narrow / the most narrow
polite → politer / the politest; more polite / the most polite

❗ **Irregular forms:**
bad - worse - the worst | good - better - the best |
far - further / the farther - furthest / the farthest

- You use the **comparative** form to describe the results of change or how something is in the process of changing, e.g.
  Your teeth will be **whiter** (than before).
  Batteries are getting **more efficient**.
- You use the **superlative** form to show that one thing or person in a group has got more or less of a quality than all the others in the same group, e.g.
  Compared to going by car and flying, walking has the **lowest** carbon emissions.
- You use the phrase **as + adjective + as** to express that people, animals or things are the same with regard to a particular quality, e.g.
  The expensive toothbrush is **as good as** the cheap toothbrush.
- You use the phrase **not as + adjective + as** or **comparative + than** to express that people, animals or things aren't the same with regard to a particular quality, e.g.
  A tomato is**n't as sweet as** an apple.
  An apple is **sweeter than** a tomato.

❗ Don't mix up **than** *(als)*, **then** *(dann)* and **when** *(als, wenn)*, e.g.
It was much more expensive **than** I had expected.
He bought a new T-shirt, **then** another and **then** another.
I loved watching commercials **when** I was a kid.
Call me **when** you've finished.

b) How to make an adverb

To make an adverb you use the adjective + **-ly** or **-ally**:

	example
– adjective + -ly:	Some storylines in commercials aren't understood **easily**.
– adjective ending in -ic + -ally:	Some films end **dramatically**.

❗ **Spelling rule:**
- adjectives ending in -y: angr**y** → angr**i**ly; happ**y** → happ**i**ly; except for: shy → shyly
- adjectives ending in -le: comfortab**le** → comfortably; terrib**le** → terribly

❗ **Good or well:**
Good is an **adjective** and **well** is the **adverb**, e.g.
- This storyline is **good**.
- It was written **well**.

Well can also be used as an **adjective** to talk about health, e.g.
If you don't feel **well**, try to eat more fruit and vegetables.

❗ Some adjectives and adverbs have **the same form**:
fast → fast, e.g. a **fast** runner; to run **fast**
early → early, e.g. an **early** night; to get up **early**
late → late, e.g. a **late** night; to get up **late**

❗ **Two different adverb forms:**
hard → hard *(schwer, schwierig)* / hardly *(kaum)*, e.g. to work **hard**; he **hardly** works
late → late *(spät)* / lately *(in letzter Zeit)*, e.g. to arrive **late**; I haven't been to London **lately**

c) Comparison of adverbs

	adverb	comparative	superlative
	adverbs that have the same form as the adjective		
comparison with -er/-est	(to drive) fast	fast**er**	(the) fast**est**
	(to sleep) late	lat**er**	(the) lat**est**
	(to jump) high	high**er**	(the) high**est**
	(to work) hard	hard**er**	(the) hard**est**
	(to fly) low	low**er**	(the) low**est**

	adverbs ending in -y or -ally		
comparison with more / most	(to change) quickly	**more** quickly	(the) **most** quickly
	(to come) easily	**more** easily	(the) **most** easily
	(to talk) quietly	**more** quietly	(the) **most** quietly
	(to end) dramatically	**more** dramatically	(the) **most** dramatically

Irregular forms:

(to drive) badly – worse – (the) worst
(to get up) early – earlier – (the) earliest
(to go) far – further / farther – (the) furthest / farthest
(to drink) little – less – (the) least
(to eat) much – more – (the) most
(to swim) well – better – (the) best

- To show similarity, you use **as + adverb + as**, e.g.
  The electric car works **as well as** a traditional car.
- To show difference, you use **not as + adverb + as** or the **comparative + than**, e.g.
  The engine isn't running **as quietly as** it should.
  Our new model goes from 0 to 100 **faster than / more quickly than** other models.

Test yourself

Exercise 1

Read the draft version of an advertisement for a payment card and correct the mistakes.

One of the better things about growing up is starting to take control of your money. **TEENpay** is the nation's popularest payment card for teenagers who want to pay for things quick and easyly and find carrying cash inconveniently. Applying for a card is the most simple thing you can imagine!
Just go online, open an account and get an adult to send some money to it electronicly. We'll send you your newly card, and when it arrives, you'll be able to use it immediatally. Of course, you can top up your account as frequent as you like. Happy shopping!

Exercise 2

Complete a customer review of the Rototronic AquaVibes electric toothbrush (see p. 40). Think carefully whether you need the adjective, the adverb or a comparative or superlative form.

★☆☆☆☆ **Very disappointing, not as advertised!**
The advert claimed it was [1] (good) electric toothbrush you could buy for under £30. I can't say it's [2] (bad) because I haven't tried all the others, but I'm sure there are much [3] (effective) ones available for the price. Firstly, I thought the brush head would be [4] (big). This one has [5] (tiny) head I've ever seen. It is [6] (not good) my old electric toothbrush and it doesn't clean my teeth [7] (good) a normal toothbrush either. The advert said it was '[8] (medical) tested', but of course that means nothing – maybe the result of the test was that it's [9] (useless) electric toothbrush ever made! I don't know if that was a [10] (lazy)-written ad copy or [11] (intentional) misleading. There's only one way in which it's [12] (good) my old electric toothbrush. It charges [13] (fast) and it lasts [14] (long) between charges. Having said that, after charging it feels [15] (significant) [16] (hot) than I'd expect. I hope it is [17] (not dangerous) those [18] (terrible)-designed gadgets you read about that explode in people's hands! I'd give it zero stars if I could.

〈G6〉 Revision: Tenses referring to the future

→ Unit 2, p. 53

a) The will future

You use the **will future** (will + infinitive) …

	example
– to say that something is certain to happen in the future. The speaker cannot influence these states or events, e.g. the weather.	The students are going to be homeschooled tomorrow as the Southwest of Britain **will see** severe storms.
– to express that you think something might happen. Often with: verbs like to hope, to expect, to be sure and adverbs like probably, perhaps, possibly	I'm sure the school **will buy** some new equipment before the start of the new term. Our teachers **will** probably **get** some training on how to use this equipment in the classroom.
– for spontaneous decisions, promises and general predictions.	I**'ll call** you later today to talk about the school dance.
– to ask for help or to offer help without having planned to do this before.	**Will** you **have** a look at my phone, please? It doesn't seem to be working. – OK, I**'ll help** you in a minute. / I**'ll have** a look at it in a minute.

b) The going-to future

You use the **going-to future** (am / is / are + going to + infinitive) …

	example
– to talk about future plans and intentions of the speaker, listener or writer.	I**'m going to study** Computer Science.
– to talk about a strong possibility of an event happening in the future. There are clear signs that indicate this.	Due to a technical problem, there **isn't going to be** any connection to the internet today.

c) The simple present

You use the **simple present** (infinitive; third person singular: infinitive + -es / -s) …

	example
– to talk about events that are officially fixed, e.g. in timetables, programmes and schedules. Often with: verbs like to arrive, to begin, to depart, to leave, to start, to end	The first lesson **starts** at 8:00. The lunch break **begins** at 12:30 and **ends** at 1:15. I've just checked and the 6:30 train from London **doesn't arrive** in Coventry until 7:50.

d) The present progressive

You use the **present progressive** (am / is / are + present participle) …

	example
– to talk about (personal) arrangements you have made for the future. Often with: verbs of movement and time phrases like tomorrow, this weekend, on Saturday, next week	We**'re meeting** at 3:30 p.m. tomorrow to carry on with our project.

Test yourself **Exercise 1**

*The head teacher is talking about a new school database during assembly. Complete the conversation with forms of **will** and **be going to**. In some instances you have to be careful about the word order.*

Head teacher: As I think you all know, next term we **1** (future plan) launch our new student database. It **2** (general prediction) be very useful for planning lessons and monitoring students' individual progress. Any questions?

Student 1: How **3** (certain to happen) the system protect students' data?

Head teacher: I don't know exactly. I'm sure it **4** (general prediction) be insecure in any way, but I **5** (spontaneous offer) ask and get back to you. **6** (ask for help) you give me a couple of days to find out? I can tell you that we **7** (future intention) do everything we can to protect your data.

Student 2: I **8** (future possibility) probably want to see my record. **9** (future plan) let students and parents be able to do that?

Head teacher: Yes, they **10** (future plan) have access. The feedback we've had so far suggests that many students and parents **11** (signs indicate this) find it very useful.

Exercise 2

Use the notes for a technology workshop to write a post for the school website.
*Use the **simple present** and the **present progressive**.*

- *next Saturday – the student council – offer a one-day technology workshop*
- *start: 10 a.m. – finish: around 4 p.m.*
- *workshop – start with overview of the latest tech introduced in school recently*
- *continue with chance to try some new gadgets*
- *lunch break – start at 1 p.m. at the latest*
- *Jack Manson (Year 10) – bring his famous vegetable curry sandwiches – sell them for 50p each*
- *Ms Gledhill – the computer science teacher – give short talk – at the end of this workshop*

G7 The will-future perfect

→ Unit 2, p. 53

You use the **will-future perfect** (will have + past participle) …

	example
– to express that an action or event will have been completed at a given point in the future. Often with: by tomorrow, by then, by 2060, by the time, in 50 years' time, when my parents come back	The trial programme to test our new approach to learning **will have finished** by the end of the year.

Test yourself **Exercise 1**

Tarun is 16 and very ambitious. He wants to start a tech company. Read his notes for his future plans. For each note, write a sentence with the ***will-future perfect****.*

- *start my first tech company – before I finish university*
- *make my first million – by the time I'm 25*
- *at that point – millions of people – buy my gadgets*
- *when I'm in my fifties – become a billionaire*
- *by then – I stop working – retire to my private island*
- *marry my girlfriend?*
- *how many (if any) children I have?*

G8 The will-future progressive

→ Unit 2, p. 53

You use the **will-future progressive** (will be + present participle) …

	example
– to describe an action in progress at a certain time in the future. Often with: this time next week / month / year, over the coming days / weeks / months / years	Over the coming months, we **will be developing** an exciting VR-based collaborative learning programme.
– to describe a future action that overlaps with a shorter action or time.	When we open the first school of this type in September, we **will be offering** a more personalised approach to education.
– to say that something will happen repeatedly in the future.	Students **will be rehearsing** for the school play on Tuesday afternoons from the beginning of October.

Test yourself **Exercise 1**

Match the words and phrases from the three different columns and write sentences that include the ***will-future progressive*** *to predict the future of technology. Many different answers are possible. Perhaps add your own predictions too.*

a few years from now in 20 years' time when I next buy a new one by 2050 when I start work at the next big tech fair	nobody / everybody only a few people smartphones tech companies VR systems artificial intelligence	still use big desktop computers talk to us as if it was a real person launch their latest gadgets (not / still) use social media (still) get better and better do what seems impossible today

〈G9〉 Revision: Relative clauses

→ Unit 2, p. 56

a) Defining relative clauses and contact clauses

You use defining relative clauses to **give necessary information**. Without this information the meaning of the main clause would be unclear. You use the relative pronoun …

	example
– who or that for people. (Note: The object form whom is used in formal style in BE. It is commonly used in AE.)	Rankin's goal during the photo project wasn't to blame the people **who / that** had created editing apps. The people **who / that / whom** Rankin used in the project didn't usually edit their own photos.
– which or that for things or animals if not personalised.	Many teenagers use the same social media **which / that** their friends use.
– whose to express what belongs to somebody.	People **whose** goal is to become a well-known influencer will have to work very hard.

❗ **No comma** is used between the defining relative clause and the noun (in the main clause) it refers to.

❗ In defining relative clauses, you can leave out the **relative pronoun** if it's the object of the relative clause (i.e. the relative pronoun is followed by a **subject**), which then becomes a contact clause, e.g. The people (**who / that / whom**) **we** interviewed were all using filters.

b) Participles in place of defining relative clauses

You can replace a defining relative clause with a participle construction. You use …

	example
– the present participle to replace a defining relative clause with a verb form in the active voice. It can replace the simple form (a badge which states …) or the progressive form (girls who are playing …).	In a competition each player has a badge **which states** their gaming names. → … a badge **stating** their gaming names. The girls **who are playing** in the final match started doing e-sports at the age of 11. → The girls **playing** in the final match …

	example
– the past participle to replace a defining relative clause with a verb form in the passive voice.	I read the job description **which** was included in the advertisement very carefully. → I read the job description **included** in the advertisement very carefully.

c) **Non-defining relative clauses**

You use non-defining relative clauses to **add extra information** about a person or thing. This makes the sentence more interesting. But the main clause is complete and understandable without the non-defining relative clause. You use the relative pronoun …

	example
– who for people. (Note: The object form whom is used in formal style in BE. It is commonly used in AE.)	Social media influencers, **who** are mostly in their teens and twenties, can earn a lot of money. Mr Shirky, **whom** you may have seen on the internet, is an expert on the social effects of technology.
– which for things.	Rankin explored photo editing apps in a recent photo series, **which** is titled 'Selfie Harm.'
– whose to express what belongs to somebody.	The photographer, **whose** photography subjects have included celebrities, took portraits of 15 individuals wearing minimal make-up.

! **Never** use the relative pronoun **that** in non-defining relative clauses.

! **There is a comma** before the relative pronoun to separate the main clause from the relative clause. When speaking, you pause at the comma.

Test yourself **Exercise 1**

a) *Complete part of an article about changing standards of beauty. Make the meaning of the sentences clear by joining them using a* ***defining relative clause****.*

1. In the past it was often monarchs. They were the most important influencers.
2. Portraits of them were often copied and distributed around the country. They were painted at the time.
3. Many of these portraits showed them with looks. They can seem strange to us today.
4. However, many people tried to copy the monarch's appearance. They lived at the time.
5. Today pop stars and actors are the people. Their appearance is most likely to influence how others want to look.
6. Many celebrities have a 'personal stylist'. They work with them before they are seen in public.
7. Celebrities may ask the stylist to give them an innovative look. They want to be noticed.

Queen Elizabeth I reigned 1558–1603

b) *Replace the defining relative clause with a participle construction* ***where possible****.*

Exercise 2

Continue the article by joining the sentences so they have a ***non-defining relative clause****.*

1. Thanks to stylists, photos of celebrities often don't show their everyday appearance. They may also have been heavily retouched.
2. These photos may be seen by millions of people. Those people then share them with others on the internet.
3. A look created by a stylist can influence a very large number of people. It may be very different from the everyday appearance of the celebrity.
4. Perhaps one day these photos of celebrities will seem as strange as portraits of kings and queens from past centuries do to us today. They will probably exist electronically far into the future.

Rihanna
international celebrity,
c. 2005 –

G10 The relative pronoun *which* to comment on the main clause

→ Unit 2, p. 56

You already know the relative pronoun **which**. It can be used in defining and non-defining relative clauses to refer back to a noun in the main clause (→ G9). You can also use …

	example
– a non-defining relative clause with which *(was)* to comment on the main clause. It then refers to the entire main clause.	I recently tried VR for the first time, **which was an amazing experience.** Technology keeps changing, **which can make it difficult to keep up.** There are lots of free apps available, **which is good news if you don't have much money.**

There is a comma to separate the main clause from the relative clause. When speaking, you pause at the comma.

Test yourself

Exercise 1

Match each main clause with a suitable comment. Then write sentences with ***which*** *to join them.*

1. Nowadays, standards of beauty are mostly defined by celebrities, the fashion industry and internet influencers.
2. We're told that famous actors, singers, footballers etc. are the most successful people in the world.
3. Many internet video channels focus on fashion and beauty.
4. It may be that everybody in a social group is watching the same influencers' channels.
5. Social media can have a huge impact on the lives of its users.

a) This can put a lot of pressure on people in that group to look the same.
b) This raises questions about whether there should be more checks and regulations.
c) It's very different to how things were in the past.
d) It means new ideas can instantly reach a very large international audience.
e) This, of course, makes people want to copy their favourite celebrity's appearance.

G11 Relative clauses with where and when

→ Unit 2, p. 57

You already know the relative pronouns **who**, **which**, **that** and **whose** (→ G9, G10).
Two more relative pronouns are **where** and **when**. You can use them in defining and non-defining relative clauses. If a relative clause refers …

	example
– to a place, you can use where instead of in which / at which.	That was the e-gaming camp **where** we stayed last summer. (= … **at which** we stayed last summer.) Photo editing has become an open secret in the world of social media, **where** image is everything. (= …, **in which** image is everything.)
– to a period in time, you can use when instead of in which / on which / at which.	I can't remember the date **when** the e-gaming competition starts. (= … the date **on which** the e-gaming competition starts.) Summer is the time **when** most gaming tournaments are held. (= … the time **in which** most gaming tournaments are held.)

! If you use expressions like **the year …**, **the day …** or **the time …**, you can use **when** or **that** or **leave out the relative pronoun**. e.g.
Monday is **the day (when)** we usually meet for lunch.
I can't remember **the year (that)** they moved the school to a new location.

Test yourself **Exercise 1**

*Complete the sentences so they use a relative clause. Write two versions for each: one with **in / on / at which** and one with **where / when**.*

1. There has probably never been a time ___ people did not think about their appearance.
2. Norway is one country ___ they have laws to fight unrealistic beauty standards.
3. Schools are one place ___ there can be a lot of peer pressure.
4. The 2010s was the decade ___ social media really became part of everyday life.
5. There are social media platforms ___ some people spend a very significant amount of their time.

⟨G12⟩ Revision: Tenses referring to the present

→ Text and media smart 2, p. 74

a) The simple present

You use the **simple present** (infinitive, third person / singular: infinitive + -es / -s) …

	example
– to express facts.	40% of UK parents and guardians **use** location-tracking apps daily.
– to express what people accept as true.	Devices like computers and smartphones **don't work** without electricity.

	example
– to talk about things that happen regularly or about permanent states. Often used with: always, often, never, regularly, sometimes, usually	A summary of a news report **is** usually 1/3 of the original text and **leaves out** details, personal opinions and interpretations.
– to describe a series of actions or events that happen one after another. It is often used in sports commentaries, in comments on texts and in summaries.	Tim Lewis **begins** his article by referring to a survey on apps used by parents. He **goes on** to quote an expert. In the next part he **explains** … He **concludes** the article by pointing out that …

b) **The present progressive**

You use the **present progressive** (am / is / are + present participle) …

	example
– to describe activities that are happening at the moment. Often used with: at the moment, just, just now, right now	The girl **is sitting** in front of the computer and **playing** a computer game. She **is wearing** headphones.
– to express gradual developments.	According to recent surveys, the number of parents who track the location of their children **is increasing**.

Test yourself **Exercise 1**

Complete the transcript of a radio news report by putting in the ***simple present*** *or the* ***present progressive*** *form of the verb in brackets.*

Reporter: I **1** (to stand) near London's Houses of Parliament and the noise you can hear **2** (to come) from a protest. A group of around 500 people **3** (to chant) the slogan 'No to spy cameras!', which **4** (to refer) to the security cameras in our streets. With me is Ethan Davies, one of the protest organisers. Tell me, why exactly **5** (you / to protest)?

Protester: Every time we **6** (to leave) our homes, cameras **7** (to photograph and film) us without our permission. The UK **8** (currently / to have) around 5 million surveillance cameras, and the number **9** (still / to rise). Recent research **10** (to suggest) that a person who **11** (to spend) an active day in a city centre is caught on camera up to 300 times. No doubt several surveillance cameras **12** (to film) us right now. My group **13** (to call) for a law to limit the number of cameras in our streets.

Reporter: Arguments for these cameras **14** (usually / to start) with the point that they **15** (to help) to protect us from crime. **16** (you / to disagree) with that?

Protester: I **17** (to accept) that it is true in some cases, but companies and other organisations **18** (to put) more and more cameras in our streets not to protect us but to collect information about us. It **19** (to get) to the point where it feels like somebody **20** (to watch) us all the time.

Exercise 2

Look at the photo from the website of a radio station which goes with the news report in ex. 1. Use the ***simple present*** *or the* ***present progressive*** *forms of the verbs and verb phrases below to write a description.*

to face away from | to look towards | to give the impression that | to include | (not) to try to stop | to show | to stand

⟨G13⟩ Revision: Tenses referring to the past

→ Unit 3, pp. 89–90

a) Present perfect simple

You use the **present perfect simple** (has / have + past participle) …

	example
– to stress the result of an activity or event. The activity itself happened in the past, but the result is still relevant in the present. Often with: already, just, ever, so far, twice, three times	Leon **has taken** so many photos with his smartphone that he must save some of them to the cloud.
– for an activity or event that began in the past and has continued until now. Often with: for, since	He **hasn't seen** his parents for eight months.
– to express that something hasn't happened yet or to ask whether something has taken place yet. Often with: never, (not) yet	They are really excited about going to Canada because they **have never been** there before. **Have** you **paid** for the tickets yet?

❗ You use **for with a period of time** (e.g. for hours, for years, for a long time) and **since with a point in time** (e.g. since 1996, since yesterday, since she got up this morning).

❗
- **Stative verbs** (to be, to believe, to know, to see etc.) are normally used in the present perfect simple, e.g.
  Leon's family **has** always **loved** active holidays.
- **Dynamic verbs** (to live, to play, to work etc.) are used in the present perfect progressive, e.g.
  Leon's dad **has been trying** to speak French since they arrived in Montreal.

b) **The present perfect progressive**

You use the **present perfect progressive** (have / has + been + present participle) …

	example
– to describe an activity which began in the past, is still happening in the present and may continue in the future. The duration and continuation of an activity are stressed.	Leon **has been enjoying** life in Toronto.
– to say how long an action has lasted. Often with: all week / day / year, since, for	Leon **has been living** in Toronto for almost eight months now. He **has been planning** things all week that he can do with his parents.
– to express that an action is repeated.	He **has been taking** kayaking lessons every second weekend this summer.

c) **The simple past**

You use the **simple past** (irregular simple past form or infinitive + -ed for regular verbs) …

	example
– to describe states, events or activities that were completed in the past and are now over. Often with: last week / month / year, two days / weeks / years ago, yesterday, in 2021, when	My parents and I **travelled** more than 600 miles while they were in Canada.
– to describe a series of actions or events. This makes it the basic tense in narrative texts (stories, novels) and in reports about past events.	We **spent** the first day sightseeing in Toronto and **visited** the CN Tower. On the second day …

d) **The past progressive**

You use the **past progressive** (was / were + present participle) …

	example
– to describe an activity or event that was in progress at a certain time in the past. It is often used to describe something that was still going on when something new happened. In this case you use the past progressive for the background action and the simple past for the new action or event. Often with: while	While I **was taking** a photo of the falls, a wave hit me.

	example
– to talk about several activities that were happening at the same time in the past.	Lots of people **were watching** us while we **were doing** the Edge Walk.
– to describe gradual developments.	It **was getting** dark by the time Leon and his parents returned from their bike trip around Ottawa.

e) The past perfect simple

You use the **past perfect simple** (had + past participle) …

	example
– to describe an activity or event that happened before another activity or event in the past. The past perfect simple is often used with the simple past (active or passive). In this case the simple past describes what happened at a certain time in the past and the past perfect simple states what happened before that time. Often with: after, before, by the end of …, ever, never, still, just, (not) yet	The host family **had exchanged** emails with Leon before he **came** to stay. Leon **was shown** around on the first day at his new school after he **had met** the principal. He still **hadn't seen** all of the school by the end of his first week.

Test yourself **Exercise 1**

Peyton is Leon's host sister in Canada. Read her email to a friend and put in the most suitable form of the verb in brackets: ***simple past, past progressive, present perfect simple*** *or* ***present perfect progressive****.*

Hi Jo!
Hope you're OK. You know that Leon **1** (to stay) with us for a while now. When he **2** (to arrive), he was a little shy, but he **3** (to become) a lot more relaxed since then. He still **4** (not to tell) us a huge amount about his life back in Germany, though. We'll probably find out more soon because his parents **5** (to come) to visit him here. Their plane **6** (to land) early this morning while I **7** (still/to have) breakfast. They **8** (already/to make) it to downtown Toronto. They **9** (to invite) me to go with them, but I thought they **10** (just/to be) polite and so I **11** (not to accept). Since then, though, I **12** (to think) that maybe I **13** (to make) a mistake. Leon (just/to send) **14** me photos from where they **15** (to go) this morning. Seems like they **16** (to do) lots of sightseeing all morning. It looks as though they're having an amazing time.
Bye for now!
Peyton

Exercise 2

Choose the ***present perfect simple*** *or the* ***past perfect simple*** *to complete Peyton's next email to her friend.*

Hi Jo!
Leon and his parents are back from their trip around Eastern Canada. 1 (We've/We'd) just had dinner with them, and they told us all about their trip. They 2 (haven't/hadn't) expected to enjoy Niagara Falls as much as they did – 3 (they've/they'd) never seen anything like it! Now they're feeling that they 4 (haven't/hadn't) seen enough of Canada's natural landscapes, and so 5 (they've/they'd) decided to stay a bit longer. Luckily, 6 (they've/they'd) booked the kind of flight you can change quite easily, and Leon's mom 7 (has/had) moved the return flight forward to next Sunday. Of course, school 8 (has/had) started again now. Before dinner, Leon 9 (has/had) asked me about taking a few days off school. I told him it doesn't work like that here, but he 10 (has/had) decided to do it anyway. He 11 (hasn't/hadn't) planned to miss school, but he doesn't want his parents to travel alone. I hope he doesn't get in trouble!
Looking forward to seeing you next week.
P.

⟨G14⟩ The past perfect progressive

→ Unit 3, pp. 89–90

You use the **past perfect progressive** (had been + present participle) …

	example
– for actions that were already in progress and ended at or just before a point in the past.	Mum **had been sleeping** for some time on the plane when she was woken up by a strange noise.
– to express that an activity or event was in progress before it was interrupted by another activity or event. Often with: for, since	They **had been walking** around Toronto since 10 o'clock when they discovered a police museum.

Test yourself

Exercise 1

Complete part of a travel blog about a visit to Toronto by putting in the verbs below using the ***past perfect progressive*** *(1–7) and the* ***signal words*** *(A–D).*

to discuss | not to expect | to hope | not to look around | to prepare | to rain | to travel

for months | for 12 hours | for more than a few minutes | since the start of the week

When we finally got to Toronto, we 1 A, so we were quite tired. Being in Canada woke us up, though! Of course, we 2 for good weather, and we weren't disappointed. Apparently, it 3 almost non-stop B, but when we walked out of the airport it was warm and sunny. We 4 for our trip to Canada C, and 5 which places to see a lot. In the end, though, we decided to start by just wandering along some streets and seeing what we could find. I knew that Canadians were friendly people, but I 6 them to be quite so friendly in their biggest city. We 7 central Toronto D before somebody started a conversation with us.

⟨G15⟩ Revision: Indirect speech

→ Unit 3, p. 90

a) Indirect speech without backshift

You use **indirect speech without backshift** to report what somebody has just said or what you have just read, e.g. to quote from a text. The reporting **verb in the introductory sentence** is in the **simple present** and **what you report is in the same tense as in direct speech**.

"My parents and I **spent** the first day sightseeing in Toronto."
→ In his blog Leon **says** in line 6 that he and his parents **spent** the first day sightseeing in Toronto.

b) Indirect speech with backshift

You use **indirect speech with backshift** to report what somebody said some time ago. The reporting **verb in the introductory** sentence is in the **past tense** and the **tense in the reported sentences changes** (= backshift).

direct speech	indirect speech with backshift
simple present → Host dad: The job in the forest industry **is** suited to my interests.	simple past He explained to Leon (that) the job in the forest industry **was** suited to his interests.
present progressive → I**'m going** to work now.	past progressive He told his family (that) he **was going** to work then.
present perfect simple → Leon's mom: I**'ve** never **been** to Toronto before.	past perfect simple She explained that she **had** never **been** to Toronto before.
simple past → I **saw** a police officer wearing a turban.	past perfect simple She mentioned that she **had seen** a police officer wearing a turban
past perfect simple = We **hadn't realised** French is the main language in Montreal.	past perfect simple They admitted they **hadn't realised** that French is the main language in Montreal.
can + infinitive → Host dad: You **can't visit** Montreal without trying poutine!	could + infinitive He told us we **couldn't visit** Montreal without trying poutine.
will + infinitive → Leon: I**'ll send** you some photos from Niagara Falls.	would + infinitive Leon said he **would send** his host family some photos from Niagara Falls.

! Remember to change **pronouns and possessive determiners**, e.g.
Leon: **I** have just checked **my** emails. → He said **he** had just checked **his** emails.

❗ When using indirect speech with backshift, remember to change **phrases of time and place** if things are reported on another day or if people are in different places. You may also need to change the **verbs** to come (→ to go) and to bring (→ to take), e.g.

Richard: I don't have time to help you **now**.
→ Richard said he didn't have time to help me **then**.
Sally: I couldn't wait to **come here**.
→ Sally said she couldn't wait to **go there**.

now → then
today → that day
this evening → that evening
yesterday → the day before
two weeks ago → two weeks before
tomorrow → the next day
last year → the previous year, the year before
here → there

❗ **Questions in indirect speech:**
- For **questions with a question word**, use **asked** or **wanted** to **know + question word**, e.g.
  Taxi driver: **Where** do you want to go?
  → The taxi driver asked **where** the passenger wanted to go.
- For **questions without a question word**, use if, e.g.
  Taxi driver: Will you stay in Toronto for long?
  → The taxi driver wanted to know **if** the passenger would stay in Toronto for long.

❗ **Requests and commands in indirect speech:**
Use **tell sb to do sth** for commands and **ask sb to do sth** for requests, e.g.
Friend: Don't get your hopes up too high, Leon.
→ A friend **told** Leon **not to get** his hopes up too high.
Host mom: Please be polite to Leon.
→ The host mom **asked** her daughter **to be** polite to Leon.

Test yourself Exercise 1

*Leon called Peyton from Niagara Falls. A few days later, she tells her grandparents what Leon said. Put in the correct forms of the verbs in brackets (1–12) using **indirect speech with backshift**. Also change the **verbs, phrases of time and place** (A–F).*

Leon: We've just arrived at the falls, and it feels amazing to be here. I'd already seen them on TV last night, but that really didn't prepare me for how spectacular they are! We're really enjoying it. I just wish I'd brought a better camera than the one on this phone.
Peyton: How long will you be there?
Leon: Until late this afternoon, and then we're getting the bus back to Toronto. I think I'll sleep very well tonight after a such a long day, and that's a very good thing because we're leaving for Montreal on the six o'clock train tomorrow morning!

"When he called me, he said that he and his parents 1 (just / to arrive) at the falls, and it 2 (to feel) amazing to be A. He mentioned that he 3 (already / to see) the falls on TV B, but that really 4 (not to prepare) him for how spectacular they 5 (to be). He said they 6 (really / to enjoy) it, but he 7 (to wish) he C a better camera with him. After that, if I remember it correctly, he told me that they 8 (to stay) until late D, and then they 9 (to get) the bus back to Toronto. Then I think he said something about how he 10 (to think) he 11 (to sleep) well E, which was good because they 12 (to leave for) Montreal on an early train F."

Exercise 2

*Read the emails. Then complete the conversation using **asked (sb to), told (sb to), wanted to know** and **indirect speech with backshift**.*

Hi Leon! I'm emailing you in English to show how good my English is! I have some questions for you. Can I apply for a place on the school exchange programme too? Where can I find out more about it? Will you help me with the application form? Please email me all the info you have. One more question: Is it OK for me to give your name as a reference with my application? All the best, Nico	Dear Nico, Below there's a link to the exchange programme website. You'll find all the info you need there. Don't get too excited, though. Last year there were about ten applications for every place. Please don't give me as a reference. You'll need a teacher for that. Best wishes, Leon

Leon: I got an email from Nico, one of my classmates back home, with lots of questions.

Peyton: What did he want to know?

Leon: He **1** apply for a place on the school exchange programme too. He **2** find out more about it and he also **3** with the application form! He **4** all the information I had. He also **5** my name as a reference with his application.

Peyton: What did you say?

Leon: I sent him a link to the exchange programme website. I **6** too excited because last year there were many more applicants than places, and I **7** my name as a reference with his application.

⟨G16⟩ Expressing probability

→ Unit 3, p. 92

You use **to be supposed to, to be likely to, to be said to, to be certain to** and **to happen to + infinitive** to express chances of probability. The emphasis is on the activity that is expected to happen and not on the chances of something happening. The speaker/writer may or may not be able to prove that the event in question is true.

to be supposed to	= to be generally believed or expected to be/do sth
	The resort town of Whistler **is supposed to be** environmentally friendly. *Der Ferienort Whistler **gilt als** umweltfreundlich.*
to be likely to	= very probably
	In just one generation, the glacier **is likely to disappear**. *Innerhalb nur einer Generation wird der Gletscher **wahrscheinlich** verschwunden sein.*
to be said to	= They say …; to be believed to be / do sth
	The chemicals **are said to endanger** and **pollute** nearby rivers. *Die Chemikalien **sollen** die nahe gelegenen Flüsse gefährden und verschmutzen./**Man sagt, dass** die Chemikalien …*

to be certain to	= sth that you can rely on to happen or to be true
	Environmentalists believe that the experience **is certain to change** the behaviour and lifestyle of the visitors. *Umweltschützende sind der Meinung, dass diese Erfahrung* ***sehr wahrscheinlich / mit hoher Wahrscheinlichkeit*** *das Verhalten und den Lebensstil der Besuchenden ändern wird.*
to happen to	= (to do or be something) by chance
	The areas where fracking is done also **happen to have** a higher risk of earthquakes. *In den Gebieten, in denen Fracking betrieben wird, besteht* ***zufällig / zufälligerweise*** *auch ein höheres Risiko für Erdbeben.*

Test yourself Exercise 1

Choose the correct phrases to complete another news report extract about environmental issues on Canada's West Coast.

If you travel around Canada's countryside, you **1** (are supposed to / are certain to / are said to) see lots of cows. Cattle farming is an important part of the country's economy, and many of its twelve million cattle are on farms along the West Coast. Happy cows in nice grassy fields **2** (are supposed to / are certain to / happen to) be part of sustainable agriculture, right? Unfortunately, their stomachs produce methane, a gas which **3** (is likely to / is supposed to / happens to) be a significant cause of climate change. Cattle farming **4** (does not happen to / is not likely to / is not said to) end in Canada any time soon. However, reducing the amount of meat and milk products we consume **5** (is said to / is certain to / is likely to) be one of the best ways to reduce our personal carbon footprints.

⟨G17⟩ Revision: The passive

→ Text and media smart 3, p. 130

You use the active voice to stress what the subject does, but the **passive voice to stress what is done**. You form the passive voice using **a form of to be + past participle** (irregular form or infinitive + ed).

tense	form of to be + past participle	example
simple present	am/is/are + past participle	The play **is directed** by a new director.
simple past	was/were + past participle	The music **was composed** by Andrew Lloyd Webber.
present perfect simple	have/has been + past participle	Flyers **have been printed** and need to be distributed.
past perfect simple	had been + past participle	The show **had been sold out** long before the premiere.

tense	form of to be + past participle	example
going-to future	am/is/are going to be + past participle	Rehearsals **are going to be held** in the assembly hall on Tuesday afternoons.
will future	will be + past participle	Lots of VIPs **will be invited** to the show.

When changing an active sentence into a passive one, the **object of the active sentence becomes the subject of the passive sentence**. The subject of the active sentence is often left out when it isn't important to say who causes the action. However, if you need to include the person who causes the action in order to make the passive sentence clearer or easier to understand, you use 'by'.

Active voice: **Andrew Lloyd Webber** composed the music.
Passive voice: The music was composed **by Andrew Lloyd Webber**.

! News headlines often use the past participle only, e.g. 'New London theatre **opened**' instead of 'New London theatre **was opened**'.

Test yourself

Exercise 1

Complete the announcement on a school website from the Drama Club with suitable ***passive forms*** *of the verbs in brackets.*

Coming soon: New Drama Club production!

"The Comedy of Errors" **1** (to write) by William Shakespeare around 1594, and it **2** (to perform) on stage thousands of times since then. It **3** (also/to do) on the radio and **4** (to film) a number of times. In 1938 it **5** (to adapt) by Rogers and Hart for a stage musical called "The Boys from Syracuse". Of course, every play **6** (to do) in a different way by everybody who attempts to do it, and it isn't easy to bring something new to one of Shakespeare's most popular works.
We thought, 'How can we do something different?' Unlike a professional production, it **7** (only/to see) by the friends and family of the cast, and it **8** (not to review) by a national newspaper so we can afford to take some risks. Also, we **9** (to give) a challenge by Ms Hollis, the drama teacher. "Do something that surprises me," she said. "OK, we'll try," we promised. Did you know that back in Shakespeare's time, all the female parts **10** (to play) by male actors? We've decided to find out what it's like if the roles **11** (to cast) the other way round. All the male roles **12** (to act) by female actors and all the female roles ... you get the idea. We're pretty sure that **13** (not to try) before!

Exercise 2

Read the notes that a member of the Drama Club took. Rewrite them as questions with ***passive forms****.*

1. *Did we print out enough copies of the playscript?*
2. *How much rehearsal time will we need?*
3. *Have we booked the assembly hall for the evening of the production?*
4. *Has the head teacher given permission to use the assembly hall?*
5. *Where does the school store costumes from previous plays?*
6. *Have any other local websites mentioned our production?*
7. *Is the local newspaper going to review the production?*
8. *How will we sell the tickets?*

⟨G18⟩ Revision: Conditional sentences

→ Text and media smart 3, p. 137

There are three basic types of conditional sentences. They all have two parts: an if-clause and a main clause. The if-clause expresses a condition and the main clause describes a consequence.

a) **Realistic condition: The condition may be fulfilled in the future.**

	example
You use type 1 sentences for actions that are probable / possible. The verb in the if-clause is in the simple present; the verb in the main clause is in the will future, a modal verb + infinitive or an imperative.	If you **give** the wrong answer to a CAPTCHA, the system **will generate** a new one and ask you to try again. If you **need** help, you **can call** the help desk or **look for** FAQs or tutorials online. If the help desk line **is** busy, **try** again later.

b) **Theoretical condition: The condition is unlikely to be fulfilled in the future; it is purely theoretical.**

	example
You use type 2 sentences for actions that are (currently) hypothetical. The verb in the if-clause is in the simple past; the verb in the main clause is in the conditional tense (= would / could / might + infinitive).	Maybe it **would help** if I **understood** how the bees got in your house. You **would get** a better reaction if you **were** more polite.

c) **Condition no longer possible: The condition can no longer be fulfilled because it refers to a situation in the past which is over now.**

	example
You use type 3 sentences to say that the condition can no longer be fulfilled because it refers to a situation in the past. The verb in the if-clause is in the past perfect simple; the verb in the main clause is in the conditional perfect (would / could / might have + past participle).	I **wouldn't have called** the help desk if I **hadn't needed** advice from an expert. You **could have saved** some time if you **had called** earlier and asked for help.

! If the if-clause comes first, you need to put a **comma** between the if-clause and the main clause.

❗ **When** or **if**:

when	– meaning 'as soon as' / *sobald* – time matters – something is sure to happen	**When** I see my cousin tomorrow, I'll tell him about my computer problems. ***Sobald** ich meinen Cousin morgen sehe, werde ich ihm von meinen Computerproblemen erzählen.*
if	– meaning *falls* – the condition matters – it's not sure whether something will happen	**If** I see my cousin tomorrow, I'll tell him about my computer problems. ***Falls** ich meinen Cousin morgen sehe, werde ich ihm von meinem Computerproblemen erzählen.*

Test yourself **Exercise 1**

a) *Write a conditional sentence for each situation. Put the **if**-clause or **when**-clause first.*

I need help   ask for it

1. The speaker may need help.
2. The speaker will need help.
3. It's unlikely that the speaker will need help.
4. The speaker didn't need help.

b) *Rewrite the sentences with the if-clause or when-clause second.*

Exercise 2

Correct the mistakes in the sentences from conversations between customers and help desk assistants.

1. If you will return the product to us, we give your money back.
   (The caller will probably return the product.)
2. If there's more information on the website, I don't need to keep calling the help desk.
   (There isn't much information on the website.)
3. It probably didn't break if you have read the instructions properly.
   (The caller didn't read the instructions properly.)
4. I won't have ordered it if I have known it was such bad quality.
   (I didn't know it was such bad quality.)
5. I could help you if I would.
   (I can't help you.)
6. We ship your order when we will receive payment from you.
   (As soon as the customer pays for the item, it will be shipped.)

Start:
1. If you **return** the product to us, we …
2. If there **were** …

Vocabulary

In *Green Line* 6 G9, all the important words and phrases in each module are listed chronologically in the **Vocabulary**. These words are obligatory, which means you should learn them and be able to understand and use them.

All new obligatory vocabulary items are listed separately for each module. For example, an obligatory item which appears in two modules is listed in both. Therefore, the three modules in *Green Line* 6 G9 can be worked on chronologically or in any chosen order.

Words which help you to understand a text but which are not obligatory, are explained in annotations below the text itself. This also applies to new words in the optional ⟨Story 2⟩ of each Unit as well as to items in Check-out. Words that are less frequent or not directly relevant for understanding a text are not listed at all, whether the text is obligatory or optional. In this case, or if you come across any other new words, we would encourage you to look them up in a(n online) dictionary. In contrast to your previous student's books, there is no alphabetical Dictionary at the end of *Green Line* 6 G9.

A list of the most frequent and important operators can be found on p. 272, followed by the list of irregular verbs on p. 273.

In *Green Line* 6 G9, terms that have become widely accepted as self-designations are used to designate marginalized groups. Some terms that appear in original texts and cannot be changed, are controversial. These have been placed in single inverted commas to indicate that they are no longer acceptable. In the discussion on correct designations or terms used by the communities themselves, there is a wide variety of positions that should also be respected in English language learning.

Abbreviations and symbols

sg/pl	*singular/plural*	5	*The words are part of this exercise.*
sb/sth	*somebody/something*	!	*Watch out!*
jmd./jmdn./jmdm./etw.	jemand/jemanden/jemandem/etwas	↔	*is the opposite of*
fml/infml	*formal/informal*	→	*is related to*
coll	*colloquial; informal*	=	*corresponds to*
ugs.	umgangssprachlich; informell	≠	*doesn't correspond to*
slang	*very informal*	**Fr./Lat.**	*related words in French/Latin*
vulg	*vulgar; rude*	*f/m/nt*	*feminine/masculine/neuter*
AE	*American English*		
BE	*British English*		

Across cultures 1 Making your voice heard

	to **make one's voice heard** [ˌmeɪk wʌnz ˌvɔɪs ˈhɜːd]	sich Gehör verschaffen	How can we *make our voices heard*?
	to **have a voice** [ˌhæv‿ə ˈvɔɪs]	ein Mitspracherecht haben	*Having a voice* and making a difference are important to me.
	democracy [dɪˈmɒkrəsi]	Demokratie	In a *democracy* the people vote for the government. ! Watch the spelling and the pronunciation.
	participation [pɑːˌtɪsɪˈpeɪʃn]	Mitwirkung; Beteiligung	*participation* → to participate *Fr.* participation *(f)*
	level [ˈlevl]	Ebene	You can make your voice heard at different *levels*.
1	**student council** [ˌstjuːdnt ˈkaʊnsl]	Vertretung der Schüler/-innen	The *Student Council* meets every Thursday after school.
	election [ɪˈlekʃn]	Wahl	The first free *elections* in South Africa were in 1994. *Fr.* élection *(f)*; ***Lat.*** eligere
	vote [vəʊt]	Stimme; Stimmrecht; Wahl; Wahlrecht; Abstimmung	A candidate has to earn my *vote*; then I might vote for them. a *vote* → to vote
	to **make one's point** [ˌmeɪk wʌnz ˈpɔɪnt]	seinen Standpunkt deutlich machen; seine Meinung vertreten	= to clearly express one's opinion
	fur [fɜː]	Pelz-; Pelz; Fell	= the thick hair that covers the skin of many animals
	politics *(pl only)* [ˈpɒlətɪks]	Politik	! I think *politics* **is** important. *Fr.* politique *(f)*
2	to **persuade** [pəˈsweɪd]	überreden; überzeugen	= to convince *Fr.* persuader; ***Lat.*** persuadere
	to **sit back** [sɪt ˈbæk]	sich zurücklehnen	*Sit back* and relax!
	to **take the lead** [ˌteɪk ðə ˈliːd]	die Führung übernehmen	*to take the lead* → to lead
3	**representative** [ˌreprɪˈzentətɪv]	Vertreter/-in; Stellvertreter/-in; Repräsentant/-in; Sprecher/-in	*representative* → to represent
4	to **point out sth** [ˌpɔɪnt‿ˈaʊt]	auf etw. hinweisen	If you *point out a fact*, you tell somebody about it.
5	to **debate** [dɪˈbeɪt]	debattieren	to *debate* → a debate *Fr.* débattre
	voting [ˈvəʊtɪŋ]	Wahl-	The *voting* age in most countries is 18.
	to **lower** [ˈləʊə]	etw. herabsetzen; etw. senken; etw. vermindern	*to lower* ↔ to raise *to lower* → low
	retirement age [rɪˈtaɪəmənt eɪdʒ]	Rentenalter; Renteneintritts-alter	*Retirement ages* are rising worldwide.
	voter [ˈvəʊtə]	Wähler/-in	*voter* → voting → vote → to vote
	to **poll** [pəʊl]	befragen	In this survey people of all ages *are polled*.
	minimum age [ˈmɪnɪməm eɪdʒ]	Mindestalter; Altersgrenze	What's the *minimum age* for getting a part-time job in Germany?

6	**power** *(no pl)* [paʊə]	Macht; Kraft; Stärke	*power* → powerful
7	**Supreme Court** [suːˌpriːm 'kɔːt]	Oberster Gerichtshof *(der USA)*	The case will have to be taken to the *Supreme Court*.
9	to **adopt** [ə'dɒpt]	verabschieden	The new policy will be *adopted* soon.
	government body [ˌɡʌvnmənt 'bɒdi]	Regierungsbehörde; staatliche Einrichtung	= an organisation which is part of the state
	well-being ['welˌbiːɪŋ]	Wohlergehen; Wohlbefinden	Doing sports is important for my mental *well-being*.
	sanitation [ˌsænɪ'teɪʃn]	Sanitäreinrichtungen; sanitäre Anlagen	The village did not have access to clean water and *sanitation* until recently.
	decent ['diːsnt]	angemessen; fair	Everybody should have access to *decent* pay and working conditions.
	reduced [rɪ'djuːst]	weniger; reduziert; verringert	= made less or smaller
	consumption [kən'sʌmpʃn]	Konsum; Verbrauch	The country's energy *consumption* is too high.
	partnership [ˌpɑːtnə'ʃɪp]	Partnerschaft	*partnership* → partner

Making your voice heard

have	to have a voice / a say / your say	ein Mitspracherecht haben; mitbestimmen
	to make one's voice heard	sich Gehör verschaffen
	to have / make an impact	Wirkung zeigen; Eindruck auf jmdn. machen
	to have a point	nicht ganz Unrecht haben
make	to make a choice	eine Wahl treffen
	to make / take a decision	eine Entscheidung treffen
	to make a difference	etwas verändern; einen Unterschied machen
	to make change happen	Veränderungen / Wandel bewirken/erreichen
	to make a noise	Lärm machen
	to make one's point	seinen Standpunkt deutlich machen; seine Meinung vertreten
	to make a statement	sich äußern; eine Stellungnahme abgeben
	to make progress	vorankommen; Fortschritte machen
	to make sb think about sth	jmdn. zum Nachdenken anregen
take	to take responsibility / the blame for sth	die Verantwortung / Schuld für etw. tragen; etw. auf seine Kappe nehmen
	to take part in (a protest)	teilnehmen an
	to take a vote (on)	abstimmen (über)
get	to get involved (in)	sich für etw. engagieren; sich involvieren; sich beteiligen
	to get sb's attention	jmdn. auf sich aufmerksam machen; Interesse bei jmdm. wecken
feel	to feel strongly about sth	etw. ernst nehmen; jmdm. am Herzen liegen; auf etw. Wert legen
stand up	to stand up for sb/sth	sich für jmdn./etw. einsetzen; für jmdn./etw. einstehen
	to stand up for one's beliefs	sich für seine Überzeugungen einsetzen; für seine Überzeugungen einstehen

Unit 1 Never enough?

Check-in

	consumerism [kən'sju:mərɪzm]	Konsum; Konsumdenken	= the buying and using of goods and services
	consumer [kən'sju:mə]	Verbraucher/-in; Konsument/-in	*consumer* → consumerism
1	to **consume** [kən'sju:m]	konsumieren; verbrauchen; verzehren	= to eat or drink; to use sth up ***Fr.*** consommer; ***Lat.*** consumere
	disposable [dɪ'spəʊzəbl]	Wegwerf-; Einweg-	= to be thrown away after use
	to **exceed** [ɪk'si:d]	überschreiten	The amount of money paid for repairs *exceeds* that of last year.
	packaging ['pækɪdʒɪŋ]	Verpackung; Verpackungsmaterial	*packaging* → to pack
	to **take away** [ˌteɪk‿ə'weɪ]	etw. mitnehmen; zum Mitnehmen	One coffee to *take away*, please.
	impact *(no pl)* ['ɪmpækt]	Auswirkung; Einfluss	***Fr.*** impact *(m)*
3	**activism** ['æktɪvɪzm]	Aktivismus	*activism* → activist
	cause [kɔ:z]	Sache; Anliegen	One *cause* I feel strongly about is the environment. ***Fr.*** cause *(f)*; ***Lat.*** causa *(f)*
	achievement [ə'tʃi:vmənt]	Leistung; Erfolg; Errungenschaft	One of the government's greatest *achievements* is its contribution to the peace process in the region. *achievement* → to achieve sth
	to **let sb off sth** [let 'ɒf]	jmdn. von etw. freistellen; jmdn. von etw. befreien	Have you got homework to do? – No, we *were let off* homework because of the sports event in the afternoon.
	to **boycott** ['bɔɪkɒt]	boykottieren	= to refuse to buy sth or take part in sth
	party ['pɑ:ti]	Partei	Which *party* did you vote for? ***Fr.*** parti *(m)*
	to **flee, fled, fled** [fli:; fled; fled]	flüchten; fliehen	The animals *fled* from the fire.

Station 1: The life cycle of a T-shirt

	life cycle ['laɪf ˌsaɪkl]	Lebenszyklus; Lebensdauer	Can you describe the *life cycle* of a butterfly?
1	**on average** [ɒn‿'ævrɪdʒ]	durchschnittlich; im Durchschnitt	*On average* around 10,000 people visit the shopping centre every day.
	to **dispose of sth** [dɪ'spəʊz‿əv]	etw. entsorgen	= to get rid of; to throw away
	textile ['tekstaɪl]	Textil-; textil	My grandparents worked in the *textile* industry all their lives.
	carbon dioxide (CO_2) [ˌkɑ:bn daɪ'ɒksaɪd]	Kohlendioxid; Kohlenstoffdioxid	Plants turn *carbon dioxide* into oxygen.
	ecological footprint [i:kəˌlɒdʒɪkl 'fʊtprɪnt]	ökologischer Fußabdruck	Think of how you can lower your *ecological footprint*.

textiles *(pl)* ['tekstaɪlz]	Textilien	I work for a company that designs *textiles*.
shipping ['ʃɪpɪŋ]	Versand; Transport *(von Gütern)*; Schifffahrts-; See-	= transportation of goods
disposal (of sth) [dɪ'spəʊzl]	Entsorgung; Beseitigung	*disposal* → disposable → to dispose of sth
as though [əz 'ðəʊ]	als ob	I can't believe it! You behave *as though* nothing has happened.
metric ton [ˌmetrɪk 'tʌn]	(metrische) Tonne	= 1,000 kg

Numbers and measurements

Be careful with these words because they are used differently in different countries!

million	Million	A **million** is a thousand times a thousand = 1,000,000 = 10^6.
billion	Milliarde	A thousand times a million is a **billion** in the US, the UK, Australia and Canada. 1,000 x 1,000,000 = 10^9 = 1 **billion**
trillion	Billion	1,000,000 x 1,000,000 = 10^{12} = 1 **trillion** In Germany a thousand times a million is a Milliarde, and a million times a million is a Billion.
ton / tonne	Tonne	A **tonne** is 1,000 kg in the metric system. A **ton** can be a long ton, i.e. ca. 1,016 kg (in the UK and the Commonwealth) or a short ton, i.e. ca. 907 kg (in the US).
pound	Pfund	A **pound** is 500 g in the metric system. In the UK and the Commonwealth as well as in the US it is ca. 454 g.

organic [ɔ:'gænɪk]	Bio-; aus biologischem Anbau	Nowadays, there are lots of *organic* products in most supermarkets.
profitable ['prɒfɪtəbl]	Gewinn bringend; rentabel; profitabel	Their new business is highly *profitable*. They make a lot of money with it.
harmful ['hɑ:mfl]	schädlich; nachteilig; verletzend	Does it contain any *harmful* substances?
raw [rɔ:]	roh; unverarbeitet; unbearbeitet; unbehandelt	I feed my dog *raw* meat.
production site [prə'dʌkʃn saɪt]	Produktionsstätte	They're building a huge *production site* near our village.
to **spin, span, spun** [spɪn; spæn; spʌn]	spinnen	First, raw cotton *is spun* and then it is made into fabric.
to **bleach** [bli:tʃ]	bleichen	= a process that removes the colour from sth, e.g. fabric
to **dye** [daɪ]	färben	Have you ever *dyed* your hair?
chemical ['kemɪkl]	Chemikalie	Workers in the textile industry, e.g. in Bangladesh, often come into contact with dangerous and harmful *chemicals*.
to **contaminate** [kən'tæmɪneɪt]	verschmutzen; verunreinigen; verseuchen; vergiften; kontaminieren	Don't use the water. It's *contaminated*.
groundwater ['graʊndˌwɔ:tə]	Grundwasser	There hasn't been a lot of rain this year. The *groundwater* level is rather low.

	finished ['fɪnɪʃt]	fertiggestellt	the *finished* product = the final product
	a load of washing [ə ˌləʊd‿əv 'wɒʃɪŋ]	Wäscheladung	At the weekend we always wash several *loads of washing*.
	landfill ['lænfɪl]	Mülldeponie	Garbage is disposed of at a *landfill*.
5	to **reduce** [rɪ'dju:s]	reduzieren; vermindern; verringern	If you *reduce* waste, you produce less waste. *Fr.* réduire
	fashion label ['fæʃn ˌleɪbl]	Modelabel; Marke	My favourite influencer has created his own *fashion label*.
6	**torn** [tɔ:n]	zerrissen	I need to sew my jacket. It's *torn* at the sleeve.
	to **regift** [ˌri:'gɪft]	weiterverschenken	= to give away sth as a gift which you yourself got as a present
	item ['aɪtəm]	Ding; Gegenstand	We'll get a few cents for every *item* we donate.
	living ['lɪvɪŋ]	Lebensweise	For sustainable *living*, it's important to give clothes a longer and more useful life cycle, among many other things.
7	**clothing swap** ['kləʊðɪŋ swɒp]	Kleidertauschbörse	Wow, where did you buy that cool skirt? – I didn't buy it. I got it at a *clothing swap*.
	to **swap** [swɒp]	tauschen	= to exchange
8	to **be trapped** [bi 'træpt]	gefangen sein; eingeschlossen sein	After the storm they *were trapped* in their house for two days.
	shopping trolley ['ʃɒpɪŋ ˌtrɒli]	Einkaufswagen	We spent a lot of money in the supermarket today – two *shopping trolleys*, filled up to the top.
	upside down [ˌʌpsaɪd 'daʊn]	umgedreht; auf den Kopf gestellt	Look, that street sign is *upside down*.
	bar [bɑ:]	Gitterstab; Stab; Stange; Strebe	The animal escaped because one *bar* of the cage was loose.
9	**head buyer** [ˌhed 'baɪə]	leitende/-r Einkäufer/-in; Chefeinkäufer/-in	*head* = main; leading
	to **have a/an … feel** [fi:l]	sich … anfühlen	The fabric of this hoodie *has a* very strange *feel*. I don't feel comfortable in it.
	cost [kɒst]	Preis; Kosten	*cost* → to cost
	to **refund** [ri:'fʌnd]	rückerstatten; zurückzahlen	When you return a product, the price *is* usually *refunded*.
	prepayment [ˌpri:'peɪmənt]	Vorauszahlung	= payment made ahead of getting a product
	managing director [ˌmænɪdʒɪŋ daɪ'rektə]	Geschäftsführer/-in	My mother is one of the *managing directors* of the company.
	revised [rɪ'vaɪzd]	überarbeitet	The leaflet had to be *revised* because some of the information was incorrect.
	increase ['ɪnkri:s]	Erhöhung; Anstieg; Zunahme; Wachstum	! Watch the pronunciation: an **in**crease – to in**crease**

Abbreviations in formal letters

Re	(= regarding)	Betr.	(= Betreff)
Attn	(= for the attention of)	z. Hd.	(= zu Händen von)
pp	(= per procurationem)	i. A.	(= im Auftrag)
Ref.	(= reference)	AZ	(= Aktenzeichen)
Enc. / Encl.	(= enclosed)	Anlage; Anhang	
c./o.	(= care of)	c/o	(= bei)

Station 2: What shall I cook for dinner?

Overshoot Day ['əʊvəʃu:t ˌdeɪ]	Weltüberlastungstag; Erdüberlastungstag	It's important to bring *Overshoot Day* back by several days, or even better months, each year.
to **become aware of sth** [bɪˌkʌm ə'weər‿əv]	sich einer Sache bewusst werden; sich etw. vor Augen führen	They were really shocked when they *became aware of* what had really happened.
resources *(pl)* [rɪ'zɔ:sɪz]	Ressourcen; Rohstoffquellen	= things that are available to be used when needed *Fr.* ressource *(f)*
to **regenerate** [ri:'dʒenreɪt]	erneuern; regenerieren	= to grow again
the years ahead [ðə ˌjɪəz‿ə'hed]	die kommenden Jahre	= the (near) future
to **calculate** ['kælkjəleɪt]	rechnen; berechnen; kalkulieren	= to work out *Fr.* calculer
guide [gaɪd]	Richtwert; Anhaltspunkt	We haven't worked out the final numbers yet, but these are still a good *guide* to see how things have developed.
to **generate** ['dʒenreɪt]	erzeugen; generieren; herstellen; bilden	= to produce *Fr.* générer
by [baɪ]	um	The world's population is expected to increase *by* nearly 2 billion people in the next 30 years.
vegan ['vi:gən]	vegan; Veganer/-in	**!** Watch the pronunciation.
diet [daɪət]	Ernährung; Ernährungsweise; Nahrung; Diät	A balanced and healthy *diet* is important for your health.
preferably ['prefrəbli]	vorzugsweise; möglichst	*preferably* → to prefer
dairy product ['deəri ˌprɒdʌkt]	Milchprodukt; Milcherzeugnis; Molkereiprodukt	= milk, cheese, yoghurt, etc.
treat [tri:t]	(besonderes) Vergnügen; Genuss	The meal was delicious. What a *treat*!
use-by date [ˌju:zbaɪ 'deɪt]	Mindesthaltbarkeitsdatum; Verfallsdatum	Very often, food can still be consumed after its *use-by date*. Check it before you throw it away.
heated ['hi:tɪd]	beheizt; geheizt; erhitzt	*heated* → heat
greenhouse ['gri:nhaʊs]	Gewächshaus; Treibhaus	We grow our own salad, tomatoes and strawberries in a *greenhouse* in our garden.
fertiliser ['fɜ:tɪlaɪzə]	Dünger; Düngemittel	We only use organic *fertiliser* on our farm.

	to **do sb a favour** [ˌduː ə 'feɪvə]	jmdm. einen Gefallen tun	Can you *do me a favour* and help me carry the bags, please?
	beef [biːf]	Rindfleisch	*Fr.* bœuf *(m)*
	pork [pɔːk]	Schweinefleisch	*Fr.* porc *(m)*
	farmed salmon [ˌfɑːmd 'sæmən]	Zuchtlachs	*farmed salmon* ↔ wild salmon
	post- [pəʊst]	Nach-; nach-; Post-; post-	= after
	processing ['prəʊsesɪŋ]	Verarbeitung	My grandparents used to do everything themselves on their farm: from growing and harvesting food to *processing* and selling it.
	retail ['riːteɪl]	Einzelhandel	Internet shops make money in online *retail*.
3	**menu** ['menjuː]	Speisekarte; Speiseplan	Chips are always on the *menu* of fast-food restaurants.
4	**apple crumble** [ˌæpl 'krʌmbl]	*mit Streuseln überbackener Apfelauflauf*	= a popular dessert in the UK
	chicken wing ['tʃɪkɪn ˌwɪŋ]	Hähnchenflügel; Hühnerflügel	*Chicken wings* came originally from Buffalo, New York.
	baked potato [ˌbeɪkt pə'teɪtəʊ]	Ofenkartoffel	A *baked potato* can be a main dish or a side dish served with meat, for example.
	rice [raɪs]	Reis	Would you like *rice* or bread with the curry? *Fr.* riz *(m)*
	cherry ['tʃeri]	Kirsche; Kirsch-	*Cherries* are my favourite fruit.
6	**global warming** *(no pl)* [ˌgləʊbl 'wɔːmɪŋ]	globale Erwärmung; Erderwärmung; Erwärmung der Erdatmosphäre	One of today's biggest challenges is slowing down *global warming*.

Action! Beware of 'greenwashing'

	Beware of ...! [bɪ'weər‿əv]	Vorsicht, ...! ; Achtung! ...!	*Beware of* the dog!
1	**eco-conscious** ['iːkəʊ ˌkɒnʃəs]	umweltbewusst	An *eco-conscious* lifestyle can help to reduce pollution.
	to **define** [dɪ'faɪn]	bestimmen; definieren; bestimmen	*to define* → definition *Fr.* définir
	biodegradable [ˌbaɪəʊdɪ'greɪdəbl]	biologisch abbaubar; kompostierbar	These takeaway boxes are *biodegradable*.
	to **mislead (sb)** [ˌmɪs'liːd]	(jmdn.) täuschen; (jmdn.) in die Irre führen	= to make sb believe sth that isn't true
	claim [kleɪm]	Behauptung	a *claim* → to claim
	the fine print *(no pl)* ['faɪn ˌprɪnt]	das Kleingedruckte	Do you always read *the fine print* on documents?
	certification [sətɪfɪ'keɪʃn]	Zertifizierung; Bescheinigung	The 'Blauer Engel' is a German symbol of *certification* for environmentally friendly products or services.
2	**documentary** [ˌdɒkjə'mentri]	Dokumentarfilm; Dokumentation	I watched a fascinating *documentary* about the rainforest last night.
3	**producer** [prə'djuːsə]	Produzent/-in; Hersteller/-in	*producer* → production → to produce
	eco-friendly ['iːkəʊ ˌfrendli]	umweltfreundlich	We try to buy *eco-friendly* products only.

Story 1: The Garbage Eater

1	**garbage can** *(AE)* ['gɑ:rbɪdʒ ˌkæn]	Mülleimer; Abfalleimer	*garbage can (AE)* = dustbin *(BE)*
	edible ['edɪbl]	essbar	*edible* → to eat
	to **freak out** [ˌfri:k‿'aʊt]	ausflippen	They *freaked out* when our dog started to bark again.
	kind of *(coll)* ['kaɪnd‿əv]	ziemlich; irgendwie	It's *kind of* a long way from New York to Los Angeles. – *Kind of*? It's a huge distance!
	to **strike sb as …** [ˌstraɪks 'mi]	jmdm. … scheinen	Our new neighbours *strike me as* odd. We hardly ever see them, and if we do, they never say hello.
	pretentious [prə'tenʃəs]	angeberisch; überheblich	My new neigbour is really *pretentious*. He talks all the time about famous people he knows. *Fr.* prétentieux/-euse
	dude *(AE) (coll)* [du:d]	Typ; Kerl	Hey, *dude*! What's up?
	apparently [ə'pærntli]	anscheinend	*apparently* → to appear *Lat.* apparere
	Big deal. *(coll)* [bɪg 'di:l]	Na und?	= So what?
	intense [ɪn'tens]	intensiv; heftig	an *intense* feeling = a very strong feeling *Fr.* intense
	I'm not buying it. *(coll)* [ˌaɪm nɒt 'baɪɪŋ ɪt]	Das kannst du sonstwem erzählen.; Das nehm' ich dir nicht ab.	Lots of people believe him but *I'm not buying it.*
	daring ['deərɪŋ]	gewagt	= unusual or involving danger or risks
	charming ['tʃɑ:mɪŋ]	charmant; reizend; bezaubernd	What a *charming* person!
	What is up with that? *(AE) (coll)* [ˌwɒt‿ɪz‿'ʌp wɪ‿ðæt]	Warum?; Was ist der Grund dafür?	= Why? For what reason?
	trashed *(AE) (coll)* [træʃt]	kaputt; demoliert	My shoes are so *trashed*. I need a new pair.
	to **pull sth off** *(coll)* [pʊl 'ɒf]	etw. durchziehen	They never thought we'd *pull it off*. They were so wrong!
	supposedly [sə'pəʊzədli]	angeblich; anscheinend; scheinbar	*Supposedly*, the new smartphone is the best you can get at the moment. I'm not buying that kind of advertising.
	to **kiss sb's ass** *(vulg) (coll)* [kɪs 'æs]	jmdm. in den Arsch kriechen	I can't believe how my best friend tries to impress our new classmate. She so kisses her ass.
	to **approve** [ə'pru:v]	genehmigen; billigen	The Student Council finally got the regulations on smartphone use *approved*.
	to **forbid, forbade, forbidden** [fə'bɪd; fə'bæd; fə'bɪdn]	verbieten; untersagen	*to forbid* ↔ to allow
	authority [ɔ:'θɒrəti]	Autorität; Amt; Behörde	*Fr.* autorité *(f)*; Lat. auctoritas *(f)*
	Here's the killer. *(coll)* [ˌhɪəz ðə 'kɪlə]	Und jetzt wird's spannend.	And *here's the killer* … – Stop, don't tell me how the story ended.
	to **rip sth off** [rɪp]	sich etw. vom Leib reißen	They *ripped off* their clothes and ran into the sea.
	jerk *(coll)* [dʒɜ:k]	Vollidiot; Blödmann; Depp	= idiot

in the meantime [ˌɪn ðə ˈmiːntaɪm]	in der Zwischenzeit	= meanwhile
to **be stuck** [bi ˈstʌk]	festsitzen; feststecken; hängen bleiben	If you*'re stuck* in a place, you can't get out.
rad *(AE) (slang)* [ræd]	cool; toll; abgefahren	= cool
to **bust sb** *(coll)* [bʌst]	jmdn. auffliegen lassen	They cheated in the test and the teacher *busted them*.
to **be all worked up (about sth)** *(coll)* [bi‿al ˌwɜːkt ˈʌp]	(über etw.) total aufgebracht sein	= to be very upset or excited about sth
earnest [ˈɜːnɪst]	ernsthaft; aufrichtig	= serious
to **roll with sth** *(coll)* [ˈrəʊl wɪθ]	die Dinge nehmen/akzeptieren, wie sie sind	= to accept things the way they are
barely [ˈbeəli]	kaum	I can *barely* see him. = I can hardly see him.
to **acknowledge sb/sth** [əkˈnɒlɪdʒ]	jmdn./etw. wahrnehmen; jmdn./etw. bemerken	= to admit or accept that sb or sth exists
self-righteousness [ˌselfˈraɪtʃəsnəs]	Selbstgerechtigkeit	*Self-righteousness* and criticism often don't go well together.
self-esteem [ˌselfɪˈstiːm]	Selbstwertgefühl; Selbstachtung	People who have low *self-esteem* often expect to do badly.

Skills: How to choose the appropriate register and style

1	**aka** *(= also known as)* [ˌeɪkeɪˈeɪ]	alias; auch bekannt als	Spider-Man, *aka* Peter Parker
	to **do harm** [ˌduː ˈhɑːm]	Schaden anrichten	*to do harm* → harmful → harm
	to **expel sb** [ɪkˈspel]	jmdn. verweisen; jmdn. hinauswerfen	You can be *expelled* from school if you repeatedly break the school rules. ***Lat.*** expellere
	consistently [kənˈsɪstntli]	wiederholt; ständig, immer wieder	= again and again
	to **disobey** [ˌdɪsəˈbeɪ]	missachten	= to refuse to do what sb or a rule tells you to do
	on top of that *(coll)* [ɒn ˌtɒp‿əv ˈðət]	zu alledem; und dann auch noch	= what's more
	grade *(AE)* [greɪd]	Klasse; Jahrgang	What *grade* is your little brother in? – In second *grade*.
	expulsion [ɪkˈspʌlʃn]	Ausschluss; Schulausschluss; Verweisung	*expulsion* → to expel
	to **request** *(fml)* [rɪˈkwest]	bitten	= to ask for sth in a polite way
	reinstatement [ˌriːɪnˈsteɪtmənt]	Wiederaufnahme; Wiedereinstellung	The lawyer fought for the *reinstatement* of the workers.
	in advance [ɪn‿ədˈvɑːns]	im Voraus	If you order things online, you usually pay *in advance*.
	consideration [kənˌsɪdrˈeɪʃn]	Überprüfung; Berücksichtigung	*consideration* → to consider ***Fr.*** considération *(f)*
	matter [ˈmætə]	Angelegenheit; Sache	They talked to a lawyer about the *matter*.

Participles used as adjectives

Participles (present participle: verb + -ing, past participle: verb + -ed or irregular form of the verb) are often used as adjectives, as in the following examples.

recycled cotton	**reduced** price
finished product	**trapped** animal
unwanted effect	**broken** machine
consumed food	**written** instruction
(un)restricted access	**torn** clothes
revised price list	**surprising** facts
farmed salmon	**growing** industry
heated greenhouse	**daring** activity

Unit task: A challenge to reduce waste

reduction [rɪˈdʌkʃn]	Reduzierung; Verminderung	*reduction* → to reduce *Fr.* réduction *(f)*
to **put sth into practice** [ˌpʊt‿ɪntə ˈpræktɪs]	etw. (in die Praxis) umsetzen	Let´s *put* the theory *into practice*.

Non-standard English

You have already heard about different registers. In informal English people often use informal words or grammar and fillers.

Colloquial words / usage

a no-brainer	ein Kinderspiel	The carbon maths is **a no-brainer**. = It's easy to work out that long-distance shipping by plane causes more carbon emissions than transport over a short distance in a lorry.
a real no-no	ein echtes Tabu	Flights are **a real no-no**. = You're not even supposed to speak or think about flying.
so	so sehr, dermaßen	That was **so** the best thing about unrestricted carbon. = I can't stress enough how much that meant to me when there were no restrictions.

Shortened/simplified words or sentences

Looks like …	It looks like …	! *The subject (pronoun) is left out in these sentences.*
Reminds me of …	It / That reminds me of …	
thru	through	
wanna	want to	
gonna	going to	
cept	except	! *These words or phrases are shortened.*
cos	because	
temp	temperature	
aircon	air-conditioning	

Text and media smart 1 Dealing with advertising

Check-in

	advertising *(no pl)* ['ædvətaɪzɪŋ]	Werbung; Reklame; Werbe-	All this *advertising* on social media is getting on my nerves.
	print ad ['prɪnt æd]	Printanzeige	Do you pay attention to *print ads* in magazines or TV ads at all? – No, I only watch online ads.
	commercial [kə'mɜ:ʃl]	Werbespot	= an advert on TV or radio
1	**advertiser** ['ædvətaɪzə]	Werbefachmann/-frau; Werbeträger; Inserent/-in	*advertiser* ⟶ ad(vertisment) ⟶ advertising
	sceptical ['skeptɪkl]	skeptisch	= when you have doubts about sth
	brand [brænd]	Marke	= a particular product or line of products made by one company and sold under a special name
	sample ['sɑ:mpl]	Probe; Probepackung; Muster	My favourite cosmetics company was giving away *samples* at the supermarket today.
	bar [bɑ:]	Riegel; Tafel	What's your favourite chocolate *bar*?

Station 1: Did you see that new ad?

1	to **introduce** [ˌɪntrə'dju:s]	einführen; einleiten	*to introduce* ⟶ introduction *Fr.* introduire
	formula ['fɔ:mjələ]	Formel	! Watch the spelling and the pronunciation.
	target ['tɑ:gɪt]	Ziel-; Ziel	Who is the *target* group of this advertisement?
	desire [dɪ'zaɪə]	Begierde; Verlangen	= a strong wish *Fr.* désir *(m)*
	ad copy ['æd ˌkɒpi]	Werbetext	We've got the visuals for the new ad, but we still need the *ad copy* for it.
	dignity *(no pl)* ['dɪgnəti]	Würde	= behaviour that is calm and controlled *Fr.* dignité *(f)*; *Lat.* dignitas *(f)*
	out of ['aʊt‿əv]	von	Buying fair trade products helps the producers to live *out of* their work.
	this/that way [ðɪs/ðæt 'weɪ]	so; auf diese Weise	It doesn't work *that way*!
2	**toothbrush** ['tu:θbrʌʃ]	Zahnbürste	*toothbrush* ⟶ tooth
	FOMO *(fear of missing out)* ['fəʊməʊ]	FOMO *(Angst, etwas zu verpassen)*	A friend of mine has severe *FOMO*.
	hard-to-reach [ˌhɑ:d tə 'ri:tʃ]	schwer zugänglich; schwer erreichbar	The house is at the end of a very narrow dirt road. It's *hard-to-reach*.
	enamel [ɪ'næml]	Zahnschmelz	The *enamel* protects your teeth.
3	**solar-powered** ['səʊləpaʊəd]	solarbetrieben	We're going camping this weekend. I must buy a *solar-powered* torch.
4	**storyline** ['stɔ:rilaɪn]	Handlung	*storyline* ⟶ story

	lively ['laɪvli]	lebendig; lebhaft; munter	Their presentation was really convincing – very interesting and *lively*.
	playful ['pleɪfʊl]	spielerisch; scherzhaft	↔ serious
	tracking shot ['trækɪŋ ˌʃɒt]	Kameraschwenk	*tracking shot* → medium shot → long shot
	fast motion [ˌfɑ:st 'məʊʃn]	Zeitraffer	The clip is even funnier when you look at it in *fast motion*.
	slow motion [ˌsləʊ 'məʊʃn]	Zeitlupe	*slow motion* ↔ fast motion

Station 2: How advertising works

1	**added** ['ædɪd]	zusätzlich	There is no *added* sugar in this product.
	artificial [ˌɑ:tɪ'fɪʃl]	künstlich	*artificial* ↔ natural *Fr.* artificiel/-le
	fat [fæt]	Fett	Butter is a kind of *fat*.
	goodness ['gʊdnəs]	wertvolle Inhaltsstoffe	Don't cook vegetables for too long or all the *goodness* in them will get lost.
	iron [aɪən]	Eisen	I'm always tired. Maybe it's lack of *iron*.
	preservative [prɪ'zɜ:vətɪv]	Konservierungsmittel; Konservierungsstoff	We avoid products that contain lots of *preservatives*. *preservative* → to preserve
	nutritious [nju:'trɪʃəs]	nährstoffreich; nahrhaft	A *nutritious* diet is important for your health.
	whole grains *(pl)* ['həʊl greɪnz]	Vollkorn	Bread made from *whole grains* is healthier than white bread.
2	to **contribute to** [kən'trɪbju:t tə]	beitragen zu	= to play a part/role in *Fr.* contribuer; ***Lat.*** contribuere
	childhood ['tʃaɪldhʊd]	Kindheit	I had a happy *childhood*.
3	**watchdog** ['wɒtʃdɒg]	Aufsichtsbehörde; Aufsichtsstelle; Aufsicht	= an organisation or body of people who check that companies follow the laws
4	**steel** [sti:l]	Stahl; Stahl-	Germany's *steel* industry is very big.
	needle ['ni:dl]	Nadel	Have you got a *needle*? I need to sew on this button.
	reasonably ['ri:znəbli]	halbwegs; einigermaßen	*reasonably* comfortable = comfortable, but not extremely
	promotion of [prə'məʊʃn‿əv]	das Bewerben von	the *promotion of* a product = advertising a product
	to **apply (to)** [ə'plaɪ tə]	gelten (für); zutreffen (auf)	This method of working *applies to* other tasks too.
	to **examine** [ɪg'zæmɪn]	untersuchen; kontrollieren	*to examine* → examination *Fr.* examiner
	to **promote sth** [prə'məʊt]	für etw. werben	*to promote sth* = to advertise sth
	to **break the law** [ˌbreɪk ðə 'lɔ:]	gegen das Gesetz verstoßen	= not to follow the law
	to **police** [pə'li:s]	überwachen; kontrollieren	= to check that rules and laws are followed
	progressive [prə'gresɪv]	fortschrittlich; progressiv	My school is *progressive*. They try out lots of new methods.
	awareness [ə'weənəs]	Bewusstsein; Interesse	*awareness* → to become aware of sth

	to **have a poor record (as)** [ˌhævˌə pɔː ˈrekɔːdˌæz]	eine schlechte Bilanz (in Bezug auf/hinsichtlich) aufweisen	The company *has a* very *poor* environmental *record*.
	equal opportunity [ˌiːkwəlˌɒpəˈtjuːnəti]	Chancengleichheit	= the same chances for everyone
	care [keə]	Pflege; Betreuung; Aufmerksamkeit; Sorgfalt; Versorgung	= attention or thought you give to sth
	promotional [prəˈməʊʃnl]	Werbe-	*promotional* → to promote → promotion of
	to **be aware of sth** [biˌəˈweərˌəv]	sich etw. bewusst sein	I'*m aware of* the negative effects of media overuse. You don't have to remind me all the time.
7	**targeted** [ˈtɑːɡɪtɪd]	gezielt	*targeted* ads = ads aimed at a specific person or group of people
	to **disable** [dɪsˈeɪbl]	deaktivieren	Cookies on websites can be *disabled*.
	clickbait [ˈklɪkbeɪt]	Klickfang; Klickköder; Clickbait; Klickbait	= catchy headline or material on a website which leads you to another website or ad

Options

1	**advertising agency** [ˈædvətaɪzɪŋˌeɪdʒənsi]	Werbeagentur	= a company that designs and creates adverts
	ice cream parlour [aɪs ˈkriːm ˌpɑːlə]	Eisdiele; Eiscafé	Let's go to the new *ice cream parlour* around the corner.
	Creative Commons (licence) [kriˌeɪtɪv ˈkɒmnz ˌlaɪsns]	lizenzfrei; frei nutzbar	Always use *Creative Commons* photos for presentations or publications.

Advertising

advertisement	Anzeige; Werbung; Reklame
advertising	Werbung; Werbebranche
advertising agency	Werbeagentur
advertising campaign	Werbekampagne
ad copy	Werbetext
advertiser	Werbeträger/-in; Werbefachmann/-frau; Inserent
to advertise (for)	werben (für); Werbung machen; anpreisen; inserieren
to place an advertisement	eine Anzeige platzieren
to design an ad / a campaign	eine Anzeige(nkampagne) entwerfen
to hire	beauftragen; anheuern
internet ad	Onlinewerbung
TV / radio commercial	Werbespot; Fernsehwerbung / Radiospot
brochure	Prospekt; Broschüre
catalogue	Katalog; Broschüre
flyer	Flyer
leaflet	Prospekt; Faltblatt
street banner	Werbebanner; Werbetransparent
(electronic) billboard	(elektronische) Anzeigentafel / Werbetafel
brand	Marke
product	Produkt
launch	Markteinführung
to launch a product	ein Produkt auf den Markt bringen / einführen / lancieren
to promote a product	ein Produkt vermarkten
promotion (of)	das Bewerben (von); Werbeaktion
target group	Zielgruppe
to target a market	auf einen Markt abzielen
market leader	Marktführer/-in
market research	Marktforschung
market share	Marktanteil
retail outlet	Einzelhandelsgeschäft
retail price	Einzelhandelspreis
to attract attention	Aufmerksamkeit erregen
to catch sb's attention	jmdn. auf sich aufmerksam machen; Interesse wecken
to evoke feelings	Gefühle hervorrufen
to identify with (sb/sth)	sich identifizieren mit
to persuade (sb)	(jmdn.) überzeugen; (jmdn.) überreden

Across cultures 2 Exploring culture in new dimensions

	dimension [daɪˈmenʃn]	Dimension; Aspekt	It took me a very long time to realise the full *dimension* of the situation.
1	**VR headset** [viː; ˌɑːr ˈhedset]	VR-Brille	I always feel sick when I use a *VR headset*.
	AR goggles *(pl)* [eɪ; ˌɑːr ˈɡɒɡlz]	AR-Brille	I got the latest *AR goggles* for my birthday. They're amazing.
	to **immerse oneself in sth** [ɪˌmɜːs ˈɪn]	in etw. eintauchen	They *immersed themselves in* the new game. = They got completely involved in the new game.

	to **interact (with sb/sth)** [ˌɪntəˈækt]	(mit jmdm./etw.) interagieren; (mit jmdm.) kommunizieren	= to communicate *Fr.* interagir
	to **enhance** [ɪnˈhɑːns]	anreichern; aufbereiten	= to add digital information, photos, etc.
	real-life [ˌrɪəlˈlaɪf]	real; wirklich	*real-life* ↔ fake
	computer-generated [kəmˌpjuːtəˈdʒenreɪtɪd]	computergeneriert; computererzeugt	= produced by/with a computer
	image [ˈɪmɪdʒ]	Bild; Abbildung	= picture; photo *Fr.* image *(f)*; ***Lat.*** imago *(f)*
	written [ˈrɪtn]	schriftlich	Please hand in your application in *written* form.
2	**metaverse** [ˈmetəvɜːs]	Metaversum *(virtuell erzeugter, dreidimensionaler Raum, in dem man sich z.B. mit Freunden/ Freundinnen treffen kann)*	Let's meet in the *metaverse*.
	immersive [ɪˈmɜːsɪv]	vollständig eintauchend; immersiv	*immersive* → to immerse oneself in sth
	unwieldy [ʌnˈwiːldi]	unhandlich; sperrig	Can you imagine how *unwieldy* mobile phones used to be in the beginning?
4	**in person** [ɪn ˈpɜːsn]	persönlich	You have to pick up the documents *in person*.
	best-kept secret [ˌbestkept ˈsiːkrət]	bestgehütetes Geheimnis	Don't worry, I won't tell anyone. It'll remain the *best-kept secret* ever.
	change [tʃeɪndʒ]	Abwechslung	*change* → to change
	to **hike** [haɪk]	wandern	We *hiked* all the way from Stuttgart to Lake Constance.
	take a (quick) peek inside sth [ˌteɪk‿ə ˈpiːk]	einen (kurzen) Blick in etw. hineinwerfen	*to take a peek inside sth* = to have a quick look at sth
	from the comfort of … [ˌfrəm ðə ˈkʌmfət‿əv]	bequem von … aus	Nowadays, you can order almost anything *from the comfort of* your sofa.
	advertising disclosure *(no pl)* [ˈædvətaɪzɪŋ dɪsˌkləʊʒə]	Kenntlichmachung von Werbung	= to indicate advertising
	affiliate link [əˈfɪlieɪt lɪŋk]	Affiliate-Link; Link zu einem Werbepartner	Follow the *affiliate link* if you want more information.
	advertising *(no pl)* [ˈædvətaɪzɪŋ]	Werbung; Reklame; Werbe-	*advertising* → to advertise → advertisement → advertiser
	to **regulate** [ˈregjəleɪt]	regulieren; regeln	= to control sth by introducing rules *to regulate* → regulation
	by law [baɪ ˈlɔː]	gesetzlich; rechtlich	= legally
	disclaimer [dɪsˈkleɪmə]	Disclaimer; Haftungsausschluss	You can find the *disclaimer* at the bottom of the page.
5	**hybrid** [ˈhaɪbrɪd]	hybrid	! Watch the pronunciation.
	with regard to [ˌwɪð rɪˈgɑːd tə]	im Hinblick auf	*With regard to* safety rules, there is a lot you have to consider.
	volume [ˈvɒljuːm]	Lautstärke	It's too loud! Please turn the *volume* down.
	kinda *(= kind of) (infml)* [ˈkaɪndə]	ziemlich; irgendwie	This is *kinda* weird.

	frozen ['frəʊzn]	eingefroren; gefroren; erfroren; vereist	The internet connection in this hotel is terrible. Only *frozen* pictures! *frozen* → to freeze
7	**interaction** [ˌɪntə'ækʃn]	Interaktion; Kommunikation	*interaction* → to interact
	via ['vaɪə]	über; per	Let's talk *via* messenger.
	basic ['beɪsɪk]	einfach	Breakfast was *basic*, but nice.
	pandemic [ˌpæn'demɪk]	Pandemie	How did you get through the *pandemic*?
	educational [ˌedʒʊ'keɪʃnl]	Bildungs-; Lehr-; Erziehungs-	What do you think of *educational* computer games?
	digital imaging technician (DIT) [ˌdɪdʒɪtl ˌɪmɪdʒɪŋ tek'nɪʃn]	Techniker/-in für digitale Bildgebung	*DIT* sounds like the perfect career job for me.
	to **encourage sb to do sth** [ɪn'kʌrɪdʒ]	jmdm. (dazu) raten, etw. zu tun; jmdn. (dazu) ermuntern, etw. zu tun	My parents *encouraged* me to apply for this job. ***Fr.*** encourager
	in the wild [ˌɪn ðə 'waɪld]	in freier Wildbahn	*in the wild* → wild
	to **adopt** [ə'dɒpt]	übernehmen; annehmen; adoptieren	My team liked the draft and *adopted* it without changing anything.
	gaming ['ɡeɪmɪŋ]	Spielen; Zocken; Spiele-	I would love to work in the *gaming* industry.
	advance [əd'vɑ:ns]	Fortschritt	This new gadget is a huge technological *advance*.
	excessive [ɪk'sesɪv]	übermäßig; überschüssig	They took an *excessive* interest in video games.
	enemy ['enəmi]	Feind/-in	*enemy* ↔ friend ***Fr.*** ennemi/-e *(m), (f)*; ***Lat.*** inimicus/-a *(m), (f)*
	two-tier ['tu:tɪə]	gespalten; Zweiklassen-	↔ fair
	immersion [ɪ'mɜ:ʃn]	Eintauchen; Immersion	*immersion* → immersive → to immerse oneself in sth
8	**Creative Commons (licence)** [kriˌeɪtɪv 'kɒmnz ˌlaɪsns]	lizenzfrei; frei nutzbar	Always use *Creative Commons* photos for presentations or publications.
	to **enable sth** [ɪ'neɪbl]	etw. aktivieren	I can't use the internet. – Maybe you forgot to *enable* WiFi on your computer?

Digital tools and devices

Using your smartphone, tablet, display, touchscreen
- to tap and swipe
- to charge a battery / a rechargeable battery
- to lock ↔ to unlock your SIM card
- SIM = subscriber identity module (Teilnehmer-Identitätsmodul)
- to switch on power save mode
- to change settings
- to install ↔ to deinstall apps / an operating system (Betriebssystem)
- to get (regular / automatic) updates / bugfixes (Fehlerbehebung)
- to upload ↔ to download files
- to make a purchase
- the amount is charged / credited to your account

Using a network
- there's no signal / my phone has got no reception
- to log on / sign into a secure / open network
- internet security, firewall ↔ virus, Trojan horse
- VPN = virtual private network
- to store data in a cloud
- to import / to transfer / to read in data

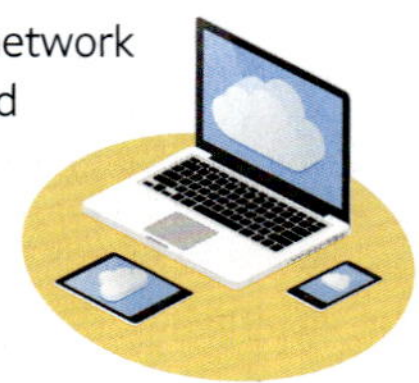

IT words

Most IT words are English and are universally understood. German translations are only used for some of them. Some are used with German endings.

access	Zugang
account	Konto
app [æp]	App; Anwendung
AI (= artificial intelligence)	künstliche Intelligenz (KI)
AR (= augmented reality)	Augmented Reality
browser	
button	Knopf
cable	Kabel
clip	
computer	Rechner
connection	Verbindung
console	Konsole
controller	
data	Daten
device	Gerät
digital	
format	Format; formatieren
hardware / software	
headset	
influencer	
to install / to deinstall	
key; keyboard	Taste, Tastatur
laptop; notebook	
mouse; mousepad	
network	Netzwerk
offline / online	
operating system	Betriebssystem
password	Passwort
platform	Plattform
robot	Roboter; Automat
screen	Bildschirm
search engine	Suchmaschine
server	
service	Dienst
settings	Einstellungen
smartphone	
streaming	
tab	
tablet	
update	
user	
VR (= virtual reality)	VR (= virtuelle Realität)
web design	
wifi	WLAN
window	Fenster

English verb + German *-en*

to chat	chatten
to check	checken
to hate	haten
to like	liken
to post	posten
to reset	resetten
to scan	scannen
to stream	streamen

Unit 2 The digital age

Check-in

1	to **be willing to do sth** [bi ˈwɪlɪŋ tə]	gewillt sein, etw. zu tun; bereit sein, etw. zu tun	How much *are* you *willing to* pay for the bike? = to be prepared to do sth
	to **embrace sth/sb** [ɪmˈbreɪs]	etw. (bereitwillig) annehmen	She *embraced* the opportunity.
	to **relate (to sb/sth)** [rɪˈleɪt]	sich (mit etw./jmdm.) identifizieren; eine Vorstellung (von etw./jmdm.) haben	In advertisements you have to present input and pictures your target group can *relate to*. Otherwise it doesn't work.
	I don't get it. [aɪ ˌdəʊnt ˈget_ɪt]	Ich verstehe es nicht.; Ich kapiere es nicht.	*I don't get it.* ↔ I get it!
	to **perceive** [pəˈsiːv]	wahrnehmen	How do you *perceive* this story? *Fr.* percevoir
	to **contribute to** [kənˈtrɪbjuːt tə]	beitragen zu	= to play a part/role in *Fr.* contribuer; *Lat.* contribuere
	footprint [ˈfʊtprɪnt]	Fußabdruck	Remember that every time you do sth on social media, you leave a digital *footprint*.

	brand [brænd]	Marke	= a particular product or line of products made by one company and sold under a special name
	to **foster sth** ['fɒstə]	etw. fördern	= to help the development or growth of sth = to support
	mindset ['maɪndset]	Denkweise; Einstellung	How is your generation's *mindset* different from that of your parents?
2	**temptation** [temp'teɪʃn]	Versuchung	The child ate some of the cake before her birthday. The *temptation* was too big.
	to **leaf through sth** ['li:f θru:]	etw. durchblättern; in etw. herumblättern	After *leafing through* the book, I decided not to read it. It seemed boring.
	to **feel trapped** [fi:l 'træpt]	sich gefangen fühlen	If you *feel trapped* in a habit, for example, it's difficult not to act according to that habit.
	viewfinder ['vju:ˌfaɪndə]	Bildsucher; Sucher	I prefer to look through the *viewfinder* of my camera when I take pictures, not at the screen.
	to **miss out (on sth)** [ˌmɪs‿'aʊt]	(etw.) verpassen	Of course I'm coming to the party. I don't want to *miss out on* the event of the year!
	beauty ['bju:ti]	Schönheit; Schönheits-	*Fr.* beauté *(f)*

Station 1: The future of school and learning

approach [ə'prəʊtʃ]	Herangehensweise; Vorgehensweise; Ansatz	We get the same results but we have different *approaches*. *Fr.* approche ***(f)***
textbook ['tekstbʊk]	Lehrbuch; Schulbuch	I forgot my *textbook*. Can I have a look at yours?
curriculum, *(pl)* **curricula** [kə'rɪkjələm; kə'rɪkjələ]	Lehrplan	The Ministry of Education works out the *curricula* for the different school subjects.
emphasis ['emfəsɪs]	Schwerpunkt; Fokus	If you stress sth, you give it *emphasis*.
to **collaborate** [kə'læbreɪt]	zusammenarbeiten; kollaborativ arbeiten	= to work together ***Lat.*** laborare
to **adapt** [ə'dæpt]	(sich) anpassen	*Adapting* to quickly changing situations will become an important skill for future generations.
personalised ['pɜ:snlaɪzd]	personalisiert; individualisiert	*personalised* → personal → person
trial-and-error learning [ˌtraɪəl‿ən‿'erə ˌlɜ:nɪŋ]	Lernen durch Ausprobieren	= by trying out
coming ['kʌmɪŋ]	kommend; herannahend; bevorstehend	= future
-based [beɪst]	-bezogen; -basiert	In the future education will also be digital-*based*.
trial program ['traɪəl]	Probelauf	During the *trial program* a team of young students and developers will test the new game.
to **perform well/badly** [pəˌfɔ:m 'wel/'bædli]	gut/schlecht sein; gut/schlecht abschneiden; mehr/weniger leisten	Most of the class didn't *perform* very *well* in the test.
to **benefit from sth** ['benɪfɪt frəm]	von etw. profitieren; aus etw. Nutzen ziehen	*to benefit* → a benefit

	higher education [ˌhaɪər‿edʒʊˈkeɪʃn]	Hochschulbildung; weiterführende Schulbildung	Universities and colleges are institutions offering *higher education*. *higher education* ↔ primary/secondary education
	enrollment [ɪnˈrəʊlmənt]	Anmeldung; Registrierung	= registration
3	**in progress** [ɪn ˈprəʊgres]	im Verlauf; im Gange	The construction work in our road hasn't been finished yet: it's still *in progress*.
	point [pɔɪnt]	Zeitpunkt	The project will have to be finished at a certain *point* in the future.
4	**regular** [ˈregjələ]	regelmäßig; gleichmäßig	*Fr.* régulier/ière
6	**pen pal** [ˈpen pæl]	Brieffreund/-in	I have three *pen pals*: two in the US and one in France.

Station 2: Creating your own reality

1	to **modify** [ˈmɒdɪfaɪ]	verändern; modifizieren	= to change *Fr.* modifier
	image [ˈɪmɪdʒ]	Darstellung; Image	Usually, the public *image* of stars or politicians is different from who they are in private. *Fr.* image *(f)*
	to **retouch** [ˌriːˈtʌtʃ]	retuschieren; nachbessern; korrigieren	My friends and I did a challenge on not *retouching* photos we post online at all for one month.
	to **determine** [dɪˈtɜːmɪn]	bestimmen; feststellen; entscheiden	Look at these pictures and try to *determine* those which have been retouched and those which haven't. *Fr.* déterminer
	to **enable sb** [ɪˈneɪbl]	jmdn. befähigen; jmdm. ermöglichen	= to make it possible for sb to do sth
	to **perpetuate** [pəˈpetʃueɪt]	aufrechterhalten; festigen; fortbestehen lassen	= to make sth continue for a long time ***Lat.*** perpetuus/-a/-um *(adj)*
	homogenized [həˈmɒdʒənaɪzd]	homogenisiert	Milk nowadays is usually *homogenized*.
	as opposed to [ˌəz‿əˈpəʊz‿tə]	im Gegensatz zu; statt; anstatt	= in contrast to
	potential [pəˈtenʃl]	potenziell; möglich	= possible *Fr.* potentiel/-le
	harmful [ˈhɑːmfl]	schädlich; nachteilig; verletzend	Does it contain any *harmful* substances?
	to **be titled** [bi ˈtaɪtld]	betitelt; mit dem Titel versehen	*to be titled* → a title
	harm [hɑːm]	Schaden; Verletzung	= damage; injury
	before and after [bɪˌfɔːr‿ənd ˈɑːftə]	vorher-nachher	Wow, the *before and after* effect is really amazing.
	striking [ˈstraɪkɪŋ]	markant; auffällig; bemerkenswert	= interesting and attracting attention
	to **alter** [ˈɔːltə]	abändern; ändern; verändern	= to change
	to **come up with sth** [ˌkʌm‿ˈʌp wɪð]	auf etw. kommen	= to think of sth

	particularly [pə'tɪkjələli]	insbesondere; vor allem	The app attracts young people, *particularly* young women.
	to **be scared by sth** [bi 'skeəd baɪ]	von etw. erschrocken sein	= to be worried by sth
	inadequate [ɪ'nædɪkwət]	unzulänglich; nicht ausreichend; mangelhaft	= not good enough
	to **note** [nəʊt]	anmerken; erwähnen	*to note* → a note
	to **come along** [ˌkʌm‿ə'lɒŋ]	entstehen; herkommen	We didn't expect an opportunity like that to *come along*.
	subject ['sʌbdʒɪkt]	*hier:* fotografierte Person	The *subjects* you take pictures of always have to agree to be photographed.
	variety (of) [və'raɪəti‿əv]	Vielzahl (an); Vielfalt (von)	I love to cook with a great *variety* of ingredients. *Fr.* variété *(f)*
	precondition [ˌpri:kən'dɪʃn]	Voraussetzung; Bedingung	The *precondition* for taking part in the project is that you have to be 18 years old.
	to **witness sb do sth** ['wɪtnəs]	sehen, wie jmd. etw. tut; beobachten, wie jmd. etw. tut	= to see sth happen
	to **enlarge** [ɪn'lɑ:dʒ]	vergrößern	This photo is beautiful. You should *enlarge* it and put it up on the wall.
	to **plump** [plʌmp]	prall machen; prall werden	Do you think *plumping* lips makes them more beautiful?
	reflection [rɪ'flekʃn]	Ausdruck; Zeichen	a *reflection* of = a sign of
	altered ['ɔ:ltəd]	verändert	= changed
	homogenous [ˌhɒmə'dʒi:nəs]	gleichartig; homogen	*homogenous* → homogenized
2	**evaluation** [ɪˌvæljueɪʃn]	Einschätzung; Beurteilung	Regular *evaluation* of the healthcare system is important.
	modified ['mɒdɪfaɪd]	verändert	= changed; altered *Fr.* modifié/-e
5	**unflattering** [ʌn'flætrɪŋ]	wenig schmeichelhaft; unvorteilhaft	I'd rather not buy that dress. It's *unflattering*.
8	**counter** ['kaʊntə]	Gegen-	= against; opposite
	to **label** ['leɪbl]	bezeichnen; kennzeichnen	*to label* → a label
	to **apply (to)** [ə'plaɪ tə]	gelten (für); zutreffen (auf)	This method of working *applies to* other tasks or situations too.
9	**due to** ['dju: tə]	wegen; infolge von	The project wasn´t completed *due to* a lack of money. = because of
	to **restrict** [rɪ'strɪkt]	begrenzen; beschränken	Social interaction was *restricted* during the pandemic.
	to **homeschool** ['həumsku:l]	(jmdn.) zuhause unterrichten; Hausunterricht erteilen	= to teach children in their own homes
10	**disorder** [dɪ'sɔ:də]	Störung; Erkrankung	*disorder* ↔ order
11	**accountant** [ə'kaʊntənt]	Buchhalter/-in; Steuerberater/-in	I like working with numbers. Maybe I should consider becoming an *accountant*.

Story 1: Video game murder

1	to **slay, slew, slain** [sleɪ; slu:; sleɪn]	töten; erschlagen	= to kill
	to **strike sb, struck, struck** [straɪk; strʌk; strʌk]	jmdm. auffallen	The headline *struck me.* I couldn't believe what it said!
	at the reminder of [ˌət ðə rɪ'maɪndər‿əv]	bei der Erinnerung an	= when remembering sth
	coder ['kəʊdə]	Programmierer/-in	= a person who develops computer programmes
	to **suspect** [sə'spekt]	vermuten; verdächtigen	I strongly *suspect* that they are not telling the truth. *Lat.* suspicari
	in a row [ˌɪn‿ə‿'rəʊ]	nacheinander; hintereinander; in Folge	They had three pieces of cake *in a row.*
	tear [tɪə]	Träne	a *tear* → to burst into tears → to cry
	to **stream** [stri:m]	strömen; laufen; fließen	The child couldn't stop crying. Tears *were streaming* down his face.
	damn *(infml)* [dæm]	verdammt; Scheiß-	Stop making that *damn* noise. It's really getting on my nerves.
	to **freeze sb, froze, frozen** [fri:z; frəʊz; 'frəʊzn]	jmdn. erstarren lassen	Her nasty words *froze me.*
	to **process** ['prəʊsəs]	verarbeiten; verstehen	The experience was intense. It took them a while to *process* it.
	to **throw up** *(coll)* [ˌθrəʊ‿'ʌp]	erbrechen; sich übergeben	I felt sick in the car and *threw up.* = to be sick
	to **stack** [stæk]	stapeln	= to put objects, e.g. chairs, on top of each other
	dude *(AE) (coll)* [du:d]	Typ; Kerl	Hey, *dude*! What's up?
	to **wash over sb** [ˌwɒʃ‿'əʊvə]	jmdn. überkommen	= to affect sb strongly
	to **navigate through sth** [ˌnævɪgeɪt 'θru:]	sich einen Weg durch etw. bahnen	They had to *navigate through* a big crowd in order to get to the exit.
	swarm [swɔ:m]	(Menschen)Schar; Schwarm	= a large group of people
	sweaty ['sweti]	verschwitzt; feucht	*sweaty* → to sweat
	Egyptian [ɪ'dʒɪpʃn]	ägyptisch; Ägypter/-in	Have you ever been to the *Egyptian* Museum in Berlin?
	epic ['epɪk]	episch; heroisch	There are lots of *epic* characters in stories from Scandinavia.
	universe ['ju:nɪvɜ:s]	Universum; Welt	*Fr.* univers *(m)*
	to **trade sth (for sth)** ['treɪd fɔ:]	etw. (gegen etw.) eintauschen; etw. (durch etw.) austauschen	= to buy, sell or exchange things
	I can't shake this feeling that ... [aɪ 'kɑ:nt ˌʃeɪk ðɪs 'fi:lɪŋ ðæt]	Ich werde das Gefühl nicht los, dass ...	*I can't shake this feeling that* there's something really wrong here.
	to **whip out** ['wɪp‿aʊt]	zücken; parat haben	The journalist *whipped out* a pen and took notes.
	to **want sth badly** [wɒnt 'bædli]	etw. unbedingt wollen	= you want sth very much

	dragon ['drægn]	Drache	Harry Potter fought a *dragon* in ***Harry Potter and the Goblet of Fire***.
	loss [lɒs]	Verlust	*a loss* → to lose
	to **have sth at one's fingertips** [ˌhæv æt ˌwʌnz 'fɪŋgətɪps]	etw. zum Greifen nah haben; etw. schnell zur Hand haben	The attraction of games like this is that you can *have* a whole world *at your fingertips*.
	to **be shy of sth** *(after noun)* [bi 'ʃaɪ‿əv]	fehlen	The team *is* still *shy of* two players.
	time-consuming ['taɪmkənˌsjuːmɪŋ]	zeitintensiv; zeitaufwändig	If sth is *time-consuming*, it takes a lot of time to do it.
3	**downside** ['daʊnsaɪd]	Kehrseite; Schattenseite	= the negative side of sth
6	**intended** [ɪn'tendɪd]	beabsichtigt; intendiert	We expected that to happen. It was an *intended* result.
	outcome ['aʊtkʌm]	Ergebnis; Resultat	= result
	to **ensure** [ɪn'ʃɔː]	sicherstellen	We try to *ensure* that everyone is treated equally.
	be out of proportion (to) [bi ˌaʊt‿əv prə'pɔːʃn]	in keinem Verhältnis (zu etw.) stehen	The effort *is out of proportion* with the result.

Hyphenation

In English hyphens are used in the following cases:

1. When two or more words act as a single idea (compound adjectives) and describe the noun that follows:

   world-famous influencer
   eco-conscious shopping
   black-and-white picture
   real-life visit
   computer-generated image
   time-consuming activity

   ! Exceptions to the rule include, for example, **all-important**:

   These computers are all important. These computers are **all-important**.

2. Between numbers in fractions:
   one-fifth, **one-third**, etc.

3. To separate a word at the end of a line along its syllables.

   ! A one-syllable word cannot be separated with a hyphen.

Skills: How to work in a team

1	**further** ['fɜːðə]	weiter	Are there any *further* questions? = Are there any other questions?
	to **set, set, set** [set; set; set]	festlegen; festsetzen	It's better to *set* small goals and achieve everything than to *set* large goals and not reach them.
	milestone ['maɪlstəʊn]	Meilenstein	We've achieved three out of four *milestones* already. Almost there!
	to **stick to sth** [stɪk tə]	sich an etw. halten	*Stick to* the rules!
	progress ['prəʊgres]	Fortschritt	= improvement; development *Fr.* progrès *(m)*

	to **assess** [ə'ses]	einschätzen; beurteilen	We need to *assess* the results. = to judge; to evaluate
2	to **visualise** ['vɪʒuəlaɪz]	visualisieren; sichtbar machen	= to show; to make seen

Check-out

1	**sales** *(pl)* [seɪlz]	Umsatz; Absatz	Oil companies have had record *sales* due to the energy crisis.
2	to **strive (for), strove, striven** [straɪv; strəʊv; 'strɪvn]	streben (nach)	What do you think it is important to *strive for* in life? Happiness? Health? Wealth? …
	perfection [pə'fekʃn]	Perfektion; Vollkommenheit	! Watch the spelling and the pronunciation.
3	**queer** [kwɪə]	queer *(Begriff, den manche Personen aus der LGBTQ+ Community als Eigenbezeichnung benutzen)*	
4	**sideways** ['saɪdweɪz]	seitwärts; seitlich	Crabs move *sideways*.
	to **dive** [daɪv]	(sich) ducken; (ab)tauchen	They *dived* to avoid the low-flying insects.
	to **stumble** ['stʌmbl]	stolpern; straucheln	I *stumbled* and fell.
	to **spot** [spɒt]	erkennen; entdecken	= to recognise; to notice
	trunk [trʌŋk]	Stamm; Baumstamm	A lot of tree *trunks* were blocking the roads after the storm.
	immediately [ɪ'mi:diətli]	sofort; gleich	I don't want to wait any longer. Let's go *immediately*.
	to **view** [vju:]	ansehen; anschauen	= to look at
	underneath [ˌʌndə'ni:θ]	unter; darunter	= below
	literally ['lɪtrəli]	wörtlich	= used to emphasize the truth of sth
	shame [ʃeɪm]	Scham; Schande; Schmach	The situation was so embarrassing and painful that they felt great *shame*.
	weapon ['wepən]	Waffe	I would never ever want to have a *weapon* in my house.
	barely ['beəli]	kaum	I can *barely* see him. = I can hardly see him.
	desperate ['desprət]	verzweifelt; hoffnungslos; ausweglos	= with little hope *Fr.* désespéré/-e; ***Lat.*** desperare
5	**killer** *(coll)* ['kɪlə]	toll; super; Wahnsinns-	We had a *killer* weekend!
7	**coding** ['kəʊdɪŋ]	Programmier-	*coding* → coder

Digital communication and cooperation

Activities

- to create / to maintain a blog / a vlog
- to post / to publish on the internet
- to upload content to the internet
- to subscribe to / to use a messenger service / a streaming service / a dating service
- to collaborate
- to contribute to a wiki
- to block / to disable / to unblock an account
- to mute a chat (stummschalten)
- to follow somebody
- fashion / lifestyle / fitness influencer – haul girl / boy
- unboxing
- to crop / to edit pictures

Trends/Developments

- gamification
- technology based methods of learning
- lifelong learning

Problems

- phishing Ausspionieren von Daten
- fake news
- copyright issues / copyright violation urheberrechtliche Fragen / Verletzung des Urheberrechts
- to control your privacy
- cyber bullying
- hate speech

Exercise Sounds and spelling: Word stress in word families

a) *Read the following sentences with words from the same word family out loud. If you aren't sure where to put the stress, you can use an online dictionary.*

1. Would you like to **contribute** a comment? All **contributions** are welcome.
2. Those bargains are **tempting**, but I must ignore the **temptation**.
3. Working on projects helps people to develop collaborative **strategies**. A **strategic** approach is always important in teamwork.
4. He noticed that people often **modified** the same things in their photos. The **modifications** were mainly to the eyes and mouth.
5. In the test people could **combine** filters with retouching techniques. In fact, a **combination** of both was the most common.
6. With a simple app you can **alter** photos of yourself, and nobody can see the **alterations**.
7. The models in **various** adverts show a little more **variety** than in the past.
8. In group projects there can be a **progressive** decrease in interest so you should check the group's **progress** regularly.

A 54 **b)** *Listen to check your answers.*

Text and media smart 2 Dealing with factual texts

Check-in

	argumentative text [ɑ:gjəˌmentətɪv 'tekst]	Erörterung; Aufsatz	An *argumentative text* needs to be convincing, but sorry, this text isn't.
1	**everyday** ['evrideɪ]	alltäglich, Alltags-	An *everyday* situation is sth that happens every day.
2	**intention** [ɪn'tenʃn]	Absicht; Intention	= what sb wants to do *intention* → intended

Station 1: Summary and analysis

	summary ['sʌmri]	Zusammenfassung	*summary* → to sum up
1	**honey** ['hʌni]	Schatz	Hey *honey*! = Hey darling!
	to **quote** [kwəʊt]	zitieren	*to quote* → a quotation
	rise [raɪz]	Anstieg; Zunahme	There's a *rise* in the world's population every year.
	parental [pə'rentl]	elterlich; Eltern-	She left her *parental* home at the age of 18. *parental* → parents
	surveillance *(no pl)* [sɜ:'veɪləns]	Überwachung; Überwachungs-	*Fr.* surveillance *(f)*
	guardian ['gɑ:diən]	Erziehungsberechtigte/-r; Vormund	*guardian* → guard → to guard
	on a daily basis [ˌɒn‿ə deɪli 'beɪsɪs]	täglich; tagtäglich	Let's look at how much we spend *on a daily basis*.
	whereabouts ['weərəbaʊts]	Aufenthaltsort; Verbleib	The police had no information on the *whereabouts* of the criminal.
	extension [ɪk'stenʃn]	Erweiterung; Vergrößerung; Ausdehnung; Ausbau	*extension* → to extend
	helicopter ['helɪkɒptə]	Helikopter; Hubschrauber	The *helicopter* landed on the roof of the hospital.
	parenting ['peərntɪŋ]	Kindererziehung	Can you recommend a book on *parenting*?
	battleground ['bætlgraʊnd]	Reizthema; Schlachtfeld	Media-use and gaming are probably a *battleground* in most families.
	contentious [kən'tenʃəs]	strittig; kontrovers; umstritten	Both your opinions are highly *contentious*.
	solicitor [sə'lɪsɪtə]	Rechtsanwalt/Rechtsanwältin; Anwalt/Anwältin	We should ask a *solicitor* for legal advice.
	to **last** [lɑ:st]	durchhalten; (an)dauern; (an)halten	My motivation for doing sports at least once a week didn't *last* for long.
	not necessarily [ˌnɒt nesə'serəli]	nicht unbedingt	Only because a product is more expensive than another one of the same kind does*n't necessarily* mean that it is better quality.
	meanwhile ['mi:nˌwaɪl]	derweil	You can cut the grass today. *Meanwhile* I'll be working in the greenhouse.

	to **go along with sb/sth** [ˌgəʊ‿ə'lɒŋ wɪð]	jmdm./etw. zustimmen; sich jmdm./etw. anschließen	I liked the idea and *went along with it.*
	request [rɪ'kwest]	Bitte; Wunsch; Anfrage	= wish
	to **catch sb out doing sth** ['kætʃ‿aʊt ˌdu:ɪŋ]	jmdn. bei etw. erwischen	The teacher *caught them out smoking* in the playground.
	frankly ['fræŋkli]	ehrlich gesagt; offen gestanden	= to tell you the truth
	anxious ['æŋʃəs]	besorgt; ängstlich	= worried
	to **mess up** *(infml)* [ˌmes‿'ʌp]	Mist bauen	= to do sth badly or wrong
	childhood ['tʃaɪldhʊd]	Kindheit	I had a happy *childhood.*
	worrier ['wʌriə]	jmd., der sich ständig Sorgen macht; Pessimist/-in	*a worrier* → to worry → to be worried
	to **keep sb sane** [ki:p 'seɪn]	jmdn. bei Verstand halten	Going for long walks at the weekend *keeps me sane.*
	neither … nor … ['naɪðə; 'ni:ðə ... nɔ:]	weder … noch …	*neither … nor* → not either
	evil ['i:vl]	böse; schlecht	*evil* ↔ good
	boundary ['baʊndri]	Grenze	= (imaginary) line that marks where something (e.g. an area of land) ends and something else begins
	negotiation [nɪˌgəʊʃi'eɪʃn]	Verhandlung	= a discussion in which (different groups of) people try to agree on sth and make a decision
	dismissive [dɪ'smɪsɪv]	abweisend; ablehnend	What's all this *dismissive* behaviour about? Is there a problem?
	to **confide in sb** [kən'faɪd‿ɪn]	sich jmdm. anvertrauen	*to confide in sb* → confident → confidence
	mute [mju:t]	still; schweigsam	= silent
	rupture ['rʌptʃə]	Bruch; Riss	My sister and I had a big fight many years ago. Unfortunately, we've never been able to fully repair the *rupture.*
	to **be disputed** [bi dɪ'spju:tɪd]	umstritten sein	The negative effects of the medicine *are* highly *disputed.*
	offspring ['ɒfsprɪŋ]	Nachwuchs; Nachkommen	= one's children, grandchildren, etc.
	abridged [ə'brɪdʒd]	gekürzt	An *abridged* text is a text that has been made shorter.
2	**entitled** [ɪn'taɪtld]	mit dem Titel	*entitled* → title
	to **negotiate sth** [nɪ'gəʊʃieɪt]	etw. aushandeln; etw. verhandeln	They have been *negotiating* better working conditions for many years. *to negotiate* → negotiation *Fr.* négocier
	to **advise (sb to do sth)** [əd'vaɪz]	(jmdm.) raten (etw. zu tun)	! *to advise sb to do sth* = to give sb advice
3	to **reduce** [rɪ'dju:s]	reduzieren; vermindern; verringern	We have to *reduce* CO_2 emissions worldwide. *Fr.* réduire
	to **state** [steɪt]	nennen; darlegen; darstellen	*to state* → a statement
5	**partly** ['pɑ:tli]	teilweise; zum Teil	= not fully

6	**restriction** [rɪ'strɪkʃn]	Begrenzung; Beschränkung; Einschränkung; Restriktion	My parents are so strict – we have too many *restrictions*! *Fr.* restriction *(f)*
	fixed [fɪkst]	festgesetzt; festgelegt	Sorry, I can't grant any reduction. The price is *fixed*.
	ID (identification) [ˌaɪ'di (aɪˌdentɪfɪ'keɪʃn)]	Identifizierung; Identifikation	Can I see your *ID*, please.
	purchase ['pɜːtʃəs]	Kauf	A house is the most expensive *purchase* most people ever make.
	mental ['mentl]	psychisch; seelisch	*mental* ↔ physical ***Lat.*** mens *(f)*
	habit ['hæbɪt]	Gewohnheit; Angewohnheit	= sth one usually does *Fr.* habitude *(f)*
	concern [kən'sɜːn]	Sorge	*concern* → to be concerned
	increasingly [ɪn'kriːsiŋli]	zunehmend	Young people's lives are *increasingly* shaped by social media.
	rowing ['rəʊɪŋ]	Rudern	*Rowing* can also be done as esport.
	sailing ['seɪlɪŋ]	Segeln	*sailing* → sailor
	eventually [ɪ'ventʃuəli]	schließlich; endlich; irgendwann	*eventually* = finally
	to **tend to** ['tend tə]	neigen zu; tendieren zu	= to be likely to do sth
7	**complaint** [kəm'pleɪnt]	Beschwerde; Beschwerde-	*a complaint* → to complain *Fr.* plainte
	to **be pleased** [bi 'pliːzd]	froh sein; sich freuen; erfreut sein	= to be happy about sth
	to **raise** [reɪz]	vorbringen; aufwerfen *(Fragen)*	to *raise* a problem or a question
	objective [əb'dʒektɪv]	sachlich	! Watch the spelling and the pronunciation.
	to **justify** ['dʒʌstɪfaɪ]	rechtfertigen	Give examples from the text to *justify* your opinion. = Give examples from the text to support your opinion. *Fr.* justifier

Station 2: Argumentative texts

1	to **harm sb** [hɑːm]	jmdm. schaden; jmdn. verletzen; jmdm. etw. antun	= to hurt or damage *to harm* → harm → harmful → harmless
	to **be confronted with** [bi kən'frʌntɪd wɪð]	konfrontiert werden mit	= to face something that you have to deal with or react to
	disability *(no pl)* [ˌdɪsə'bɪləti]	Behinderung; Beeinträchtigung	People with a *disability* are still not visible or represented enough in our society.
	slim [slɪm]	schlank	I'm sick of only seeing *slim* people on the internet and on social media.
	confidence ['kɒnfɪdns]	Selbstvertrauen	*confidence* → confident
	plastic surgery *(no pl)* [ˌplæstɪk 'sɜːdʒəri]	Schönheitschirurgie; Schönheitsoperation	*Plastic surgery* is expensive and can be dangerous.

	diet [daɪət]	Ernährung; Ernährungsweise; Nahrung; Diät	A balanced and healthy *diet* is important for your health.
	professional [prə'feʃnl]	professionell; Profi-; ausgebildet	I love photography. After school I would really like to work as a *professional* photographer.
3	**well-founded** [ˌwel'faʊndɪd]	fundiert; stichhaltig; begründet	The lawyer had *well-founded* evidence of the crime.
	to **take a stand** [ˌteɪk‿ə 'stænd]	Stellung beziehen; Position beziehen	Whose side are you really on? *Take a stand*!
4	**student council** [ˌstju:dnt 'kaʊnsl]	Vertretung der Schüler/-innen	The *Student Council* meets every Thursday after school.
5	**minimum age** ['mɪnɪməm eɪdʒ]	Mindestalter; Altersgrenze	What's the *minimum age* for getting a part-time job in Germany?

Options

1	**deprivation** [ˌdeprɪ'veɪʃn]	Entbehrung; Entzug	Sleep *deprivation* over a long period of time can be really bad for your health.
	depressed [dɪ'prest]	deprimiert; bedrückt; depressiv	*depressed* → depression
	twist [twɪst]	Clou; Knackpunkt	I'm sure you'd never have expected that, so *here's the twist …*
	to **overuse** [ˌəʊvə'ju:z]	übermäßig nutzen	= to use excessively
	co-founder [ˌkəʊ'faʊndə]	Mitgründer/-in	Only two of the original *co-founders* are still in the company.
	chief executive [ˌtʃi:f‿ɪg'zekjətɪv]	Vorstandsvorsitzende/-r	The head of a company or an organisation is called the *chief executive*.
	overuse [ˌəʊvə'ju:s]	übermäßiger Gebrauch	*overuse* → to overuse
	access ['ækses]	Zugang	The internet offers very fast *access* to information. *Fr.* accès *(m)*
	to **shut down** [ʃʌt 'daʊn]	herunterfahren; abschalten	Stop playing and *shut down* your computer now.
	after bedtime [ˌɑ:ftə 'bedtaɪm]	nach dem Schlafengehen	My parents always say "No mobiles *after bedtime*!" It really gets on my nerves.
	to **be aware of sth** [bi‿ə'weər‿əv]	sich etw. bewusst sein	I'*m aware of* the negative effects of media overuse. You don't have to remind me all the time.
	to **complain** [kəm'pleɪn]	sich beschweren; sich beklagen	The soup was cold, so I *complained*.
	to **characterise** ['kærəktraɪz]	charakerisieren; bezeichnen	= to describe the main qualities of sb or sth *to characterise* → character → characteristic
	to **respond to** [rɪ'spɒnd tə]	reagieren auf; erwidern auf; antworten auf	= to answer *to respond to* → response *Fr.* répondre; *Lat.* respondere
	well-adjusted [ˌwelə'dʒʌstɪd]	ausgeglichen	My friend is always relaxed. He's very *well-adjusted*.
	policymaker [ˌpɒləsi'meɪkə]	Politiker/-in; Entscheidungsträger/-in	A lot of *policymakers* were involved in the decision-making process.
	workable ['wɜ:kəbl]	brauchbar; geeignet; praktikabel	This is a highly *workable* plan. I'm sure it'll all work out nicely.
	in the meantime [ˌɪn ðə 'mi:ntaɪm]	in der Zwischenzeit	You can go and buy some milk and *in the meantime* I'll do the dishes.

Across cultures 3 Canada

1	**franc** [fræŋk]	Franc *(Währung)*	The currency in France used to be the *franc.*
	glacier ['glæsiə]	Gletscher	The longest *glacier* in the world is in Alaska.
	maple leaf ['meɪpl ˌli:f]	Ahornblatt	There is a red *maple leaf* on the Canadian flag.
	beaver ['bi:və]	Bieber	*Beavers* have changed the Canadian landscape by building dams.
	agricultural [ˌægrɪ'kʌltʃrl]	landwirtschaftlich	*agricultural* → agriculture
	head of state [ˌhed‿əv 'steɪt]	Staatsoberhaupt	= the official leader of a country
	governor-general ['gʌvnəˌdʒenrl]	Generalgouverneur/-in	The *governor-general* represents the British monarch in Canada.
	official language [əˌfɪʃl 'læŋgwɪdʒ]	Amtssprache	In India English is an *official language.*
	time zone ['taɪm ˌzəʊn]	Zeitzone	There are seven different *time zones* in Europe.
	ice hockey ['aɪs ˌhɒki]	Eishockey	= a popular winter sport in Canada
	lacrosse [lə'krɒs]	Lacrosse *(kanadischer Nationalsport)*	*Lacrosse* is played with a ball and a stick with a net at one end.
2	**forestry** ['fɒrɪstri]	Forstwirtschaft; Forst-; forstwirtschaftlich	*forestry* → forest
	democracy [dɪ'mɒkrəsi]	Demokratie	In a *democracy* the people vote for their government. ! Watch the spelling and the pronunciation.
3	**mosaic** [məʊ'zeɪɪk]	Mosaik	= a picture made with small colourful stones
4	**Indigenous Peoples** [ɪnˌdɪdʒɪnəs 'pi:plz]	Indigenous Peoples *(Überbegriff für die in Kanada lebenden Gesellschaften der First Nations, Métis und Inuit)* *Außerhalb des kanadischen Kontextes wird der Begriff ‚indigenous' und dessen Verwendung als Fremdbezeichnung immer wieder diskutiert. Er gilt als nicht neutral, da er ausschließlich für außereuropäische Gesellschaften verwendet wird und weiterhin ‚Rückständigkeit' impliziert.*	
	Métis ['meti]	Metis	= Indigenous peoples in Canada
	Inuit ['ɪnuɪt]	Inuit	The *Inuit* live where the land is covered in snow and ice.
	inhabitant [ɪn'hæbɪtnt]	Einwohner/-in; Bewohner/-in	= sb who lives in a place *Fr.* habitant/-e *(m), (f)*
	census ['sensəs]	Volkszählung	The *census* showed that 10% of the population had moved from the country to a city or town.
	heritage ['herɪtɪdʒ]	Herkunft; Erbe	= traditions and values that have continued over many years in a country, community, group or family
	fur [fɜ:]	Pelz; Fell	= the thick hair that covers the skin of many animals
	trader ['treɪdə]	Händler/-in	*trader* → trade → to trade
	hence [hens]	daher; deshalb	= for this reason
	homeland ['həʊmlænd]	Heimat; Heimatland	= the place where sb is or was born

to **be located** [bi ləʊ'keɪtɪd]	liegen; gelegen sein	Where *is* the region *located*? = Where exactly is the region? *to be located* → location
distribution [ˌdɪstrɪ'bjuːʃn]	Verteilung	*Fr.* distribution *(f)*; ***Lat.*** distribuere
to **compare to sth/sb** [kəm'peər‿tə]	mit etw./jmdm. vergleichbar sein	How do the figures of 2014 *compare to* this year's figures? *Fr.* comparer; ***Lat.*** comparare
5 **impact** *(no pl)* ['ɪmpækt]	Auswirkung; Einfluss	*Fr.* impact *(m)*
to **pass (a law)** [ˌpɑːs (ə lɔː)]	(ein Gesetz) verabschieden	= to agree to introduce a law
act [ækt]	Gesetz	to pass an *act* = to pass a law
to **reserve** [rɪ'zɜːv]	vorbehalten; reservieren	= to only allow a specific group to use sth
governance ['gʌvnəns]	Verwaltung; Kontrolle	*governance* → government → governor
elected [ɪ'lektɪd]	gewählt	*to elect* → election *Fr.* élu/-e
appointed [ə'pɔɪntɪd]	ernannt; berufen	= chosen to do a specific job
Band Council ['bænd ˌkaʊnsl]	*Vertretung der First Nations Gesellschaften innerhalb der kanadischen Regierung. Die bestehenden politischen und sozialen Strukturen der First Nations peoples wurden von der kanadischen Regierung abgewertet, unterdrückt und abgeschafft und 1876 schließlich im Zuge des ‚Indian Acts' durch die ‚Band councils' ersetzt.*	
unit ['juːnɪt]	Einheit	= small part of sth bigger
'chief' [tʃiːf]	*Bezeichnung eines politischen Amtes/einer politischen Position, die den bestehenden Strukturen der First Nations peoples im Zuge des ‚Indian Acts' übergestülpt wurde. Während des Kolonialismus, der gezielt die bestehenden politischen Strukturen der kolonisierten Gebiete ignorierte, unterdrückte und abschaffte, wurde der Begriff pauschal für sehr diverse Ämter verwendet, wodurch diese abgewertet wurden. Der Begriff ist somit nicht neutral und sollte wie auch die dt. Entsprechung ‚Häuptling' nicht als Fremdbezeichnung verwendet werden.*	
councillor ['kaʊnslə]	Ratsmitglied; Rat/Rätin	= sb who is a member of a group which is elected by the people
pass system ['pɑːs ˌsɪstəm]	*Passierschein-System*	Under the *pass system* the First Nations peoples could not leave the reserves without permission.
Roman Catholic [ˌrəʊmən 'kæθlɪk]	katholisch; Katholisch-	= belonging to the Christian church whose head is in Rome, Italy
to **convert sb (to sth)** [kən'vɜːt]	jmdn. (zu etw.) bekehren	= to persuade sb to change to another religion ***Lat.*** convertere
to **pave the way for sth** [ˌpeɪv ðə 'weɪ fə]	den Weg für etw. ebnen; den Weg für etw. bahnen	= to prepare sth so that sth else can happen
creation [kri'eɪʃn]	(Er)Schaffung; Gründung; Einführung	Job *creation* is an important task for the new government. *Fr.* création *(f)*
consent [kən'sent]	Zustimmung; Einwilligung	You must ask for sb's *consent* before you post their photo on social media.
remote [rɪ'məʊt]	abgelegen; fern	They lived in a *remote* part of the country. = far away; distant
to **deny** [dɪ'naɪ]	verweigern; leugnen; abstreiten	Some states *deny* the people the right to free speech.

access ['ækses]	Zugang	The internet offers very fast *access* to information. *Fr.* accés *(m)*
to **introduce** [ˌɪntrə'djuːs]	einführen; einleiten	*to introduce* → introduction *Fr.* introduire
to **prevent** [prɪ'vent]	verhindern; abhalten	= to stop sth from happening
to **segregate** ['segrɪgeɪt]	trennen *(anhand rassistischer Zuschreibungen, z.B. hier die Trennung von First Nations people und weißen Personen, u.a. um fruchtbares Land von den First Nations peoples zu rauben)*	*to segregate* ↔ to integrate
to **take away** [teɪk‿ə'weɪ]	wegnehmen; berauben	= to remove
unless [ən'les]	es sei denn, (dass) …; wenn nicht	You can't board the plane *unless* you show your passport first.
agent ['eɪdʒnt]	Vertreter/-in; Verwalter/-in	! Watch the pronunciation.
representative [ˌreprɪ'zentətɪv]	Vertreter/-in; Stellvertreter/-in; Repräsentant/-in; Sprecher/-in	*representative* → to represent
residential school *(Canada)* [rezɪ'dentʃl skuːl]	*staatliches Internat für Kinder der Indigenous peoples in Kanada*	The government took thousands of Indigenous children from their communities and sent them to *residential schools* so that they would forget their culture and language.
Christian ['krɪstʃən]	christlich	Christmas is a *Christian* holiday.
to **adopt** [ə'dɒpt]	übernehmen; annehmen; adoptieren	The teachers in the residential schools forced the Indigenous children to *adopt* European culture.
forced removal [ˌfɔːst rɪ'muːvl]	Zwangsumsiedlung; gewaltsame Umsiedlung	*Forced removals* of Indigenous children have caused a lot of damage.
to **estimate** ['estɪmeɪt]	schätzen; annehmen	The doctor *estimated* she would need to stay in hospital for a week. *Fr.* estimer; ***Lat.*** aestimare
sexual ['sekʃʊəl]	sexuell	*sexual* → sex
fate [feɪt]	Schicksal; Fügung; Vorsehung	= things that happen to you that you can't control ***Lat.*** fatum *(nt)*
to **concern** [kən'sɜːn]	betreffen; beschäftigen; beunruhigen	= to involve = to be worried about sth
compensation [ˌkɒmpən'seɪʃn]	Entschädigung; Wiedergutmachung; Schadensersatz	= money sb gets from another person who has hurt them in some way
on sb's behalf [ˌɒn bɪ'hɑːf]	im Namen von jmdm.; in jmds. Interesse; im Auftrag von jmdm.	I'm calling you *on behalf of* Mr Smith who is on holiday at the moment.
'idol worship' ['aɪdl ˌwɜːʃɪp]	‚Götzenanbetung' *(kolonialistischer Begriff, der die Religionen und die Spiritualität der kolonisierten Gesellschaften abwertete und damit die Unterdrückung und Christianisierung der Menschen rechtfertigte)*	
potlatch ['pɒtlætʃ]	Potlatch *(eine komplexe soziopolitische/spirituelle Zeremonie der First Nations peoples der Westküste Nordamerikas, bei der Besitz/Reichtum umverteilt wird und den Mitgliedern einer Gemeinschaft ihr soziopolitischer Status sowie Rechte über Jagd- und Fischerei-Territorien (neu) verliehen werden)*	

	ceremonial [ˌserɪˈməʊniəl]	festlich; Fest-; zeremoniell	*ceremonial* → ceremony
6	**Inuktitut** [ˌɪnʌktiˈtʌt]	Inuktitut	= one of the main languages spoken by the Inuit
7	**abroad** [əˈbrɔːd]	im Ausland; ins Ausland	! They live *abroad*. (= im Ausland) They went *abroad*. (= ins Ausland)
	savings *(pl)* [ˈseɪvɪŋz]	Ersparnisse	*savings* → to save
	to **adapt (to sth)** [əˈdæpt]	(sich an etw.) anpassen	= to change so that one fits in better
8	to **annoy sb** [əˈnɔɪ]	jmdn. ärgern; jmdn. aufregen	= to make sb angry

Unit 3 Discover Canada!

Check-in

	adaptation [ˌædæpˈteɪʃn]	Bearbeitung; Adaption	The children enjoyed the film *adaptation* of the Roald Dahl novel ***Matilda***.
1	**citizen** [ˈsɪtɪzn]	Bürger/-in	She is a British *citizen*. *citizen* → citizenship *Fr.* citoyen/-ne *(m)*, *(f)*
	to **make up** [ˌmeɪk ˈʌp]	zusammensetzen; zusammenstellen	Boys *make up* only 30% of the students at our school.
	Asian [ˈeɪʒn]	asiatisch; Asiat/-in	*Asian* → Asia
	to **take the oath of citizenship** [ˌteɪk ðiˌəʊθˌəv ˈsɪtɪznʃɪp]	den Eid auf die Staatsangehörigkeit/Staatsbürgerschaft ablegen	When you *take the oath of citizenship*, you promise to follow the rules and laws as a citizen.
	faithful [ˈfeɪθfəl]	treu	*faithful* → faith
	constitution [ˌkɒnstɪˈtjuːʃn]	Verfassung	*Fr.* constitution *(f)*
	caribou [ˈkærɪbuː]	Karibu; Rentier	= an animal that is normally found in cold areas in North America and Canada
	entirety *(no pl)* [ɪnˈtaɪrəti]	Gesamtheit; Gänze	*entirety* → entirely
	mountain range [ˈmaʊntɪn ˌreɪndʒ]	Bergkette	The Rocky Mountains are a *mountain range*.
	natural resources *(pl)* [ˌnætʃrl rɪˈzɔːsɪz]	Bodenschätze	Canada is rich in *natural resources*, such as oil, gas and coal.
	reserve [rɪˈzɜːv]	Vorkommen; Reserve	= a big amount of sth which can be used in the future
	extraction [ɪkˈstrækʃn]	Förderung; Gewinnung	The *extraction* of oil is not good for the environment.
	to **export** [ɪkˈspɔːt]	exportieren; ausführen	= to send products to other countries for sale
	waterproof [ˈwɔːtəpruːf]	wasserdicht	My jacket is not *waterproof* so if it rains, I'm going to get wet.
	smart [smɑːt]	elegant; schick; gepflegt	= formal; elegant
	snowmobile [ˈsnəʊməˌbiːl]	Schneemobil	The Inuit now use *snowmobiles* when they go hunting.

	industrial park [ɪnˈdʌstriəl pɑːk]	Industriegebiet; Gewerbepark	= an area in which a lot of factories are located
	deposit [dɪˈpɒsɪt]	Vorkommen; Depot; Lager; Lagerstätte	= an amount of sth that is found underground *Lat.* deponere
	citizenship certificate [ˈsɪtɪznʃip səˌtɪfɪkət]	Einbürgerungsurkunde	Dave has applied for a *citizenship certificate* because he needs to prove that he is a citizen of Canada.
3	**maple syrup** [ˈmeɪpl ˌsɪrəp]	Ahornsirup	Most of the world's *maple syrup* is produced in Canada.
	dam [dæm]	Damm; Staumauer	A *dam* is built to form a man-made lake.
	producer [prəˈdjuːsə]	Produzent/-in; Hersteller/-in	*producer* → production → to produce
	strategic [strəˈtiːdʒɪk]	strategisch	*strategic* → strategy

Station 1: Adventures in Eastern Canada

	observation deck [ˌɒbzəˈveɪʃn ˌdek]	Aussichtsdeck; Aussichtsplatt-form	We had an amazing view of the city from the *observation deck*.
	edge [edʒ]	Rand; Kante	Don't put that bottle too near the *edge* of the table or it might fall off.
	by accident [ˌbaɪ ˈæksɪˌdnt]	zufällig; versehentlich; aus Versehen	The tourists found a great place for breakfast *by accident*.
	detective [dɪˈtektɪv]	Detektiv/-in; Kommissar/-in	! Watch the spelling and the pronunciation.
	to **board** [bɔːd]	an Bord gehen; besteigen	= to get onto a plane, boat, etc.
	kayaking [ˈkaɪækɪŋ]	Kajakfahren	*Kayaking* and canoeing are popular water sports.
	falls [fɔːlz]	Wasserfall	The boat brought the tourists very close to the *falls*.
	hydropower [ˌhaɪdrəʊˈpaʊə]	Wasserkraft	= the power we can get from water
	poutine *(Canadian English)* [puːˈtiːn]	Poutine *(Pommes frites mit Bratensoße und geriebenem Käse)*	*Poutine* was first made popular in Quebec.
	cheese curd [ˈtʃiːz kɜːd]	geriebener Käse; Käsebruch	*Cheese curd* is often used in dishes in the US and Canada.
	gravy [ˈgreɪvi]	Bratensoße	= a brown sauce made from meat
	neat *(coll)* [niːt]	interessant; cool	= interesting; cool
	to **rent** [rent]	mieten	= to pay for the use of sth
1	**body of water** [ˌbɒdi əv ˈwɔːtə]	Gewässer	A lake is a *body of water*.
	excursion [ɪkˈskɜːʃn]	Ausflug; Exkursion	= trip
	to **rush** [rʌʃ]	eilen; sich beeilen; stürzen	They were in a hurry and *rushed* to the station.
5	**arena** [əˈriːnə]	Arena; Stadion	= stadium
6	**the experience of a lifetime** [ði ɪkˌspɪəriəns əv‿ə ˈlaɪftaɪm]	ein einmaliges Erlebnis; eine einmalige Erfahrung	The trip to see the whales was the *experience of a lifetime*.
	to **rank** [ræŋk]	anordnen; einordnen	*Rank* the names alphabetically.
	to **fulfil** [fʊlˈfɪl]	erfüllen; gerecht werden	= to do sth that is expected, hoped for or promised

7	**resilience** [ri'zɪliəns]	Belastbarkeit; Resilienz	= when sb manages to be happy again after sth terrible has happened
	judgment *(Canadian English)* ['dʒʌdʒmənt]	Urteilsvermögen	! *jud**g**ment (Canadian English)* = jud**ge**ment *(BE)* *Fr.* jugement *(m)*

Canadian English

Different words – same meaning

chesterfield	couch	sofa	
dépanneur	convenience store / corner store	corner shop	a small local shop, usually with long opening hours
fire hall	fire station	fire station	
gas bar	(gas) station	petrol station	
housecoat	bathrobe	dressing gown	
parkade	parking garage	multistorey car park	
runners	sneakers	trainers	
washroom	bathroom	toilet	

Words unique to Canada

chinook	a warm wind
Eh?	Don't you think?
garburator	garbage disposal, usually installed under a kitchen sink
loonie	Canadian dollar or one-dollar coin
Mountie	Member of the highly-respected Royal Canadian Mounted Police (RCMP)
poutine	French fries with cheese curds on top, served with gravy (= meat sauce)
snowbird	A Canadian who travels south to sandy beaches and tropical waters to escape winter
Timmie's	Tim Hortons (Canadian coffeehouse and restaurant chain; the name goes back to Tim Horton, a famous Canadian ice hockey player)
toonie	Canadian two-dollar coin
toque / tuque	knitted hat

Canadian English

Different spelling

Mostly, Canadian English is spelt like British English, not American English.
! *There are some exceptions.*

col**our** / fav**our**	col**or** / fav**or**	col**our** / fav**our**
catalo**gue** / dialo**gue**	catalo**g** / dialo**g**	catalo**gue** / dialo**gue**
cent**re** / theat**re**	cent**er** / theat**er**	cent**re** / theat**re**
che**que**	che**ck**	che**que**
practi**ce** / to practi**se**	practi**ce** / to practi**ce**	practi**ce** / to practi**se**
to pre**-e**xist / to re**-e**lect	to pre**e**xist / to re**e**lect	to pre**-e**xist / to re**-e**lect
trave**ll**er	trave**l**er	trave**ll**er
! to organi**ze** / to reali**ze**	to organi**ze** / to reali**ze**	to organi**se** / to reali**se**
! to analy**ze**	to analy**ze**	to analy**se**
! li**k**able	li**k**able	li**ke**able
! judg**m**ent	judg**m**ent	judg**em**ent

Station 2: Western Canada and its environmental issues

resort [rɪ'zɔ:t]	Ferienort; Ferienanlage	We're going to a very beautiful *resort* in the Rocky Mountains for our vacation.
seldom ['seldəm]	selten	↔ often
next in line *(AE)* [ˌnekst‿ɪn 'laɪn]	als Nächstes *(amerik.)*; der/die Nächste *(brit.)*	Firstly, the tourists create a lot of pollution. *Next in line* they don't respect the wildlife.
disturbance [dɪ'stɜ:bəns]	Störung	A big problem is the *disturbance* of wildlife by tourism.
artificial [ˌɑ:tɪ'fɪʃl]	künstlich; Kunst-	If it doesn't snow in the ski resorts, they will have to make *artificial* snow. *Fr.* artificiel/-le
fossil fuel ['fɒsl ˌfju:l]	fossiler Brennstoff; fossiler Energieträger	Coal, oil and gas are *fossil fuels*.
to **put sth into practice** [ˌpʊt‿ɪntə 'præktɪs]	etw. (in die Praxis) umsetzen	Let's *put* the theory *into practice*.
to **retreat** [rɪ'tri:t]	sich zurückziehen	When a glacier *retreats*, it gets smaller.
at an alarming rate [ˌæt ən‿əˌlɑ:mɪŋ 'reɪt]	in einem alarmierenden Tempo; in einer alarmierenden Geschwindigkeit	= so quickly that it is really shocking and threatening
to **shrink, shrank/shrunk, shrunk** [ʃrɪŋk; ʃræŋk/ʃrʌŋk; ʃrʌŋk]	schwinden; schrumpfen	= to become smaller
accessibility [əkˌsesə'bɪləti]	Zugänglichkeit; Erreichbarkeit	*accessibility* → to access sth → access

	to **encourage sb to do sth** [ɪn'kʌrɪdʒ]	jmdn. ermutigen, etw. zu tun; jmdm. (dazu) raten, etw. zu tun; jmdn. (dazu) ermuntern, etw. zu tun	My parents *encouraged me to* apply for this job. *Fr.* encourager
	to **dig out, dug out, dug out** ['dɪg‿aʊt; 'dʌg‿aʊt; 'dʌg‿aʊt]	ausgraben	They *dug out* a big hole for a new building behind our school.
	habitat ['hæbɪtæt]	Lebensraum; Habitat; Standort	***Lat.*** habitare
	boulder ['bəʊldə]	Felsblock; Felsbrocken; Findling	= a huge stone
	stream [stri:m]	Bach; kleiner Fluss	The water in mountain *streams* is usually clean and clear.
	to **extract** [ɪk'strækt]	gewinnen; entnehmen; extrahieren	*to extract* → extraction
	chemical ['kemɪkl]	Chemikalie	I never use *chemicals* for dying my hair, only natural colours.
	to **break open** [ˌbreɪk 'əʊpn]	aufbrechen	= to open with force
	rock [rɒk]	Fels; Stein; Gestein	= a big stone
	to **endanger** [ɪn'deɪndʒə]	gefährden	*to endanger* → danger → dangerous
	to **pollute** [pə'lu:t]	verschmutzen; verunreinigen	*to pollute* → pollution *Fr.* polluer
2	to **contribute to** [kən'trɪbju:t tə]	beitragen zu	= to play a part/role in *Fr.* contribuer; ***Lat.*** contribuere
5	to **conserve** ['kənsɜ:v]	erhalten; bewahren	= to keep sth the way it is ***Lat.*** conservare
	vital ['vaɪtl]	lebenswichtig	= extremely important
	seed [si:d]	Saat; Samen	A lot of plants can be grown from *seed*.
	root [ru:t]	Wurzel	The *roots* of a plant are usually underground.
	food web ['fu:d web]	Nahrungskette	= the system in which animals and plants depend on one another for food
	to **breed, bred, bred** [bri:d; bred; bred]	züchten; brüten	Beavers usually *breed* between January and March.
	boardwalk ['bɔ:dwɔ:k]	Holzsteg	If you stay on the *boardwalk*, you won't damage any of the plants.
	cattle rancher *(Canadian English)* ['kætl ˌræntʃə]	Viehzüchter/-in; Rinderzüchter/-in	= sb who has a big farm with cattle
6	**precipitation** [prɪˌsɪpɪ'teɪʃn]	Niederschlag	Rain and snow are both types of *precipitation*.

Energy production

to affect	sich auswirken; etw. beeinflussen	flood / to flood	Flut; Überschwemmung / (über)fluten; überschwemmen
to break open	aufbrechen	fossil fuel	fossiler Brennstoff; fossiler Energieträger
to conserve	erhalten; bewahren	fracking	Fracking
to contaminate	verschmutzen; verunreinigen; verseuchen; vergiften	global warming	(globale) Erderwärmung; Erwärmung der Erdatmosphäre
damage / to damage	Schaden; Beschädigung / schaden; beschädigen	groundwater	Grundwasser
deforestation	Abholzung; Entwaldung	harm / to do harm	Schaden / Schaden anrichten
destruction / to destroy	Zerstörung / zerstören; vernichten	natural resources	Bodenschätze
eco-system	Ökosystem	pollution / to pollute	Verschmutzung; Verunreinigung / verschmutzen; verunreinigen
emission / to emit	Emission; Ausstoß / ausstoßen; absondern	regenerate	erneuern; regenerieren
to endanger / endangered	gefährden / gefährdet	rise / to rise	Anstieg; Zunahme / (an)steigen; zunehmen
extraction / to extract	Förderung; Gewinnung / gewinnen; fördern	to shrink	schwinden; schrumpfen

7	**materials** *(pl)* [mə'tɪəriəlz]	Material	= equipment
	to **visualize** ['vɪʒuəlaɪz]	visualisieren; sichtbar machen	= to show; to make seen

Action! Ice fishing in the Yukon

2	**documentary** [ˌdɒkjə'mentri]	Dokumentarfilm; Dokumentation	I watched a fascinating *documentary* about the rainforest last night.
4	to **portray** [pɔː'treɪ]	porträtieren; darstellen; abbilden; schildern	The film was criticised for *portraying* the topic in a very negative way.

Story 1: Migwite'tmeg: We remember it

1	**anniversary** [ˌænɪ'vɜːsri]	Jahrestag; Jubiläum	An *anniversary* is a day when you remember or celebrate sth that happened on the same date in the past.
	to **unite** [juː'naɪt]	vereinigen; verbinden; zusammenschließen	*to unite* → union
	anthology [æn'θɒlədʒi]	Sammlung; Sammelband; Anthologie; Zusammenstellung	= a collection of poems, short stories, graphic novels, etc.
2	**ally** ['ælaɪ]	Alliierte/-r; Verbündete/-r	= friend; partner

	to **hinder sb from doing sth** ['hɪndə frəm]	jmdn. davon abhalten, etw. zu tun; jmdn. daran hindern, etw. zu tun	= to stop sb from doing sth
	fowl [faʊl]	Geflügel; Federvieh	= a bird that can be eaten or that produces eggs
3	**illustrator** ['ɪləstreɪtə]	Zeichner/-in	*illustrator* → illustration → to illustrate
	colourist ['kʌlərɪst]	Colorist/-in; Farbenkünstler/-in	= an artist who uses colour in their work
	warden ['wɔ:dn]	Wache; Wächter/-in; Aufseher/-in; Kontrolleur/-in	= sb who makes sure that people follow the rules
	from the looks of it [ˌfrəm ðə 'lʊks‿əv‿ɪt]	wie es aussieht	*From the looks of it* we are going to get wet. The sky is so dark.
	good for nothing [ˌgʊd fə 'nʌθɪŋ]	nichtsnutzig; nutzlos	Those *good for nothing* neighbours have left their rubbish on the street again.
	bully ['bʊli]	Tyrann; Rabauke; Rüpel	We went to the head teacher to stop the *bully* from making trouble.
	to **take sb's livelihood** [teɪk 'laɪvlihʊd]	jmdn. seiner Existenz berauben	We depend on the salmon. They mustn't *take our lifelihood.*
	to **trespass** ['trespəs]	unbefugt betreten; unbefugt eindringen; unbefugt überschreiten	*Trespassing* is a serious crime. = to enter a place without permission
	to **break the law** [ˌbreɪk ðə 'lɔ:]	gegen das Gesetz verstoßen	The people had to *break the law* to survive.
	resources *(pl)* [rɪ'zɔ:sɪz]	Ressourcen; Rohstoffquellen	= things that are available to be used when needed *Fr.* ressource *(f)*
	to **intimidate** [ɪn'tɪmɪdeɪt]	einschüchtern; bedrohen	= to threaten
	catch [kætʃ]	Fang	*a catch* → to catch
	line [laɪn]	Leine; Schnur	If the *line* in the fishing net breaks, you must repair it.
	elder ['eldə]	*hier: respektvolle Anrede;* Älteste/-r	= old person in a community who is respected by all
	'savage' ['sævɪdʒ]	*‚Wilde/-r' (rassistischer, abwertender Begriff, der als Teil des Konstrukts von ‚zivilisierter Welt' vs. ‚die Wilden' die Versklavung, Unterdrückung und Ausbeutung der kolonisierten Menschen rechtfertigte)*	
4	**consecutive** [kən'sekjʊtɪv]	aufeinanderfolgend; fortlaufend	The panels here are arranged *consecutively*, one after the other. ***Lat.*** consequi
	onomatopoeia [ˌɒnəʊˌmætə'pi:ə]	Lautmalerei; Onomatopoesie	= a word that suggests the sound it describes, e.g. 'bong' to describe the sound of a church bell
	sound effect ['saʊnd‿ɪˌfekt]	Geräuscheffekt; Toneffekt	What would films be like without music and *sound effects*?
	baton ['bætɒn]	Schlagstock	When she hit the door with the *baton*, it made a loud noise.
	shield [ʃi:ld]	Schild	= sth someone uses to protect themselves, e.g. a police officer
6	to **swap** [swɒp]	tauschen	= to exchange
	walking stick ['wɔ:kɪŋ ˌstɪk]	Gehstock	The old man uses a *walking stick* to support himself when he walks.

	one-sided [ˌwʌn'saɪdɪd]	einseitig	If a news report is *one-sided*, it isn't objective.
	account [ə'kaʊnt]	Beschreibung; Darstellung	= a description that is written or spoken
	disconnect [ˌdɪskə'nekt]	Trennung	*disconnect* → to disconnect → disconnected
	gathering ['gæðrɪŋ]	Zusammenkunft; Versammlung	We always have a family *gathering* on my grandmother's birthday. *gathering* → to gather

Skills: How to turn a literary text into an audio adaptation

1	to **picture** ['pɪktʃə]	sich vorstellen	= to imagine
	to **reflect** [rɪ'flekt]	(sich) spiegeln; wiederspiegeln; reflektieren	The mirror opposite the window *reflects* the sunlight. *Fr.* réfléchir
	to **slide, slid, slid** [slaɪd; slɪd; slɪd]	gleiten	The boats *slid* quietly across the lake.
	narration [nə'reɪʃn]	Schilderung; Erzählung	*narration* → narrative → narrator *Lat.* narrare
	to **confiscate sth** ['kɒnfɪskeɪt]	wegnehmen; beschlagnahmen; einziehen	The teacher *confiscated* their mobile phones.
4	to **tell (sb/sth) apart** [tel ə'pɑ:t]	(jmdn./etw.) auseinanderhalten	I can't *tell* the twins *apart*. They look so much like one another.
	italics [ɪ'tælɪks]	Kursivschrift	The word *shocked* is written in *italics*.
	engine ['endʒɪn]	Motor	Almost all cars have the *engine* in front of the driver.

Unit task: Create your own audio adaptation

	audiobook ['ɔ:diəʊˌbʊk]	Hörbuch	When I don't have time to read a book, I listen to an *audiobook* instead.
	Creative Commons (licence) [kriˌeɪtɪv 'kɒmnz ˌlaɪsns]	lizenzfrei; frei nutzbar	Always use *Creative Commons* photos for presentations or publications.
	to **assign** [ə'saɪn]	zuordnen	We're going to do group work, but don't divide up into groups yourselves: I'll *assign* you to your groups.
	emphasis ['empfəsɪs]	Betonung	If you stress sth, you put *emphasis* on it. *emphasis* → to emphasize
	take [teɪk]	Aufnahme; Version	= a scene that you film or record without stopping the camera

Check-out

1	to **homeschool** ['həumsku:l]	(jmdn.) zuhause unterrichten; Hausunterricht erteilen	= to teach children in their own homes
	voluntary ['vɒləntri]	freiwillig	When you do *voluntary* work, you aren't paid for what you do. *voluntary* → a volunteer
	former ['fɔ:mə]	ehemalig	*Former* students often give presentations on Careers Day at my school.

2	**pen pal** ['pen pæl]	Brieffreund/-in	I have three *pen pals*: two in the US and one in France.
3	**on average** [ɒn‿'ævrɪdʒ]	durchschnittlich; im Durchschnitt	*On average* around 10,000 people visit the shopping centre every day.
8	**shipping** ['ʃɪpɪŋ]	Versand; Transport *(von Gütern)*; Schifffahrts-; See-	The *shipping* season in Churchill is very short because of the ice.
	frozen ['frəʊzn]	gefroren; eingefroren; erfroren; vereist	*frozen* → to freeze
	further ['fɜ:ðə]	weiter	Are there any *further* questions? = Are there any other questions?
	efficient [ɪ'fɪʃnt]	effizient; wirksam; wirtschaftlich; leistungsfähig	An *efficient* person or machine works quickly and well. ***Lat.*** efficere
9	**rail track** ['reɪl træk]	Bahngleis; Schiene	Cars travel on roads and trains travel on *rail tracks*.
	to **strike, struck, struck** [straɪk; strʌk; strʌk]	ausbrechen; zuschlagen	= when sth terrible happens, e.g. a disaster
	flooding ['flʌdɪŋ]	Flut; Hochwasser; Überschwemmung	*flooding* → to flood
	loaf [ləʊf]	Brot; Brotlaib	Please cut the *loaf* into slices.
10	**coincidentally** [kəʊˌɪnsɪ'dentli]	zufällig	= when sth happens without planning it *coincidentally* → coincidence
	fragile ['frædʒaɪl]	anfällig; labil; schwach; brüchig; zerbrechlich	Don't drop the parcel, it's *fragile*. *Fr.* fragile
	global warming *(no pl)* [ˌgləʊbl 'wɔ:mɪŋ]	globale Erwärmung; Erderwärmung; Erwärmung der Erdatmosphäre	One of today's biggest challenges is slowing down *global warming*.
	beluga whale [bə'lu:gə ˌweɪl]	Beluga; Weißwal	*Beluga whales* move south in the autum when the ice forms in the Arctic.

Text and media smart 3 Dealing with plays

Check-in

	playscript ['pleɪskrɪpt]	Theatertext; Drehbuch	= the written text of a play
1	to **stage** [steɪdʒ]	aufführen	This year our tutor group is going to *stage* a play by Shakespeare. *to stage* → the stage
	to **direct** [dɪ'rekt]	Regie führen; leiten	*to direct* → director
	set [set]	Kulisse; Bühnenbild	The play won a prize for best stage *set*.
	seating ['si:tɪŋ]	Bestuhlung	*seating* → seat
	cabaret ['kæbəreɪ]	Kleinkunst; Varieté	= entertainment with singing and dancing, performed in clubs
	nativity play [nə'tɪvəti ˌpleɪ]	Krippenspiel	= a play performed at Christmas

2	**dress circle** ['dres ˌsɜ:kl]	erster Rang	We got seats in the first row of the *dress circle*.
	upper circle ['ʌpə ˌsɜ:kl]	zweiter Rang	Seats in the *upper circle* are usually cheaper than those in the dress circle.
	aisle [aɪl]	Gang	On a plane I prefer an *aisle* seat.
	to **star** [stɑ:]	die Hauptrolle spielen *(Film, Theater)*	Her biggest dream is to *star* in a famous musical.
	pandemic [ˌpæn'demɪk]	Pandemie	How did you get through the *pandemic*?
	production [prə'dʌkʃn]	Inszenierung	*production* → to produce → producer

Station 1: Help desk

	help desk ['help desk]	Helpdesk; Hotline; Auskunft	If you have problems with the hardware, call the *help desk*.
1	**box office** ['bɒks ˌɒfɪs]	Kartenschalter; Abendkasse; (Theater)Kasse	Tickets are available at the *box office*.
2	**playwright** ['pleɪraɪt]	Dramatiker/-in; Bühnenautor/-in	The *playwright* William Shakespeare introduced thousands of new words into the English language.
	novelist ['nɒvlɪst]	Schriftsteller/-in; Autor/-in	*novelist* → novel
	to **call in** *(AE)* [ˌkɔ:l 'ɪn]	anrufen	= to call a place
	to **call out** [ˌkɔ:l‿'aʊt]	rufen	= to shout
	What's the nature of ...? [ˌwɒts ðə 'neɪtʃər‿əv]	Worum handelt es sich bei ...?	*What's the nature of your call?* = What's your call about? Why are you calling?
	network ['netwɜ:k]	Netzwerk; Netz	We couldn't log into the office *network* today.
	boy *(coll)* [bɔɪ]	oh Mann *(ugs.)*; Junge, Junge *(ugs.)*	*Boy*, what a day!
	to **pick up a call** [ˌpɪk‿ʌp ə 'kɔ:l]	einen Anruf entgegennehmen	My friend kept on talking for hours. I wish I *hadn't picked up the call*.
	go ahead [gəʊ‿ə'hed]	Nur zu!; Mach nur!	Can I use your mobile? – No problem, *go ahead*!
	ID (identification) [ˌaɪ'di (aɪˌdentɪfɪ'keɪʃn)]	Identifizierung; Identifikation; *hier:* Nutzername	I forgot both my *ID* and my password.
	to **encounter sb/sth** [ɪn'kaʊntə]	auf jmdn./etw. treffen; auf jmdn./etw. stoßen	I *encountered* quite a few difficulties in my new job. *Fr.* rencontrer
	insurmountable [ˌɪnsə'maʊntəbl]	unüberwindbar	= sth that is extremely difficult to solve or to deal with *Fr.* insurmontable
	difficulty ['dɪfɪklti]	Schwierigkeit	*difficulty* → difficult *Fr.* difficulté *(f)*
	to **prompt sb (to do sth)** [prɒmt]	jmdn. (dazu) veranlassen (etw. zu tun)	What *prompted you to say* that? = What made you say that?
	to **demand** [dɪ'mɑ:nd]	einfordern; verlangen	*to demand* → a demand *Fr.* demander
	assistance [ə'sɪstəns]	Unterstützung; Hilfe	I really need your *assistance* with this problem. I can't solve it on my own. = help

paid professional [peɪd prə'feʃnl]	bezahlte Fachkraft	My company doesn't hire *paid professionals* but students for the help desk.
to **crack a nugget** *(coll)* [ˌkræk‿ə 'nʌgət]	eine (harte) Nuss knacken; ein Problem lösen	We really thought we couldn't solve the problem. But then we *cracked the nugget* after all!
kinda *(= kind of) (infml)* ['kaɪndə]	ziemlich; irgendwie	This is *kinda* weird.
to **have an attitude** [ˌhæv‿ən 'ætɪtju:d]	eine falsche Einstellung haben	Maybe your problem is that you always *have* kind of *an attitude*.
to **mind one's own business** ['maɪnd ˌwʌnz‿əʊn 'bɪznɪs]	sich um seine eigenen Angelegenheiten kümmern	Why do you always get involved? *Mind your own business*!
all of a sudden [ˌɔ:l‿əv‿ə 'sʌdn]	plötzlich; auf einmal	= suddenly
to **be desperate for sth** [bi 'desprət fɔ:]	etw. dringend brauchen	I'*m desperate for* it. = I really need it.
to **sigh** [saɪ]	seufzen	People often *sigh* if they feel disappointed or tired.
to **keep sb occupied** [ˌki:p ɒkju:'paɪd]	jmdn. beschäftigen	I have so much homework to do. It'*ll keep me occupied* for the rest of the day.
brain [breɪn]	Gehirn; Verstand; Hirn	Think! Use your *brain*!
to **cut out** [kʌt‿'aʊt]	sich ausschalten; sich abschalten	I didn't do well in the test. It felt like my brain just *cut out*.
Are you magic? [ˌɑ: ju 'mædʒɪk]	Kannst du zaubern?; Können Sie zaubern?	How did you do that? *Are you magic?*
wand [wɒnd]	Zauberstab	I'll dress up as Harry Potter for Halloween, but I haven't got a *wand* yet.
busy ['bɪzi]	besetzt	I couldn't reach our doctor. The line was *busy* all day.
near [nɪə]	nahe; beinahe; fast	= close to a certain state, i.e. crying
tear [tɪə]	Träne	a *tear* → to burst into tears
to **fail** [feɪl]	versagen; scheitern	I tried to stop eating sugar and *failed* completely.
to **programme** ['prəʊgræm]	programmieren	*to programme* → a programme
human being [ˌhju:mən 'bi:ɪŋ]	Mensch	I'm a *human being*, not a robot!
vat [væt]	Bottich	= a large container
to **exhale** [eks'heɪl]	ausatmen; aufatmen	*Exhale* and try to relax!
dumb *(rude)* [dʌm]	dumm; doof	= stupid
beekeeper ['bi:ˌki:pə]	Imker/-in; Bienenzüchter/-in	= sb who owns and looks after bees
hood [hʊd]	Kapuze; Haube	*hood* → hoodie
apiary ['eɪpiəri]	Bienenstock; Bienenhaus	How many bees live in an *apiary*? – Between 20,000 and 60,000.
beekeeping ['bi:ˌki:pɪŋ]	Imkerei; Bienenzucht; Bienenhaltung	My family has been into *beekeeping* for centuries.
minion ['mɪnjən]	Arbeiterin *(in einem Bienenvolk)*	The worker bees (*minions*) feed the queen bee.

pollinator ['pɒləneɪtə]	Bestäuber	*pollinator* → to pollinate
to **fear** [fɪə]	(sich) fürchten; Angst haben	= to be scared of sb/sth
to **chuckle** ['tʃʌkl]	in sich hineinlachen	The story she was reading made her *chuckle* all the time.
Just kidding! *(AE)* [ˌdʒʌst 'kɪdɪŋ]	Kleiner Scherz am Rande!	*Just kidding! (AE)* = Only joking! *(BE)*
threat [θret]	Bedrohung	a *threat* → to threaten (sb)
classic ['klæsɪk]	*hier:* typisch	*Classic* mistake! Almost everybody does that.
hive [haɪv]	Bienenstock	= where the bees live
to **be frightened (of)** [bi 'fraɪtnd]	Angst haben (vor); sich fürchten (vor)	*Are* you *frightened* of dogs? = to be afraid of
high-pitched ['haɪpɪtʃt]	schrill; hellklingend	a *high-pitched* voice = a very high voice
whimper ['wɪmpə]	Winseln; Wimmern	The little dog gave a *whimper* of pain.
to **assert one's dominance** [əˌsɜ:t wʌnz 'dɒmɪnəns]	sich durchsetzen; sich behaupten	Do you always have to *assert your dominance*?
combat ['kɒmbæt]	Kampf; Gefecht	= fight *Fr.* combat *(m)*
to **extrude** [ɪk'stru:d]	ausstoßen	A volcano *extrudes* lava.
fragrant ['freɪgrənt]	duftend; wohlriechend	The room was *fragrant* with the smell of flowers.
odor *(AE)* ['əʊdə]	Geruch; Duft	= an unpleasant smell *odor (AE)* = odour *(BE)*
to **navigate** ['nævɪgeɪt]	sich orientieren; navigieren; steuern	They *navigated* with the help of the GPS on their mobile.
high fiber *(AE)* ['haɪ faɪbər]	ballaststoffreich	You should eat more *high fiber* food, like dried fruits.
diet [daɪət]	Ernährung; Ernährungsweise; Nahrung; Diät	A balanced and healthy *diet* is important for your health.
to **entrance sb/sth** [ɪn'trɑ:ns]	jmdn./etw. verzaubern; jmdn./etw. in seinen Bann ziehen	They *were entranced* by the beauty of the music.
scent [sent]	Duft; Parfüm	I love your *scent*. What's the name of the perfume?
pied-piper ['paɪdpaɪpə]	wie ein Rattenfänger	She led the group, *pied-piper* style.
on the count of ... [ˌɒn ðə 'kaʊnt‿əv]	bei ...	*On the count of* three – go!
Charge! [tʃɑ:dʒ]	Los!	= Go!
to **crawl** [krɔ:l]	kriechen; krabbeln	Our son is just starting to *crawl*.
to **complain** [kəm'pleɪn]	sich beschweren; sich beklagen	My soup was cold, so I *complained*. *Fr.* se plaindre
delivery [dɪ'lɪvri]	Lieferung; Auslieferung; Zustellung	*delivery* → to deliver
thrilled [θrɪld]	aufgeregt; außer sich vor Freude	= excited

honk [hɒŋk]	Hupen; Gehupe	What's that loud *honk*?
horn [hɔ:n]	Hupe	Must be the *horns* of a lot of cars.
vehicle ['vɪəkl]	Fahrzeug; Vehikel	= car; lorry
to **careen** *(AE)* [kə'ri:n]	rasen	= to drive very fast and in a dangerous way
screech [kri:tʃ]	Quietschen	The car turned around the corner with a loud *screech*.
tire *(AE)* [taɪə]	Reifen	*tire (AE)* = tyre *(BE)*
to **hurl** [hɜ:l]	schleudern; werfen	At the protests they *hurled* stones through shop windows.
to **ricochet** ['rɪkəʃeɪ]	abprallen	The ball *ricocheted* off the wall.
stoop *(AE)* [stu:p]	offene Veranda	We sat on the *stoop* and watched the sunset.
maniacally ['meɪniækli]	wie ein Wahnsinniger/eine Wahnsinnige	She rang the bell *maniacally*.
to **gun the engine** [ˌɡʌn ðə 'endʒɪn]	den Motor aufheulen lassen	There's a traffic light in front of my bedroom. It drives me crazy when people *gun the engine* at night.
to **speed off, sped off, sped off** [spi:d 'ɒf; sped 'ɒf; sped 'ɒf]	schnell davonfahren; losdüsen	They got into the car and *sped off*.
battered ['bætəd]	ramponiert; verbeult	My neighbours have a very old, *battered* car.
imaginable [ɪ'mædʒɪnəbl]	vorstellbar	*imaginable* → to imagine → imaginary *Fr.* imaginable
shard [ʃɑ:d]	Scherbe	After the accident there were *shards* everywhere.
shattered ['ʃætəd]	zerschlagen; zertrümmert; zerbrochen	After the storm lots of windows were *shattered*.
whiner ['waɪnə]	Quengler/-in; Jammerlappen	Oh, stop it! You're such a *whiner*!
properly ['prɒpli]	richtig; anständig; ordentlich	= well; correctly
terms and conditions [ˌtɜ:mz‿ən 'kəndɪʃnz]	allgemeine Geschäftsbedingungen (AGBs)	You can't continue with your order unless you accept the *terms and conditions*.
to **launch** [lɔ:nʃ]	abschießen	The satellite was successfully *launched*.
the fine print *(no pl)* ['faɪn ˌprɪnt]	das Kleingedruckte	Do you always read *the fine print* on documents?
It states that ... [ɪt ˌsteɪtz 'ðæt]	Darin steht, dass ...	Look, *it states that* you can't return the shoes.
landing ['lændɪŋ]	Landung	*landing* ↔ take-off
item ['aɪtəm]	Ding; Gegenstand	We'll get a few cents for every *item* we donate.
discount ['dɪskaʊnt]	Rabatt; Preisnachlass	Let's buy this laptop, it's really cheap. There's a 50% *discount*.
jello *(AE)* ['dʒeləʊ]	Götterspeise; Wackelpudding	*jello (AE)* = jelly *(BE)*

Layout and format

italics	Kursivschrift
quotation marks	Anführungszeichen
colon	Doppelpunkt
brackets	(runde / eckige) Klammern *(BE)*; eckige Klammern *(AE)*
parenthesis, parentheses *(pl)*	Einschub; eingeschobener Satz(teil); (runde) Klammern *(AE)*
indented	eingerückt
centred	zentriert
-aligned	-bündig

Station 2: A humorous scene

1	**read-through** ['riːdθruː]	Probedurchgang; Probelesen	Check your script by doing a *read-through*.

Options

3	**dress rehearsal** ['dres rɪˌhɜːsl]	Generalprobe	= the final practice before the first performance

Exercise **Intonation: When you step into a character role**

A 55

a) *You can use falling intonation at the end of a sentence to show that you are neutral or not interested in something, or you can ask a question to which you don't expect an answer. Rising intonation shows interest, surprise or strong emotion, or you can use it to ask a question to which you expect an answer. Listen to the examples to hear the difference.*

1. What seems to be the problem?
2. I can't remember my password.

b) *Work in pairs. One person reads the examples out loud with either rising or falling intonation. The other person gives an appropriate response.*

1. So, I'm talking to an expert in problem solving, am I?
2. Why do you think I'm phoning you?
3. Did you type in the correct password?
4. Is it my problem that your computer isn't working?
5. I'm having a really difficult day here.
6. Thanks for all your help.

Operators

operator	explanation	example
analyse	describe and explain in detail	*Analyse* the narrative perspective in the extract.
assess	express an opinion about sb / sth and give reasons for this opinion	*Assess* the work you have done so far.
comment (on)	give one's opinion and support it with evidence or reasons	*Comment on* the language in the extract.
compare	show how sth is similar and / or different to sth else	*Compare* the graphic novel to a comic and a 'normal' novel.
describe	give a detailed description of what sb / sth is like	*Describe* how Anna's feelings change.
discuss	give arguments for and against sth so that you can come to a conclusion	*Discuss* the pros and cons of the photos.
evaluate	express an opinion about the nature or quality of sb / sth and give reasons for this opinion	*Evaluate* the success of the steps taken to reduce pollution.
examine	describe and explain in detail	*Examine* how the relationship between the characters changes.
explain	give reasons for / details about sth	*Explain* what this quotation means to you.
give / write a characterisation of	give an analysis of a character	*Write a characterisation of* the narrator, Esther.
illustrate	use examples to explain sth or make it clear	*Illustrate* the differences between a virtual and a normal concert.
interpret	explain the meaning, purpose or message of sth	*Interpret* the results of ratings and open-ended questions.
outline	give the main aspects of sth	*Outline* the role of the monarchy.
point out	find and explain aspects of sth	*Point out* information which the writer didn't feel was relevant enough to include in the summary.
state	present the main aspects of sth	*State* your opinion.
summarise; sum up	give a concise description of the main points or ideas of sth	*Summarise / Sum up* the three problems that the article identifies.
write (+ text type)	produce a text with specific features	*Write* an email. / *Write* a rough draft of your playscript.

Irregular verbs

infinitive	simple past	past participle	German
be [bi:]	was [wɒz] / were [wɜ:]	been [bi:n]	sein
beat [bi:t]	beat [bi:t]	beaten ['bi:tn] / beat [bi:t]	schlagen; besiegen
become [bɪ'kʌm]	became [bɪ'keɪm]	become [bɪ'kʌm]	werden
begin [bɪ'gɪn]	began [bɪ'gæn]	begun [bɪ'gʌn]	beginnen; anfangen
bet [bet]	bet [bet] / betted ['betɪd]	bet [bet] / betted ['betɪd]	wetten
bite [baɪt]	bit [bɪt]	bitten ['bɪtn]	beißen
bleed [bli:d]	bled [bled]	bled [bled]	bluten
blow [bləʊ]	blew [blu:]	blown [bləʊn]	blasen; pusten
break [breɪk]	broke [brəʊk]	broken ['brəʊkn]	(zer)brechen; kaputt machen
breed [bri:d]	bred [bred]	bred [bred]	züchten; brüten
bring [brɪŋ]	brought [brɔ:t]	brought [brɔ:t]	(mit)bringen
build [bɪld]	built [bɪlt]	built [bɪlt]	bauen
burn [bɜ:n]	burnt [bɜ:nt] / burned [bɜ:nd]	burnt [bɜ:nt] / burned [bɜ:nd]	(ver)brennen
burst [bɜ:st]	burst [bɜ:st] / bursted ['bɜ:stɪd]	burst [bɜ:st] / bursted ['bɜ:stɪd]	platzen; bersten
buy [baɪ]	bought [bɔ:t]	bought [bɔ:t]	kaufen
cast [kɑ:st]	cast [kɑ:st]	cast [kɑ:st]	werfen
catch [kætʃ]	caught [kɔ:t]	caught [kɔ:t]	fangen
choose [tʃu:z]	chose [tʃəʊz]	chosen ['tʃəʊzn]	(aus)wählen
come [kʌm]	came [keɪm]	come [kʌm]	kommen
cost [kɒst]	cost [kɒst]	cost [kɒst]	kosten
cut [kʌt]	cut [kʌt]	cut [kʌt]	schneiden
deal (with) [di:l]	dealt [delt]	dealt [delt]	sich befassen (mit); umgehen (mit)
dig out ['dɪg‿aʊt]	dug out ['dʌg‿aʊt]	dug out ['dʌg‿aʊt]	ausgraben
do [du:]	did [dɪd]	done [dʌn]	machen; tun
draw [drɔ:]	drew [dru:]	drawn [drɔ:n]	zeichnen; ziehen
dream [dri:m]	dreamt [dremt] / dreamed [dri:md]	dreamt [dremt] / dreamed [dri:md]	träumen
drink [drɪŋk]	drank [dræŋk]	drunk [drʌŋk]	trinken
drive [draɪv]	drove [drəʊv]	driven ['drɪvn]	fahren
eat [i:t]	ate [et]	eaten ['i:tn]	essen
fall [fɔ:l]	fell [fel]	fallen ['fɔ:lən]	(hin)fallen
feed [fi:d]	fed [fed]	fed [fed]	füttern; ernähren
feel [fi:l]	felt [felt]	felt [felt]	fühlen
fight [faɪt]	fought [fɔ:t]	fought [fɔ:t]	kämpfen; (sich) streiten
find [faɪnd]	found [faʊnd]	found [faʊnd]	finden
fit [fɪt]	fit [fɪt] / fitted ['fɪtɪd]	fit [fɪt] / fitted ['fɪtɪd]	passen
flee [fli:]	fled [fled]	fled [fled]	flüchten; fliehen
fly [flaɪ]	flew [flu:]	flown [fləʊn]	fliegen
forbid [fə'bɪd]	forbade [fə'bæd/fə'beɪd]	forbidden [fə'bɪdn]	verbieten; untersagen
forget [fə'get]	forgot [fə'gɒt]	forgotten [fə'gɒtn]	vergessen
forgive [fə'gɪv]	forgave [fə'geɪv]	forgiven [fə'gɪvn]	vergeben; verzeihen

infinitive	simple past	past participle	German
freeze [fri:z]	froze [frəʊz]	frozen ['frəʊzn]	gefrieren; erstarren
get [get]	got [gɒt]	got [gɒt] / gotten ['gɒtn]	bekommen; erhalten
give [gɪv]	gave [geɪv]	given ['gɪvn]	geben
go [gəʊ]	went [went]	gone [gɒn]	gehen; fahren
grow [grəʊ]	grew [gru:]	grown [grəʊn]	wachsen; anbauen; züchten
hang [hæŋ]	hung [hʌŋ]	hung [hʌŋ]	hängen
have [hæv]	had [hæd]	had [hæd]	haben
hear [hɪə]	heard [hɜ:d]	heard [hɜ:d]	hören
hide [haɪd]	hid [hɪd]	hidden ['hɪdn]	(sich) verstecken
hit [hɪt]	hit [hɪt]	hit [hɪt]	schlagen; treffen
hold [həʊld]	held [held]	held [held]	(fest)halten
hurt [hɜ:t]	hurt [hɜ:t]	hurt [hɜ:t]	verletzen; sich weh tun
keep [ki:p]	kept [kept]	kept [kept]	(auf)bewahren; behalten
know [nəʊ]	knew [nju:]	known [nəʊn]	kennen; wissen
lay [leɪ]	laid [leɪd]	laid [leɪd]	legen; verlegen
lead [li:d]	led [led]	led [led]	(an)führen
lean [li:n]	leant [lent] / leaned [li:nd]	leant [lent] / leaned [li:nd]	(sich) lehnen
learn [lɜ:n]	learnt [lɜ:nt] / learned [lɜ:nd]	learnt [lɜ:nt] / learned [lɜ:nd]	lernen
leave [li:v]	left [left]	left [left]	(ver)lassen
lend [lend]	lent [lent]	lent [lent]	(ver)leihen
let [let]	let [let]	let [let]	lassen
lie [laɪ]	lay [leɪ]	lain [leɪn]	liegen
light [laɪt]	lit [lɪt]	lit [lɪt]	beleuchten; erhellen; anzünden
lose [lu:z]	lost [lɒst]	lost [lɒst]	verlieren
make [meɪk]	made [meɪd]	made [meɪd]	machen; tun
mean [mi:n]	meant [ment]	meant [ment]	bedeuten; meinen
meet [mi:t]	met [met]	met [met]	treffen
pay [peɪ]	paid [peɪd]	paid [peɪd]	(be)zahlen
prove [pru:v]	proved [pru:vd]	proved [pru:vd] / proven [pru:vn]	belegen; nachweisen; beweisen
put [pʊt]	put [pʊt]	put [pʊt]	legen; setzen; stellen
read [ri:d]	read [red]	read [red]	lesen
ride [raɪd]	rode [rəʊd]	ridden ['rɪdn]	fahren; reiten
ring [rɪŋ]	rang [ræŋ]	rung [rʌŋ]	klingeln; läuten
rise [raɪz]	rose [rəʊz]	risen ['rɪzn]	steigen; sich erheben; aufstehen
run [rʌn]	ran [ræn]	run [rʌn]	laufen; rennen
say [seɪ]	said [sed]	said [sed]	sagen
see [si:]	saw [sɔ:]	seen [si:n]	sehen
sell [sel]	sold [səʊld]	sold [səʊld]	verkaufen
send [send]	sent [sent]	sent [sent]	senden; verschicken
set [set]	set [set]	set [set]	stellen; legen; (den Tisch) decken
sew [səʊ]	sewed [səʊd]	sewn [səʊn] / sewed [səʊd]	nähen
shake [ʃeɪk]	shook [ʃʊk]	shaken ['ʃeɪkn]	schütteln
shine [ʃaɪn]	shone [ʃɒn]	shone [ʃɒn]	scheinen; glänzen
shoot [ʃu:t]	shot [ʃɒt]	shot [ʃɒt]	schießen

infinitive	simple past	past participle	German
show [ʃəʊ]	showed [ʃəʊd]	shown [ʃəʊn] / showed [ʃəʊd]	zeigen
shrink [ʃrɪŋk]	shrank [ʃræŋk] / shrunk [ʃrʌŋk]	shrunk [ʃrʌŋk]	schwinden; schrumpfen
shut [ʃʌt]	shut [ʃʌt]	shut [ʃʌt]	zumachen; schließen
sing [sɪŋ]	sang [sæŋ]	sung [sʌŋ]	singen
sink [sɪŋk]	sank [sæŋk]	sunk [sʌŋk]	untergehen; sinken
sit [sɪt]	sat [sæt]	sat [sæt]	sitzen
slay [sleɪ]	slew [slu:]	slain [sleɪn]	töten; erschlagen
sleep [sli:p]	slept [slept]	slept [slept]	schlafen
slide [slaɪd]	slid [slɪd]	slid [slɪd]	rutschen
smell [smel]	smelt [smelt] / smelled [smeld]	smelt [smelt] / smelled [smeld]	riechen; duften
sneak [sni:k]	snuck [snʌk]	snuck [snʌk]	schleichen
speak [spi:k]	spoke [spəʊk]	spoken ['spəʊkn]	sprechen
speed off [spi:d 'ɒf]	sped off [sped 'ɒf]	sped off [sped 'ɒf]	schnell davonfahren; losdüsen
spell [spel]	spelt [spelt] / spelled [speld]	spelt [spelt] / spelled [speld]	buchstabieren
spend [spend]	spent [spent]	spent [spent]	ausgeben; verbringen
spill [spɪl]	spilt [spɪlt] / spilled [spɪld]	spilt [spɪlt] / spilled [spɪld]	verschütten; auslaufen
spread [spred]	spread [spred]	spread [spred]	(sich) verbreiten
stand [stænd]	stood [stʊd]	stood [stʊd]	stehen
steal [sti:l]	stole [stəʊl]	stolen ['stəʊln]	stehlen
stick [stɪk]	stuck [stʌk]	stuck [stʌk]	kleben; stecken
sting [stɪŋ]	stung [stʌŋ]	stung [stʌŋ]	stechen
strike [straɪk]	struck [strʌk]	struck [strʌk]	ausbrechen; zuschlagen
strive (for) [straɪv]	strove [strəʊv] / strived [straɪvd]	striven ['strɪvn] / strived [straɪvd]	streben (nach)
swear [sweə]	swore [swɔ:]	sworn [swɔ:n]	schwören
sweep [swi:p]	swept [swept]	swept [swept]	fegen; kehren
swim [swɪm]	swam [swæm]	swum [swʌm]	schwimmen
swing [swɪŋ]	swung [swʌŋ]	swung [swʌŋ]	baumeln; schwingen; schaukeln
take [teɪk]	took [tʊk]	taken ['teɪkn]	nehmen
teach [ti:tʃ]	taught [tɔ:t]	taught [tɔ:t]	unterrichten; lehren; beibringen
tell [tel]	told [təʊld]	told [təʊld]	erzählen
think [θɪŋk]	thought [θɔ:t]	thought [θɔ:t]	(nach)denken; glauben
throw [θrəʊ]	threw [θru:]	thrown [θrəʊn]	werfen
understand [ˌʌndə'stænd]	understood [ˌʌndə'stʊd]	understood [ˌʌndə'stʊd]	verstehen
upset [ʌp'set]	upset [ʌp'set]	upset [ʌp'set]	aus der Fassung bringen
wake up [ˌweɪk‿'ʌp]	woke up [ˌwəʊk‿'ʌp]	woken up [ˌwəʊkn‿'ʌp]	(auf)wachen; (auf)wecken
wear [weə]	wore [wɔ:]	worn [wɔ:n]	anhaben; tragen
weave [wi:v]	wove [wəʊv]	woven ['wəʊvn]	weben
win [wɪn]	won [wʌn]	won [wʌn]	gewinnen; siegen
write [raɪt]	wrote [rəʊt]	written ['rɪtn]	schreiben

Unit 1

Check-out

1 Speech at a protest
1. a); **2.** b); **3.** c); **4.** b); **5.** a); **6.** b)

2 Buy Nothing Day
a) F; A; G; E; C; B; D
b) Model answer:
1. The protest is held on Black Friday, a day when people usually buy lots of products both in the shops and online. The protesters want to persuade people to buy less.
2. They will continue to raise awareness about the level of consumption in rich countries and try to persuade people to consume less.
3. The writer suggests that the protesters should try to persuade politicians and business leaders to do something.
4. In the letter to the editor, the writer is unhappy about the traffic delay which was caused by the protest. The writer wants to point out that people might associate the protest with problems for themselves.

c) Student's own answer

3 What do you think?
Student's own answer

4 Water: a key resource
1. b) material; **2.** a) consumerism; **3.** c) impact; **4.** a) groundwater; **5.** b) regenerate; **6.** c) dispose of; **7.** c) chemicals; **8.** b) thrown away; **9.** a) landfills; **10.** b) contaminate; **11.** c) greenwashing; **12.** b) pesticides; **13.** b) textile; **14.** c) cotton

5 Apps and food waste
Model answer:
Hey,
There are two apps that I've read about. The first app offers recipes that you can make with food that is left over. The app combines a limited number of ingredients and suggests a suitable recipe. The other app has an English name, "Too Good To Go", and as its name says, it tells users where they can get the food which restaurants, cake shops and supermarkets would otherwise throw away. The food products are sold at a reduced price.

6 Your ideas ...
Student's own answer

7 A family conversation
a)
Imogen: Do you think we **ought to try** becoming vegetarians?
Dad: Maybe. I **used to be** a vegetarian when I was younger.
Imogen: I know, but Mum **might not be** very happy about it.
Dad: When we were at university, we often **used to cook** vegetarian food.
Imogen: **Shall** we **ask** Mum what she thinks?

b)
Imogen: How often **did you use to cook** together in those days?
Dad: Quite often. We **used to live** in the same student house, so we shared a kitchen. That's how we got to know each other.
Imogen: **Did you use to go** to protests together too?
Dad: No, we **used to have** very different interests. She **didn't use to like** my protests and I **didn't use to do** much else!

8 You, the consumer
a)/b) Student's own answers

Diff pool

1 Negative aspects and solutions
a)/b)/c) Student's own answers

2 Young activists
1 b); **2** b); **3** a); **4** c)

3 Meet some young activists
See answer in ex. 2

4 An online survey
Student's own answer

5 What we could do better
1 e); **2** d); **3** g); **4** c); **5** f); **6** b); **7** a)

6 How to: Understand a formal letter
1. pp.; **2.** c/o; **3.** Re; **4.** Attn; **5.** Enc./Encl.; **6.** Ref.

7 Talking about figures
- 29: the date in July in 2021 on which Overshoot Day happened
- 40: the number of kilos of carbon dioxide that are generated by one kilo of lamb
- 50: the percentage by which we need to reduce meat consumption to push back Overshoot Day by 17 days
- 17: the number of days by which we can push back Overshoot Day if we reduce meat consumption by 50%
- 1,300,000,000: the amount of food in tonnes that is wasted every year
- $^1/_3$: the amount of the total production of food that is wasted every year

8 Words to talk about environmental issues
1 c); **2** e); **3** d); **4** h); **5** a); **6** g); **7** f); **8** b)

9 Talking about the environment
Model answer:
1. In order to waste less food, we ought to plan meals before we go shopping.
2. Cycling or walking more would reduce my ecological footprint.
3. If we don't stop wasting resources, we might have serious shortages of food/none left for future generations.
4. As a species we must ask ourselves, "Shall we destroy our planet or shall we take care of it?"
5. Governments and big companies ought to do more to protect the environment.
6. Repairing broken things would be better than throwing them away and buying something new.

10 What shall we do?
See model answer in ex. 9

11 Why greenwashing matters

products	claims	reasons
can of lemonade	100% recyclable aluminium container	It takes a lot of energy to recycle metal.
children's toy	Made with 20% recycled plastic	The other 80% is probably new plastic.
supermarket dessert	All the products in our fridges come in eco-friendly packaging	It doesn't say why it is eco-friendly'.
packet of sausages	Meets our Green Label farm quality standards	It doesn't say what the standards are, or if they are checked by another organisation.
light bulb	Energy-saving LED	The claim is nothing special as LED bulbs are usually energy-saving.

12 The problem with greenwashing
See answer in ex. 11

13 What is the story about?
1. E; **2.** B; **3.** A; **4.** D; **5.** C

14 Create headings
See answer in ex. 13

15 Yearbook article about the new guy
Student's own answer

16 Formal and informal letters

informal phrases in letter A	formal phrases in letter B
What he did in the cafeteria did no harm …	The actions he took … were completely harmless.
In fact,	Furthermore,
Did you know that …?	They would like to point out …
We've checked all the school rules	Having examined the school rules,
We think the teachers ought to show …	They respectfully ask the school authorities to produce …
Jedediah was expelled because …	The reason given for expelling Mr. Strock was …
On top of that,	Moreover,
Thanks,	Thank you in advance

Grammar

〈G1〉 Exercise 1
1 Everywhere; **2** As soon as; **3** While; **4** because; **5** before; **6** since; **7** than; **8** when; **9** until; **10** where

Exercise 2
1 as / because / since; **2** while; **3** before / until; **4** where; **5** even though / although; **6** whereas / while

G2 Exercise 1
a) **1** as / just as / like; **2** as; **3** as though / as if; **4** like

b) Model answer:
1. … in order to protect the environment for future generations.
2. … so that you can make sustainable choices when you go shopping.
3. … so you know how far they have travelled.
4. … in case there is a long period of very dry weather.

〈G3〉 Exercise 1
1. You **have to** wash your hands before touching the food.
2. Customers **aren't allowed to** touch the food at all.
3. Customers **are allowed to** taste something before they buy it, but it **has to** be given to them on a plate. They **aren't allowed to** just take things.
4. You **are allowed to** chat with customers to make them feel welcome, but only if you **are able to** do all your other work too.
5. You **don't have to** ask me if you need to take a toilet break.
6. Starting next month, we **won't be able to** offer our customers any coffee. This is because we **weren't able to** get any more coffee without packaging, so we **wouldn't be able to** say it's zero waste.

Exercise 2
Partner A: 1 must; **2** needn't; **3** couldn't; **4** must; **5** can; **6** must; **7** must; **8** can

Partner B: 1 have to; **2** don't have to; **3** wasn't able to; **4** will have to; **5** will be able to; **6** has to; **7** will have to; **8** will be allowed to

G4 Exercise 1
1 Might; **2** might; **3** would; **4** should / ought to; **5** should / ought to; **6** would; **7** would; **8** would; **9** might not / wouldn't; **10** might not / wouldn't; **11** would / 'd; **12** Would; **13** Shall; **14** shouldn't / ought not to

Exercise 2
1 used to be; **2** didn't use to use; **3** used to sell; **4** didn't use to offer; **5** used to stock; **6** used to throw away

Text and media smart 1

Diff pool

1 The vocabulary of advertising

1. advertisement; **2.** celebrity; **3.** bargain; **4.** customer; **5.** to catch sb's attention; **6.** to persuade sb; **7.** to exaggerate; **8.** claim

2 Talking about advertising

See answer in ex. 1

3 Buy it now!

1 video; **2** phone battery; **3** power; **4** muesli bar; **5** ingredients; **6** sugar; **7** toothbrushes; **8** electric toothbrush; **9** mouth

4 Understand and analyse a commercial

Student's own answer

5 What does it really mean?

Model answer:

	claims	reasons
1	Made with whole grains	Even if it is made "with" whole grains, the food could still contain unhealthy ingredients.
2	No added sugar	It could still have a lot of natural sugar (e.g. from fruit, honey) as well as unhealthy ingredients.
3	low fat	'Low fat' doesn't have to be good for you and it could still contain unhealthy ingredients.
4	Forms part of a balanced diet	The claim doesn't mean anything as almost any food can be part of a balanced diet.
5	Part of a nutritious diet	The product may contain only small amounts of nutritious ingredients.
6	Bursting with natural goodness	The claim doesn't mean anything even if it sounds healthy.
7	All natural ingredients	Large amounts of some natural ingredients, e.g. sugar, animal fat, are unhealthy and 'natural' isn't officially defined.
8	Contains six vitamins	Some unhealthy products can contain healthy ingredients, but they still aren't good for you.
9	High in iron	The other ingredients in the product may not be good for you.
10–11	Free from artificial colours, flavours and preservatives	The food could still contain other unhealthy ingredients.
12	Gives you the energy you need to start your day	The product could have a lot of sugar.

6 Food advertising

1 b); **2** c); **3** a); **4** b); **5** b); **6** c)

7 The problem with food advertising

Model answer:

1. Children and teens see between 12 and 21 TV or media food ads each day.
2. The types of food that are advertised the most to children and teens are fast food and drinks with sugar.
3. Food advertisers make the food look attractive by using tricks and food stylists.
4. Advertisers use older children to make products seem cool to younger viewers.
5. Food advertisers use misleading phrases such as "made with whole grains" or "part of a nutritious breakfast" to make people think that the product is healthy even though it isn't.
6. You should look at the labels on food products to see whether they have unhealthy ingredients.

8 Sum up the problems

Model answer:

1. … to advertise products.
2. … make money.
3. … has different values to the influencer's own well-known values.

Grammar

‹G5› Exercise 1

One of **the best** things about growing up is starting to take control of your own money. **TEENpay** is the nation's **most popular** payment card for teenagers who want to pay for things **quickly** and **easily** and find carrying cash **inconvenient**. Applying for a card is **the simplest** thing you can imagine! Just go online, open an account and get an adult to send some money to it **electronically**. We'll send you your **new** card, and when it arrives, you'll be able to use it **immediately**. Of course, you can top up your account as **frequently** as you like. Happy shopping!

Exercise 2

1 the best; **2** the worst; **3** more effective; **4** bigger; **5** the tiniest; **6** isn't/not as good as; **7** as well as; **8** medically; **9** the most useless; **10** lazily; **11** intentionally; **12** better than; **13** faster; **14** longer; **15** significantly; **16** hotter; **17** isn't/not as dangerous as; **18** terribly

Unit 2

Check-out

1 Edutainment

Model answer:

1. It's a form of entertainment that educates as well.
2. c)
3. It makes learning more fun.
4. Sales have increased a lot.
5. They can distract students from learning; not all students have equal access to technology; a reliance on technology and gamification can lead to less interpersonal connection.
6. b)

2 Your experiences

a)/b) Student's own answer

3 Online friendships

Student's own answer

4 A fresh start

Model answer:

a) Anna is bullied by some boys at school who have found out about her past. When she was at her last school, an embarrassing photo was taken of her at a party and posted online. She tried to delete all copies of the photo, but now someone has posted it again on a Facebook profile and everyone at her new school can see it.

b) Anna feels shocked when one of the boys calls her Anna Reeves (l. 16). When she sees the photo on the new Facebook page, she feels shame (l. 42) and then she feels sick (ll. 47–48). After having thought about who could have seen the photo, she starts to panic (l. 56). At the end of the extract, Anna seems to be desperate (l. 66): She can't decide which option to click when she is asked about the reason for reporting the photo. She is sad and embarrassed by it (ll. 62–66).

c) Student's own answer

5 VR in every home and school?

1 free-time; **2** immersive; **3** game console; **4** screen-based; **5** enables; **6** celebrated; **7** benefits; **8** use; **9** potential; **10** all-important

6 The future of digital media

1 will have been; **2** won't be writing; **3** will have become; **4** will have changed; **5** will have learned; **6** will be using; **7** will have understood; **8** will be cyberbullying

7 Mixed bag

1. I never play video games, which makes me unusual at my school.
2. That's the classroom **in which** we're going to start a coding club.
3. Can you remember a time **when** you didn't use social media every day?
4. We found that AR software is really easy to use, **which** we weren't expecting.
5. Major esports competitions, **where** players can win a lot of money, attract thousands of spectators.
6. During people's teenage years, **when** cyberbullying can become a serious problem, it is especially important to be careful on social media.

Diff pool

1 What I want you to know

Student's own answer

2 Describing music

Model answer: The song belongs to the musical genre pop. At first, the only instruments that the listener hears are a guitar/an electric guitar as well as the vocals. Later drums and a piano are added. The music gets louder, more dynamic and more complex in the second half of the song. In the first half of the song it is sad, melodious and moody, in the second half it sounds more hopeful. The rhythm is quite slow and regular at the beginning of the song. In the second half it is a little bit faster.

3 Future forms

1. B; **2.** D; **3.** C; **4.** A

4 Alexis' day at NewSchoolUS

1 will be riding; **2** will have planned; **3** will be walking; **4** will be finishing; **5** won't have prepared; **6** will have had; **7** will be catching; **8** will have talked

5 Alexis' plans for tomorrow

See answer in ex. 4

6 Selfie Harm

Student's own answer

7 Holiday posts

Ryan: That was the beach next to our hotel **1 where** you took a really nice photo of me.
Ellie: Oh, I remember. The day **2 when** I took this photo was very cloudy.
Ryan: Do you think I should post it? I don't usually put photos of myself on social media, **3 where** there's always a risk of getting negative comments.
Ellie: That's true. I'd really like to live in a perfect world **4 where** everybody is polite on social media.
Ryan: Do you remember this time last year **5 when** you first started posting content?
Ellie: I do. Fortunately, I haven't had any negative experiences so far. But at my school, **6 where** cyberbullying has become very common, they've decided to ban mobile phones.
Ryan: That's so sad. I don't know. Maybe I shouldn't post it.
Ellie: It's your choice. Sometimes I wish I hadn't started using social media last year **7 when** I didn't care so much about my online image.

8 Video games

1 avatar; **2** horns; **3** skulls; **4** typing; **5** looking; **6** female; **7** wings; **8** inventive; **9** uninteresting; **10** making fun of; **11** boring; **12** irony; **13** violent; **14** hanging; **15** terrified; **16** wide open; **17** video game; **18** informs; **19** reflects; **20** criticises

9 Help with cyberbullies

1. d); **2.** b); **3.** c); **4.** a); **5.** i); **6.** j); **7.** g); **8.** h); **9.** f); **10.** e); **11.** m); **12.** k); **13.** n); **14.** l)

10 SLAY

	advantages and possibilities	downsides and real-life consequences
developers	- video games can be a form of art / creative expression (ll. 5–6); - they can create a new world for people who need one (ll. 100–102)	- they are responsible for the negative effect of games on users (ll. 6–8) - video games can be taken too seriously (ll. 18–21) - people don't always respect the rules of a game (ll. 67–70)
users	- video game characters can be seen and used as an extension of one's own personality (ll. 8–9) - people can make money by doing something they love: playing video games (l. 36) - people can be whoever they want to be (ll. 62–64, ll. 85–87) - people are free to do whatever they want within the limits of the games without risking anything (ll. 85–89)	- playing a video game for too long can have negative effects on one's health (ll. 15–18) - they might meet dangerous people online (ll. 40–43) - games are not always designed to be inclusive and can therefore be discriminating towards minorities (ll. 74–81) - harmful actions don't have any consequences in real life; anonymity of games can be abused (ll. 90–94)

11 ⟨The narrator's language⟩

1 informal; **2** relaxed; **3** short; **4** simple; **5** knew; **6** easier; **7** humorous; **8** humour; **9** exaggerated; **10** tone

Grammar

⟨G6⟩ Exercise 1

1 are going to; **2** will; **3** will; **4** won't; **5** will; **6** Will; **7** are going to; **8** will; **9** Are … going to; **10** are going to; **11** are going to

Exercise 2

Model answer:

Dear Students,

Next Saturday the student council **is offering** a one-day technology workshop. It **starts** at 10 a.m. and **finishes** around 4 p.m. The workshop **starts** with an overview of the latest tech introduced in school recently and **continues** with the chance to try some new gadgets. The lunch break **starts** at 1 p.m. at the latest. Jack Manson (Year 10) **is bringing** his famous vegetable curry sandwiches and **is selling** them for 50p each. Ms Gledhill, the computer science teacher, **is giving** a short talk at the end of this workshop.

G7 Exercise 1

I'**ll have started** my first tech company before I finish university.
I'**ll have made** my first million by the time I'm 25.
At that point millions of people **will have bought** my gadgets.
When I'm in my fifties, I'**ll have become** a billionaire.
By then I'**ll have stopped** working and **will have retired** to my private island.
Will I have married my girlfriend?
How many (if any) children **will** I **have had**?

G8 Exercise 1

Model answer:
A few years from now, nobody **will be using** social media.
When I next buy a new one, smartphones **will be doing** what seems impossible today.
By 2050 artificial intelligence **will be talking** to us as if it was a real person.
In 20 years' time, VR systems **will** still **be getting** better and better.
When I start work, only a few people **will** still **be using** big desktop computers.
At the next big tech fair, tech companies **will be launching** their latest gadgets.

⟨G9⟩ Exercise 1

a) **1.** In the past it was often monarchs **who / that** were the most important influencers.
2. Portraits of them **which / that** were painted at the time were often copied and distributed around the country.
3. Many of these portraits showed them with looks **which / that** can seem strange to us today.
4. However, many people **who / that** lived at the time tried to copy the monarch's appearance.
5. Today pop stars and actors are the people **whose** appearance is most likely to influence how others want to look.
6. Many celebrities have a 'personal stylist' **who / that** works with them before they are seen in public. / Many celebrities have a 'personal stylist' **with whom** they work before they are seen in public.
7. Celebrities **who / that** want to be noticed may ask the stylist to give them an innovative look.

b) **2.** Portraits of them **painted** at the time were often copied and distributed around the country.
4. However, many people **living** at the time tried to copy the monarch's appearance.
6. Many celebrities have a 'personal stylist' **working** with them before they are seen in public.
7. Celebrities **wanting** to be noticed may ask the stylist to give them an innovative look.

Exercise 2

1. Thanks to stylists, photos of celebrities, **which may also have been heavily retouched**, often don't show their everyday appearance.
2. These photos may be seen by millions of people**, who then share them with others on the internet**.

3. A look created by a stylist, **which may be very different from the everyday appearance of the celebrity,** can influence a very large number of people.
4. Perhaps one day these photos of celebrities, **which will probably exist electronically far into the future,** will seem as strange as portraits of kings and queens from past centuries do to us today.

G10 Exercise 1

1. Nowadays, standards of beauty are mostly defined by celebrities, the fashion industry and internet influencers, **which is very different to how things were in the past.** (c)
2. We're told that famous actors, singers, footballers etc. are the most successful people in the world, **which, of course, makes people want to copy their favourite celebrity's appearance.** (e)
3. Many internet video channels focus on fashion and beauty, **which means new ideas can instantly reach a very large international audience.** (d)
4. It may be that everybody in a social group is watching the same influencers' channels, **which can put a lot of pressure on people in that group to look the same.** (a)
5. Social media can have a huge impact on the lives of its users, **which raises questions about whether there should be more checks and regulations.** (b)

G11 Exercise 1

1. There has probably never been a time **in which** people did not think about their appearance.
   There has probably never been a time **when** people did not think about their appearance.
2. Norway is one country **in which** they have laws to fight unrealistic beauty standards.
   Norway is one country **where** they have laws to fight unrealistic beauty standards.
3. Schools are one place **in/at which** there can be a lot of peer pressure.
   Schools are one place **where** there can be a lot of peer pressure.
4. The 2010s was the decade **in which** social media really became a part of everyday life.
   The 2010s was the decade **when** social media really became a part of everyday life.
5. There are social media platforms **on which** people spend a very significant amount of their time.
   There are social media platforms **where** people spend a very significant amount of their time.

Vocabulary

Sounds and spelling: Word stress in word families

a)/b)

1. con**tri**bute [kənˈtrɪbjuːt]; contri**but**ions [ˌkɒntrɪˈbjuːʃnz]
2. **temp**ting [ˈtemptɪŋ]; temp**ta**tion [tempˈteɪʃn]
3. **stra**tegies [ˈstrætədʒiz]; stra**te**gic [strəˈtiːdʒɪk]
4. **mod**ified [ˈmɒdɪfaɪd]; modifi**ca**tions [ˌmɒdɪfɪˈkeɪʃənz]
5. com**bine** [kəmˈbaɪn]; combi**na**tion [ˌkɒmbɪˈneɪʃən]
6. **al**ter [ˈɔːltə]; alte**ra**tions [ˌɒltəˈreɪʃənz]
7. **va**rious [ˈveəriəs]; va**ri**ety [vəˈraɪəti]
8. pro**gress**ive [prəˈgresɪv]; **pro**gress [ˈprəʊgres]

Text and media smart 2

Diff pool

1 Analysing a text
Student's own answer

2 Your checklist for summary writing
- reduce the text to 30–40% of the original / one to three pages for longer texts
- introduction: state title, **author** and main point (plus source and publication date if it's an article)
- main part: structured in paragraphs; **every** new point needs a new paragraph
- conclusion: not needed
- order of points: either **thematically** (combined in a new, logical way) or **chronologically** (as in the original)
- **don't** include details, examples, quotations and your own opinion
- **don't** copy original lines word for word
- use a **formal** register
- use the **present** tense if you describe the actions of the author, e.g. "The author concludes …"

3 Judging an analysis
Student's own answer

4 Making a difference
Student's own answer

5 Smartphones at school

a)

pros	cons
- makes it easier to meet friends in breaks etc. - normal now to have a smartphone at all times - very helpful in an emergency - most students aged 15–16 can be trusted to behave sensibly - useful for research in lessons	- many classrooms have computers, tablets etc. - emergencies in which you need a smartphone are very unusual - students without smartphones feel left out - distracts students from lessons - stops students joining in with face-to-face school life - rude posts about other students, cyberbullying etc. cause disruption

b) Student's own answer

6 Structuring an argumentative essay

for a minimum age	against a minimum age
- makes it illegal for social media platforms to collect the personal data of kids for advertising - more time to teach kids about online safety, cyberbullies and the dangers of meeting strangers online - older teens are more likely to spot misinformation and fake news - easier for parents to argue against social media - without social media kids have more time for meaningful activities like being creative or doing sport	- impossible to make sure kids respect the age limit - social media are an important part of the everyday life of kids aged 13–15 too - kids have already learned about online safety, cyberbullies and the dangers of meeting strangers online by the age of 13 - social media help them to connect with or make new friends - one age limit for all ignores the fact that every kid is different - the current age limits are ignored, and any other age limit will be too

Grammar

〈G12〉 Exercise 1

1 'm standing; **2** is coming; **3** are chanting; **4** refers; **5** are you protesting; **6** leave; **7** photograph and film; **8** currently has; **9** is still rising; **10** suggests; **11** spends; **12** are filming; **13** is calling; **14** usually start; **15** help; **16** Do you disagree; **17** accept; **18** are putting; **19** 's getting; **20** is watching

Exercise 2

Model answer: The photo **shows** a crowd of protesters near the Houses of Parliament. The protesters **are facing away from** the camera and **are looking towards** the Houses of Parliament. The scene **includes** some police officers who **are standing** with the protesters, but they **are not trying to stop** them from protesting. The photo **gives the impression that** it is a peaceful protest.

Unit 3

Check-out

1 School in Canada

1. c); **2.** c); **3.** b); **4.** b); **5.** a); **6.** c)

2 Life on a ranch in Canada

Model answer:

Dear Ben,

You told me that your family is thinking about moving to a remote part of Canada. I heard this interview with a German woman who went to live on a ranch in the Rocky Mountains with her family, so I thought I'd tell you about it. Their daily lives involve looking after the animals and vegetable garden as well as repairs and building work. The whole family also collects and cuts wood for the fire. The ranch gets its power from solar cells and batteries, which means that they can't always use the fridge or computer or telephone. They must also be careful of the wild animals when they are outside. It seems as if you can get used to them and learn to judge their behaviour. The woman's children are between eight and 16. They are homeschooled in the morning by their mother and are free to go out in the afternoon. The children do lots of things like hunting and fishing and riding as well as reading or listening to music. It sounds different to your life in Coventry, but that doesn't mean it would be boring. Write soon and tell me what your family decides to do.

All the best, …

3 Canada, a huge country

a)/b) Student's own answer

4 A travel blog from the Rockies

–

5 Understanding Cindy's blog

a) Model answer:

1. … her family (mother, father and brother).
2. … the water is very cold.
3. … construction.
4. … Cindy's dad was tired of driving.
5. … they wanted to drive on the glacier/they couldn't walk across the glacier.
6. … it was in the motorhome.

b) **1.** true: I took so many pictures!
2. false: Our engine has to work really hard.
3. false: Never seen that before!
4. true: … there was construction; … it started to rain
5. false: … my brother even tried to walk on the ice
6. true: … not far away from me.

c) **1.** Banff National Park; Lake Louise; Jasper
2. the Canadian Rockies (when the sun was going down); Lake Louise; the snow coach trip across the Columbia Icefield
3. sun; rain; snow
4. go on a boat at Lake Louise; go shopping at Lake Louise; walk on the glacier

6 Your choice

Student's own answer

7 A huge country
1 natural; **2** endless; **3** live; **4** travel; **5** flight; **6** settlers; **7** dangerous; **8** crossing

8 Churchill – bears and ships
1 polar; **2** winter; **3** migration; **4** industry; **5** season; **6** extend; **7** cargo has; **8** transport; **9** efficient

9 ⟨Disaster hits Churchill⟩
1 had already been worrying; **2** hit; **3** flooded; **4** struck; **5** had been expecting; **6** destroyed; **7** cut off; **8** stopped; **9** have been flying; **10** have been paying; **11** had been planning; **12** couldn't

10 ⟨What will happen to Churchill?⟩
Model answer:
Churchill **happens to stand** on a very fragile kind of landscape called permafrost. The infrastructure there **is said to depend** on the frozen ground to support it. However, Churchill **is likely to lose** up to 70% of this permafrost by the year 2100 because of global warming and increased precipitation. The 900 people who live there year round and their income **are certain to be affected**. Beluga whale and polar bear tourism make up about 60% of its economy, but forecasts predict that these animals and the tourists **are certain to stay away** if temperatures continue to rise. The tundra buggies that **are supposed to transport** tourists across the permafrost ground to see the polar bears may not have any ground to drive on. There may be small lakes instead. But it's not only about tourism. About 51% of the population identifies as Indigenous. According to studies, at least one quarter of these people **are said to hunt** for their meat. But as the ground changes, so too will the wildlife. Some animals that are traditionally hunted **are certain to disappear**.

Diff pool

1 The Canadian mosaic
Student's own answer

2 First impressions
Student's own answer

3 ⟨Find the rule⟩
a) **1.** d; **2.** a; **3.** b; **4.** f; **5.** c; **6.** e
Model answer: You use the past perfect progressive to describe actions that were already in progress and ended at or just before a point in the past. You use the present perfect progressive to describe an action that started in the past, is still happening now and may continue into the future.
b) **1.** You use the past perfect progressive to stress how long an activity had continued before another event in the past happened.
2. It emphasises that an activity had happened several times up to a point in the past.
c) Model answer:
- We'd been walking around Toronto since 10:00 a.m. (l. 11) – rule 1
- We'd been hoping to take the train to Niagara Falls (l. 20) – rule 2
- We … hadn't been planning on staying overnight (ll. 21–22) – rule 1
- We'd been talking about booking a package tour (l. 24) – rule 2

4 ⟨Working in the forestry industry⟩
1 arrived; **2** have been trying; **3** has been working; **4** had been planning; **5** lost; **6** didn't have; **7** didn't give up; **8** found; **9** has been; **10** has been working

5 The interview
a) **1.** B; **2.** D, K; **3.** A, E, F; **4.** C, H; **5.** J, L; **6.** G, I
b) Student's own answer

6 ⟨Find the rule⟩

form of to be	form of verb	past participle	adjective	infinitive
is		supposed		to be
is			likely	to disappear
are			certain	to change
is		said		to be
	happen			to have

7 A cartoon
1 is covering; **2** is still raining; **3** is standing; **4** is wearing; **5** is throwing; **6** is trying; **7** snows; **8** raining

8 Your own backyard
Student's own answer

9 Could you write the subtitles, please?
a)/b) Student's own answers

10 Mi'gmaq culture
Model answer:
- gwis: means 'son'; a father says this to his son to show their special relationship
- farming tools: things which the community can use to grow their own food and, if necessary, to fight the police
- to clean fish: a skill which people need to get food; it is passed on from father to son
- to repair nets: a skill which people need to get food; it is passed on from father to son
- elder: someone who has experience of the world; this person is respected and when they can no longer fish, they are supported by the community
- thousands of years: the length of time that the community has fished for their food
- salmon run: part of the salmon's life cycle; a good run means that there will be enough fish for the community to catch and eat
- to respect the cycle: the community knows that they must respect the salmon's life cycle or else the numbers of fish will go down; then there won't be enough fish for the community to live on
- government: the Canadian / state government tries to make the community fish less and they send in the police to stop them; the community doesn't accept this as they have their own laws and rights

- to ring the church bells: the bells warn the community that there is trouble; everyone answers the call
- rules and laws: the community has its own rules and laws, which depend on the laws of nature and the best way for the community to survive; the community does not accept laws that come from outside e.g. from the government, as they are not good for the community or the environment

11 Writing a characterisation
Model answer:
1. The elder is wearing a shirt and a pair of trousers with braces as well as a hat. His skin is wrinkled and his hair is white. It looks like he can't walk very well as he uses a walking stick.
2. He seems very independent and he often refuses when people offer to help him. On the other hand, he is pleased when the young fisherman brings him fish. Whenever there is trouble, he stands with his community. At the end of the graphic novel, he acts like a warrior and tries to protect his community.
3. I think that he feels strongly about his people and their rights. He seems to be worried when the trouble starts and he probably thinks that the situation will repeat itself, which it does a year later. He is determined not to let the police win.

12 Emotions
a)/b) Model answer:
- disgust: p. 99, the third panel on the page which shows the woman's reaction when her son tells her the QPP are taking the salmon
- anger: p. 100, the last panel on the page where the head of the community and the policeman shout at one another
- confusion: p. 111, the top panel when the people don't know what is happening
- surprise: p. 91, the top-right panel when the boy wakes up the girl while it is still dark
- dismay: p. 113, the second panel on the page when the people look up at the helicopter
- fear: p. 116, the middle panel where the boy sees the police arresting his father
- sadness: p. 108, the last panel on the page where the boy looks into the distance
- anxiety: p. 110, the bottom panels that show the family's reaction when the father does not come home
- relief: p. 101, the last large panel on the page where the police finally leave the community in peace
- pride: p. 104, the last panel in the bottom left-hand corner when the father tells his son he has done a good job cleaning the fish
- happiness: p. 105, the panel where the old man smiles and thanks the other man for the fish
- excitement: p. 103, the panel which shows the reaction of the community when the head of the community says that they won't let the minister intimidate them

13 ⟨Dividing the short story "Oil and Ivory" into sections⟩
a) Model answer:
Section A ll. 1–9: The oil platform explodes
Section B ll. 10–33: Zack wakes up in the igloo
Section C ll. 34–47: Only the Inuit are affected by the oil spill
Section D ll. 48–74: The problem with the narwhals' migration
Section E ll. 75–134: Zack's opinion of the Inuit
Section F ll. 135–183: Zack's drill cuts holes in the ice
Section G ll. 184–242: Meri saves the narwhals/the narwhals clean up the oil spill
b) Student's own answer

14 ⟨Conflict in the short story "Oil and Ivory"⟩
Student's own answer

Grammar

⟨G13⟩ Exercise 1
1 has been staying; **2** arrived; **3** 's / has become; **4** hasn't told; **5** have come; **6** landed; **7** was still having; **8** 've / have already made; **9** invited; **10** were just being; **11** didn't accept; **12** 've / have been thinking; **13** made; **14** has just sent; **15** went; **16** 've / have been doing

Exercise 2
1 We've; **2** hadn't; **3** they'd; **4** haven't; **5** they've; **6** they'd; **7** has; **8** has; **9** had; **10** has; **11** hadn't

⟨G14⟩ Exercise 1
1 'd / had been travelling; **A** for 12 hours; **2** 'd / had been hoping; **3** had been raining; **B** since the start of the week; **4** 'd / had been preparing; **C** for months; **5** (had been) discussing; **6** hadn't been expecting; **7** hadn't been looking around; **D** for more than a few minutes

⟨G15⟩ Exercise 1
1 had just arrived; **2** felt; **A** there; **3** 'd / had already seen; **B** the night before / the previous night; **4** hadn't prepared; **5** were; **6** were really enjoying; **7** wished; **C** had taken; **8** would stay; **D** that afternoon; **9** were getting; **10** thought; **11** would sleep; **E** that night; **12** were leaving for; **F** the next day / the next morning

Exercise 2
Model answer: **1** asked (me) if he could; **2** wanted to know where he could; **3** asked if I would help him; **4** asked me to email him; **5** asked (me) if it was OK to give; **6** told him not to get; **7** asked him not to give

⟨G16⟩ Exercise 1
1 are certain to; **2** are supposed to; **3** happens to; **4** is not likely to; **5** is said to

Text and media smart 3

Diff pool

1 Jobs in the theatre
a)/b) Student's own answers

2 Jobs in the theatre
a)/b) Student's own answer

3 It's your decision!
Student's own answer

4 Formal vs informal
a)/b)
- **Assistants:** **1.** nature; **2.** help; **3.** possibly; **4.** sorry; **5.** understood; **6.** instead; **7.** insurmountable, prompted; **8.** demands; **9.** nugget, Impossible; **10.** attitude, desperate; **11.** look; **12.** about; **13.** doing; **14.** welcome, glad
- **Customers:** **1.** just; **2.** wonder; **3.** complain; **4.** change; **5** saved; **6.** wonderful, indeed

c) impolite / informal: 7, 8, 9, 10. The rest of the phrases are polite or formal.

5 Formal vs informal
See answer in ex. 4

6 Write your scene
Student's own answer

Grammar

〈G17〉 Exercise 1
1 was written; **2** has been performed; **3** has also been done; **4** (has) been filmed; **5** was adapted; **6** is done; **7** is only going to be seen / will only be seen; **8** isn't going to be reviewed / won't be reviewed; **9** were given; **10** were played; **11** are cast; **12** will be acted; **13** hasn't been tried

Exercise 2
1. **Were** enough copies of the playscript **printed out**?
2. How much rehearsal time **will be needed**?
3. **Has** the assembly hall **been booked** for the evening of the production?
4. **Has** permission to use the assembly hall **been given** by the head teacher? / **Has** permission **been given** by the head teacher to use the assembly hall?
5. Where **are** the costumes from previous plays **stored**?
6. **Has** our production **been mentioned** on / by any other local websites?
7. **Is** the production **going to be reviewed** by the local newspaper?
8. How **will** the tickets **be sold**?

〈G18〉 Exercise 1
a) 1. If I need help, I'll / will ask for it.
2. When I need help, I'll / will ask for it.
3. If I needed help, I'd / would ask for it.
4. If I'd/had needed help, I'd / would have asked for it.

b) 1. I'll/will ask for help if I need it.
2. I'll/will ask for help when I need it.
3. I'd/would ask for help if I needed it.
4. I'd/would have asked for help if I'd / had needed it.

Exercise 2
1. If you **return** the product to us, we **will give** your money back.
2. If there **was / were** more information on the website, I **wouldn't need** to keep calling the help desk.
3. It probably **wouldn't have broken** if you **had read** the instructions properly.
4. I **wouldn't have ordered** it if I **had known** it was such bad quality.
5. I **would help** you if I **could**. / If I **could help** you, I **would**.
6. We **will ship** your order when we **receive** payment from you.

Vocabulary

Intonation: When you step into a character role
a)/b) Student's own answers

Bildquellennachweis:

U1.1 Unsplash, Montréal, QC (Daniel Novykov); **U1.2** plainpicture GmbH & Co. KG RF, Hamburg (DEEPOL); **3.1** ShutterStock.com RF, New York (suicidecrew); **3.2** ShutterStock.com RF, New York (granata1111); **5.1** ShutterStock.com RF, New York (suicidecrew); **7.1** stock.adobe.com, Dublin (vospalej); **10.1** ShutterStock.com RF, New York (Olga Gladkikkh); **10.2** jani lunablau, Barcelona; **11.1** Fosseway Films, London; **11.2** Fosseway Films, London; **12.1** ShutterStock.com RF, New York (Olga Gladkikkh); **12.2** ShutterStock.com RF, New York (suicidecrew); **12.3** ShutterStock.com RF, New York (BearFotos); **13.1** stock.adobe.com, Dublin (Oleksandr Dibrova); **13.2** Preiselbeerdesign Miriam Brusniak, Berlin; **13.3** https://www.un.org/sustainabledevelopment; The content of this publication has not been approved by the United Nations and does not reflect the views of the United Nations or its officials or Member States; **14.1** stock.adobe.com, Dublin (EdNurg); **14.2** ShutterStock.com RF, New York (Lisa S.); **14.3** stock.adobe.com, Dublin (chika_milan); **14.4** ShutterStock.com RF, New York (Maridav); **15.1** Getty Images, München (s0ulsurfing - Jason Swain); **15.2** stock.adobe.com, Dublin (Sonja Birkelbach); **15.3** VISUM Foto GmbH, München (Mauricio Bustamante); **15.4** Alamy stock photo, Abingdon (Rob Crandall); **15.5** ShutterStock.com RF, New York (suicidecrew); **16.1** ShutterStock.com RF, New York (Valentina Razumova); **16.2** stock.adobe.com, Dublin (Studio Light & Shade); **17.1** stock.adobe.com, Dublin (PRASANNAPIX); **18.1** Picture-Alliance, Frankfurt/M. (dpa-Themendienst); **19.1** Mauritius · Images, Mittenwald (Brendan Bell/Alamy); **20.1** Environmental Working Group, www.ewg.org; **22.1** Kramer, Peer, Düsseldorf; **22.2** Kramer, Peer, Düsseldorf; **22.3** Kramer, Peer, Düsseldorf; **22.4** Kramer, Peer, Düsseldorf; **22.5** Kramer, Peer, Düsseldorf; **22.6** Kramer, Peer, Düsseldorf; **30.1** Romo, Virginia, Stuttgart; **31.1** Kramer, Peer, Düsseldorf; **35.1** Mauritius Images, Mittenwald (Peter Marshall/ Alamy); **37.1** Getty Images Plus, München (Fly View Productions); **39.1** OXFAM INTERMON, Barcelona; **40.1** ShutterStock.com RF, New York (Creative Family); **40.2** ShutterStock.com RF, New York (Maridav); **40.3** ShutterStock.com RF, New York (Krakenimages.com); **42.1** 2017, Boclips/Wonderscape; **44.1** ShutterStock.com RF, New York (Master1305); **44.2** ShutterStock.com RF, New York (Olesia Bilkei); **44.3** ShutterStock.com RF, New York (TY Lim); **45.1** ShutterStock.com RF, New York (granata1111); **45.2** ShutterStock.com RF, New York (Dalaifood); **45.3** ShutterStock.com RF, New York (Tyler Olson); **45.4** ShutterStock.com RF, New York (Elena Veselova); **45.5** ShutterStock.com RF, New York (Nina Buday); **45.6** ShutterStock.com RF, New York (MSPhotographic); **45.7** ShutterStock.com RF, New York (SunKids); **46.1** ShutterStock.com RF, New York (Olga Gladkikkh); **46.2** ShutterStock.com RF, New York (Andrey_Popov); **46.3** ShutterStock.com RF, New York (Zyabich); **46.4** ShutterStock.com RF, New York (RossHelen); **46.5** stock.adobe.com, Dublin (Davizro Photography); **47.1** ShutterStock.com RF, New York (elRoce); **47.2** ShutterStock.com RF, New York (Sophie James); **47.3** ShutterStock.com RF, New York (Stephen Moehle); **48.1** ShutterStock.com RF, New York (Olga Gladkikkh); **48.2** ShutterStock.com RF, New York (kasha_malasha); **48.3** ShutterStock.com RF, New York (donatas1205); **50.1** stock.adobe.com, Dublin (Jacob Lund); **51.1** ShutterStock.com RF, New York (MDV Edwards); **51.2** ShutterStock.com RF, New York (Lenscap Photography); **51.3** ShutterStock.com RF, New York (metamorworks); **51.4** ShutterStock.com RF, New York (Ground Picture); **52.1** stock.adobe.com, Dublin (Jess rodriguez); **55.1** Trunk Archive, New York (Rankin); **55.2** Trunk Archive, New York (Rankin); **56.1** ShutterStock.com RF, New York (RapunzielStock); **57.1** ShutterStock.com RF, New York (ileela); **58.1** Preiselbeerdesign Miriam Brusniak, Berlin; DAK-Gesundheit; aus: Mediensucht während der Corona-Pandemie: Ergebnisse der Längsschnittstudie zu Gaming und Social Media, S.17/S.18; (Vorlagegraphik: DAK Statistik Nutzungszeiten Gaming/Nutzungszeiten sozialer Medien und Gaming über vier Messzeitpunkte: Soziale Medien Werktags); **58.2** CartoonStock Ltd, Bath (Len Hawkins); **58.3** CartoonStock Ltd, Bath (Chris Wildt); **59.1** Aus dem Video Gone too far. Licensed edition with the kind permission of Childnet International, London, UK www.childnet.com, 2022; **59.2** Aus dem Video Gone too far. Licensed edition with the kind permission of Childnet International, London, UK www.childnet.com, 2022; **59.3** Aus dem Video Gone too far. Licensed edition with the kind permission of Childnet International, London, UK www.childnet.com, 2022; **59.4** Aus dem Video Gone too far. Licensed edition with the kind permission of Childnet International, London, UK www.childnet.com, 2022; **59.5** Aus dem Video Gone too far. Licensed edition with the kind permission of Childnet International, London, UK www.childnet.com, 2022; **59.6** Aus dem Video Gone too far. Licensed edition with the kind permission of Childnet International, London, UK www.childnet.com, 2022; **60.1** ShutterStock.com RF, New York (Mariia Korneeva); **61.1** stock.adobe.com, Dublin (Aschura Takuya); **66.1** ShutterStock.com RF, New York (suicidecrew); **67.1** ShutterStock.com RF, New York (Rawpixel.com); **68.1** CartoonStock Ltd, Bath; **71.1** ShutterStock.com RF, New York (Eugenio Marongiu); **72.1** ShutterStock.com RF, New York (fizkes); **72.2** stock.adobe.com, Dublin (fizkes); **75.1** ShutterStock.com RF, New York (fizkes); **76.1** ShutterStock.com RF, New York (antoniodiaz); **78.1** ShutterStock.com RF, New York (Monkey Business Images); **80.1** ShutterStock.com RF, New York (Studio Romantic); **82.1** stock.adobe.com, Dublin (vospalej); **82.2** ShutterStock.com RF, New York (James A Boardman); **83.1** ShutterStock.com RF, New York (PJ-Photography); **83.2** stock.adobe.com, Dublin (vospalej); **84.1** stock.adobe.com, Dublin (vospalej); **85.1** Metroland Media Group Ltd., Toronto (Published in Canadian Immigrant Magazine/Hemeterio); **85.2** ShutterStock.com RF, New York (chakkraphong jinthawet); **86.1** Alamy stock photo, Abingdon (THE CANADIAN PRESS/Andrew Vaughan); **86.2** Mauritius Images, Mittenwald (louise murray/ Alamy); **87.1** stock.adobe.com, Dublin (IBRESTER); **87.2** ShutterStock.com RF, New York (Russ Heinl); **87.3** stock.adobe.com, Dublin (_panya_); **88.1** jani lunablau, Barcelona; **88.2** jani lunablau, Barcelona; **88.3** stock.adobe.com, Dublin (Tharanga); **88.4** jani lunablau, Barcelona; **88.5** stock.adobe.com, Dublin (tammykayphoto); **88.6** jani lunablau, Barcelona; **88.7** jani lunablau, Barcelona; **88.8** jani lunablau, Barcelona; **88.9** jani lunablau, Barcelona; **89.1** stock.adobe.com, Dublin (TOimages); **91.1** stock.adobe.com, Dublin (Adam); **91.2** Alamy stock photo, Abingdon (RM USA); **91.3** ShutterStock.com RF, New York (LeonWang); **91.4** Alamy stock photo, Abingdon (Michael Wheatley); **93.1** www.CartoonStock.com, Bath (David Beningfield); **94.1** © BBC Motion Gallery — British Broadcasting Corporation — Media Centre, London; **94.2** © BBC Motion Gallery — British Broadcasting Corporation — Media Centre, London; **94.3** © BBC Motion Gallery — British Broadcasting Corporation — Media Centre, London; **94.4** © BBC Motion Gallery — British Broadcasting Corporation — Media Centre, London; **95.1** ShutterStock.com RF,

New York (Aewphoto); **95.2** stock.adobe.com, Dublin (vospalej); **96.1** Migwite'tmeg: We Remember it: pages 196-218 from This Place: 150 Years Retold copyright 2019 by, Brandon Mitchell (Text) and Tara Audibert (Illustrations) Reproduced with permission from HighWater Press, Winnipeg. https //www.portageandmainpress.com; **97.1–** Migwite'tmeg: We Remember it: pages 196–218 from This Place: 150 Years Retold copyright 2019 by Brandon Mitchell (Text) and Tara Audibert (Illustrations) Reproduced with permission from HighWater Press, Winnipeg. https://www.portageandmainpress.com; **98.1** Migwite'tmeg: We Remember it: pages 196-218 from This Place: 150 Years Retold copyright 2019 by, Brandon Mitchell (Text) and Tara Audibert (Illustrations) Reproduced with permission from HighWater Press, Winnipeg. https://www.portageandmainpress.com; **99.1** Migwite'tmeg: We Remember it: pages 196-218 from This Place: 150 Years Retold copyright 2019 by, Brandon Mitchell (Text) and Tara Audibert (Illustrations) Reproduced with permission from HighWater Press, Winnipeg. https://www.portageandmainpress.com; **100.1** Migwite'tmeg: We Remember it: pages 196-218 from This Place: 150 Years Retold copyright 2019 by, Brandon Mitchell (Text) and Tara Audibert (Illustrations) Reproduced with permission from HighWater Press, Winnipeg. https://www.portageandmainpress.com; **101.1** Migwite'tmeg: We Remember it: pages 196-218 from This Place: 150 Years Retold copyright 2019 by, Brandon Mitchell (Text) and Tara Audibert (Illustrations) Reproduced with permission from HighWater Press, Winnipeg. https://www.portageandmainpress.com; **102.1** Migwite'tmeg: We Remember it: pages 196-218 from This Place: 150 Years Retold copyright 2019 by, Brandon Mitchell (Text) and Tara Audibert (Illustrations) Reproduced with permission from HighWater Press, Winnipeg. https://www.portageandmainpress.com; **103.1** Migwite'tmeg: We Remember it: pages 196-218 from This Place: 150 Years Retold copyright 2019 by, Brandon Mitchell (Text) and Tara Audibert (Illustrations) Reproduced with permission from HighWater Press, Winnipeg. https://www.portageandmainpress.com; **104.1** Migwite'tmeg: We Remember it: pages 196-218 from This Place: 150 Years Retold copyright 2019 by, Brandon Mitchell (Text) and Tara Audibert (Illustrations) Reproduced with permission from HighWater Press, Winnipeg. https://www.portageandmainpress.com; **105.1** Migwite'tmeg: We Remember it: pages 196-218 from This Place: 150 Years Retold copyright 2019 by, Brandon Mitchell (Text) and Tara Audibert (Illustrations) Reproduced with permission from HighWater Press, Winnipeg. https://www.portageandmainpress.com; **106.1** Migwite'tmeg: We Remember it: pages 196-218 from This Place: 150 Years Retold copyright 2019 by, Brandon Mitchell (Text) and Tara Audibert (Illustrations) Reproduced with permission from HighWater Press, Winnipeg. https://www.portageandmainpress.com; **107.1** Migwite'tmeg: We Remember it: pages 196-218 from This Place: 150 Years Retold copyright 2019 by, Brandon Mitchell (Text) and Tara Audibert (Illustrations) Reproduced with permission from HighWater Press, Winnipeg. https://www.portageandmainpress.com; **108.1** Migwite'tmeg: We Remember it: pages 196-218 from This Place: 150 Years Retold copyright 2019 by, Brandon Mitchell (Text) and Tara Audibert (Illustrations) Reproduced with permission from HighWater Press, Winnipeg. https://www.portageandmainpress.com; **109.1** Migwite'tmeg: We Remember it: pages 196-218 from This Place: 150 Years Retold copyright 2019 by, Brandon Mitchell (Text) and Tara Audibert (Illustrations) Reproduced with permission from HighWater Press, Winnipeg. https://www.portageandmainpress.com; **110.1** Migwite'tmeg: We Remember it: pages 196-218 from This Place: 150 Years Retold copyright 2019 by, Brandon Mitchell (Text) and Tara Audibert (Illustrations) Reproduced with permission from HighWater Press, Winnipeg. https://www.portageandmainpress.com; **111.1** Migwite'tmeg: We Remember it: pages 196-218 from This Place: 150 Years Retold copyright 2019 by, Brandon Mitchell (Text) and Tara Audibert (Illustrations) Reproduced with permission from HighWater Press, Winnipeg. https://www.portageandmainpress.com; **112.1** Migwite'tmeg: We Remember it: pages 196-218 from This Place: 150 Years Retold copyright 2019 by, Brandon Mitchell (Text) and Tara Audibert (Illustrations) Reproduced with permission from HighWater Press, Winnipeg. https://www.portageandmainpress.com; **113.1** Migwite'tmeg: We Remember it: pages 196-218 from This Place: 150 Years Retold copyright 2019 by, Brandon Mitchell (Text) and Tara Audibert (Illustrations) Reproduced with permission from HighWater Press, Winnipeg. https://www.portageandmainpress.com; **114.1** Migwite'tmeg: We Remember it: pages 196-218 from This Place: 150 Years Retold copyright 2019 by, Brandon Mitchell (Text) and Tara Audibert (Illustrations) Reproduced with permission from HighWater Press, Winnipeg. https://www.portageandmainpress.com; **115.1** Migwite'tmeg: We Remember it: pages 196-218 from This Place: 150 Years Retold copyright 2019 by, Brandon Mitchell (Text) and Tara Audibert (Illustrations) Reproduced with permission from HighWater Press, Winnipeg. https://www.portageandmainpress.com; **116.1** Migwite'tmeg: We Remember it: pages 196-218 from This Place: 150 Years Retold copyright 2019 by, Brandon Mitchell (Text) and Tara Audibert (Illustrations) Reproduced with permission from HighWater Press, Winnipeg. https://www.portageandmainpress.com; **117.1** Migwite'tmeg: We Remember it: pages 196-218 from This Place: 150 Years Retold copyright 2019 by, Brandon Mitchell (Text) and Tara Audibert (Illustrations) Reproduced with permission from HighWater Press, Winnipeg. https://www.portageandmainpress.com; **118.1** Migwite'tmeg: We Remember it: pages 196-218 from This Place: 150 Years Retold copyright 2019 by, Brandon Mitchell (Text) and Tara Audibert (Illustrations) Reproduced with permission from HighWater Press, Winnipeg. https://www.portageandmainpress.com; **127.1** stock.adobe.com, Dublin (Autumn Sky); **127.2** jani lunablau, Barcelona; **128.1** stock.adobe.com, Dublin (Sergii Figurnyi); **130.1** ShutterStock.com RF, New York (sirtravelalot); **131.1** Don Zolidis, . (Anne C Godfrey); **137.1** Satzkiste GmbH, Stuttgart; **137.2** ShutterStock.com RF, New York (Pormezz); **137.3** ShutterStock.com RF, New York (YAKOBCHUK VIACHESLAV); **137.4** Mauritius Images, Mittenwald (Aleksey Popov/Alamy); **137.5** Alamy stock photo, Abingdon (Hero Images Inc.); **137.6** stock.adobe.com, Dublin (Alliance); **137.7** ShutterStock.com RF, New York (Bannafarsai_Stock); **138.1** Mauritius Images, Mittenwald (Wavebreak Media ltd/Alamy); **149.1** ShutterStock.com RF, New York (Gorodenkoff); **151.1** ShutterStock.com RF, New York (SeventyFour); **152.1** stock.adobe.com, Dublin (cbies); **153.1** stock.adobe.com, Dublin (alexkich); **153.2** Alamy stock photo, Abingdon (Valerii Honcharuk); **155.1** Mauritius Images, Mittenwald (Paul Andrew Lawrence/Alamy); **156.1** ShutterStock.com RF, New York (LightField Studios); **157.1** ShutterStock.com RF, New York (AleksOrel); **158.1** ShutterStock.

com RF, New York (Iakov Filimonov); **162.1** Romo, Virginia, Stuttgart; **163.1** Romo, Virginia, Stuttgart; **166.1** Migwite'tmeg: We Remember it: pages 196-218 from This Place: 150 Years Retold copyright 2019 by, Brandon Mitchell (Text) and Tara Audibert (Illustrations) Reproduced with permission from HighWater Press, Winnipeg. https://www.portageandmainpress.com; **167.1** Ernst Klett Verlag GmbH, Stuttgart; **167.2** Ernst Klett Verlag GmbH, Stuttgart; **167.3** Ernst Klett Verlag GmbH, Stuttgart; **167.4** Ernst Klett Verlag GmbH, Stuttgart; **168.1** www.CartoonStock.com, Bath (Matthew Diffee); **168.1** www.CartoonStock.com, Bath (Matthew Diffee); **170.1** Romo, Virginia, Stuttgart; **170.2** Romo, Virginia, Stuttgart; **170.3** Romo, Virginia, Stuttgart; **170.4** Romo, Virginia, Stuttgart; **170.5** Romo, Virginia, Stuttgart; **170.6** Romo, Virginia, Stuttgart; **170.7** Romo, Virginia, Stuttgart; **170.8** Romo, Virginia, Stuttgart; **170.9** Romo, Virginia, Stuttgart; **175.1** stock.adobe.com, Dublin (Pixel-Shot); **175.1** stock.adobe.com, Dublin (Pixel-Shot); **178.1** Getty Images, München (Onfokus); **181.1** From THE SUSTAINABLE DEVELOPMENT GOALS REPORT 2022: UNSTATS.UN.ORG/SDGS/REPORT/2022/ ©(2022) United Nations. Reprinted with the permission of the United Nations.; **184.1** ShutterStock.com RF, New York (fizkes); **186.1** Thomas Weccard Fotodesign BFF, Ludwigsburg; **188.1** ShutterStock.com RF, New York (VH-studio); **198.1** stock.adobe.com, Dublin (Web Buttons Inc); **200.1** stock.adobe.com, Dublin (Iryna); **203.1** stock.adobe.com, Dublin (Ljupco Smokovski); **206.1** ShutterStock.com RF, New York (ViDI Studio); **209.1** ShutterStock.com RF, New York (Dragon Images); **211.1** Thinkstock, München (photos.com); **212.1** ShutterStock.com RF, New York (Fred Duval); **215.1** ShutterStock.com RF, New York (rightclickstudios); **218.1** jani lunablau, Barcelona; **218.2** ShutterStock.com RF, New York (TRphotos); **222.1** Mauritius Images, Mittenwald (Chris Cheadle/lamy); **225.1** ShutterStock.com RF, New York (Bojan Milinkov); **230.1** ShutterStock.com RF, New York (Thomas La Mela); **236.1** stock.adobe.com, Dublin (Mix and Match Studio); **242.1** ShutterStock.com RF, New York (mayrum); **260.1** stock.adobe.com, Dublin (Tarik GOK); **260.2** ShutterStock.com RF, New York (granata1111); **260.3** ShutterStock.com RF, New York (suicidecrew); **260.4** stock.adobe.com, Dublin (Tarik GOK); **261.1** stock.adobe.com, Dublin (Tarik GOK); **261.2** ShutterStock.com RF, New York (granata1111); **261.3** ShutterStock.com RF, New York (suicidecrew); **Vorsatz hinten** Dekelver, Christian, Weinstadt

Textquellennachweis:
24.1 From Destroy All Cars, Blake Nelson, 2009; **29.1** From: The Carbon Diaries © 2008, Saci Lloyd; **36.1** Die Bundesregierung, 2019; **37.2** Emma Watson in The Climate is Changing, Why Aren't We?: A practical guide to how you can make a difference ©2020 Daisy Kendrick; **50.1** Ian Jukes, 2012 in Literacy Is NOT Enough: 21st Century Fluencies for the Digital Age; **50.2** Amy Jo Martin © 2019 Information Age Publishing Inc.; **50.3** Nolan Bushnell, 09.03.2012, https://americanart.si.edu; **54.1** 2020, Dr. Daniel Dettling, https://schulen-der-zukunft.freiheit.org; **55.1** From HuffPost. © 2019 BuzzFeed. All rights reserved. Used under license.; Zur besseren altersgemäßen Verständlichkeit wurde der Originaltext verändert, ohne den Inhalt und/oder Sinn zu verändern.; **60.1** From: SLAY ©2019 Brittney Morris; **65.1** From: The Disconnect ©2019 Keren David; **68.1** Attributed to Emily Atack; **70.1** From: The Burning ©2019 Laura Bates; Zur besseren altersgemäßen Verständlichkeit wurde der Originaltext verändert, ohne den Inhalt und/oder Sinn zu verändern.; **73.1** Tim Lewis, ©2022 Guardian News & Media Ltd.; **81.1** Jean M Twenge Copyright Guardian News & Media Ltd 2018; **84** British North America Act, 1867 - Enactment no. 1 §41 (24); **95** Peace and Friendship Treaty (1752) between His Majesty the King and the Jean Baptiste Cope; **96–118** Migwite'tmeg: We Remember it: pages 196-218 from This Place: 150 Years Retold copyright 2019 by, Brandon Mitchell (Text); **119.1** Wayne Arthurson, https://quillandquire.com; **122.1** ©2020 Jennifer Lee Rossman; **131** Help Desk: A Stay-At-Home Play, Don Zolidis, https://www.playscripts.com/; **157.Ex. 4** Help Desk: A Stay-At-Home Play, Don Zolidis, https://www.playscripts.com/; **162** from Laura by Robert O'Neill. „Who Needs open-ended texts?", Praxis des neusprachlichen Unterrichts 50, Berlin: Pädagogischer Zeitschriftenverl. 2003, S. 80; **163.1** From Destroy All Cars, Blake Nelson, 2009; **164.1** Leanne Guenther; DLTK's Educational Activities for Kids (Website), Calgary, Alberta, Canada, www.dltk-kids.com; **164** Leanne Guenther; DLTK's Educational Activities for Kids (Website), Calgary, Alberta, Canada, www.dltk-kids.com; **178.1** Casey Magloire, 07.12.2021, https://news.sky.com; **194.1** Wörterbuchauszug PONS Schülerwörterbuch ISBN 978-3-12-517539-6, S. 423 („mean")

CANADA
Arctic Ocean
ALASKA (USA)
Dawson
YUKON
NORTHWEST TERRITORIES
NUNAVUT
Baker Lake
Yellowknife
Rocky Mountains
CANADA
BRITISH COLUMBIA
ALBERTA
SASKAT-CHEWAN
MANITO
Pacific Ocean
Edmonton
Jasper
Banff
Whistler
Calgary
Saskatoon
Vancouver
Regina
Winnipeg
0
500 km
1000 km
USA